BRITISH SHIPS OF WAR IN THE HARBOR

G. Griffin's Wharf   H. Gates Shipyard   I. Old North Meeting (church)   J. Christ Church

RED DAWN at LEXINGTON

"Stand your ground.
Don't fire unless fired upon,
But if they mean to have a war,
Let it begin here!"

Captain John Parker
Lexington Minute Company
April 19, 1775

RED DAWN at LEXINGTON

"If They Mean to Have a War, Let It Begin Here!"

L OUIS   B IRNBAUM

B O S T O N

HOUGHTON MIFFLIN COMPANY

1986

Library of Congress Cataloging in Publication Data

Birnbaum, Louis, d. 1983.
Red dawn at Lexington.

Bibliography: p.
Includes index.
1. Massachusetts — History — Revolution, 1775–1783 —
Campaigns.   2. Boston (Mass.) — History — Revolution,
1775–1783 — Campaigns.   I. Title.
E263.M4B57   1986   973.3'11   85-24703
ISBN 0-395-38814-7

Printed in the United States of America

P 10 9 8 7 6 5 4 3 2 1

Endpaper map adapted from 1941 map by Samuel H. Bryant
in *Paul Revere and the World He Lived In* by Esther Forbes.
Copyright 1942 by Esther Forbes and copyright © renewed
by Linwood M. Erskine. Reprinted by permission
of Houghton Mifflin Company.

Contents

ILLUSTRATIONS AND MAPS

COLOR INSERTS

Preface

WRITTEN HISTORY usually lacks a sense of how events appeared to those who experienced them. And, in fact, the diaries and journals of both British and American participants in the early days of the American Revolution reveal no awareness of participating in cataclysmic events. Rather, the reader senses a matter-of-fact, day-by-day involvement in experiences occasioned simply by place and time.

To achieve a similar view of these historic events, the modern reader must understand a world unlike his own in both manner and substance. It was an era when shocking inequities among men were considered part of Nature's law. Injustice, disease, poverty, and suffering, ghosts, curses, spirits, and witches — all were taken for granted.

Time was measured by months rather than by days or minutes. The fastest means of travel was by horseback or horse-drawn conveyance, and the controversy between England and the American colonies resulted in part from that fact and the immense distances between the two areas. Depending on the weather and time of year, a ship took from two to three months to cross the Atlantic Ocean one way. Thus the reply to a letter sent in January could be expected by May or June.

The distance in time and space was largely responsible for the lack of mutual understanding between the colonists in America and those who controlled the British Parliament and made the laws governing the colonies. During the 1770s the Whigs (or Liberals, as they would later be called) were out of power, and the arch-conservative Tories were in control under the corrupting influence of King George III, who was attempting to reverse the ascendancy of Parliament that had been established with the "Glorious Revolution" of 1689.

The lack of communication fostered an unrealistic English conception of the nature of America. Parliament viewed the Americans across the sea as Englishmen no different from those living in London, Manchester, Chester, or the villages of England. History proved them wrong.

During the first 150 years of colonial experience, which spanned seven or eight generations, intermarriages between the original English colonists and the descendants of German, Dutch, Swedish, Norwegian, French, and Danish cultures created a distinct cultural mix that, by 1773, was only partially loyal to Britain in tradition and attitude.

From the inception of the English colonies in 1607, a continuous series of conflicts between England and France created a permanent state of warfare between English and French colonists. The latter were usually supported by their fierce Indian allies. Out of necessity, the predominantly British colonists created a military society in which every able-bodied male from age sixteen to sixty automatically became a member of the organized militia. He was required to furnish and care for his musket or, if he were fortunate enough to possess one, the new Pennsylvania or Kentucky rifle. Battling French and/or Indian encroachments on colonial settlements, the average American experienced years of service in the field as a combat soldier.

Parliament and King George III consistently failed to understand this simple truth. They did not realize they were dealing with an armed population. In letters sent home to their families, British army officers recounted the details of their shocking discovery regarding the military preparedness in the northern colonies, particularly in Massachusetts. New England had been the major area of conflict with the French and Indians for nearly a century and a half, and most men were veterans of provincial regiments.

The New England colonies had created a prosperous economy in which employment was available for anyone who wanted a job. There was a tremendous shortage of labor, and free workers were highly paid. Thousands of indentured servants were able, upon receiving their freedom, to save enough to open their own shops or businesses and become prosperous artisans or farmers. Land was cheap and plentiful and produced abundant foodstuffs. Forests teemed with wild game, and rivers and inlets were alive with fish easily caught by the use of hand nets.

Given an abundant diet of wide variety, Americans grew taller, stronger, and healthier and they lived longer than their European counterparts. The birth rate was the highest in the world, and families of ten or twelve living children were not uncommon. In 1775 the population of Massachusetts alone was 349,094; in Connecticut it was 197,856. The letters and diaries of British soldiers are filled with descriptions of these large, well-built Americans and their clear, unblemished skin. The women of the colonies received special tribute from the British, who described their lithe, slim bodies and beautiful complexions. When French troops arrived to aid the Americans late in the Revolutionary War, they delightedly described American women as the most beautiful in the world.

British officers throughout the war were hard-put to prevent wholesale desertions among their men. The life that could be theirs as deserters in America was so much better than they could hope for in England that thousands deserted to the Americans despite brutal punishments meted out to those who were caught.

It was also a life of comparative freedom. Before 1765, the colonies had, in actual practice, lived without any serious interference or regulations from the mother country. The long distance from England discouraged attempts to control the colonists, so long as the products of the colonies continued to enrich British merchants. Royal governors sent to oversee the colonies discovered upon arrival that their pay depended upon the decisions of local colonial legislatures, and they quickly found it expedient to accept the situation of local autonomy rather than jeopardize the regularity of their income.

It was only in 1765, when the king and Parliament attempted to collect money in a new manner to help defray the immense cost of the recently ended Seven Years' War, known in America as the French and Indian War, that difficulties arose. Instead of asking the legislatures to vote funds to England as previously had been done, the combined power of the king and his ministers was used to pass a stamp tax that would be gathered by tax collectors not under the control of the colonial legislatures. Although the Stamp Acts were soon repealed in the face of violent colonial protest, the British decided to send additional troops to America to maintain a semblance of authority and to shift onto the colonies the burden of feeding some of the numerous regiments of the British army.

Despite occasional outbreaks of violence, including the so-called Boston Massacre, tensions gradually lessened, and by 1773 it appeared that the troubles in New England were over. Just at this time, the fatal decision was made by Parliament to revive the tax question as a means of saving the nearly bankrupt East India Company. This move may have been hastened by the fact that most Tory members owned shares in the huge import-export company. The colonial response to the British monopoly and tax on tea came in December 1773, when a horde of disguised militiamen of Boston and the surrounding towns destroyed Boston's allotment of tea in what came to be known as the Boston Tea Party. The entire affair was organized by England's greatest enemy, Samuel Adams, one of a handful of colonists who dreamed of eventual independence from England.

The ministry's angry reaction was to close the Port of Boston and send additional regiments there to overawe the population and quell opposition. Shortly thereafter, a series of laws that the Americans called the Intolerable Acts abolished trial by jury, town meetings, and other privileges that Americans had enjoyed for a century and a half, privileges they thought of as the "rights of Englishmen." The Intolerable Acts were followed by other laws that soon destroyed the economy of New England, largely by prohibiting American fishing rights on the Grand Banks in the north Atlantic. In a move certain to give the Southern colonies common cause with New England, Parliament surprisingly extended the same prohibitions to them.

Inevitably, thousands of unemployed sailors, fishermen, stevedores, shipbuilders, craftsmen, clerks, warehousemen, and wagon drivers were available for the Massachusetts militia. Gradually New England became an armed camp, with hundreds of militia companies drilling along village greens. British officers stationed in Boston watched the developments with growing apprehension, and they wrote of the burgeoning power and size of a New England army.

Back in London, the colonial militia was ridiculed as a bad joke. The British ministry apparently had forgotten the colonial contribution to victory in the French and Indian War. Americans had furnished nearly 100,000 troops during the war, many of whom were now ready to use again what they had learned. Hundreds of Americans had risen from the ranks to become officers, and some were recognized as superb combat officers by the British themselves. Such men as George Washington, Israel Putnam, William Prescott, Artemas Ward, William Heath, and John Stark represented many years of military experience. Also, a sense of military pride had developed among the officers and men during the successful conclusion of the French and Indian War, which ended in 1763. The science of supplying large numbers of men had been developed to a high degree by American military planners, and the strategy of eighteenth-century warfare had been refined under combat conditions to relate to American terrain and circumstances.

During the eighteenth century, battlefield differences between the trained soldiers of the king and American militiamen were not great. Modern weapons that give industrial nations of the twentieth century immense advantages, such as trucks, tanks, and planes, were unknown. Consequently, military decisions depended on men carrying muskets into battle, with the occasional use of field cannon. If the British had any advantage, it was in the massed firepower created by close formations of highly disciplined men supported by the Royal Artillery.

It has been estimated that over 700,000 men of military age were available to the American forces during the Revolutionary War, most of them trained members of militia companies scattered throughout the colonies. Although most of those men never saw combat, they were available whenever needed. And in fact, two of the greatest American victories of the war, Bennington and King's Mountain, were won by quickly organized, local militia regiments. The British armies at Bennington and King's Mountain did not realize that there were any American forces nearby until the moment of attack.

The account of events that follows draws heavily on the first-hand reports of men and women who wrote of the first riots in Boston, of General Thomas Gage's raid on Concord, of the Battle of Bunker Hill (fought, in fact, on Breed's Hill), and of the long siege of Boston. Some of this material is rare or has come to light only recently; all of it offers the modern reader the detail and sense of immediacy found only in eyewitness accounts. My intent is to enliven the events recounted here, events that too often seem to be stale folklore. There are mysterious hints of treason, a spy in the central council of the Massachusetts Committee of Safety, and details of daily life among the British regulars, the colonial militiamen, and their families.

The story progresses through three years of confrontation, from April 1773 to March 1776. In the beginning, demands for independence from Britain came only from a few zealots. By the final days of March 1776, the proud British army of General Sir William Howe had been forced by an army of New England militiamen to evacuate Boston. The fight had captured the imagination of many colonists, and the Declaration of Independence and an irrevocable break with England were less than four months away.

RED DAWN at LEXINGTON

Voyage to America

THE PAINFUL BEAUTY of the scene would haunt the passengers for the rest of their lives. It was Sunday morning, April 27, 1773, and the seven ships of the British convoy had waited eight days for the fair winds necessary to start them on their voyage to the colonies. Four of the converted East Indiamen — HMS *Friendship, Pallas, Henry,* and *Brudenell* — were assembled to carry the full regimental complement of the Royal Welsh Fusiliers, numbered the 23rd Foot, to duty in the colony of New York. Three other transports were bound for Quebec with members of the Royal Fusiliers of the 7th Regiment of Foot.

The decks of the ships, beneath bristling masts, were awash with the scarlet uniforms of British soldiers and the variegated colors worn by their women and children. Everyone was on deck to witness the departure, and the excitement of the impending adventure was transferred to the ships themselves as shouts of "Make sail!" boomed through speaking trumpets, and smooth billows of canvas ballooned and crackled in the winds.

On the four ships bound for New York, 450 officers and men augmented by dependents swelled the passenger lists to over a thousand. And as the ships glided across the blue waters of Plymouth Sound and Catwater Inlet into the English Channel, passengers crowded the decks and were tossed about as bows lifted to meet the seas and towering waves broke across the vessels. To starboard the green hills of Cornwall slid slowly by; not until Tuesday morning did the convoy pass Point Lizard and watch the last land they would see for seven weeks drop below the horizon.

Atop the quarterdeck of HMS *Friendship*, Lieutenant Frederick Mackenzie watched with a strange sense of foreboding as the rocky coastline disappeared. He braced himself against the lurch and lift of the ship as he listened to the slow, rhythmical creaking of the rigging, the groan of the timbered hull.

Mackenzie, like his fellow officers, was a member of England's upper class. The only son of an English father and a French Huguenot mother who had escaped to England from the religious persecution of France, he joined the British army in 1745 at age seventeen, when his parents paid £400 for a second lieutenant's commission in the prestigious 23rd Foot. (It was the only regiment in the army in which the lowest commissioned rank, that of ensign, was called second lieutenant, as is the modern custom.)

Although Mackenzie had proven an outstanding infantry officer, both in combat and during peacetime, the army's promotion system of the time necessitated payment of over £1200 (more than $5000) for the next highest rank of captain. Mackenzie's family obligations precluded that; consequently, in twenty-eight years he had risen only to first lieutenant. Now second-in-command of a battalion company of twenty-eight men, he was also the regimental adjutant or chief executive officer. Considered the best junior officer in the 23rd Foot, he was known for his pleasant manner and a stern but friendly attitude toward his men.

With Mackenzie on the *Friendship* were his wife Nancy and their three children. Accommodations aboard ship were meager and living conditions often very difficult, for officers as well as for enlisted men. The ship was in fact a converted cargo vessel, and Nancy Mackenzie and daughters Charlotte, age two, and Fanny, age six, shared a seven-foot-square cubicle with the wife of Lieutenant Gibbings, her seven-year-old daughter, and a fourteen-year-old indentured Scottish servant girl.

Protruding from the sides of the cabin were two built-in bunks, each two and a half feet wide, which left only two feet of space between the wooden frames. Nancy slept in one of the bunks with her younger daughter at her feet. Frederick had fashioned a shallow box in the far end of the space between the frames for the older girl to sleep in. Mrs. Gibbings occupied the other bunk with her daughter suspended from the overhead by a hammock two feet above her head. The indentured servant girl slept on bedding under Mrs. Gibbings's bed. A one-foot-square opening into the passageway at the foot of the ladder to the main deck provided the only ventilation.

Six people would find such an existence difficult under ordinary conditions, but the situation worsened during rough weather and illness. Mrs. Gibbings was chronically seasick for virtually the entire voyage, and when frequent storms kept everyone below decks, the chamber pots beneath Nancy's bunk were in continual use and usually full. This combined with the sudden pitch and roll of the ship and a dearth of fresh air to create an intolerable environment for Nancy and the children. Similar circumstances prevailed among others on board. Officers enjoyed no better quarters, and in Lieutenant Mackenzie's cabin his ten-year-old son Jem slept in a hammock suspended over his father's bunk.

Much of the time, however, pleasant weather permitted everyone to spend some time topside, and the main deck was often crowded with several hundred people milling about. Both men and women sat along the sides, backs against the gunwales, smoking the long clay pipes popular at the time. Above them in the rigging and throughout the vessel, the ship's crew were hard at work, while around them children played and women washed, mended, and chatted.

On the quarterdeck, seven feet above the main deck, families of the officers enjoyed the sun, fresh air, and the view of the open sea. Captain Evans, the ranking regimental officer, delighted Fanny Mackenzie with the task of collecting eggs. Jem fed the fowl and ducks and covered them at night. Mackenzie worried about Jem as the boy clambered up and over the rigging with the captain's son, but the youngsters, given the run of the ship, had the time of their lives as they helped the crew with endless shipboard tasks.

Each regimental officer had a specific shipboard assignment during the crossing. Watch sections were established with three officers to a section. Mackenzie's section stayed on deck until 2:00 A.M., seeing that all galley fires were extinguished by 8:00 P.M. and checking all berthing spaces between decks. After reveille they saw that all spaces were cleaned and sprinkled with vinegar (the disinfectant of the time), and they supervised the airing of bedding on deck, weather permitting.

In addition, each officer had certain other assigned functions. Captain Evans had the care of sixty-three fowl kept in pens on deck to provide fresh eggs during the voyage. Lieutenant Gibbings had charge of seven sheep and two hogs, which furnished occasional fresh meat. Captain Grove looked after the rum, brandy, beer, porter, and wines. Another officer had charge of teas and breakfasts, while Lieutenant Mackenzie supervised the preparation of dinners and suppers.

Such provisions were carried solely for officers and their families, however. Among the enlisted men, sergeants supervised the storage and preparation of provisions available from the enlisted men's own organization. Many enlisted men's wives helped prepare and serve meals, which were cooked in the ship's galleys in open fireplaces located at the stern of the ship.

Lacking the cabin accommodations of the officers, enlisted men and their dependents slept in hammocks slung fourteen inches apart from hooks attached to the overhead in the berthing spaces. Each night at eight o'clock the boatswain's pipe sounded "hammocks," and within a few minutes, in a scene reminiscent of bats hanging from the roof of a cave, everyone not on watch was suspended from the overhead in long, tight rows swaying with the motion of the ship.

Although the ship's crew were awakened at 5:00 A.M., soldiers and their dependents were allowed to sleep until 7:00. Five minutes were allocated to lash up and stow hammocks, while the decks were scrubbed and sprinkled with vinegar. Breakfast was piped at 8:00, when the enlisted men received the entire day's ration. (Women and children were each allowed half rations.) The women would then prepare breakfast with part of the food, reserving some for later meals. Officers' families enjoyed the aid of servants in meal preparation, and single men were formed into various small "messes" to prepare their meals.

The diet was generous compared to that of the average Englishman of the time. A full daily ration consisted of one pound of salt pork or beef, one pound of ship's biscuit, and one gallon of beer. This was augmented by a weekly allowance of two pints of peas, three pounds of oatmeal, eight ounces of butter, and a pound of cheese. Occasionally rice replaced oatmeal and olive oil supplanted butter.

Sanitary facilities were minimal on board ship. In good weather the ship's carpenter rigged temporary latrines above the gunwales above deck. These consisted of a safety line to hold on to, a sheet of canvas for privacy, and short lengths of rope hung alongside the facility. The last item, which performed the function now filled by toilet paper, has contributed an expression to naval terminology, for the end of the rope was dipped into the sea before and after use, and this "bitter end" became the unsecured end of line found in today's seagoing jargon.

During the convoy's voyage the weather changed frequently. On the second day, off Point Lizard and within fifty miles of the English coast, massive mountains of water roared into the ships from the northwest. To maintain their course the ships tacked, exposing their sides to the force of the sea, and the small vessels were lifted high above the enormous swells and dropped sideways into deep troughs of apparently solid, dark blue water. Under the great weight of sodden yardarms and sail, the towering masts heeled the ships alarmingly, and within a few hours virtually everyone was seasick.

Though the seven ships were separated and reunited after that storm, within a week they were again separated, and the *Friendship* did not see its sister ships for the remainder of the voyage. Again, on May 7, the *Friendship* was struck by seas of such raging fury that parts of the rigging were carried away; the topsail was badly split and the mainmast sprung. During the storm all hatches were battened down tightly, and only crew members were allowed on deck as dark, angry waves smashed across the decks, rolling the vessel from side to side and plunging the gunwales under water. To the Mackenzies and others below decks, clinging to whatever they could, the ship felt as though it must surely go all the way over. Time after time, miraculously, the *Friendship* righted itself, then slowly, very slowly, it would shudder and start the other way. Everyone was aware that one out of ten ships was lost at sea each

year, and while many on board the *Friendship* were resigned to
their fate, others were crazed with fear. Conditions below decks in
humid and stinking cubicles like that of Nancy Mackenzie were
sickening and terrifying.

Two children of enlisted men died during this storm. When the
weather cleared, a short sermon and ceremony was held on deck,
and the two small bodies, sewed into white canvas hammocks,
were slid into the waves as the entire assemblage stood, tragically
moved.

During good weather, efforts were made to repair the mainmast, but the attempt was soon abandoned, and the *Friendship*
continued the voyage carrying only one yardarm on the weakened
mast, which reduced their speed.

On May 30, the worst storm of the voyage struck without warning. Again, everyone stayed below decks as the ship fought for its
life. Despite great fear that the sprung mainmast could not withstand the quick rolls and pitches and would snap like a matchstick,
the *Friendship* miraculously survived.

As time passed these storms were followed by beautiful days of
white clouds, blue water, and calm winds, although rains occasionally battered the ship. Now and then excitement swept over the
ship as it came upon a school of porpoises. The voyagers marveled
at the speed maintained by the huge animals, and they tried to
explain the source of the power that propelled them so quickly
through the water. The officers organized shooting matches to see
if anyone was enough of a marksman to hit a porpoise, but the
records show that not a single hit was scored during the voyage.

Frequently they ran into schools of flying fish, which to their
amazement leaped out of the water and flew through the air for
nearly twenty yards before splashing back into the sea. On several
occasions, huge sea turtles were seen paddling about in the water,
and the officers petitioned the captain to lower a boat so they
could improve their menu, but he refused, much to their chagrin.

In 1773, ship captains, using a chronometer developed only
eleven years before by a self-taught Yorkshire carpenter named
John Harrison, were able to plot both their latitude and longitude
within thirty miles of their objective. A sextant developed in 1731

and considerable knowledge concerning winds, currents, and coastlines that had been collected over the centuries were available to determine the ship's position. The captain of the *Friendship* also had at his disposal reliable charts of water depths and sailing directions.

On June 3, when the lookout aboard the *Friendship* sighted a sloop, the captain, believing himself close to land, signaled for her to approach so he could check his position. The sloop, an American ship, quickly changed its course and approached until it was within three hundred yards. Then suddenly it turned away and sped off. The British were surprised, but they felt that the sloop might have been smuggling and was frightened off by the scarlet British army uniforms on the *Friendship*'s decks. The episode was Lieutenant Mackenzie's first taste of the growing tensions that awaited the Royal Welsh Fusiliers in America.

Another ship was soon encountered which stopped and confirmed the captain's calculations that they were at longitude 72. New York City, their destination, was at longitude 74, latitude 41. Great caution was now required, for they were close to the continental shelf of North America and the dreaded Nantucket shoals, where the water frequently and unexpectedly reaches a depth of only three feet.

The leadsman was in the chains taking soundings throughout that day and night. On June 4, the sounding lead found bottom at 135 fathoms. On the night of June 7, a reading of 86 fathoms assured them they were over the continental shelf. Their charts showed them to be at longitude 72 west of London and 41.50 north. The next night land was sighted — the northeastern end of Long Island. The *Friendship* sailed south on June 9 along the coast of Long Island, and as the sun set, the lookout spotted the famous light at Sandy Hook. They signaled for a local pilot, who was soon brought aboard and guided the vessel skillfully across the bay in pitch darkness. Within four hours they were alongside a wharf at what is now the Battery of New York Harbor. It was 11:00 P.M., June 9, 1773. The crossing of the Royal Welsh Fusiliers had taken seven weeks and a day.

To their surprise the *Friendship* was the first ship of their convoy to arrive in the colonies, despite their disabled mast.

The next morning, Lieutenant Mackenzie and Captain Edward Evans, as the two senior army officers on board, went ashore to call on General Tryon, the colonial governor of New York. After a short report of their voyage and the exchange of social amenities over tea, the two officers returned to their ship.

Passing one of New York's famous outdoor markets, they purchased quantities of bread, butter, milk, meat, fish, salad greens, cherries, strawberries, and pineapples. Their return to the ship laden with fresh food caused a sensation, and officers and non-commissioned officers raced to the closest market to duplicate their feat.

On June 11, the *Pallas* and the *Henry* arrived in New York. Smallpox, a dreaded disease of the time, had caused the death of four children on board the *Pallas*. Five children had recovered after a long and violent illness. Two soldiers also had died, their deaths vaguely attributed to "fever and consumption." On board the *Henry,* Lieutenant Douglas and his family of four were gravely ill with smallpox when they reached New York. The youngest son died shortly after their arrival, although the rest of the family, permanently scarred, survived.

On June 17 the remainder of the regiment arrived aboard the *Brudenell.* There had been no deaths on the crossing, but the ship had sprung its mainmast in two places, and rough seas had opened some seams in the hull, necessitating pumping every two hours.

With arrival of the *Brudenell,* the redcoated 23rd Foot of the Royal Welsh Fusiliers was marched through the streets of New York to barracks on the outskirts of the city. Blue-uniformed fifers and drummers led the way as the regiment swung through the city, rank after rank of scarlet and white faced with blue, under gleaming bayonets and regimental flags. Their show of strength brought cheers from proud British citizens, for New York was comparatively loyal to the Crown at this time. Some 350 miles to the north, however, lay Boston, a major seat of dissension and one reason for the regiment's embarkation for the colonies.

The New York barracks consisted of long rows of identical houses with four identical rooms in each house. Each room measured eighteen by fifteen feet, with a ceiling slightly over six feet high and three windows. Two soldiers were assigned to a room.

An enlisted man's family occupied one half of a house, sharing it with another family.

As an officer, Frederick Mackenzie had the use of a house for himself and his family. Those officers with larger private means leased fine homes in the city and kept elegant horses and carriages. Many were soon actively involved in the lively social life of New York's upper class.

The Mackenzies purchased a horse and chaise also, and each morning at 6:00 Nancy drove a half mile through the clean, wide streets to shop in the crowded open-air market. The heat was extreme that summer, so markets opened at 5:00 A.M. and closed by 10:00 A.M. Animals were butchered early in the morning and sold that day. In the absence of refrigeration, meat not disposed of by closing time had to be destroyed. To allow people to buy meat on the Sabbath, the markets opened briefly from 5:00 A.M. to 8:00 A.M. on Sundays.

Top-grade fresh meat sold for six cents a pound. Chickens sold for nine cents each and a nine-pound quarter of lamb for forty-five cents. Lobsters cost three cents a pound. Vegetables were somewhat cheaper, and fruit was plentiful. Pineapples as large as quart mugs were shipped in from the West Indies daily and sold for twelve cents each. Cherries cost four cents a pound, strawberries six cents a quart, raspberries eight cents a quart, and freshly baked bread two cents a pound.

The currency used in the markets was mostly the Spanish "*dolar*," and the rate of exchange for the British soldiers was based on eight shillings to the *dolar* or dollar.

Among the problems plaguing Lieutenant Mackenzie and other officers was the low cost and availability to their troops of intoxicating liquor. Good beer and rum were plentiful and cheap: twelve gallons of beer cost forty-seven cents; rum cost forty-three cents a gallon; the finest French brandy was one dollar a quart. Consequently, drunkenness among both officers and men was common and became a perpetual source of trouble during the next ten years in America. Despite attempts to restrict the use of liquor by the men, wives or camp followers could always find ways to smuggle it in.

Generally, however, life in New York was good to the men of the

Royal Welsh Fusiliers. In addition to his rations and quarters, a private received four shillings and sixpence a month. After deductions he could still afford all the liquor he wanted; the girls were friendly, and so was the general citizenry of New York.

The Mackenzies were content with their new quarters and spent many hours together in walks around the beautiful town. New York was like a typical eighteenth-century Dutch city, and in letters to his father, Mackenzie enthusiastically described the friendly people and broad, spacious streets lined with stately trees and elegant brick buildings. In 1773 the city was located on the south end of the peninsula that is now Manhattan, which Mackenzie described as an island twelve miles long, surrounded by water on three sides, with breathtaking views in every direction. Across the two-mile-wide Hudson River lay an area known as the Jerseys, which appeared to him to be a "nobleman's park."

Like many other Englishmen, the Mackenzies thoroughly enjoyed New York and its beauty, and they eagerly looked forward to the coming years of duty there. Yet, in little over a year, they would once again be on board ships bound for the colony of Boston and a tragically different way of life.

Boston in 1774

DESPITE THE CHARMS of New York, Boston was the most flour-
ishing colony in North America in the 1770s. Its shipyards built
ships cheaper than anywhere else in the world; its merchant fleets
carried goods for other colonies; its merchants, often evading re-
strictive British mercantilistic laws, traded with Europe, Africa,
Asia, and above all with the West Indies.

Until 1750 Boston had the largest population in the colonies,
but first Philadelphia and then New York surpassed it. Boston's
population remained frozen at 16,000 while, by 1774, New York
had climbed to 25,000 and Philadelphia had rocketed to 40,000.

Boston was built on a rocky, pear-shaped peninsula that was
virtually an island attached to the mainland by a narrow, marshy
neck of land, often swept by water and spray. The town consisted
of only 782 acres of hilly and irregular land dominated by three
peaks called the Tri-mountains.

Of the hills that towered over Boston in 1774, only Copp's Hill
still exists. Fort Hill, where the Royal Welsh Fusiliers were
stationed during their two years in Boston, has entirely disappeared, the result of 200 years of leveling and filling the adjacent marshes. Mountain Vernon, the western peak of the Tri-
mountains and once the most conspicuous feature of Boston, and
its eastern peak, Cotton or Pemberton Hill, were leveled in building developments between 1799 and 1835. The central peak, Beacon Hill, had sixty feet shorn from its top between 1811 and 1834.

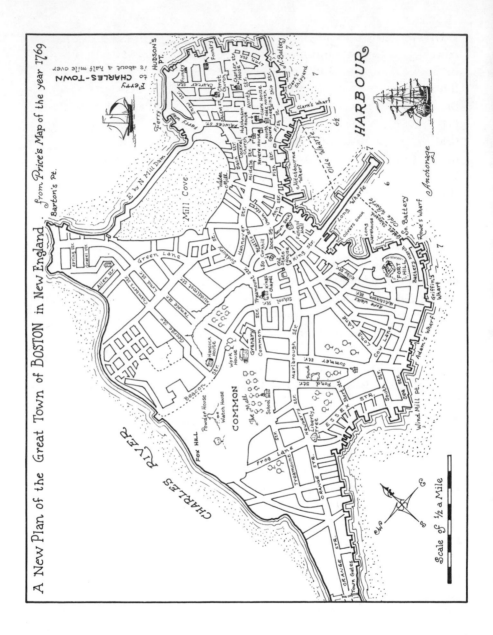

A New Plan of the Great Town of BOSTON in New England. from Price's Map of the year 1769

Ferry to CHARLES-TOWN is about a half mile over

HARBOUR

CHARLES RIVER

Mill Cove

COMMON

Scale of ½ a Mile

In 1774 Boston had the dubious distinction of having the narrowest, crookedest, and most winding streets of any town in North or South America. Built mostly of wood, the city presented a low, flat skyline, pierced here and there by an occasional church steeple. The waterfront, which included the entire seaward or southern side, was crowded by warehouses built on top of the wharves that extended out into the harbor, some for a considerable distance. Long Wharf stretched out into the water for half a mile. Clark's Wharf, Griffin's Wharf, and Rowe's Wharf were far shorter. Since Long Wharf was the official entrance to the town, it continued inland to become King Street, which led to Province House, the Governor's residence in the heart of Boston.

Of the seventeen churches in Boston, most were Congregationalist, descended from the original Puritan church. Others were Episcopal, Anabaptist, French Huguenot, and Quaker. Though the religious test for voting had been abolished, the selectmen of the town continued to grant the Congregational church large sums of public money collected from all Boston citizens, regardless of faith.

The population of Boston depended on the commercial success of the merchants, large and small. Money that came to the town through commerce and shipping found its way to the small shopkeepers, mechanics, sailors, stevedores, artisans, apprentices, and the farmers who fed them all. These men worked twelve to fourteen hours a day, six days a week.

The town craftsmen or artisans, working with their hands and a few simple tools, created all the necessities of life and made up the bulk of the population. The craftsman's work was conducted in a small shop with living quarters above. He worked side by side with his apprentices and journeymen helpers to produce the articles that had been ordered in advance. By custom, wives handled the customers in the front showroom of the shop, while husbands worked in the back.

In addition to countless shops throughout Boston, there were several industries that were large, even by modern standards. One of these was the manufacture of rum, New England's favorite drink as well as one of its most profitable sources of jobs and income. Using molasses brought in from the West Indies in exchange for slaves, Massachusetts alone supported sixty distilleries in 1793, with an annual output of 2,700,000 gallons.

However, the major industry of Boston and New England was shipbuilding. With an abundance of lumber of every necessary kind, the New England shipbuilders of 1773 led the entire world. One third of Britain's merchant fleet had been built in New England ports. To handcraft a ship employed hundreds of men and was a long and complex operation that took over a year to complete. The master shipwright had complete charge of the construction and made use of carpenters, blacksmiths, painters, carvers, coopers, ropemakers, tanners, and sailmakers.

Unlike modern large cities, which have separate areas of affluence and poverty, Boston housed wealthy merchants next door to the impoverished poor and modest shops. In the north and south ends of Boston the epitome of London elegance lived next to poverty and vice. Through crooked, cobblestoned streets that sloped down toward a central gutter poured a mixture of humanity. Living in crowded tenements, mews, and abandoned warehouses were the families of the poor, toughs, jacktars, brawling bullies, harlots, the neglected old, the insane, and the hopelessly crippled. Toward North Park and the Boston Common the houses were less crowded; many had their own yards, and large mansions boasted exquisite lawns and gardens.

Between the poor and the wealthy lived the large middle class of artisans, brewers, shipwrights, blacksmiths, and other shopkeepers. However, the small acreage of Boston and the hills of the Trimountains compressed everyone into the streets. Horse- and oxen-drawn carts and wagons, heavily laden with farm produce and manufactured goods, competed for room along the cobblestoned and dirt streets that twisted and turned through the town. When goods recently unloaded from the holds of ships met materials moving toward the ships for export, monumental traffic jams occurred.

During winter, when rain and snow turned the streets into canals and the roads to bottomless rivers of mud, conditions became acute. Horses were used primarily for riding or to pull two-wheeled carts. Heavy wagons drawn by oxen hauled most goods and sank deep into the unpaved thoroughfares.

Ferries were privately owned and were usually barges operated by oars or by a rope tied to each shore. Most people traveled by foot or horseback. Cross-country travel was improved in the mideighteenth century with the introduction of the stage coach. It took five days to travel the 350 miles from Boston to New York and two days to go to Portsmouth from Boston, a distance of sixty miles. Travelers usually arrived after dark at some candlelit wayside inn, ate supper, smoked a clay pipe of tobacco, and went to sleep, to be awakened before dawn to resume the journey.

The Puritan church required that everyone be able to read his Bible, and the founders of the Massachusetts Bay colony saw in that dictum the need for public education. This revolutionary idea was put into practice in 1647 with a law that required every town with at least fifty householders to appoint a teacher. Towns that had a hundred householders were to maintain secondary or grammar schools "able to instruct youths [boys] so far as they shall be fitted for the University." Over the years, smaller communities had difficulty fulfilling the dictates of the law, especially towns in the interior. Boston, however, followed the regulations to the letter and consequently became an educational seat of considerable note.

The high birth rate in the American colonies was a phenomenon of the time. Benjamin Franklin stated in 1770 that the American population doubled every twenty years. He claimed to have proof that there were twice as many marriages as there were in Europe, and that each marriage produced twice as many offspring. Many children had from ten to fifteen brothers and sisters. Franklin himself was one of seventeen children; John Marshall was one of fifteen; Paul Revere was one of twelve, and he himself fathered sixteen. Such large families were generally born of more than one mother, for many women died young in childbirth.

In Boston boys of sixteen bore the responsibilities of manhood, including those of taxpayer and membership in the militia. The number of young people in America was startling. More than half the population in 1774 were youngsters fifteen years of age and under. The short average life span, coupled with the high birth rate, heavily weighted statistics toward the young.

Ostensibly to safeguard the stability of marriage, the law gave the husband total authority over the person and property of the wife, who lost title to her land, money, and other possessions, including clothes and intimate articles, the day she married. She could neither sue nor be sued in court. *Blackstone's Commentaries* summed it up: "The very being or legal existence of the woman is suspended during marriage, or at least incorporated and consolidated into that of her husband."[1]

The issues of legal rights and economics were singularly joined in the matter of the slave trade or "triangular trade," as it was called. During the early eighteenth century, New England ships began to sail from Boston, Newport, Salem, Providence, or New London loaded with rum, fish, dairy products, and other commodities bound for one of the fourteen English "factories" along the coast of West Africa. These factories, guarded by soldiers, had been built in cooperation with the local chief as collection and storage depots where native rulers could accumulate slaves captured on forays into the interior.

The trade had existed for centuries throughout Africa, where dominant tribes held their captives of war as slaves and raided their neighbors for women. In these black kingdoms and tribes, large numbers of slaves were sacrificed in religious ceremonies, on the death of the chief or their owners. While bartering for ivory, which they carried to Portugal, the Portuguese had been offered a number of these slaves in 1442. For centuries, Arab slave traders brought thousands of blacks out of Africa, the women to be used in the harems and the men to work in estates in Mohammedan kingdoms, such as Morocco, Egypt, and Zanzibar, and the Christian kingdom of Abyssinia. They also supplied a great demand for slaves in the African kingdoms of Uganda, Benin, and Dahomey.

Eventually the practice grew, as Europeans recognized the substantial profits to be made and began to bring slaves to Europe to work as servants and laborers. When the New England ships arrived at the factories along the African coast, traders would spend three or more weeks bartering for slaves, ivory, or other goods. The chiefs would display their wares, and after gifts and exchanges of goods, the ships would sail for the British or Spanish sugar colonies in the West Indies — Jamaica, Barbados, or Cuba. Of the captives, 13 percent were expected to die during the difficult six- to eight-week voyage, which was called the "middle passage." Most of the survivors were unloaded in the West Indies in exchange for molasses that was produced by other slaves working in the sugarcane fields or boiling houses. These people were worked under such brutal and merciless conditions that deaths ran as high as 30 percent during the first three or four years.

Most of the slaves that were sold on the mainland of North America, in colonies like South Carolina and Virginia, came from the West Indies after they had been conditioned to bondage there.

Finally, laden with barrels of molasses and occasionally a few slaves that had not been sold in the West Indies, the ships would sail for home ports in New England. There, rum distilleries would purchase the molasses, the major ingredient in rum, and the slaves would be sold as servants to wealthy merchants or landowners.

The total number of blacks, both slave and free, in New England was 20,000, in 1774. In the colony of Massachusetts Bay there were 5249 blacks in a white population of 343,845. Unlike the Southern colonies, the Puritan traditions of New England dictated that black men and women be converted to Christianity. The Calvinistic doctrine of the Congregationalist church held that everyone read the Bible for himself; consequently hundreds of schools were established for blacks to learn "reading, catechizing and writing." A majority of the blacks became Congregationalists, but others chose the Anglican church or became Quakers.

The Puritan tradition also precluded the casual sexual relationships between white or black men and black women that were often encouraged in the South. In New England, marriage was required of everyone, black or white.

By 1774, hundreds of New England slaves had been freed by their masters and, compared to the South, those still in bondage lived less difficult lives as porters, clerks, and messengers, working with their masters rather than for them. Although blacks were barred from military service early in the eighteenth century, by 1774 many militia companies included a small number of freed blacks, as well as slaves who were promised their freedom in return for military service.

THREE

Samuel Adams
and Colonial Unrest

ALTHOUGH the New York reception of the 23rd Foot reflected the loyalty many colonists felt toward the mother country, there were a few dissidents anxious to weaken or end British authority in America. Much of the strife between the colonies and England can be traced to dissident Samuel Adams and his Bostonian Whigs. It was he who coined the phrase "Boston Massacre" after the isolated incident in May 1770, and he marshaled support for the repeal of the Stamp Act, the Townshend Acts, and other unpopular British legislation.

Deacon Adams, Samuel's father, was a wealthy brewer in Boston. In 1747 he founded a bank called the Land Bank, using contributions from eight hundred prosperous Boston merchants who signed mortgages to secure their share of the assets. Deacon Adams was elected director of the bank and issued paper money, secured by the assets of the bank.

At the time, Samuel Adams was twenty-five years old. As the son of a very wealthy man, he lived in solitary splendor as an honor student at Harvard. His meals were prepared and served to him by his own staff of servants, and he never attended the Commons, where the average students took their meals.

The colonial lieutenant governor of Massachusetts, Thomas Hutchinson, was opposed to the Land Bank, which he believed to be inflationary. He wrote a series of tracts and letters to the British Parliament and was eventually successful in convincing them to abolish Deacon Adams's Land Bank. As a result, eight hundred Boston merchants lost their money and many were financially ruined. Adams not only lost the greater part of his fortune, but his reputation as well. His son was forced to move from his luxurious quarters at Harvard and was reduced to waiting tables in the Commons in return for his meals.

Samuel completed his education in that fashion and received a master's degree. But the traumatic experience fostered in him a lifelong hatred of the British government, men of great wealth and privilege, such as Thomas Hutchinson, and the institution of money itself. He became obsessed with a passionate desire to improve the lot of the common man, with whom he now identified.

Following graduation, Adams attempted one unsuccessful enterprise after another. Finally his father hired him to work in the dilapidated brewery left to him after his financial collapse. When the elder Adams died, Samuel lost the brewery by poor management.

Eventually Adams was elected as a tax collector for the city of Boston. In identifying closely with the common man, he was easily dissuaded from collecting many overdue taxes or pressing delinquent taxpayers. As a result, he was loved by the poor but distrusted by the propertied class. The votes of the poor being more numerous, Adams was re-elected year after year. There was talk among the merchants that he was "short" in his accounts, and some favored sending him to jail, but nothing came of the situation.

Throughout his life Samuel Adams was never able to understand money or the keeping of books. What he did understand — and better than any other man of his time — was the use of political power. Seldom in her history has England had a more dangerous enemy. It is a fact of history that Adams, prematurely gray, his shaking voice betraying the symptoms of palsy before he was forty, seedily dressed in clothes that marked him as a failure, cost Great Britain her American colonies. By his remarkable influence over other people he was able to generate the first successful colonial revolution in history.

THE DESTRUCTION OF TEA AT BOSTON HARBOR
Courtesy of the Museum of the City of New York

The Boston Tea Party according to Nathaniel Currier, who issued this as a colored lithograph in 1846, eleven years before he started the famous firm with James M. Ives.

As early as 1764, Adams had built his Whig Party into one of the most powerful and disciplined political machines the world had seen. He recruited his younger cousin — a superb lawyer named John Adams — and James Otis, a brilliant orator who tended toward instability. In his major coup, Adams persuaded one of the wealthiest men in the colonies, John Hancock, and Hancock threw his great wealth into the Whig cause. Adams's "great cause," of which he never uttered a word in public, was complete independence from England.

Through oratory, tireless intrigue, and the liberal use of John Hancock's money and jobs, Samuel Adams captured the imagination of the workingmen and rural laborers of New England, who soon organized into powerful mobs that dominated Boston.

Guy Fawkes Day is celebrated in England on November 5 as a reminder of a Catholic plot to blow up Parliament in 1605. In the American colonies during the eighteenth century it was celebrated in every village and town as "Pope's Day." Festivities included fireworks, the consumption of vast quantities of rum, and considerable fighting; it was, in fact, a day when ordinary citizens stayed home and locked their doors. As local doggerel put it, "Powder plots is not forgot. 'Twil be observed by many a sot."

The celebration, blatantly anti-Catholic, usually featured a large float carrying an effigy of the pope with other figures representing monks, friars, and devils. After a day of revelry and roughhouse, the climax occurred in the evening when the floats, effigies, and anything nearby were burned in a huge bonfire. Afterward everyone capable of doing so staggered home, usually after midnight.

Boston, over a period of years, had seen Pope's Day grow into an annual armed conflict between the north end of Boston and the south end. Each side prepared its own float, complete with the proper effigies. After marching around most of the day in their own section of Boston and forcing merchants to dispense free rum, the large mob, drunken and unruly, headed toward the other section of town. When the two mobs met, a wild brawl would break out in an attempt to capture the other's float. The fight, carried on with fists, clubs, and rocks, usually raged into the night. Often hundreds were injured, and occasionally people were killed. The few town constables were helpless to stop the riot, which then continued through the narrow streets of Boston.

Over the years both the north and the south sides developed a semipermanent organization that planned the next November 5 celebration. In 1764, the south-enders were led by a Captain Mackintosh and the north-enders by a Captain Swift, both planning to win the Pope's Day fracas. On November 5, 1764, the fights surpassed any that had gone before. In the end several people lay dead, many were seriously injured, and Boston was a shambles.

In the early morning of November 6 the two mobs, exhausted with fighting and drinking, had joined in burning their effigies in a monstrous bonfire. Then, arms about each other's shoulders, the weary warriors staggered home. By consummate skill, Samuel Adams was able to bring the two leaders together and gain control of the combined factions for his own purposes.

The next year brought great economic distress to Boston. Many businesses failed, and thousands of idle workers thronged the streets. Many could not pay their rent or debts, and farmers were unable to sell their produce. The French and Indian War had brought prosperity to New England, but it was over, and the troops, supplies, and jobs were gone.

Meanwhile, Parliament acted to replenish the war-depleted treasury by creating a Stamp Tax calling for a stamp to be affixed to every legal document, newspaper, or commercial paper. These new stamps were scheduled to go on sale in November 1765.

On the night of August 14 in that year, amid a roar of protest organized by Samuel Adams, Captain Mackintosh led the combined mobs of north and south Boston to the home of Andrew Oliver, who had been appointed stamp collector for Boston. They ripped his fences apart, smashed his windows, and poured into his house to steal his alcoholic beverages. Governor Sir Francis Bernard was reluctant to face the unruly crowd, but Lieutenant Governor Thomas Hutchinson showed his courage by bringing in the constables to restore order. The crowd pelted them with bricks but eventually withdrew when Adams signaled them to do so. The excited men and boys then marched to the largest of a group of elms, which they christened the Liberty Tree, and designated themselves the "Sons of Liberty." For many years after, August 14 was celebrated in New England as the day that the liberty movement began in the colonies.

A week later, on the night of August 21, an enormous crowd

formed in front of the State House, where a large bonfire had been built. Under the leadership of Captain Mackintosh, the crowd headed toward the most beautiful house in Boston, that of Lieutenant Governor Hutchinson, who had been for years the special object of Sam Adams's enmity.

On the way, members of the mob broke into several homes and ransacked them for rum. When they reached Hutchinson's house they wasted no time. The front door was smashed in with axes and the wild crowd rushed in. Hutchinson led his three sons, two daughters, their governess, and five servants out through the back, thereby probably saving their lives. The house was completely destroyed. Famous paintings were slashed; everything that could be carried — cash, silver, jewelry, rum, and wine — was stolen away as if by a colony of ants. Hutchinson's famous orchard of beautiful fruit trees was cut down; the roof of the house was torn off in great chunks and hurled into the gardens; wood panels were pried off the walls, as was the carved wainscoting, and carted away. The famous library, which included hundreds of leather-bound books, was thrown into the street and destroyed. And Hutchinson's manuscript on the history of Massachusetts Bay, which represented years of research and was due to be published, was torn to shreds.

The attack was condemned by most educated people of the colonies, and it cast a pall over Adams and his unruly mobs. He publicly expressed his regret and claimed to be outraged at the actions of Captain Mackintosh and his followers. Adams blamed "vagabonds" as the ones responsible, but when Mackintosh was jailed, Adams threatened more violence unless he was allowed to go free. Mackintosh was released, and he and Captain Swift met on November 5, 1765, and turned Pope's Day into a peaceful occasion. The former north- and south-enders were now members of the Sons of Liberty, and their proud march through the streets of Boston ended in a huge "unity feast" attended by prominent Whigs, including Samuel Adams.

As a result of the colonial boycott of the Stamp Tax, the merchants of England prevailed on Parliament to repeal the Act. That was done in 1766, and thereafter Samuel Adams and his Whigs continued to organize clubs, demonstrations, and projects. But the sacking of Hutchinson's home had made most people ashamed, and the ordinary people of Boston, as well as the merchant class, had lost their desire for confrontation.

In 1767 England passed the Townshend Acts, calling for new import duties on glass, lead, paint, paper, and tea. Again Sam Adams marshaled the mobs of Boston, and once again the colonies boycotted, with nonimportation agreements that caused British merchants to plead with Parliament to repeal the new taxes. It was then that Adams circulated a letter to all the other colonies making the point that "Taxation without representation is illegal" and endangered other liberties as well.

The king's minister ordered Governor Bernard to dissolve the Massachusetts Legislature for refusing to rescind Adams's circular letter, and two regiments of British regulars arrived to protect the customs officials attempting to enforce the Townshend Acts.

Many of the other colonies passed resolutions in sympathy with Boston, one of which, "the Virginia Resolves," was introduced by a wealthy planter and soldier of Virginia, Colonel George Washington. It was adopted in May 1769.

Again as a result of the financial distress that British merchants felt at the American boycott of British goods, Britain yielded when Lord North asked Parliament to repeal all of the duties established by the Townshend Acts except the one on tea. With the repeal, tension eased in New England, but not on the part of Samuel Adams.

On the night of March 5, 1770, an Adams-inspired mob badgered a lone British sentry on guard duty in front of the Boston Customs House. When the crowd began pelting the sentry with snowballs and other objects, he called for help and was soon joined by a squad of men from the 29th Regiment.

Finally the crowd attacked the British soldiers, who lost their heads and fired at the rioters. Five men died and a number were wounded. The soldiers were arrested by the Town Watch and tried for murder, but John Adams, although an ardent Whig and Samuel Adams's cousin, defended them on the ground that they had been in danger of being killed and had fired in self-defense. In a verdict historic in the annals of justice they were acquitted by an American jury. Two of the soldiers were found guilty of manslaughter but were released after minor punishment.

However, Samuel Adams did not let the people forget what he

called the "Boston Massacre." On March 5 of each year thereafter
a Whig leader would deliver a "Boston Massacre" oration. Several
years later, one of these highly inflammatory speeches read like
this:

> Has the grim savage rushed again from the wilderness? Or does
> some fiend, fierce from the depths of hell, with all the rancorous
> malice which the apostate damned can feel, twang her deadly arrows
> at our breast? No, none of these — it is the hand of Britain that
> inflicts the wound.[1]

By 1773, however, Adams's Whig Party was beginning to disin-
tegrate. It was divided into two conflicting groups: the conservative wing, which only wanted Britain to stop interfering with the
commercial life of the colonies; and the radical wing, which had in
mind a social revolution for the underprivileged and, in the case
of Samuel Adams, a secret desire for independence.

The conservative wing, in reality over a hundred years ahead of
its time, was in effect asking for dominion status: an independent
America that would be loyal to the king. Parliament, not ready for
that concept, rejected any such suggestions. When the conservative wing had abandoned the radical ideas and mob rule of Samuel
Adams, his nonimportation policy against British goods collapsed.
Most people were tired of the agitation and extremism of mob rule
in Boston and elsewhere. Adams's cousin, John Adams, had retired, and even John Hancock was flirting with the idea of joining
the Tory Party and Thomas Hutchinson, who had been elevated
to governor of the Massachusetts Bay colony.

All that remained of the Townshend Acts, which Adams called
"tyranny," was a small tax on tea, and the total price of tea, including the tax, was still cheaper in America than it was in England.
Americans settled down to coexist with the mother country. There
were no more riots, no more mobs, and in London Edmund
Burke, the colonists' friend who defended their rights in Parliament, felt that the revolt was now "deadness and vapidity."

Incredibly, the British East India Company blundered to the
rescue of Samuel Adams and his radicals. On the edge of bank-
ruptcy as the result of mismanagement and corruption, the company begged Parliament to save it. Many influential Englishmen,

including members of Parliament, were deeply involved in the company's financial affairs, and Parliament moved to ease the crisis.

It deprived the British East India Company of its right to govern India, but at the same time it undertook to refinance the shaky economic base of the company. Its warehouses in England contained seventeen million pounds of tea; to help move the tea Parliament passed the fateful Tea Act of 1773, which played into the hands of the rebellious Whigs.

The British East India Company was given a monopoly to ship tea to America without paying import duties and to sell it through their own agents to American retailers. Even after paying the threepence duty per pound, the American consumer would still be able to buy tea cheaper than the smuggled Dutch tea he had been drinking.

Suddenly, however, Samuel Adams rose up with new support from the conservative Whigs. Merchants who had purchased their tea from non-British sources would be ruined if only the chosen agents or consignees of the company were able to sell tea in the colonies.

John Hancock, in particular, came out roaring in opposition to the Tea Act, despite his disinterest in Samuel Adams's political agitation (caused, some said, by Hancock's courting of the beautiful Dolly Quincy). Hancock was the leading smuggler of Dutch tea in the colonies, although he wisely avoided mention of the financial injury he would suffer under the Tea Act. Instead, he argued that if it were possible for Parliament to give a monopoly to sell tea in America to a private company of its choice, what would prevent it from granting similar monopolies to other companies for other commodities?

The merchants of Rhode Island, Philadelphia, and New York angrily agreed with Hancock and exercised their control over Whig supporters to terrorize pro-British merchants into refusing to sell the tea arriving from England.

The rural areas of Massachusetts, without newspapers of their own, were bombarded by Whig papers like the *Boston Gazette*, which frightened uneducated farmers with imaginary dangers of impending heavy land taxes and confiscations.

One of the Tory blunders of the period now took place in Boston. Governor Hutchinson slyly arranged to have his two sons, Thomas Jr. and Elisha, appointed to lucrative positions as consignees for the tea monopoly. This fact, coupled with the Tea Act itself, gave Adams the ammunition he needed. Once again, he commanded unruly crowds of workers, farm laborers, and young apprentices; and the self-styled "Sons of Liberty" completely controlled the town of Boston.

Pro-British sentiment was brutally stilled by violence. Even the young Hutchinson consignees were forced to seek refuge outside of Boston among the British troops stationed at Castle William nearby. Mass meetings and inflammatory oratory became a common feature of Boston daily life, always organized by Samuel Adams and John Hancock, the latter now in the forefront of the fight.

On November 29, 1773, when the first tea ship, the *Dartmouth*, tied up at Griffin's Wharf, an immense crowd met at Faneuil Hall to decide the fate of the tea. The owner of the dock was told that if the tea were unloaded he personally would suffer. Twenty-five armed Sons of Liberty stood guard at the dock to see that no one attempted to unload the tea; among them was Paul Revere, a thirty-eight-year-old veteran of the French and Indian War and the leading silversmith of Boston.

Within the next few days, two more tea ships, the *Beaver* and the *Eleanor*, arrived at Griffin's Wharf. The meetings at Faneuil Hall continued, but the building was too small to hold the multitude, which now called itself the "Body." The gatherings were moved to Old South Meeting, and thousands poured into the huge structure. Sam Adams and his lieutenants brought hundreds of people from the countryside to Boston, mostly poor men and women who saw a glimmer of hope in resistance to what they called tyranny. Schoolboys, young girls, and unemployed youths marched to Boston and found their way to Old South Meeting. Adams took charge of the "Body" and transformed it so that it took over the authority of the regular town meeting. The Body voted that the tea must be returned to England, but Governor Hutchinson stubbornly refused to allow the ships to leave until they had unloaded their cargoes, as was required by Massachusetts law.

On December 16, over seven thousand people waited impatiently in or near Old South Meeting for Mr. Rotch, owner of the *Dartmouth*, to return from the town of Milton, fourteen miles away. He had gone there to see Governor Hutchinson and beg him to allow the tea ships to return to England with their cargoes. While waiting, the crowd grew more and more restive as they listened to speakers promising violent action. About 6:00 P.M. Rotch returned with the news: the governor had refused to allow the ships to sail.

Then, in a dramatic historical moment, Samuel Adams climbed atop a bench. There was an immediate, breathless silence, and he spoke the words his men were waiting for: "This meeting can do nothing more to save the country." Instant pandemonium broke out amid cheers, yells, and war whoops. The crowd poured out of the Old South Meeting and headed for Griffin's Wharf.

The demonstration had been carefully organized, and Adams's statement was the signal. Indian disguises had been prepared as camouflage by young men from neighboring towns, but many young members of the Boston Sons of Liberty refused to be kept from the festivities.

While thousands watched along the docks, the "Indians" split into three groups and silently and efficiently filed onto the three tea ships. Without opposition from the ships' crews, they went below, hoisted the tea chests upon the decks, broke them open, and dumped them into the harbor.

The harbor was filled with British warships under the command of Admiral Montague, and many ships rode at anchor less than four hundred yards from Griffin's Wharf. Montague himself watched the affair from the home of a Tory friend, but no attempt was made to interfere with the destruction of the tea. Even the 64th and 65th regiments of foot garrisoned on Castle Island made no move to apprehend the fewer than 150 "Indians."

The next morning, Paul Revere rode from Boston to Cambridge, to Watertown, Worcester, Springfield, Hartford, New Haven, New York, and finally Philadelphia. He carried dispatches from the Boston Committee of Correspondence to acquaint other Committees with what had transpired on the night of December 16, 1773. What had been achieved was an act of defiance so rebellious that the British government could not ignore it. Boston would be punished.

FOUR

The Punishment of Boston

ON THE MORNING of January 19, 1774, the British merchantman *Hayley* landed at the English port of Dover. Her captain carried a copy of the *Boston Evening News* article describing the attack on the tea ships in Boston Harbor. A week later, the official report arrived from Governor Hutchinson describing the destruction of 340 chests of tea. He also reported his difficulties in summoning a meeting of the council that governed Massachusetts, and how the Sons of Liberty had intimidated all members friendly to the king. Many had pleaded illness rather than attend, and even some Whig members had done so. The governor asserted that it was impossible to prosecute the perpetrators of the crime, because all had been disguised, and no one could be found to testify against anyone who was accused.

Other dispatches soon arrived. Admiral Montague charged in blunt language that the destruction of the tea was caused by John Hancock and Samuel Adams. Lieutenant Colonel Alexander Leslie, who commanded the 64th Regiment at Castle William, reported that the council had prevented him from marching his men into the city to protect the tea. He charged that Hancock, as captain of the Governor's Colonial Militia Guard, had used the men of his company to take possession of the three tea ships. A later dispatch from Governor Hutchinson announced that, while he had at long last formed his council, he was unable to have the Grand Jury prosecute, for he could not find "any persons willing to give an account of the persons who were most active."

Late in January, a British customs officer named John Malcolm was involved in a dispute with a Boston merchant. The dispute grew into a heated shouting match, and insults were traded in a torrent of angry sound. Malcolm lost control, pulled out his ceremonial sword, and wounded the merchant. The crowd that gathered included many members of the Sons of Liberty, and as the merchant slumped bleeding to the ground, they seized Malcolm and dragged him through the streets to a nearby two-wheeled cart. There they tied his wrists to the tailgate, ripped off his clothes, poured hot tar over him, and showered him with the feathers of two torn pillows.

The jeering mob dragged the cart, the victim jerked along behind it, to the Liberty Tree. Under the arching elm branches Malcolm was lifted on a platform before a crowd of several thousand and threatened with instant death unless he renounced his commission as customs officer. Though in intense pain from his burns, Malcolm refused, whereupon he was dragged to a ladder placed against the tree. A noose was put around his neck, and he was told that unless he renounced his commission at once, he would be sent "straight to hell." When he again refused, the mob relented. He was taken back to the cart, tied to the tailgate, and flogged with a cat-o'-nine-tails on his blistered, tar-covered back. When several Sons of Liberty closed in on him with drawn hunting knives and threatened to cut his ears off, Malcolm capitulated. He renounced his commission and was taken home to his distraught family. The merchant he had wounded recovered and had actually suffered only a slight flesh wound.

The affair was reported by Governor Hutchinson to the secretary of the colonies, the Earl of Dartmouth. At no time, wrote Hutchinson, did anyone in Boston, high or low, attempt to save John Malcolm during his ordeal. It was impossible to prosecute for the crime, for fear of violent retaliation undoubtedly prevented witnesses from coming forward to testify. No one in Boston or in all of New England would protect anyone who did, and it became clear to Parliament that Samuel Adams and his mobs ruled Boston, and British troops would be necessary to protect loyal citizens in the troubled colony.

The rebellion exercised by the mobs of Boston was found in government circles, as well. In 1772 Parliament had taken from the colonial legislatures control of the salaries of governors and judges of the superior courts. This was done to make those officials independent of the popularly elected legislatures, which had controlled them by their power to delay or withhold salaries.

When the General Assembly reconvened in Boston on January 26, 1774, the Whigs rekindled this as a central political issue. The law, they said, enabled the ministers in London to tax the Massachusetts colony to pay the governor and judges from England, thus enabling them to drastically alter the democratic nature of the government. The General Assembly attacked the Salaries Law of 1772 as a breach of their colonial charters.

The Whigs applied pressure to the judges to renounce their salaries if paid by the Crown. One judge, Edmund Trowbridge, immediately yielded to the General Assembly and issued a declaration that, "In compliance with the resolve of the honorable House of Representatives of June 1773, I do declare that I am determined still to receive the grants of the General Assembly of this province for my services as a justice of the Superior Court, without receiving any grant from the Crown for the same service." Justices Foster, Hutchinson, Cushing, and Ropes also agreed to receive their salary from the General Assembly. Chief Justice Peter Oliver, however, sent a letter to the House of Representatives on February 3 refusing to disobey his king, "Lest I should incur a censure from the best of monarchs."

Consequently, on February 11 the General Assembly passed a series of resolutions condemning Justice Oliver as "an enemy of the constitution of this province and obnoxious to the good people." A motion that he be removed by the governor was passed by a vote of 96 to 9 in the House. However, Governor Hutchinson refused to remove Oliver and further informed the House that he had no intention of accepting his own salary from the General Assembly. He reminded the Assembly that they were powerless under the charter to do anything except to "advise and assist," and that any refusal to accept the salary prepared by the royal authority for the payment of the justices would be a display of "contempt of this royal authority."

On February 24 the General Assembly adopted articles of impeachment of the Chief Justice for "high crimes and misdemeanors." He was charged with accepting money from the king, which constituted a "continual bribe in his judicial proceedings," and a committee of nine was appointed to appear before the governor to impeach Chief Justice Oliver.

Governor Hutchinson replied that he was not aware of any crimes or misdemeanors, nor was he aware that the council had any concurrent jurisdiction under the charter to try cases with the governor.

The council answered the governor by accusing him of making false representation in order to gain profit and places of honor. And on March 9, 1774, Hutchinson adjourned the General Assembly and advised George III that, "The course of the law is now wholly stopped. All legislative as well as executive power is gone." In short, an impasse had been reached.

Meanwhile, on March 31, King George III signed the fateful Boston Port Bill. Effective June 1, 1774, the bill was a sharp reprimand to rebellious Boston in the form of completely closing the Port of Boston to seagoing traffic until the damages created by the destruction of the tea were paid in full by the town. The governor was to come to London and report to Parliament; during his absence the new governor would be Major General Thomas Gage, holding the double responsibility of commander-in-chief of all British military forces in North America.

Additional regiments of regulars were to be sent to Boston to enforce the new law. The capital of the Massachusetts Bay colony was moved from Boston to Salem, and the Boston Customs House was closed and relocated in Plymouth.

On May 10 the official copy of the Boston Port Bill reached Boston with the arrival of the British warship *Lively*. Three days later, fifty-two-year-old Major General Thomas Gage arrived in Boston Harbor. He did not go ashore, however, but spent four days in conference aboard his ship with his predecessor, Governor Hutchinson, and other leading Loyalists of Boston. Together they held around-the-clock discussions of the best ways to implement the Port Bill.

Gage, no stranger to America, had lived there nearly twenty years. He had led the vanguard during General Braddock's campaign in the French and Indian War, and he had gallantly helped carry the mortally wounded Braddock from the battlefield. Gage was responsible for the development of the light infantry concept during the war, and as a colonel he had commanded the first light infantry regiment in the British army against the French with outstanding success. At the end of the war he had been appointed military governor of Montreal, where he had distinguished himself by his tact and mildness in dealing with the French inhabitants.

Gage was married to an American woman, the daughter of Peter Kremble of New Jersey, and he had replaced Lord Jeffrey Amherst as commander-in-chief in North America. As such he had shown great tact in dealing with the colonial authorities during crises arising from the Stamp Tax confrontations.

His appointment was greeted by the Americans with delight, and he was royally received by the people of Boston, where he immediately proclaimed that all officeholders would retain their positions.

During four continuous days of discussions with the Loyalists, Gage formed some definite opinions of the situation he faced. He was convinced that the Whig leaders were self-seeking, selfish demagogues who had no real grievances but were treasonably involved in a plot to overthrow the beneficent British government in hopes of finding themselves top positions in a new government.

When the Boston Port Bill went into effect, Gage immediately set to work to enforce its provisions. Under Admiral George Montague, all British warships were put on stations that tightly sealed the port, and the teeming docks were soon completely deserted. Two weeks later, two regiments fresh from duty in Ireland arrived and marched through the streets of Boston. They were the first British troops there since the British garrison was removed to Castle William after the Boston Massacre in 1770.

Amid rumors of impending violence by the "faction," as the radical Whigs were called, the 4th Regiment, the King's Own, filed off their ships on June 14 and marched through the tense city to the Boston Common, where they pitched their white tents. Thirty-two-year-old Captain William Glanville Evelyn and his company led the regiment through the narrow streets, peering into cross-streets and alleys. They were expecting trouble, but there were no incidents. In the rear of the company marched Ensign George Evelyn Boscawen, Captain Evelyn's seventeen-year-old cousin.

The following day the 43rd Regiment of Foot disembarked and, after marching through the town, pitched their tents next to the line of the King's Own. On July 6, the 5th Regiment under Colonel Lord Percy arrived and was followed by the 38th. Soon the four regiments were all camped on the Common.

Shortly after his arrival, Captain Evelyn wrote his father in England expressing the attitude of the newly arrived British troops. As he saw the situation, the great majority of the people of Massachusetts appeared loyal to the king. However, the radical Whigs had succeeded in terrorizing anyone whom they found to hold opinions contrary to their own. Those who disagreed with them were brutally beaten, tarred, and feathered. The captain felt that the arrival of the British troops in Boston had restored liberty and freedom of speech to the city.

The three transports that brought the 4th Regiment to Boston sailed for New York as soon as they had landed the troops. There they embarked the Royal Welsh Fusiliers, the Mackenzie family among them, and returned to Boston in early August, tying up at Rowe's Wharf. The first man to step ashore was the regimental adjutant, Lieutenant Mackenzie.

Redcoated infantrymen followed Mackenzie down the gangways as hoarse-voiced sergeants bellowed commands. The beat of the drums sounded a note of urgency and men raced to line up by companies. Amid this welter of confused and discordant sounds, the rolling of the drums abruptly stopped; it was silent. The regiment was formed.

Staccato reports from right to left rippled across the lines of rigid men as each company commander reported his company present and all men accounted for. A sharp command, the men faced right, the drums pounded out the cadence, the fifes shrilled, and in perfect step the 23rd Royal Welsh Fusiliers moved down the dock toward adjacent Fort Hill. Barracks were not yet available for either the troops or their dependents, and temporary quarters had to be found for the families while the men lived in tents on Fort Hill.

As the men marched off, the wives and children of officers began making arrangements with draymen to move their belongings to suitable lodgings. Then came the wives and children of the enlisted men, struggling laboriously down the dock laden with bags and bundles.

Nancy Mackenzie looked desperately for a house to rent. After a long and weary day, as the sun was setting, she moved into a flat in a two-story building nearly a mile from Fort Hill, where her husband's regiment had erected their tents.

Winter was approaching, and Gage was anxious for the welfare of his troops. It would be impossible for them to live in tents during the severe New England winter. His plans to build barracks were temporarily halted when the workingmen of Boston, obeying orders from Samuel Adams and the radical Whigs, refused to work for the British army. In addition, merchants were prevented from selling the army blankets, tools, and other necessary materials.

Luckily, the winter of 1774–75 was the mildest in the memory of older New Englanders. Soon Loyalist laborers and carpenters from New York began to work on the barracks, together with workers drawn from warships in the harbor.

Some troops were quartered in abandoned warehouses and distilleries, but Gage planned to move those men living in tents on Boston Common and Fort Hill into new barracks before the snows arrived.

Meanwhile, officers like Captain W. Glanville Evelyn, his cousin Ensign Boscawen, and Captain Champagne of the 4th Regiment were comfortable in rented houses, with servants to clean, cook, and serve, both for them and for their guests at frequent parties.

On November 15, winter housing was completed, and the 4th, 5th, 38th, and 43rd Regiments left their tents and marched to newly constructed barracks. Mackenzie and the 23rd Welsh Fusiliers moved into new barracks on Fort Hill. The 59th Regiment was quartered in an empty distillery near Roxbury Neck, where they manned the fortifications. And four regiments — the 10th, 18th, 47th, and 52nd — disembarked from the transports they had been living on in the harbor and marched to new barracks.

The new quarters were cold, dismal, and unfinished, lacking fireplaces and stoves. Men were put to work completing the unfinished tasks under pressure of the advancing cold, and soon the barracks were clean and warm. The tent cities were stored by the Quartermaster for future use, and shacks that had been erected around the camps were burned down, forcing dependents of the various regiments to find other quarters wherever possible. Unable to pay high rents, most of them were forced into other crowded, squalid, and unhealthy hovels.

By August, Gage had eleven regiments in Boston, including a Royal Artillery train and a battalion of the Royal Marines under the command of Major Pitcairn. This brought the number of British soldiers there to slightly less than three thousand.

Late in November 1774 Gage reorganized the British army in Boston into three brigades of approximately one thousand men each. The First Brigade, under the command of Lord Percy, consisted of the 4th Regiment (the King's Own), the 23rd Regiment (Royal Welsh Fusiliers), and the 47th Regiment, plus 460 Royal Marines under Pitcairn. The Second Brigade, under the command of General Pigot, consisted of the 5th Regiment, the 38th Regiment, and the 52nd Regiment. The Third Brigade, under the command of General Jones, included the 10th Regiment, the 43rd Regiment, the 59th Regiment, and the three detached companies of the 65th Regiment.

There have been various estimates of the total British strength in Boston on the eve of Lexington and Concord. Numerous figures have been quoted by historians, but the most reliable were the result of a minute study of British strength conducted by hundreds of American agents and reported to a special committee appointed for that purpose by the Provincial Congress. On March 20, 1775, one month before Lexington, the committee reported the following figures: "The total British strength consisted of about 2,850 men distributed as follows: on Boston Common, about 1,700; on Fort Hill, 400; on Boston Neck, 340; in barracks at the Castle [William], 330; quartered in King Street, 80."[1]

The impact of the British military presence soon increased tensions within the city. Hundreds of Loyalists fled to Boston as their homes were looted in the countryside, and no Loyalist was safe in the suburbs of Boston, where mobs smashed windows and burned homes. Many upper-class families living in Boston had enjoyed a second home in the country; but these were now falling into the hands of wandering bands of the Sons of Liberty.

The British became convinced that a shooting war would soon begin, and officers were concerned with the reputed marksmanship of American militiamen. Consequently, General Gage ordered target practice for all regiments.

Lieutenant Mackenzie had charge of this exercise, in which life-sized figures fashioned from thin boards were placed on small rafts anchored at various distances from the open side of the wharf. As the targets bobbed up and down with the tide, an officer pointed out the target figures. Six rounds were allocated per man daily for this firing practice.

As regimental adjutant, Mackenzie was also concerned about excessive drunkenness among the men. Regardless of efforts to prevent liquor from being sold to the troops, soldiers' wives and other people were able to smuggle low-priced New England rum to them. Intoxicated men staggered about the camp day and night; two men died in one night as a result of this excessive drinking.

On the morning of December 1, a private in the Light Infantry Company of the King's Own 4th Regiment was found dead on sentry duty. He lay among the rocks just below the high water mark, his face and head badly bruised, and his commanding officer believed he had fallen over the embankment in a drunken stupor. Others, however, suspected foul play by the Americans.

Mackenzie and other officers also suspected the Americans of secretly supplying the regulars with rum to induce them to desert. Desertion was a major problem in the British army in Boston and elsewhere during the Revolutionary War. Many factors encouraged it: the prosperous American towns and countryside; the desperate need for colonial workers; jobs paying high wages; opportunities to acquire land; the friendly encouragement of the colonists toward the desertion of enlisted regulars; and the great distance from home and family, which weakened ties with England. Many English soldiers with wives and children back home started a new life in America by simply walking away from the army, and their families never heard from them again.

Initially Gage was lenient with deserters, but the case of Robert

Vaughan of the 52nd Regiment hardened him to future desertions. Vaughan had been caught trying to escape by way of the Charlestown ferry. He was tried and sentenced to be shot, but Gage stayed the execution and pardoned him. In a few days Vaughan successfully attempted to desert again, and Gage immediately announced that, "As clemency has had so little effect," Vaughan would be the last man he would pardon for desertion. From then on, deserters were shot or hanged whenever captured.

Regulars continued to desert at an alarming rate. Almost every morning's muster revealed that someone had disappeared during the night, and frequently the desertion of two or three men at the same time would be discovered.

Some officers criticized General Gage's method of conducting the execution of deserters. Lieutenant John Barker of the 4th Regiment felt that it was a mistake to shoot them in front of only a firing squad and a few spectators. He favored public executions before the entire army for, as he wrote in his diary on December 24, 1774, "Punishments were never meant only to affect criminals, but also as examples to the rest of mankind."[2]

Death in various forms struck the British army in Boston frequently. The *Evening Post* of January 30, 1775, stated that during the six months from July 10, 1774, to January 10, 1775, "There had died in the British Army occupying Boston one captain, one lieutenant, and 123 soldiers, women and children, besides several seamen from the men-of-war and transports."[3] The British cemetery at the foot of Boston Common grew larger each week. Among the individual deaths:

Lieutenant John Boadil of the Royal Welsh Fusiliers died in January of consumption;

A soldier of the 4th Regiment died two days after receiving 500 lashes for selling his musket to a townsman;

Several men of the 18th Regiment, the Royal Irish, died when the three companies in Boston came down with spotted fever. The men were rushed on board their transport to keep them from infecting the rest of the army. The infection occurred because their barracks, which had previously been a distillery, had a large reservoir of stagnant water under the building;

Captain Gabriel Maturin, General Gage's private secretary, died of a throat distemper which was prevalent in the Army;

Ensign Jackson of the 64th Regiment died after being ill only two days;

On the day before Christmas, a soldier of the 10th Regiment was shot for desertion;

On the day after Christmas, a soldier in the Light Infantry Company of Lieutenant Barker's 4th Regiment died suddenly in the middle of the night from unknown causes.[4]

The state of medical knowledge contributed to the death toll, also. During the last quarter of the eighteenth century, the science of medicine and surgery was little better than it had been for over two hundred years. Scant progress had been made since the discovery of the circulation of blood seventy years earlier. Medicine generally was practiced by men who placed great faith in strong drugs and cathartics, emetics, blisters, blood-letting, opium, and Peruvian bark. Virtually the only capital operations were amputations and trepanation, in which sections of the skull were cut away. The great cavities of the body were beyond medical skills, and anesthesia was seventy years away.

Smallpox, which had been a deadly killer, was the one infectious disease that medical men of the time understood and could combat with some degree of success. Vaccination was not discovered until twenty years later; the weapon therefore was inoculation.

First introduced by the Hindus, the concept of inoculation passed to the Turks, who brought it into Europe at the beginning of the eighteenth century. The idea was to fight fire with fire; to prevent a disease by inoculation with its own virus. Smallpox inoculation was usually done in the summer. The virus was taken on the twelfth or thirteenth day from young and healthy subjects who had contracted mild cases of smallpox. The process was also carried out occasionally from dried scabs, which might have lost some of their virulence. It was believed that there was less malignancy in the disease inoculated through the skin into the capillaries than when it entered the body through the lungs. The method was based on a statistical truth: natural smallpox destroyed one out of six of its victims; smallpox produced by inoculation killed only one in three hundred.

Despite the proven results of inoculation, the process had many opponents, who argued that, while it was true that the number who died from smallpox derived from inoculation was smaller, mass inoculations spread smallpox to vastly more people. Thus, although the percentage of mortality was less, the total number of deaths was greater than if the disease were left in its natural state.

In 1774 the city of Boston was known as a medical center, but the government was officially opposed to the practice of inoculation. Many affluent citizens had their own physician secretly inoculate them. However, if their light case was reported, they were treated as though they had the most virulent form and were quarantined in a hospital at New Boston.

Smallpox first broke out among the British troops in 1774 in a house near the barracks of the 59th Regiment, where a sergeant kept his common-law wife and her five children, three of whom were by another man. The November 21, 1774, Minutes of the Boston Selectmen read:

> Information given the Selectmen, that the Smallpox has broken out in a house near the Corn Fields occupied by a Sergeant of Colonel Hammilton's Regiment (59th) and that five of his children are now under the Distemper.
>
> Dr. Jarvis returned and reported that he had been at the house and by enquiry thinks there is no doubt of the children having Smallpox.
>
> Mr. Scollay and Mr. Newell a committee to wait upon the Governor [General Gage] with information of this event, and to settle with him the charge of their removal etc. and to motion an examination of the several barracks.
>
> The committee returned and reported that the Governor had given orders for an examination of the several barracks and that a return would be made immediately.

The November 22 Minutes of the Boston Selectmen read:

MORNING SESSION

> The five children with the Smallpox in the house of one Magraw, a soldier of the 59th Regiment, Colonel Hammelton, were removed this morning to the hospital at New Boston under the care of Mr. Dorrington, the parents of the children consenting to the same.
>
> Selectmen voted that Dr. Jarvis have the care of the children as their physician. The mother of three of the Smallpox children, and

the father of two of them were permitted to go to the hospital, to attend their children.

Agreed with Mr. Joseph Vose to supply the hospital with mutton for three weeks at three coppers per pound.

AFTERNOON SESSION

Mr. Barrett was directed to smoke and clean the things at the house the children were removed from, also the rooms the children had been kept in, and a guard was provided to prevent the soldiers going into the infected rooms.

Word of the infected children spread quickly throughout Boston and caused rumors that there was a smallpox epidemic among the British troops. There were reports of bodies being buried during the night in secret, and hundreds began to clamor for permission to leave for the countryside. In order to calm the people, the selectmen placed the following advertisement in several newspapers:

ADVERTISEMENT

As the appearance of the Smallpox in this town has given rise to various reports; the public are hereby informed that last Monday night the Selectmen were acquainted by a surgeon of the Army, that five children in a house occupied by a soldier of the 59th Regiment, were seized with that disorder, all of whom were sent early the next morning to the hospital at New Boston, as was a soldier of the same Regiment in the day following. These are the only persons in town who have infections, and all in a fair way of recovery. Upon a strict enquiry made through the Regiments, by order of the Governor, no one has been found among them that appears to have even the symptoms of that distemper; the rumor that some soldiers or their children were to be inoculated is without foundation; such measures having been forbid on pain of his Excellency's highest displeasure. It is supposed that this disease was taken from a child brought from New York in one of the transports, which died a fortnight ago; and the public may be assured that the greatest care has been taken to prevent a communication of the infection.

By order of the Selectmen
November 26, 1774
William Cooper, Town Clerk

The selectmen placed another advertisement on December 7:

ADVERTISEMENT

The Public are hereby informed that the soldier and five children sent to the hospital at New Boston under the care of Dr. Jarvis as mentioned in the former advertisement are all recovered; that yesterday two children from the house the former children were taken from, and a soldier of the 59th Regiment at the barracks near the "Bunch of Grapes" who took the distemper from the same family were sent to said hospital. After strict enquiry these are all the persons who have the Smallpox in this town.

> By order of the Selectmen
> December 7, 1774
> William Cooper, Town Clerk[5]

Unfortunately, the optimism of the advertisement was unwarranted. On December 12 Private George Baldwin of the 59th came down with the dread disease and was taken to New Boston. He died several weeks later and was buried in the army burying grounds at the foot of the Common. A young child from the barracks of the 59th on Doan's Wharf was sent to New Boston, and, on December 17, Dr. Jarvis reported that a Dr. Hill's wife and three children and a Captain Trig's children had all "passed" through the smallpox. A case of inoculation by a doctor was suspected here, but under questioning all denied having received the treatment, as it was illegal in Boston.

Ten days later a Lieutenant Clarke's maidservant came down with smallpox, and General Gage announced that a transport in the harbor was being prepared to handle any army personnel who should henceforth contract the disease.

As the new year of 1775 arrived, more cases of smallpox were reported. On January 11 the son of a Mr. King was stricken and taken to New Boston, and a week later the son of a soldier of the 59th came down with the disease and was sent to the hospital ship in the harbor.

On January 12 Dr. Jarvis reported that a young woman and her child living at a house on Cross Street, which was also occupied by a sergeant of the 59th, were taken with the smallpox, and mother and child were carried by boat to the hospital ship.

Fear of a major smallpox epidemic for which the British army could be held responsible only worsened relations between the colonists and Britain. Indeed, the situation had begun to deteriorate with the first landing of British troops in Boston on June 14, 1774. Brawls between unemployed workers and British regulars occurred almost nightly, and hostilities between British officers and the Town Watch created several critical situations.

Gage and his officers were increasingly troubled by the conditions developing in New England. They saw clearly what was not apparent three thousand miles away in London: in America, England was dealing with an armed population. Every man owned some kind of firearm that he was trained to use. Militia were drilling three times a week, often more. Every day prominent families streamed into Boston as refugees seeking the protection of the British army. Most had been forced to abandon their homes in the suburbs and countryside to the Sons of Liberty, who looted and confiscated while claiming the highest motives. The British officers felt helpless to aid the men and women who were being persecuted for their loyalty, and they yearned to teach the "patriots" to respect their king and his loyal subjects. Instead, they were forced by Gage to remain in Boston and engage in training marches. The officers fumed and called Gage an old woman behind his back, praying for an opportunity to strike at the Sons of Liberty.

When the Boston Port Bill went into effect, it cut off all imports to Boston from the sea, which meant that grain shipments coming from the south could not reach Boston. The western and southern counties in Massachusetts, Rhode Island, and Connecticut came to the aid of the city, sending thousands of carts loaded with supplies to the besieged inhabitants. To American farmers and artisans, Britain's show of military force against the city of Boston was a blow aimed at the liberty of all British subjects in America. It was also a military challenge that militia companies could only interpret as an insult, and soon they began to train daily in anticipation of armed conflict.

One such militiaman, a member of the Massachusetts militia, was Nathaniel Wade, a young carpenter from Ipswich, twenty-five miles north of Boston. Out of work as a result of the Port Bill, and a devoted believer in the patriot cause, Wade became active in the formation and training of the five militia companies of Ipswich. He was a lean, hard-muscled, young bachelor, well known and liked in the community, where his parents were prosperous farmers.

The social status of artisans like Wade was much higher in America than in the closely regulated, rigid social system of England. In America, artisans stood in the middle of the social structure, particularly if they belonged to the Congregational church in Massachusetts, which claimed the major part of the middle class. Most Loyalists, on the other hand, belonged to the Episcopalian church, and there was a persistent rumor in New England that Parliament intended to create a religious hierarchy in America and appoint an Episcopal bishop for the colonies. The same rumor reported that Britain intended to introduce tithes for the support of the Church of England, as was done in Britain, and in time intended to wipe out the "heresy" of Congregationalism. The Quebec Act, which had granted religious freedom to Catholics in Canada, was interpreted as an opening move in such a program to destroy the Congregational church. As a result, nearly all the Congregational clergy of Massachusetts were active Whigs, and since virtually everyone attended church on Sunday, the sermons emanating from hundreds of Congregational pulpits fell on fertile minds, particularly those of workingmen. Such famous Boston Congregational ministers as Charles Chauncy, Samuel Cooper, Andrew Elliot, Ebeneezer Pemberton, John Lathrop, John Bacon, Simeon Howard, and Samuel Stillman were leading Whigs and ardent patriots.

The prevailing theory held by the colonists was that England, like the Roman Empire, had become corrupted by luxury, effeminacy, and venality. They believed that England had succumbed to the same poisons that had destroyed Rome. This corruption had enabled wealthy and bribable men to control the king, his ministers, and his favorites. Most Americans were certain that mysterious men were plotting to make slaves of the colonists by curtailing their liberties as Englishmen.

Even such highly educated men as Thomas Jefferson were so

persuaded. Jefferson wrote, "That single acts of tyranny may be ascribed to the accidental opinion of day-to-day series of oppressions, begun at a distinguished period and pursued unalterably through every change of ministers does plainly prove a deliberate and systematical plan of reducing us to slavery." George Washington wrote in the Fairfax Resolves in 1774 that he was fully convinced that the English government had used "a regular systematic plan to fix the shackles of slavery upon us."

The common belief of the average American emerges in the letters, journals, and diaries of the period: the immoral British government, having exhausted opportunities for plunder and profits in England and Ireland, was now seeking a quarrel with the American colonies as an excuse to plunder them of their wealth. Corrupt officials had drained both England and Ireland through taxes; therefore, the colonies were now the last remaining area for their greed. They hoped to drain the Americans quietly, but the furor over the Stamp Act had held them back, and it was then decided to destroy the colonial power to resist, so that the colonies could be broken up politically. To do so, these "corrupt forces" wished to provoke a war, which would provide the opportunity to declare Americans rebels and to conquer them. It was widely known at the time that conquered rebels must forfeit all their possessions to the king.

Unlikely as this point of view may seem to twentieth-century minds, it was firmly held by most Americans in 1774. They rejected the British charge that America opposed the Coercive Acts out of personal considerations or through the actions of a faction, or mob, of a political party. Their avowed purpose was self-defense, public faith, and preservation of the liberties of mankind.

Even as these embers of discontent smouldered, the British Parliament fed the incipient flames by the enactment of two new Acts that in effect repealed the charter of Massachusetts. The first, titled "An Act for the Better Regulating the Government of the Province of Massachusetts Bay," was passed in the House of Commons on May 2, 1774, by a vote of 239 to 64, and in the House of Lords by 92 to 20. A major blow at colonial democracy, the Act provided that the twenty-eight council members would cease to be selected by the colonial House of Representatives, and henceforth would be appointed and dismissed at the pleasure of and by the king.

In addition to rescinding the appointive power of the House of Representatives, the Act directed that all judges, sheriffs, and other civil officers in the future would be appointed by the governor or, in his absence, by the lieutenant governor. Juries were to be summoned by the sheriff, rather than selected from and by the voters. This was a major loss of democratic process, because the governor and lieutenant governor were appointed by the king, and the sheriffs were appointed by the governor. Thus all key government posts would be loyal to the king, rather than to the will of the colonial legislature. The greatest loss to the colonists, however, was their right to hold public meetings without the permission of the governor, except the annual meetings in March and May.

The second, "An Act for the More Impartial Administration of Justice in Said Province," passed on May 6 in the House of Commons by a vote of 127 to 24 and in the House of Lords by 43 to 12. It provided that any offender against the laws could be transported to another colony or to England for trial. This could be used in two ways: against any American who it was feared would be acquitted by an American jury; and in favor of a British soldier or officer who committed a crime against a colonist.

These new Acts were intended to destroy the Massachusetts political system that had grown strong in 154 years of self-government. They struck down customs that had grown, with time, into rights. The issue was no longer merely that of taxation; it cut deeply into the question of personal rights: the right to trial by a jury of neighbors and the right to elect one's own representatives. The new laws subsequently became known in the colonies as the Intolerable Acts or the Coercive Acts, and efforts to enforce them brought on the American Revolution.

On June 2, 1774, a ship from Bristol brought General Gage copies of the Acts, together with a letter from Lord Dartmouth instructing how to put them into effect. Dartmouth wrote, "Not only the dignity and reputation of the empire, but the power and

the very existence of the empire depended upon the issue, for if
the ideas of independence once took root, the colonial relations
would be severed, and destruction would follow disunion."[6]

The day the two Acts arrived in Boston, American agents informed the Boston Committee of Correspondence, and a meeting
was called. There Dr. Joseph Warren, Dr. Benjamin Church, and
Joseph Greenleaf were selected as a subcommittee to send a circular letter to every town in the Province of Massachusetts Bay,
proposing a "solemn league and covenant" to neither import, export, nor consume British goods, and to cease connections with
anyone who refused to sign. This boycott was to continue "until
the harbor of Boston shall be opened and our charter rights restored."[7]

The concept of a boycott against British goods had been a po-
tent colonial weapon since it was first used in 1764. It persuaded
many British merchants to bring their weight to bear on Parliament to repeal various measures to which the colonists objected.
In addition to urging Parliament to repeal the Coercive Acts, the
1774 boycott used psychology to reintroduce concepts of Puritan
austerity and self-sacrifice to Massachusetts. Americans were told
that they had been drawn into luxury and dissipation; the boycott
offered the opportunity to reaffirm the Puritan ethic and forsake
the delights of British goods while working to preserve liberty.

When Gage received official announcement of the new Acts on
June 8, he announced the appointment of the Mandamus Council,
representing the colony for the king. The twenty-four men
promptly accepted their appointments and held their first meeting. Judges proceeded to hold court immediately, and newly appointed sheriffs summoned juries. It appeared that Parliament
had won. The critical questions to be answered, however, were
these: Would the Americans recognize and obey these new
officials? Would the other colonies accept the situation in Massachusetts? On the answers hung the fate of the colonies and much
of the British Empire. The answers quickly came.

Although the new Acts outlawed public meetings in Massachusetts, a meeting was called for August 24, 1774, in the new capital
of Salem. Handbills were sent out by the Committee of Correspon-

dence to inform the voters that delegates were to be elected for a convention. The day before the meeting was to open, Gage issued a proclamation prohibiting anyone from attending, and he sent a company of regulars from Boston to Salem to enforce it.

The meeting was held, but soldiers burst into the meetinghouse, drove the people into the streets, and arrested the committee members. Nonetheless, a series of county conventions was held, and some county committees urged a joint meeting of the various county committees. Despite the presence of the British army, Joseph Warren called such a meeting for August 26, 1774, in Faneuil Hall in Boston.

At this meeting it was ruled that the Coercive Acts were unconstitutional and that all of the king's appointed officers were holding office illegally. The new Parliamentary policy was decried as a system of tyranny, and it was decided to form a provincial congress to counteract the tyranny imposed on Massachusetts. Each county was directed to choose members to represent it in the First Provincial Congress at Concord. Furthermore, referee committees would preside in place of the unconstitutional courts, and officers attempting to preside over the king-appointed courts, or other officers attempting to execute the two Coercive Acts, would be considered traitors and would be "shunned." Laborers were not to work for them, nor were merchants to supply them with food or other necessities.

Sentiment against British rule was finally coalescing, and early in September 1774 Massachusetts colonists made a series of resolutions that changed the course of history. The Suffolk Resolves, as they became known, bitterly denounced the actions of England and advocated two revolutionary acts: that the Provincial Congress organize military forces necessary to "secure the rights of the people," and that all commerce with Great Britain and the West Indies be suspended.

Meanwhile, the First Continental Congress had convened in Philadelphia on September 4. There Joseph Galloway, a conservative from Pennsylvania, attempted to solve the growing separation with England by a proposal that a "Grand Council" composed of representatives from all the colonies share power with Parliament in America. This Grand Council would pass laws relating to the colonies and could reject or ratify any measure initiated by Parliament.

The flaw in the plan, so far as most of the delegates were concerned, was the fact that a president general appointed by the Crown would have the power to veto decisions of the Grand Council. Consequently, Galloway's proposal was defeated, although by the narrow margin of 6 to 5, and the First Continental Congress endorsed the Suffolk Resolves. To implement them, Congress organized a Continental Association that would enforce a total boycott of Britain and British goods. Local committees throughout the colonies put their full support behind the association. From that moment on, free debate regarding Britain's role in America was over. A reign of terror descended upon the men who accepted appointments to the King's Council, or to positions of judge or sheriff. In some cases they were physically assaulted and forced from their homes, which were then ransacked and destroyed. Many more Loyalists living in the country left everything to the mobs and fled to Boston. And violence or the threat of it forced virtually all the Royal appointees to resign.

Looking back after two hundred years, it seems amazing that the Whigs were able to form nonimportation associations, organize committees of safety, elect members to illegal Provincial and Continental congresses, and organize the entire fabric of a revolutionary government under the very eyes of colonial governors. Yet they were, for the governors had no means to stop them. Mob violence forced moderates and Loyalists to keep unpopular opinions to themselves. Outside of Boston, the only police force was the colonial militia, and by 1774 it was controlled by the Whigs. Militia companies began to march throughout the colonies. Field exercises of artillery and infantry were held, and American agents were sent to Europe to purchase arms and ammunition. The war of words was at an end.

FIVE

A Century of War

THE SOURCE of the colonial military strength that was preparing to go to war with England in 1774 lay in the fact that the colonial nature of North America had provoked a hundred years of bitterly fought disputes between Britain and other European powers.

The founding of the Massachusetts Bay colony in 1630 by John Winthrop and a thousand English colonists established Boston as the nucleus of a cluster of villages that included Dorchester, Lynn, Roxbury, Cambridge, Ipswich, and Charlestown. To govern the colony, Winthrop and the Puritan leaders formed an assembly called the General Court, composed of a small group of Puritans chosen by the leaders and a handful of voters who had been carefully screened. Those who disagreed with the concepts of the ruling clique were forced to flee, usually south to Rhode Island.

By 1643 the Puritan settlements stretched westward as far as the Connecticut River, north to what are now New Hampshire, Vermont, and Maine, and south as far as Long Island Sound. This expansion brought Massachusetts into armed conflict, first with the powerful Indian tribes who occupied the territories, and later with the French settlements to the north.

In 1675, a bitter war known as King Philip's War broke out. Over forty towns were destroyed and five hundred New Englanders lost their lives. The Indians lost over a thousand men, women, and children and were defeated. All their villages were burned to the ground, and captured Indian leaders were executed. The survivors fled to Canada and ultimately became allies of the French in their war with the British. That struggle for superiority in the New World developed into a century of continuous warfare that encompassed King William's War (1689–97), Queen Anne's War, known in Europe as the War of the Spanish Succession (1702–13), the War of Jenkin's Ear (1739), King George's War, which in Europe was the War of the Austrian Succession (1745–48), and the final cataclysmic French and Indian War, part of the Seven Years' War that engulfed Western Europe.

In the face of these conflicts, colonial life was conducted among pitiless raids and heavy loss of life on both sides. Even in so-called periods of peace, the men and women of New England, particularly along the frontiers, were murdered and scalped. Consequently, at the outbreak of the American Revolution, few of the Scotch-Irish colonists who inhabited the flaming borderlands had not lost brothers, sisters, parents, children, or other relatives, murdered, captured, or tortured by the Indian allies of the Catholic French. That century of blood and fire suffered by colonists at the hands of the Indians as allies of France and later, during the Revolutionary War, of Britain, hardened attitudes toward the Indians and shaped the colonial treatment of them after America won its independence.

The French and Indian War began in 1753, although war was not officially declared until 1756. For nearly ten years it raged in a fierce, life-and-death struggle for mastery of North America. The war was fought on mountains, lakes, rivers, inlets, and forests of most of the northern portion of the continent.

By right of discovery the French claimed all land west of the Allegheny Mountains from the Great Lakes to the Ohio River, which embraced all of the tributary streams and valleys of the Ohio River. In 1682 René Robert Cavelier, Sieur de la Salle, had traveled down the Mississippi River; therefore, said the French, France owned all of the land drained by the tributary streams of the Mississippi, of which the Ohio River was one. This claim coolly included half of the North American continent.

The British, however, argued that their claim to the region was more legitimate, since they could definitely prove that they had signed a treaty with the Iroquois at Lancaster, Pennsylvania, in

1744, in which the Iroquois had given to Britain all their claims to the land west of the Alleghenies for £400 sterling.

The difficulty lay in the fact that the Iroquois did not possess a single acre of the land in question and never had. The English knew that but felt that their claim was as valid as that of France, which was based on canoes floating down the Mississippi River.

In 1749, an association was formed by a number of prominent Virginians, which included Lawrence and Augustine Washington, the two half-brothers of George Washington, to establish English settlements west of the Alleghenies and at the same time tap into the lucrative fur trade there. The association, called the Ohio Company, was chartered and granted 500,000 acres of land by the British government. On this immense tract located between the Monongahela and Kanawha rivers, the company agreed to settle a hundred families within seven years, build a fort at their own expense, and maintain a garrison there for defense.

A struggle then began between the Ohio Company and France for the support of the Indians in the region. Each side wooed the various tribes and signed a number of solemn treaties. The Indians distrusted both the French and English and consequently signed with both sides. After several years of tension, France prepared for war along the frontier, fortifying all of her trading posts and pushing out advance outposts along the Ohio River toward the English settlements.

At the urging of his two half-brothers, twenty-two-year-old George Washington was appointed a commissioner by Governor Robert Dinwiddie of Virginia and was sent to tell the French to remove their forces from the territory claimed by the Ohio Company. Washington reached Fort Le Boeuf late in 1753. He delivered his message and was politely told that France intended to take full control of the Ohio territory. Upon his return to Virginia on January 6, 1754, Washington's report to Governor Dinwiddie was forwarded to London, where it was received with great gravity and awakened Parliament to the serious nature of the French threat.

Young Colonel Washington left Williamsburg on April 17, 1754, for the site of present-day Pittsburgh on the triangle where the Allegheny and Monongahela rivers join to form the Ohio River. Agents had been sent out earlier to build a fort there that was to be garrisoned by Washington's detachment. Forty miles from the fort site, friendly Indians informed Washington and his men that the French had occupied the structure and renamed it Fort Duquesne. Washington was then in an area known as Great Meadows, and fearing immediate attack from the French, he decided to build a fort there. The site, located in a low and marshy field, was a poor choice, for it was surrounded by thick forests within rifle shot of the stockade.

Rather than wait at this fort, which he named Fort Necessity, Washington sallied out toward Fort Duquesne with part of his garrison and surprised thirty French soldiers peaceably encamped near his fort. He surrounded and rushed the camp, killing ten men, including their commander, and took the rest prisoner. Washington then marched back to Fort Necessity, unaware that he had begun the French and Indian War that would soon be escalated into the Seven Years' War in Europe and Asia. Before it was over, Britain, with Prussia and Portugal as allies, would be fighting France and her Indian allies in North America, Austria, Russia, Sweden, Spain, and many of the German states on the battlefields of Europe, in the Mediterranean, the Atlantic, the Indian Ocean, the West Indies, and in far away India and the Philippines.

In North America nearly all of the Indian tribes were enlisted on the side of the French and fought as they had always fought: by stealth and ambush, with hundreds of war parties infiltrating American colonial settlements. Thousands of men, women, and children died by unseen hands, far from the battlefronts, in the middle of the night or in the supposed security of their homes. Prisoners were usually butchered on the spot or taken as captives to be tortured and burned alive at the stake. This was the ancient and normal manner of Indian intertribal warfare, and attempts by the French to force the natives into accepted European patterns met with utter failure.

Washington's defeat of the French, although hailed as a great triumph in Virginia, was not to last long. Despite reinforcements, Fort Necessity was completely surrounded by a French army twice the size of Washington's. Spring floods turned the interior of the fort into a river, and Washington was forced to ask for terms of

surrender. The French were generous: the Americans were allowed to return to Virginia after surrendering their arms, on condition that Washington sign a document confessing to the unpro-
voked murder of the French commander during his earlier raid,
and promising that Virginia would refrain from building another
fort for a full year. Washington signed, and he and his men returned to Virginia, leaving the French in control of the entire
area.

In February 1755, Major General Edward Braddock arrived in
Virginia with two regiments of British regulars to push the French
back from Fort Duquesne and protect the lands of the Ohio Company. After much delay, the expedition set out for Fort Duquesne
across the rugged Appalachian Mountains. Braddock's total force
consisted of 1445 regulars, plus over seven hundred colonial
troops under the command of Colonel Washington. The expedition included 150 heavy wagons and five hundred pack horses
carrying heavy artillery, some pieces weighing over half a ton
each. The shot and shell for the guns had to be carried, as well as
food and forage for the horses and oxen.

It was necessary to hack a road out for the heavily laden wagons,
a slow and difficult process. After a month of backbreaking toil,
the expedition was within ten miles of Fort Duquesne when it was
ambushed by General Pierre de Contrecoeur, the French commander of Fort Duquesne, whose forces numbered 254 French
regulars and militia and over six hundred Indians. The surprise
was complete, and the British, unused to fighting in open, extended order, bunched together and fired useless volleys into the
surrounding forest. British reinforcements rushing up ran into
British troops fleeing in panic, and the entire mass of humanity
was helpless in the face of devastating fire from the French and
Indians hidden in the forest.

Only 459 of the 1445 regulars escaped death or wounds. General Braddock was badly wounded and died during the retreat.
The Americans under Washington were able to extricate the surviving British by working their way through the woods around the
flanks of the French and Indians. Washington had two horses shot
out from under him and was credited with masterminding the
retreat wherein his Americans blocked the victorious Indians

from massacring the survivors. Washington emerged from the tragedy with a reputation for coolness and valor under fire and was appointed a permanent colonel in command of all Virginia troops.

However, the defeat of Braddock exposed the entire frontier to French and Indian raids. Under the existing militia system, Americans rushed in to stem the tide in an endless series of small but deadly skirmishes in the forests. To meet the danger, the New England colonies also formed volunteer regiments and soon were able to gain the upper hand.

Throughout the first 150 years of their history the colonies followed a dual system for providing soldiers for the permanent state of war. The first method — the militia system — was founded on the old English tradition of "trained bands of men" used by the early colonial settlers.

Under this system, every able-bodied male between sixteen and sixty was required by law to provide himself with a musket and take his place in the local militia company. Those who for some reason refused could be hanged or shot. The company drilled at regular intervals, and each man was required to attend. Company officers — ensigns, lieutenants, and captains — were elected by the popular vote of the men. These officers in turn elected the field officers, who commanded regiments and brigades: majors, lieutenant colonels, and colonels.

In a society surrounded by enemies and constantly in danger of war, the system, for all its shortcomings, provided a certain degree of security. In actual practice, however, militia companies proved to be less than satisfactory. Allowing men to vote for their own company officers often resulted in their refusal to obey unpopular commands during times that required instant obedience. To keep his exalted position, an officer would attempt to remain popular with his men, for fear that failure to do so would soon send him back to the ranks. In battle, militia units were often an unruly, boisterous, and undisciplined mob. Finally, it was virtually impossible to persuade them to leave their own province to fight.

As a result of many unhappy experiences with unreliable militia units during the course of constant war, the provincial assemblies had devised an alternative method, that of regiments composed of volunteers. Officers were selected and commissioned by the colonial governor, who named and framed the entire skeletal organization of the regiment and its component companies. Still lacking were the enlisted men to fill the ranks, so a colonel chosen to command a regiment was given "beating orders," which gave him the legal authority to enlist men at specific rates of pay in the name of the governor. The colonels usually passed beating orders down to their captains to fill out their companies.

The captain would go to his home town and, with several drummers and a fifer or two, collect a crowd of men on the town green. There he would deliver a speech describing pay, bonuses, bounties, and other benefits of enlisting and, often appealing to their patriotism, explain why the colonists were needed. Most officers were able to fill the ranks of their skeletal company from a single community, usually from men of the local militia unit, who were automatically given leave of absence from their permanent militia company. In many cases, a captain selected by his colonel to recruit currently held the same rank in the local militia company, and if he were popular, men would rush to join his volunteer company.

Such volunteer companies did the bulk of the fighting in all of the colonial wars. When a war was over the men returned home and again became members of their militia units, to which they legally belonged until the age of sixty.

With the defeat of Braddock and his troops in February 1755, the major struggle against the French fell to the American volunteer regiments. In September a combined force of Americans, regulars, and Mohawk Indians defeated a large force of French and Indians at Lake George, killing over seven hundred of the enemy and capturing the French commanding general. But that was one of the few victories that England scored; English troops failed to capture Fort Niagara or Crown Point on Lake Champlain.

During the next two years, American regiments were all that stood between the French and Indians and the frontier settlements. During this time a number of American volunteer regiments became what were known as Rangers. These were men who became proficient at Indian methods of fighting well spaced out, using available cover during an advance, and maintaining contact in small but cohesive groups. All of this ran counter to the traditions of the British officers, with whom they were often associated. Most officers, products of the Frederick-the-Great school of military tactics, saw the American approach as reflecting a lack of courage to stand up and fight in the rigid lines that were fundamental to the military style of the eighteenth-century British army. What these stolid officers had forgotten was that the Prussian and British use of the linear formation on the battlefields of Europe stemmed from the fact that their recruits were unfamiliar with the musket, due to game laws in Europe that precluded their owning one, and could not be depended on to shoot accurately. Thus it was necessary to bunch the men closely in order to deliver devastating volleys from close range, firing on command. Conversely, the American recruit was a trained and often skillful shot.

The Pennsylvania rifle, often called the Kentucky rifle, was a handmade weapon developed in Pennsylvania by gunsmiths who brought their art from Germany during the first half of the eighteenth century. The rifle's long barrel had grooves (rifling) cut inside through its entire length. This rifling gave the soft lead ball a gyroscopic spin when it left the muzzle, which made it travel straight and true. The rifle had been used in Germany by the nobility for hunting in their restricted game preserves. In order to create a projectile that would receive the full force of the propellant charge of black powder, the soft lead ball was hammered into the barrel using a steel ramrod and mallet to insure a tight seal. Unfortunately, it took five minutes to reload, so the German gentry carried a number of rifles kept loaded by special servants.

The Pennsylvania gunsmith and the frontiersman combined their talents to produce the same effect while reducing the time necessary to hammer the lead ball down. Their solution was a well-greased piece of buckskin or linen called a "patch." The ball was placed in the greased patch, and the entire package was easily rammed down on top of the black powder previously measured into the muzzle. When fired, the patch created a seal and the rifling imparted a spin to the ball that carried it straight for over two hundred yards, compared with the 70-yard range of the British Brown Bess or the French Charleville musket.

Each colony had its variation of the British uniform. Some wore the scarlet coats of the British, others wore blue. The Massachusetts regiment wore blue coats with red facing; Virginia wore blue coats with buff facing.

American regiments were trained at first by British officers, who taught them the various aspects of British military life. They were equipped with British weapons and equipment, which they were expected to return when the war was over. However, a great deal of equipment used in the colonies, along with vast amounts of captured French armaments, found its way into the permanent arms of the militia units after the war.

As 1756, 1757, and 1758 passed in bloody fighting in North America, the British suffered one military disaster after another, culminating in the bloody defeat at Ticonderoga. Britain had sent an army of 6367 regulars across the Atlantic to join 5900 Provincial American volunteers from New England. The largest army of Caucasians ever assembled in North America to that time, it was equipped with eight hundred boats or bateaux and ninety whaleboats brought from Nantucket.

The force sailed up the Hudson River to Albany under the personal command of General James Abercrombie, commander-in-chief of all British forces in North America, and Brigadier General George Augustus Viscount Howe. Howe was one of those rare British generals who appreciated the unique abilities of the American fighting men and had attempted to form British regiments patterned after the American Rangers.

On July 5, 1758, the force embarked across Lake George in a long double column of boats and disembarked the next day on the northern shore of Lake George, where the waters of the lake entered a narrow gorge.

The French commander at Ticonderoga, General Marquis Louis Joseph de Montcalm, had built a huge stockade of large logs outside the fort on a narrow spur of land that led to the fort itself. The British ordered their Ranger battalions forward to scout the French defenses but immediately ran into a large French force. General Howe, who had accompanied the Americans, was killed in the first exchange of fire. Relying on the advice of his senior engineering officer, General Abercrombie decided to leave his heavy guns at the landing. It was to be his supreme error, for without the guns to smash the log wall, he was forced to send his proud regulars in series of massive frontal assaults on a narrow front against the heavy, seven-foot-high log walls.

The Americans were deployed on the flanks, but even there the casualties were heavy. The last major attack was made by the 42nd Highland Regiment (the Black Watch), in which they lost 499 men, nearly their entire number. After two thousand men had fallen and the British had failed to penetrate at a single position, the attack was called off. The surviving British forces returned to the landing, and Abercrombie, a broken man, ordered his army back to their base, abandoning much of their equipment and provisions.

By mid-1758 France was at the zenith of her power. In Europe, England and Prussia fought alone against the combined might of France, Russia, Sweden, Austria, and the rest of the German states. An army subsidized by Britain under the Duke of Cumberland had been defeated and forced to surrender its entire force of Hessian and Hanoverian troops. Despite some minor victories of Frederick the Great, King George II was seriously considering asking for an armistice. In America, as one disaster followed another, the accumulation of humiliating defeats created deep despair in both the colonies and England.

In spite of his feelings of depression, George II decided to form a new government under William Pitt, the Earl of Chatham. Miraculously, with Pitt's inspired leadership, British troops made a surprising show of offensive power and crossed the English Channel to attack the French homeland in Brittany. Some 34,000 British soldiers and sailors were committed to the assault, which, although it failed and the British withdrew, was the move that eventually won the war. France was now conscious and fearful of the British cross-channel threat, and just at the time that the war in America was reaching its climax, she refused to send reinforcements to General Montcalm in North America.

Britain increased French fears by attacking again across the English Channel, this time at Cherbourg. They captured the city and fortress, burning the fort, its military stores, and twenty-seven ships in the harbor.

The British opened 1759 with a two-pronged attack on all of the French forces in Canada. Late in 1758 the British and Americans had captured the powerful fortress of Louisbourg, which was the key to the St. Lawrence River and controlled fishing in the north Atlantic. As a result, the St. Lawrence was now open, and with a powerful fleet, General James Wolfe moved an army of fewer than five thousand regulars up the river to capture the city of Quebec.

The other prong was to attack north by way of Lake George to capture Ticonderoga and Crown Point and then capture the city of Montreal. This army, led by General Lord Jeffrey Amherst, was composed of four thousand British and over four thousand American Provincial troops.

Wolfe's campaign opened with a series of bloody battles below Quebec, where he landed his troops at the Falls of Montmorency. British frontal attacks were repeatedly repulsed, although the British navy bombarded the city and did great damage. After three months of stalemate, Wolfe moved to leave and try again the following year. However, a council of his generals advised him to try to land a force above the city and reach the high ground there.

Early on the morning of September 13, 1759, a regiment of light infantry troops, patterned after American Rangers and under command of Lieutenant Colonel William Howe, brother of the dead General Howe, landed at a small cove called Anse de Foulon (later renamed Wolfe's Cove) and climbed up the dark and rocky cliff to secure the top of the path. The rest of the army, including field guns of the American Provincial artillery, soon followed.

As dawn rose over the top of the cliff called the Plains of Abraham, it revealed the British army of 3300 men formed for battle. Montcalm rushed his troops out of the gates of Quebec and ordered an immediate attack upon the enemy. The British held their fire until the French were only forty yards away and fired a simultaneous volley that literally blew the French line away. In accordance with their method of fighting, the British volley was followed by a charge, and the battle was over. Many of the stunned survivors ran for the city gates but were overwhelmed. The French lost 1400 men, the British 664. Montcalm himself was killed and Wolfe, badly wounded, died shortly after. The few French survivors fled south to Montreal.

The army of General Amherst reached the outskirts of Ticonderoga, and American Rangers, with the aid of the artillery now
on the scene, quickly captured the fort with a loss of only sixteen
killed and fifty-one wounded. In a few weeks the army captured
Crown Point.

By 1760 Amherst's army and the troops under Wolfe's successor, General James Murray, had the city of Montreal under siege.
The French commander, Governor Pierre de Rigaud Vaudreuil,
surrendered all of Canada to Britain on September 8, 1760. The
fall of Montreal ended the fighting in America, but the war raged
on in the West Indies.

In 1762 two regiments of American Rangers were sent to Cuba
to rescue a force of ten thousand British troops that had become
bogged down around the city of Havana. The steaming climate
and yellow fever destroyed over half of the British force, but the
American presence tipped the scales, and the city was taken after
several months of fighting.

The war dragged on in Europe until France and her allies were
driven from the seas by the British navy. With British support,
Frederick the Great won the upper hand, and, with her commerce
destroyed, France agreed to an armistice in 1762 and signed the
Treaty of Paris in 1763. The long war was over. France lost all of
her North American possessions except two small islands used for
fishing, St. Pierre and Miquelon. England gave France the two
West Indian islands of Martinique and Guadeloupe she had captured, and returned Cuba to Spain.

The end of the war created new problems for the British, however. There was fear in Parliament that with the French expelled
from Canada, the American colonists would no longer feel so
dependent on the strength of the British government for protection.

In fact, the attitude of those Americans who had fought in the
war slowly changed from one of awe regarding the prowess of the
British troops to one of critical acceptance. Having survived many
British military blunders, they recognized that while the British
were good warriors, they were far from the supermen their
worldwide image proclaimed.

After the war, thousands of colonial men who had served as

soldiers returned to civilian life. Many had achieved high rank in the colonial forces, and some had so impressed British military leaders like General Lord Jeffrey Amherst that they were offered permanent rank as British officers. No doubt a number of the colonial officers were tempted to accept, and a small number did. However, the majority declined the honor. During years of combat, the preferences demanded and enjoyed at their expense by regular officers had rankled the pride of the Americans. For example, British army regulations provided that Provincial officers were subordinate to regular British officers regardless of their respective rank. Thus a British lieutenant was superior to an American major or colonel. The attitudes of the well-educated, upper-class British officers toward American officers, whom they considered their inferiors socially and militarily, was also a problem. In most cases the colonials had risen to officer status by sheer ability and leadership. They scorned the pretensions and posturing of superiority affected by their English comrades-in-arms, and they were well aware that nearly all of the king's officers had purchased their commissions and promotions with money from family fortunes.

Six

Colonial Military Leaders

IN RETROSPECT, the effects of the British-American victory in the French and Indian War were decisive in shaping the future of the North American colonies. Had there never been a decisive British victory, there would have been no American Revolution twelve years later.

The removal of the French and Indian threat from the north and west opened up the frontier to immediate westward expansion by land-hungry Americans. And as the British feared, the Americans had no further reason to depend on the mother country for military protection. Rather than offer political and economic advantages, continued dependence on Britain now involved heavy and distasteful financial obligations as England sought American participation in reducing the enormous war debt.

The removal of the threat of the French navy from the St. Lawrence estuary and fortress of Louisbourg to the fishing fleets along the Grand Banks of Newfoundland brought increasing numbers of Yankee ships into the area, with a resulting boom in shipbuilding, commerce, and economic power in New England.

Nine years of continuous warfare had brought to the forefront a large cadre of outstanding military leaders tested and hardened in the crucible of war. Such men as George Washington, Israel Putnam, John Stark, William Prescott, and Artemas Ward were only a handful of the hundreds of competent leaders available throughout the American colonies. And when the Revolution broke out, most of these men gave their allegiance to the fight for independence.

A curious mixture of circumstances — Indian defiance, British policies, religious issues, simple chance — brought this unusual body of men together to attempt what ultimately became the first successful rebellion against a major monarchy. Their lives before the American Revolution were played out against the background of the French and Indian War and the realities of frontier life, far removed from the tradition-bound societies of the old world.

One such man was George Washington of Virginia, who was descended from an old and proud English family that traced its ancestry back to the time of William the Conqueror. First mention of the family appeared in the Bolden Book of 1183, when a Norman knight, William de Hertburn, received the manor and village of Wessynton in return for services to the king.

The family changed its name from de Hertburn to de Wessynton and then to Wessyngton. Through the centuries it was altered to Weschington, Wasshington, and finally to Washington.

For two hundred years after 1183 the Wessyngtons were active as nobles in the king's service. During the English Civil War between king and Parliament, which lasted from 1642 to 1651, Colonel Henry Washington, a distinguished officer of Charles I, was the military governor of Worcester. In 1646 the king fled from Oxford in disguise, and Lord Thomas Fairfax, commander-in-chief of the Parliamentarian army, demanded that Washington surrender the city of Worcester. He defended the city with courage and determination, refusing to surrender until his king ordered him to do so. When news arrived from Charles I ordering his officers to surrender all towns, castles, and forts to the victorious Parliamentary forces, Washington refused to surrender until he was shown a copy of the order. On July 19, 1646, he capitulated on honorable terms.

The years following the execution of Charles I on January 30, 1649, were filled with attempts to restore the monarchy. Many bloody battles were fought and thousands lost their lives during the long struggle. Oliver Cromwell proceeded, in the ensuing years, to rid England of all former Cavalier supporters of Charles I.

The two Washington brothers, John and Andrew, youthful uncles of Sir Henry, the defender of Worcester, and residents for many years in the East Riding of Yorkshire, were forced to flee their ancestral home at Sulgrave, Northamptonshire. They migrated to Virginia, a colony that had become a favorite refuge for Cavalier officers seeking asylum.

Arriving in Virginia in 1657, they purchased land in Westmoreland County on the northern Neck between the Potomac and Rappahannock rivers. John Washington soon married Anne Pope and built a home on Bridges Creek. In the years that followed he became a wealthy planter and member of the House of Burgesses. As a colonel of the Virginia militia, he led his regiment against the Seneca Indians, who were then burning frontier villages.

The grandson of John Washington, Augustine, was born at Bridges Creek in 1694. He married Jane Butler and had four children by her, of whom only two sons — Lawrence and Augustine — survived. After the premature death of his wife, Augustine married the young and beautiful Mary Ball, who bore him four boys and two girls.

The eldest son of this second marriage was George Washington. Shortly after his birth on February 22, 1732, in the family home at Bridges Creek, the Washington family moved to an estate in Stafford County opposite Fredericksburg on the Rappahannock River, where George grew up.

When George was seven years old, his twenty-one-year-old half-brother Lawrence returned from England where, as was the custom among wealthy colonial planters, he had been educated. Lawrence became closely attached to his hero-worshiping younger half-brother George, who tried to model himself after him. During the War of Jenkin's Ear Lawrence obtained a commission as a captain in a newly organized Royal Regiment to fight a combined French and Spanish army in the West Indies.

In 1740, George enviously watched his scarlet-uniformed older brother march toward the embarkation point to the spine-tingling music of fife and drum. Lawrence served on the staff of General Wentworth and Admiral Edward Vernon, who had previously captured the Spanish city of Portobello. He was present at the siege of Cartagena and took part in the unsuccessful assault on that city. The ships were unable to move in close enough to hurl their shot into the town, and the scaling ladders proved to be too short. Six hundred Virginians were killed or wounded in the resulting disaster, but Lawrence returned to Virginia and his family a hero.

When at age forty-nine George's father suddenly suffered a severe attack that was diagnosed as stomach gout, he died before anyone realized the severity of the illness. His possessions were distributed among his children. Lawrence received the estate on the Potomac, along with other property and several shares in an iron works. Augustine, the second son by his first marriage, received the old homestead and the estate in Westmoreland. George, when he came of age, was to have the house and lands on the Rappahannock.

Three months after his father's death, Lawrence married Anne Fairfax, the eldest daughter of the Honorable William Fairfax of Fairfax County, and settled on the estate on the Potomac River, which he renamed Mount Vernon in honor of his former commander, Admiral Edward Vernon. Lawrence invited his younger half-brother George to live with him at Mount Vernon, where he could study surveying and mathematics.

Lawrence soon became a leading citizen of Virginia, a member of the House of Burgesses, and adjutant general of the military district with the rank of major.

Shortly after his sixteenth birthday, George Washington set out on an expedition with George William Fairfax, the twenty-two-year-old son of Sir William Fairfax. Lord Fairfax, impressed with the horsemanship of young Washington, had asked him to become a member of the expedition to survey Fairfax's property. The land consisted of over five million acres, which extended up both banks of the Potomac into the Allegheny Mountains and included a large section of the beautiful Shenandoah Valley.

The expedition traveled into the valley with the Blue Ridge Mountains on one side and the Alleghenies twenty-five miles away on the other. Young Washington proved to be an excellent surveyor, and Lord Fairfax procured an appointment for him as public surveyor, a position Washington held for the next three years. He thus became acquainted with every part of Virginia and was able to discover and purchase, with the financial backing of his brothers and William Fairfax, some of the best sections of land in the Shenandoah Valley. Thus George Washington became a wealthy landowner with hundreds of tenants working for him before he was twenty years old.

In the years before the onset of the French and Indian War, Virginia was divided into a number of military districts, each with an adjutant general holding the rank of major and responsible for organizing and arming the militia within the district. Through the influence of his brother Lawrence, nineteen-year-old George Washington was chosen as adjutant general for one of these districts. Lawrence's military friends instructed George in the art of military science as it was then known.

In the midst of military preparations, Lawrence's tuberculosis flared up suddenly and a change of climate was prescribed. When he asked George to accompany him to the West Indies, George requested a leave of absence from the militia, and the two traveled to Barbados, where George nearly died from smallpox; he recovered but carried pockmarks for the rest of his life.

George later returned to Virginia to take up his military duties, leaving Lawrence alone at Barbados. After spending the winter of 1751–52 there, Lawrence traveled to Bermuda and then to Mount Vernon, where he died at age thirty-four, only a week after his return.

Lawrence's will left Mount Vernon and all of his property to his infant daughter, Sarah, with George as the executor and heir to the estate. When Sarah died two months later, George became the head of the Mount Vernon estate, which he soon increased to eight thousand acres of land.

Following his role as a leading participant in the outbreak of the French and Indian War and his major part in the ambush that ended in the defeat of Braddock, Washington came out of the war with a reputation for coolness and determination under fire. His self-sacrifice in exposing himself to murderous fire without consideration of his own safety earned him the admiration of his countrymen as well as of British soldiers in both America and Britain. In August 1755, the twenty-three-year-old Washington was appointed a permanent colonel in command of all Virginia troops.

However, many regular British officers refused to recognize Washington's commission as equal to that of a regular officer. In 1756 he rode from Williamsburg to Boston with letters from Governor Robert Dinwiddie to settle the question. The commander of British forces in North America was Royal Governor William Shirley of Massachusetts. A captain in the British army had refused to obey Washington's orders, and Washington was determined to settle this question of a colonial officer's authority. In an important decision, Shirley supported Washington, who returned home in triumph.

For the remainder of the war, Washington protected the long Virginia frontier with a total of only seven hundred ill-equipped colonial troops, continuously feuding with the Virginia legislature over equipment and financial support. In 1757 he became gravely ill with what was diagnosed as "bloody flux," called dysentery today, and was ordered home to Mount Vernon, where he recovered.

Washington participated in the successful attack on Fort Duquesne in 1758 as commander of the Virginia regiments. The French evacuated the fort before the British army under General John Forbes closed in and burned as much of it as they could. When the British and Americans rebuilt the fort, they renamed it Fort Pitt.

Following this campaign, Washington was elected to the Virginia House of Burgesses and resigned from the army with the honorary rank of brigadier general. He had always wanted to hold a regular commission in the British army, as his brother Lawrence had done, but Lord Loudon, who commanded British forces in America at that time, refused to grant him that prize, despite General Braddock's previous promise to see that it was done.

From the day he was elected to the House of Burgesses in 1758, until the outbreak of the Revolution, Washington attended every session of that body, regardless of illness or bad weather. He also served as justice of the peace for Fairfax County, Virginia, from 1760 to 1774.

Shortly after his resignation from the army, Washington was married on January 6, 1759, to Martha Dandridge Custis, widow of Daniel Park Custis. One of the wealthiest women in America, Martha brought to the marriage over fifteen thousand acres of valuable land near Williamsburg, capital of Virginia. Washington legally adopted her two children, who soon became like his own. John and Martha Custis were only six and four years old when their mother remarried, and both looked upon Washington as their real father. He was devoted to them all his life.

As a result of his marriage, George Washington became one of the most affluent men in America. In addition to his own properties at Mount Vernon, the estate on the Rappahannock, and thousands of acres in the Shenandoah Valley and the Alleghenies, he now owned and supervised the vast Custis estate on the York River near Williamsburg. He divided his extensive properties into large farms, each under the supervision of carefully chosen overseers. Washington traveled from farm to farm inspecting the operations and rotation of the two major crops, wheat and cotton. He had his own water power, flour mill, brick and charcoal kilns, blacksmith shop, carpenters and masons, coopers to make barrels, weavers to make cotton, linen, and woolen goods, and shoemakers who turned out shoes for the workers, slaves, and overseers. He bred cattle and horses and experimented with breeding buffalo for meat. He also owned immense orchards of peaches and apples.

A typical wealthy landowner, planter, and slaveowner of the eighteenth century, Washington was well known as a concerned and kindly master. He refused to sell any of his people during his lifetime.

In the years of political and economic struggle beginning with the Stamp Act of 1765, Washington kept hoping that time would settle the difficulties and permit the colonies to enjoy more home rule. He originally believed that most of the trouble was caused by confusion and incompetence in London. But as the years passed, Washington came to believe that there was a specific plan among the Tory members of Parliament to take away the constitutional rights and liberties of Americans.

By 1774, the controversy with Britain had escalated to the stage where Washington became convinced that only force would succeed against England, for it became clear to him that the British government intended to use force against the colonists. Sitting as a representative from Virginia in the First Continental Congress in Philadelphia, he voted for the Suffolk Resolves to boycott British trade if Parliament refused to repeal the oppressive laws and to use military force to repel British troops.

The House of Burgesses, meeting on May 24, 1774, resolved that when the Boston Port Bill went into effect on June 1 all of Virginia would observe a day of "fasting, humiliation and prayer." Three days later, eighty-nine members of the Assembly met at Raleigh Tavern and entered into an association to recommend that the Committee of Correspondence send out letters asking the other colonies to join them in the formation of a General Congress representing all of the colonies. One of the members was Colonel George Washington.

The response was so enthusiastic that on June 17, 1774, the Speaker of the Massachusetts House of Representatives proposed that the Congress be held in Philadelphia. From Pennsylvania came the same suggestion: Philadelphia should be the site because there were no British troops that far south. All of the colonies, except Georgia and North Carolina, chose delegates to meet in Philadelphia in what is now called the First Continental Congress.

A second veteran who became a major figure in the American fight for independence was Israel Putnam, born in Salem Village, now Danvers, Massachusetts, in 1718. A direct descendant of the Puttenhams of Buckinghamshire in England, Putnam's great-grandfather had immigrated to America in 1634, only fourteen years after the landing of the *Mayflower*.

At age twenty Israel married Hannah Pope of Salem, who bore what was then a normal-sized family of four sons and six daughters. A few years after the marriage they moved to a tract of land near Pomfret, Connecticut, a hundred miles southwest of Boston. It was potentially excellent farm country, and after felling trees to clear the land and building fences to girdle his property, Putnam prospered. Employing methods ahead of his time, he rotated crops, fertilized fields, and used an advanced system of drainage and irrigation. His major crops were wheat, corn, and rye, but the major source of income was sheep raising. By the time he was thirty, Israel Putnam had become a man of wealth and property.

A stocky and broad-shouldered Connecticut farmer, Putnam, at thirty-seven, marched to the French and Indian War resplendent in the blue uniform of a captain. As commander of a company in the Provincial regiment of Colonel Phineas Lyman, he soon mastered the art of fighting "Indian style." Operating with the famous frontier fighter Major Robert Rogers of Rogers' Rangers, Putnam became expert at filtering through the forest to surprise and knife French and Indian sentries, cut off and destroy detached parties, waylay convoys and capture provisions, reconnoiter enemy camps, and destroy barracks and boats. He and the Rangers were officially credited with the capture of thousands of prisoners.

On one occasion Putnam and Rogers led their men in pursuit of a French and Indian raiding party of six hundred men that had destroyed a British convoy of supply wagons between Fort William Henry and Fort Edward. With only a hundred Rangers, the Americans circled ahead and ambushed the party, killing over five hundred of the enemy. The remainder fled to Ticonderoga, and within a few days the French sent out a new expedition to cut off the Rangers. The two forces met in a miniature naval battle of boats and canoes on the waters of Lake George. The result was a massacre of the French officers and their Indian allies, with the French survivors again fleeing to Ticonderoga. Only one American was killed and two were wounded.

At Abercrombie's disaster at Ticonderoga in 1758, Putnam led the Rangers against Montcalm's log wall and was with General Howe when he died.

Putnam was the principal actor in what has been described as one of the most incredible exploits of the French and Indian War. Captured by a large force of French and Indians lying in ambush, he was dragged away by his captors and struck repeatedly by the warriors' tomahawks. When the column halted for the night, deep in the forest, bloody and beaten Israel was stripped and tied to a small sapling. Dried brush and wood were piled around him as his captors prepared to burn him alive. An open area around the site was soon filled by several hundred fierce Huron warriors intoning the death chant. A flaming torch was hurled into the brush, which began to smoke and burst into flame, engulfing Putnam.

Then, unbelievably, a sudden drenching rain extinguished the flames. As smoke and steam rose through the trees, the rain stopped as suddenly as it had begun. With difficulty the Indians rekindled the fire, and as Israel tugged at his bonds the flames once again caught the damp wood, which began to burn haltingly.

Miraculously, Putnam was saved a second time. A French officer, informed of what was taking place, courageously burst through the chanting warriors and released Putnam. With the help of a unit of bayonet-wielding French regulars, they led him away from the furious Indians.

Putnam was later handed over at Ticonderoga to General Montcalm, who sent him as a prisoner of war to Montreal, where he was treated kindly and recovered from his wounds. He was exchanged shortly thereafter for a French major captured by the British.

In 1759 Putnam, now a lieutenant colonel, led the Rangers in General Jeffrey Amherst's successful campaign against Ticonderoga and Crown Point, advancing along the shores of Lake Ontario into the Thousand Island area of the St. Lawrence. There Putnam led five volunteers in a daring raid during the night against two French vessels of twelve guns each that blocked their advance. They rowed silently under the sterns of the two ships and stealthily disabled their rudders. The next morning, helpless to bring their guns to bear on the American boats closing in on them, both the ships surrendered without a fight.

In 1762, after the surrender of Montreal ended the war in North America, Putnam was called upon to lead his old regiment as part of the relief expedition to rescue the bogged-down British army on the outskirts of Havana. Surviving a shipwreck in the Caribbean, Putnam and his men participated in the capture of the city.

On May 9, 1763, Pontiac, the famous Ottawa chief who had led the attack on Braddock in 1755, united thirty-six tribes into an Indian confederacy that included most of the tribes from Lake Superior to the lower Mississippi. In simultaneous attacks on twelve settlements, eight were captured and their garrisons butchered. Hundreds of settlers on the western frontier were massacred, and relief expeditions sent to their aid were annihilated. The frontier lay abandoned and pillaged by Pontiac's triumphant warriors.

Some of the most vital forts held out, however. Even though Pontiac himself led the surprise attack on Detroit, the garrison was ready, because the chief's plans had been betrayed to the commander of the fort. The resulting siege, during which Pontiac defeated the garrison's attempted breakout in the Battle of Bloody Run, continued for five months, into October. Finally a large force collected from various colonial regiments was sent to the relief of Detroit. Newly promoted Colonel Putnam was in command of the 400-man contingent from Connecticut. They marched west through burned and devastated communities and arrived at Detroit to rescue five hundred haggard survivors. Pontiac and thousands of Indians fled at the approach of the army, and the siege ended.

Colonel Henry Bouquet of the British army later led a relief column of British and American troops to relieve Fort Duquesne, renamed Fort Pitt when it was captured by Virginia and British troops in 1758. Fort Pitt was besieged by Pontiac's Indians, and Bouquet's men smashed an Indian army that tried to ambush them on the way in the same manner they had destroyed Braddock eight years before. The resulting Battle of Bushy Run nearly annihilated the power of the Indian tribes in the Ohio Territory. Two years later Bouquet led another expedition deep into the Ohio region and forced Pontiac and all of the tribes to sign a peace treaty in 1766.

When the War of Independence broke out in 1775, the Indian tribes, convinced that the Americans intended to appropriate all of their land, would join with the British against the Americans. The Indians foresaw an American process of continuous encroachment through treacherous negotiations, and they predicted their eventual extermination by American settlers, who planned to eliminate them from the land in one way or another and drive them west across the Mississippi and beyond.

In 1763, at the close of the Indian uprising, Israel Putnam returned to his farm at Pomfret, Connecticut, to prosper as a farmer and command the Connecticut militia.

Another veteran of the French and Indian War was Scotch-Irish frontiersman John Stark. Like most colonists, his roots traced back in English history. In 1609, Protestant King James I of England conceived and put into effect a plan to dispossess the Catholics from Northern Ireland and replace them with thousands of Scots Presbyterians then living in the Scottish lowlands. These low-landers, a mixture of Scots and English, had a long history of violence and rebellion.

By the end of the seventeenth century the Scotch-Irish, as they were now called, numbered over a million in Northern Ireland. Thousands of additional lowland Scots arrived after the defeat of the Catholic armies who attempted to recover Northern Ireland in the Battle of the Boyne and later the Battle of Aughrim on June 12, 1691.

The newcomers arrived with dreams of owning land, but they soon discovered to their dismay that titles to the greater part of the land previously had been granted to wealthy English noblemen; their own role was to be that of tenant farmers to these wealthy absentee English landlords. Other undesirable conditions soon became apparent: A sacramental test excluded Presbyterians as well as Catholics from running for public office; only Anglicans were eligible. Commercial restrictions prohibited the exportation of linen and woolen goods, which could be sold only in England at prices established there. From England, linen and wool were sent to the rest of Europe at prices that enriched English merchants.

With the gradual realization of their hopeless plight, the embittered but tough and self-reliant Scotch-Irish began mass emigration to the American colonies in 1718. Upon reaching America, they discovered that the most desirable land, in a belt that stretched for a hundred miles inland from the coast, had been occupied by earlier settlers. To establish new settlements, it was necessary to move far into the interior and try to occupy lands bordering the frontier between the English, French, and Indian claims. The Scotch-Irish accepted the challenge and extended their claims along the rim of New York, New Hampshire, Massachusetts, Pennsylvania, Virginia, and North Carolina. Within twenty years they had established themselves as masters of this frontier. They seized the land they wanted and fought the Indians for the right to keep it. In sixty years they had multiplied to the extent that one person in six of the population of the English colonies was of Scotch-Irish descent.

One such individual was Archibald Stark, who with his wife had left Londonderry, Northern Ireland, in a crowded ship bound for America in 1720. Smallpox on board killed their three children, among scores of other immigrants. Arriving in what is now Maine, the Starks traveled inland and settled on the frontier, to begin their life among other Scotch-Irish settlers.

Life on the frontier had developed a culture of self-reliant, tenacious, and, by the nature of things, extremely violent people. Their lives depended on hunting, continuous guerrilla warfare with the French and their Indian allies, bare-knuckle fighting, wrestling catch-as-catch-can with gouging and no holds barred, whiskey drinking, and frequent shooting contests with their cherished Pennsylvania rifles. Their livelihood and survival depended on their marksmanship, and most men were expert shots.

On August 28, 1728, Archibald Stark's wife gave birth to her second son, John, at Derryfield, New Hampshire, now the city of Manchester. John Stark grew up to become one of the great figures of the French and Indian War and the American Revolution. He was a hard, lean, and tough frontier fighting man, who faced the Indians on their own terms and was just as dangerous as they were. Stark spent time with them as their prisoner, and was eventually legally adopted as a son by the chief of the Saint Francis tribe, who named him "Young Chief."

Unlike most frontiersmen of his time, Stark loved the Indians and their way of life, and he was fond in his old age of recalling incidents from his life among the Saint Francis.

When war broke out in 1753, Stark enlisted in the Provincial army and was commissioned a lieutenant in the famous Rogers' Rangers. His war experience paralleled that of Israel Putnam, with whom he was jointly involved in many campaigns.

At the end of the French and Indian War, John Stark retired from the Provincial army, having refused General Amherst's proffer of a commission in the British regulars. Stark built a sawmill along the banks of the Merrimac River in New Hampshire and founded a new community called Starkstown, which was later renamed Dunbarton for the part of Scotland from which his ancestors had emigrated to Ireland.

In 1774 Stark was appointed to the Provincial Committee for Safety for New Hampshire, and he was soon appointed a colonel and commander of the New Hampshire Provincial Brigade of three regiments, as well. The twelve hundred men of the brigade were handpicked by Stark from veterans of the French and Indian War, and he formed them into a volunteer organization rather than a militia unit. He personally selected all of the officers, and the brigade was considered the finest fighting force in North America. The New Hampshire Brigade of John Stark would soon have an opportunity to prove the truth of that judgment.

William Prescott, of Pepperell, Massachusetts, born on February 20, 1726, also made a notable contribution to the colonial war effort. At the outbreak of King George's War in 1745, the nineteen-year-old Prescott had marched off as a rifleman to fight the French. He participated in the capture of Louisbourg on Cape Breton, and ten years later he went off to fight in the French and Indian War, this time as a lieutenant.

Like many other colonial officers, Prescott's superb fighting qualities earned him the respect of his British superiors, and at the end of hostilities General John Winslow offered him a commission in the regular British army. Like John Stark, he refused the honor and became a prosperous farmer.

As tensions mounted in 1774, Prescott, at age forty-eight, was appointed a colonel in command of a regiment of Minutemen. Over six feet tall, he was a handsome man with blue eyes, muscular shoulders, and the trim body of an athlete. He covered a bald spot with a neat brown wig tied in back. Though self-educated, he read all books available to him. He was described by his British superiors as fearless, never in a hurry, and cool and self-possessed under fire.

When Boston was closed by the Boston Port Bill, Prescott helped supply food to the city. During Gage's raid on Concord, Prescott's regiment attempted unsuccessfully to intercept Lord Percy's beleaguered column, failing to arrive in time. From there he continued to Cambridge, where he was appointed a member of the Council of War. As the war got under way, most of Prescott's troops volunteered to stay with him.

Unlike William Prescott, Artemas Ward was college-educated. His father, Nahum Ward, was a leading citizen of Shrewsbury, Massachusetts, and served as the town's first selectman and justice of the peace. The elder Ward made his fortune as the master of a slave ship in the West Indian service. He bought a large section of land in Shrewsbury, thirty-six miles from Boston, where he built a magnificent brick house on the main road from Boston to Connecticut. He achieved prominence in local and provincial affairs and became an officer in the local militia. Like most of his contemporaries, Nahum Ward saw a great deal of action during the continuous hostilities against the French and Indians, and he saw two of his brothers lose their lives to the conflict.

Mrs. Nahum Ward gave birth to her fifth child, a son named Artemas, on the morning of November 26, 1727. As a boy, Artemas impressed his family and friends with his scholarship and ability, and it was decided that he would attend Harvard College in nearby Cambridge. In 1744, when he was sixteen, Ward entered Harvard. At that time, one hundred students comprised the total enrollment, which was well organized in accordance with the social rankings of the families. The places at the Commons where students ate, their seats in chapel, the location for recitation in the classroom, living quarters — all were determined by social rank. In the freshman class of twenty-nine students, Ward was ranked seventh.

Graduating in 1748, he accepted a teaching position in the town of Groton, where he boarded with the Congregationalist minister, the Reverend Caleb Trowbridge, and his wife. Ward and Sarah, their eldest daughter, soon became engaged and were married two years later.

Sarah Trowbridge was the great-granddaughter of the Reverend Increase Mather and the great-great-granddaughter of the Reverend John Cotton, both of whom were famous religious leaders of the early Massachusetts Bay colony. Artemas Ward's marriage to Sarah opened doors for him, and he was elected tax collector for Shrewsbury, justice of the peace, and town clerk, in turn. During the first year of his marriage, he traveled to Cambridge twice a week to complete his master's degree, which he received from Harvard in 1751.

Ward's permanent militia rank was that of captain of the First Company of Shrewsbury. When the French and Indian War broke out, he was commissioned a major by the governor and assigned to the Third Volunteer Regiment of the Provincial militia. However, while war raged on the frontier, Ward remained at Shrewsbury, for his regiment was not called to active duty.

On May 16, 1757, he was elected to the first of many terms as a representative to the General Court, the colonial legislature of Massachusetts. There he took his place among the financial, political, and social leaders of the colony.

Major Ward played a leading role in the recruiting of men for a volunteer regiment commanded by Colonel William Williams as part of the large army that was raised by General Abercrombie to capture Ticonderoga. Ward's job was to raise money to pay recruits to join; he was also charged with the accumulation of equipment necessary for the expedition. He was able to attract leading surgeons for the campaign by increasing the pay allowance for them.

Completing the administrative details of the regiment, he marched his men to the frontier. Arriving June 17, 1758, at Fort Edward, Ward found a promotion to lieutenant colonel awaiting him. His regiment became part of Abercrombie's army, which crossed Lake George in bateaux and moved toward Ticonderoga. They were in the thick of that tragic battle and were one of the last units to leave the corpse-strewn field in the darkness.

Returning to their original encampment, Ward's men were forced to remain at Fort Edward four miserable months, while men died from disease raging through the camps. Ward was soon promoted to colonel and given command of the regiment, but his health was seriously affected, and upon his return to Massachusetts, he relinquished his command and confined himself for the remainder of the war to supervising enlistments as commissioner of musters.

After the war Artemas Ward became increasingly close to Samuel Adams. They shared committee assignments in the House of Representatives, to which they had both been elected. In 1768 the House, which chose the members who would sit on the prestigious twenty-eight-man council that constituted the Upper House, elected Ward to this body. Governor Bernard vetoed the move because of Ward's close ties to Samuel Adams, and when Ward again was elected to the council in 1769, this time unanimously,

Bernard again vetoed the election. The infuriated House of Representatives voted unanimously but unsuccessfully to impeach Bernard. However, on May 5, 1770, three weeks before the House was to convene, the riot known as the Boston Massacre took place. When the House met, it elected Artemas to the council for the third time. Because of the climate created by the "massacre," which had caused the repeal of most of the Townshend Acts and the removal of the troops to Castle William, Bernard permitted Ward to take his place in the council as a means of reducing tensions that were sweeping the New England colonies.

Ward, in later years, was fond of describing the scene during the first day he attended the council meeting. The twenty-eight councilors were dressed in scarlet coats, their black hats laced with gold lying on the table before them. At the head of the table sat the lieutenant governor, Thomas Hutchinson. During the induction ceremony for newly elected members, lighted candles shone from the polished table top and reflected from the shining faces under the white wigs of the members. It was a solemn scene that dramatized for Ward the privilege and responsibility of elective office.

SEVEN

Mobilization of
the Colonial Militia

BY AUTUMN of 1774 the dispute between the Massachusetts Bay colony and Parliament had proceeded to the point where the First Massachusetts Provincial Congress, meeting in Concord, had securely taken over the actual government of the colony. When word spread of the concentration of eleven regiments of regulars in Boston, the provincial congresses in Massachusetts, Connecticut, New Hampshire, and Rhode Island had reactivated their militia regiments, officered primarily by veterans of the French and Indian War.

Some regiments, well led and well equipped, were in many respects the equal of the British regulars; others were less well prepared. A number of experienced and highly qualified military men, however, would soon achieve recognition.

To take control of the militia from the king-appointed colonial governors, the Whigs under Samuel Adams had to contend with Loyalist militia officers, who comprised over half the military staffs. Before the colonial militia could be readied to fight British troops, these men would have to be forced out.

The Whig-dominated provincial congresses lost no time. Encouraged by Whig organizers, troops in the lower ranks refused to train under Loyalist officers and were upheld by officers who were loyal to the colonial legislatures. Finally, the Provincial Congress called for a complete reorganization of the colonial militia, in which the first step would be the mass resignation of all commissioned officers and the election by popular vote within each militia company of their ensigns, lieutenants, and captains. Those officers in turn would vote for the regimental officers: majors, lieutenant colonels, and colonels.

In this way, Loyalists were eliminated from the officer corps of the militia, and control of the colonial regiments passed from the colonial governors squarely into the hands of the Provincial Congress. That placed the reins of military power throughout New England in the hands of the Whigs and left those who opposed them without military protection, except in Boston. Consequently, thousands of Loyalists abandoned their homes and farms and streamed into Boston, seeking the protection of the British garrison.

On October 27, 1774, the Massachusetts Provincial Congress, in order to provide leadership for the coming military conflict, created the powerful Special Committee of Safety. This committee had complete authority to issue orders, purchase equipment, supervise reorganization and training, and recommend promotions for the newly officered militia units.

Those selected for the Committee of Safety and the awesome responsibility that would inevitably lead to war were Dr. Joseph Warren, who was elected president of the committee, Dr. Benjamin Church, John Hancock, Richard Devens, Benjamin White, Joseph Palmer, Abraham Watson, Azor Orne, Artemas Ward, John Pigeon, William Heath, and Thomas Gardner. To assist the Committee of Safety in purchasing military supplies, a five-member Committee of Supplies was created, composed of Elbridge Gerry, David Cheever, Benjamin Lincoln, Moses Gill, and Benjamin Hall.

Within a few days the First Provincial Congress announced the selection by the Committee of Safety of five newly commissioned generals to command the Massachusetts militia and its major units. Sixty-seven-year-old Jedediah Preble, who had risen to the rank of brigadier general during the French and Indian War, was chosen the commanding general of the Massachusetts militia. Artemas Ward, a member of the Committee of Safety as well as the Provincial Congress, was selected as second-in-command. Seventy-

Successful in their search for military supplies but checked at the North Bridge by the armed resistance of militia and Minutemen, British troops turn back from Concord. The church in the background is the First Parish Church, where in 1774 the First Provincial Congress organized the Minutemen.

Alonzo Chappel was an American painter known for his portraits and landscapes, but his special field was historical illustration. An oil painting by Chappel is a rarity today, as most of his work survived as steel engravings in books like the *National Portrait Gallery of Eminent Americans*, William Cullen Bryant's edition of Shakespeare, and *History of the World, Ancient and Modern*.

Chappel lived most of his life in Brooklyn and Long Island, and was a founding member and vice president of the Brooklyn Academy of Design at the time when George Inness was president.

year-old Seth Pomeroy, who had fought against the French in 1745 and later throughout the French and Indian War, was chosen third. John Thomas, another distinguished veteran of the French and Indian War, was selected fourth, and William Heath, one of the leading military minds of New England and a member of the Committee of Safety, was chosen as the fifth general.

The newly appointed generals immediately began the task of reorganization. They accompanied various members of the committee on thorough and far-flung inspection trips throughout the colony. The regiment was reorganized into ten companies of fifty-five men each; each company was commanded by a captain assisted by ensigns and lieutenants. Each member of the regiment, if he did not own an effective firearm, was equipped with one by the committee — either a musket or a rifle — a bayonet if obtainable, pouch, knapsack, and thirty cartridges.

As the term of the First Massachusetts Provincial Congress drew to a close in December 1774, every village and town in New England resounded to the tramp of marching men, shouted commands, and the crackling of musket fire.

Veteran officers were conspicuous in the blue uniforms faced with red or white of the colonial infantry in the French and Indian War. As in the British army, both commissioned and noncommissioned officers carried a fusil, the smaller version of the Brown Bess musket.

There were no distinctive uniforms among the colonial troops until late in the Revolutionary War. The blue and buff usually associated with American Revolutionary soldiers were the Virginia militia colors and would not make their appearance in New England until the arrival of George Washington as commander-in-chief in July 1775. Until then the predominating colors were browns and greens, and if any distinctive uniform could be said to be common among the men, it was the frontiersman's shirt, soon to become famous as the rifle shirt.

In summer this shirt was made of rough linen, homespun and woven by hand. In winter the identical shirt was made from "linsey-woolsey," cloth spun from a combination of linen and wool. The shirt hung to just above the knees and was worn cinched at the waist with a large leather belt from which usually hung a tomahawk and knife. The rifle shirt did not have buttons but was doubled over from one side to the other, the excess material forming a loose pocket in front. Despite traditional accounts, frontiersmen and colonial troops who wore this shirt seldom dressed in buckskins or other animal skins. Leather or buckskin garments took a long time to dry, and the men needed clothes that dried quickly on the body if exposed to rain, snow, or streams.

The rifle shirt soon became the most popular field uniform of the American soldier. It had the advantage of being associated in the minds of British troops with the deadly marksmen of the frontier. For that reason Washington recommended in 1776 that the entire army be so uniformed:

> It is the dress which is justly supposed to carry no small terror to the enemy, who think every such person a complete marksman.[1]

By late 1774 the provincial congresses of Connecticut, Rhode Island, and New Hampshire had followed the lead of Massachusetts and seized firm control of their militia regiments. Loyalist officers had been eliminated and companies and regiments reorganized.

Israel Putnam in Connecticut and John Stark in New Hampshire were placed in command of their Provincial militia, and Rhode Island's militia was organized into a single military unit under the command of a succession of officers. Not until April 1775 would Nathanael Greene be chosen to command the Rhode Island militia.

On December 10, 1774, General Gage issued an order denouncing the purchase and storing of arms as treasonable and declaring that anyone guilty of participation would be tried for treason. Disregarding the proclamation, the Massachusetts Committee of Safety feverishly continued to stockpile large quantities of military stores in Concord and Worcester, both considered distant enough from Boston to insure their safety from capture.

On February 1, 1775, the newly elected Second Provincial Congress met in Cambridge with the Committee of Safety to consider the final selection of generals. They confirmed the selection of Preble, Ward, Pomeroy, Thomas, and Heath. When Jedediah Preble declined to accept his appointment, Artemas Ward became commander-in-chief of the Massachusetts militia.

The Committee of Safety had been increasingly worried about the Massachusetts army that had been hurriedly organized since the summer of 1774. Although the strength of the colonial militia within a radius of one hundred miles of Boston was estimated at over sixty thousand officers and men, serious organizational flaws had developed. The most pressing problem was that of the election of field officers by their own men, which brought the officers under the authority of their troops rather than the Committee of Safety. Officers understandably feared the loss of position by being voted out by their own men.

The Committee of Safety saw the entire militia system as an open invitation to disaster, and they decided to put their faith in the system that had proved so successful in previous wars, that of the volunteer regiment. It was decided to select the best officers in the existing regiments and put them in new, skeletal, regimental organizations. The committee would select the officers, and the Second Provincial Congress would legally issue the commissions and present beating orders to the newly appointed colonels to fill their ranks from the existing militia companies and regiments.

Those men not selected as officers or not wishing to serve in the new regiments would, in accordance with the law, remain in their local militia organizations.

To be ready to fight before reorganization was completed, field officers were ordered to form separate Minutemen companies of fifty privates equipped and held in readiness to march on the shortest notice. By March 1775 every town in Massachusetts had three military organizations to serve until the new reorganization was completed: a regular militia company, a Minutemen company, and an Alarm company, the last made up of older men to be called only as a last resort.

On April 14, 1775, the Second Provincial Congress of Massachusetts made their final decision to change from reliance upon militia to the formation of volunteer regiments. On the night of April 18 delegates from Massachusetts were on their way to other colonies to discuss the changeover, when the British launched their fateful expedition to Concord to destroy the military supplies there. By that sudden blow, Gage disrupted the reorganization of the New England army, and so it was a combined force of regular companies, Minutemen companies, and Alarm companies that met the British at Lexington and Concord and fought them on their way back to Boston.

During the militia buildup, British officers and men watched with a mixture of apprehension and disdain. The immense scope of the colonial military preparations was well known to General Gage, but the attitude of the British regulars toward the colonial militia was expressed in this typical letter written by a British officer to his family in England:

> As to what you hear of their taking arms to resist the force of England, it is mere bullying, and will go no further than words; whenever it comes to blows, he that can run fastest will think himself best off; believe me, any two regiments here ought to be decimated if they did not beat in the field, the whole force of the Massachusetts Province; for if they are numerous, they are a mere mob, without order or discipline and very awkward at handling their arms.[2]

In view of the colonial contribution to British victory in the French and Indian War, this low opinion is difficult to explain. Yet, despite high British regard for individual colonial soldiers during that war, such as George Washington, Israel Putnam, and John Stark, the majority of British officers professed profound contempt for the Americans as soldiers.

It was, perhaps, due to the eighteenth-century criteria for a good soldier: one who was disciplined to the point of unquestioning and submissive behavior and obedience. Accustomed to the respect shown them by their enlisted men from the English lower classes, British officers were shocked at the colonial militia, in which officers and men, both from the same social class, fraternized. The British, rigidly brought up in a society of strict class distinctions, found these and other colonial practices ludicrous.

This underestimation of the threat posed by the flexibility and marksmanship of the rebel militia became evident to the British army and the monarchy only after the Battle of Bunker Hill, which cost them a heavy price. Before that surprising performance, however, few informed military men would have felt the colonial militia a serious opponent to the widely respected and superbly organized British army of the time.

EIGHT

The British Army

WHILE COLONIAL TROOPS AND OFFICERS were drawn from an essentially one-class society, the opposite was true of the men in the British army, where upper-class men purchased their military commissions and the enlisted men came from the lower economic class and were often victims of the industrial and agricultural revolutions of the early eighteenth century.

Those revolutions had brutally affected English life. The money derived from the industrial boom was invested to a great extent in agricultural land. Consequently, England became divided into great estates, and with the improvement of roads, the need for the self-sufficient village craftsman was eliminated. Many village tailors, carpenters, brewers, millers, harness makers, and so forth found that their skills were no longer needed.

Before the industrial and agricultural revolutions, an important feature of English rural life was the open field or "common" to which all had access. Small farmers, whose land holdings would barely sustain their families, could graze their cows and sheep on the common or grow vegetables on it, or raise poultry.

Slowly, beginning under Henry VIII, by royal grant the commons became "enclosed," taken over by large landowners. By the beginning of the eighteenth century, the commons had virtually disappeared.

When the large landholders turned the land to the raising of sheep, tenant farmers who tilled small farms became an irritating surplus and a stumbling block to more profitable use of the land. Enclosure was the first step in reducing the rural population in England. As a result of the declining number of landowning farmers, the increase of landless laborers, and the rapid rise in population, the price of labor dropped to such low levels that few men could earn a living wage. England became a country of large holdings engaged in producing wool for export and employing landless laborers.

What happened to the displaced farmers? Many came to America as indentured servants; others drifted to the large cities to find work in new factories. There, they were forced to exist in degrading conditions in the infamous slums of London, Birmingham, and elsewhere. Gradually the strong family ties of the rural or "yeoman" class were stretched and broken.

With the resulting breakdown of both the farm family unit and the institution of marriage, thousands of unwanted infants were abandoned in vacant houses or left to die in the streets by desperate, unmarried mothers. In 1745 a foundling hospital was established in London to cope with the appalling infant mortality rate among the poor, especially among these deserted illegitimate children. In 1756, fifteen thousand such children were brought to the foundling home. Records indicate that only one third of them lived long enough to be apprenticed or enlisted in the army, the primary livelihoods open to them.

Britain maintained an army of over seventy thousand men, most of whom had spent their childhoods in foundling homes, workhouses, and prisons. A sign posted in front of army recruiting stations carried a clear message: a side of beef. Even the illiterate could see that if you "Join the army, you can eat." Army and navy recruiters haunted alehouses and grog shops for men. After a man was plied with rum, a shilling was placed in his hand; by British law, if the hand closed over the shilling, the man had legally enlisted for seven years of military service.

In a brutal and callous age, many men found a haven in the military. Fresh from a life of poverty, violence, and injustice, recruits were molded into tough, hardened "British regulars." This was efficiently accomplished by a calculated system of brutal discipline which imposed total regimentation in every aspect of personal life. Rules and regulations governed everything done every minute of the day. Punishment for any infraction was swift and merciless, in most cases flogging, and occasionally hanging. There were other methods, such as tying a man, stripped to the waist, to a wagon wheel and leaving him in the weather for several days and nights. By far, however, the most common punishment in use was flogging.

Through the centuries, flogging had been ritualized in European civilian life as well as in the military. Men, women, and children were commonly flogged in London and all European towns, often in a public ritual called the "tail of the cart." The victim was fastened by his wrists to the tailgate of a two-wheeled cart pulled by several oxen. In order to ensure as many spectators as possible, the cart pulled its struggling cargo to a busy or prominent location, and the driver of the cart, charged to inflict the punishment, would flog the prisoner five or six lashes or "stripes." The cart would then be moved to another location and the process repeated until the specified number of strokes had been administered. Fifty stripes "cut" into a bleeding and unconscious victim's back would usually cause death or permanent maiming.

In the army the floggings were administered under the direction of sergeants, but the actual blows were struck by the regimental drummer, always selected for his size and physical strength. The traditional "cat-o'-nine-tails" consisted of a stock covered with red baize (so the blood would not show) with nine knotted ropes of hemp attached to the end. It was a formidable weapon when swung by a powerful man. To insure that the blows were hard enough to cut the skin, each flogger would be relieved by another after six or eight lashes had been delivered.

Fifteen to twenty-five lashes were usually given for minor infractions; five hundred to a thousand, not uncommon, were tantamount to a sentence of death. Occasionally such a sentence would be administered in installments of fifty each week.

British army officers always came from the upper class, and enlisted men usually came from the lower class. The great social distance between the two groups was an unbridgeable gulf. In this age, men believed as a matter of indisputable fact in the existence of natural hereditary divisions among social classes. They were convinced that people in the lower classes were less intelligent, less moral, and could function only in an inferior manner. The attitude of upper-class officers toward lower-class soldiers was that of a master to a somewhat intelligent two-footed animal. The soldier, it was believed, had to be taught to obey any order that he received, instantly and without question. There was no doubt that only harsh discipline imposed from above could maintain the required standard of obedience in the ranks.

During the Seven Years' War, England and Prussia were allies and fought side by side on the battlefields of Europe. British officers were highly impressed by the army of Frederick the Great. The Prussians at that time produced the best drilled and disciplined troops in Europe, and the discipline imposed on the Prussian soldier, under the principles of Frederick the Great, was the envy of all European armies. The basic advice Frederick gave his officers was that soldiers must be made to fear their own officers more than they feared the enemy.

Frederick had developed a three-line formation that was adopted by the British army. To use this "linear" method effectively, troops were required who were thoroughly trained in moving from line to column to square, on command, in the face of enemy musket fire at a time when men were being hit. This formation required the most intense discipline.

Borrowing from the Prussians, British tactics were based on the principle that in order to secure maximum concentration of firepower, it was necessary to achieve maximum concentration of men. There was no need for individual initiative. A precise alignment on the field of battle was of supreme importance. The slightest deviation would cause troops to harm themselves more than the enemy.

The three-rank "line" extended across the field and marched toward the enemy at the rate of eighty steps per minute to the beat of drummers marching a few steps behind the advancing foot soldiers. In addition to marking the tempo, the drums relayed orders to the men by a variety of "beats." Every man kept in step, and the lines were perfectly straight, as if on parade. Officers usually found it necessary to halt their men during an advance under fire and coolly dress their lines.

Each soldier carried the basic weapon of the British infantry, a musket called the "Brown Bess." It weighed fifteen pounds, was four feet ten inches long, and carried a fourteen-inch, needle-sharp "socket" bayonet with a three-sided blade attached to the muzzle.

The strict game laws of England and most of Europe reserved firearms for the upper classes. No attempt was made to teach men how to shoot, and as a result, a recruit often held a musket in his hands for the first time in his life. Also, the Brown Bess was effective only within seventy yards. It was, therefore, necessary to withhold the volley and approach the enemy as close as possible to insure maximum destructive firepower.

When the British line approached to within fifty yards of the enemy, it was ordered to halt, and a volley was fired on command. The muskets were pointed, not aimed, straight ahead and low. This was done because the .75-caliber lead ball (three-quarters of an inch in diameter) had to travel the forty-two-inch length of the barrel as a result of nearly instantaneous twin explosions, one in the priming pan, the other in the base of the barrel. This usually deflected the barrel a fraction of an inch upward at the instant the ball was leaving the muzzle, causing most shots to sail over the head of the target. Much emphasis was therefore put on delivering the volley low. The approved method was to hold the musket below shoulder level.

The instant the volley was fired, the British soldiers charged toward the enemy fifty yards away, their bayonets held low in front. At that point British troops could avenge themselves for the floggings, humiliations, and injustices of their brutal training, and as they drove into the enemy, stabbing and slashing in a frenzy of cheering, shouting, and cursing, the enemy would usually turn and run, or attempt to surrender. Few soldiers were able to stand up to the twin shocks of a concentrated British volley followed by the dreaded bayonet charge. The volley that preceded the charge caused so much death and destruction at close range that the spectacle of hard-running, shouting, and merciless British regulars appearing through the smoke caused the bravest man to bolt. It was in the chilling application of the military "three R's" that England conquered her empire: "ruthless, relentless, remorseless."

In 1775 the regular British army consisted of three regiments of foot guards, two regiments of horse guards, called dragoons, one royal artillery regiment, and the backbone of the army — seventy regiments of foot, or as they are called today, infantry. Each foot regiment, such as the Royal Welsh Fusiliers, consisted of ten companies of thirty-eight men commanded by a captain. The regiment was commanded by a colonel or a lieutenant colonel. Occasionally the nominal commander was a general, although the officer who commanded the regiment in the field was usually a lieutenant colonel.

Eight of the ten companies in a regiment were called battalion companies. The remaining two were flank companies, one the grenadier company, the other the light infantry company. The men of the eight battalion companies wore black, three-cornered hats with lace on the upturned brim. Their hair was flattened in back into a black hair stock secured by a pair of brass clasps and tucked under the hat.

Officers and men wore white linen or woolen breeches that had suspenders sewed on like modern overalls. Breeches were fastened at each knee with four small buttons and a small knee buckle clasped over long, white, hand-knit stockings that fit into a pair of heavy black shoes. The shoes, fastened by a heavy round brass buckle, were kept well blacked each day. Over them and the lower part of the white wool stockings heavy black linen leggings, called gaiters or spatterdashes, about twelve inches high were worn. In bad weather the soldiers were issued heavy black gaiters that reached above the knees.

Over the waistcoat they wore the famous brick-red coat, which reached just above their knees. The coat was lined in white, with decorated sleeves and buttonholes, a flat collar, and long flat lapels and cuffs. The collar, lapels, and cuffs were faced in different colors, for each regiment had its own facing color. That of the 23rd was blue, that of the 10th yellow. The coat remained brick-red, and breeches and waistcoat were always white.

British army regulations were strict with regard to the fit and method of wearing the uniform. When new uniforms arrived, regulations required the quartermaster and other officers to inspect them to see if they were in the proper styles and colors. This had to be certified to, under penalty. Regimental tailors were then collected under the supervision of an officer and several armed sentries to insure that everyone worked his required hours.

All new coats, waistcoats, and breeches were dipped in clean fresh water and laid in the sun to dry. Each man was then fitted according to regulations, which required that when a man in a grenadier or battalion company was measured for his coat, he had to put it on and kneel on both knees. The bottom of his coat had to be exactly six inches above the ground when he was in this position; the hem had to be the same distance all around. An enlisted man or officer in the light infantry company had to have the bottom of the coat nine inches above the ground while kneeling.

Light infantry companies consisted of the best athletes in the regiment, for stamina and agility were necessary in order to run long distances and move through the countryside rather than march along roads. These companies were organized during the French and Indian War in imitation of the American Ranger battalions that had operated with the British. The Prussians borrowed the idea also and organized similar units that they called "Jagers." During the French and Indian War, Thomas Gage, then a colonel, had organized the first light infantry regiment in the British army, which operated with great success against the French at Montreal.

The soldier in a light infantry company wore a uniform similar to that of a battalion man with the exception of a shorter coat and a black leather cap with three chains in the back to keep it snug to his head. The cap resembled a modern baseball cap, but with a visor that was longer and wider than that used in the latter. This wide, long visor was pushed straight up to reveal a large regimental badge and number toward the front. The waistcoat of the light infantryman was red rather than white, and as an extra weapon he carried a hatchet at his waist.

The grenadier company, similar to the famous grenadier guards of Frederick the Great, was composed of the tallest and strongest men in the regiment. They wore a uniform like that of a battalion man with the exception of the hat. The grenadier's cap was a magnificent creation of black bearskin. On the front was the king's crest with the motto *"Nec Aspera Terrent,"* roughly "Fear Not the Use of Brutality." On the back of his cap was a metal replica of a grenade with the regimental number on it. The height of the cap — without the bearskin, which reached beyond the top — was twelve inches. Hats of such bulk and height worn by the tallest men in the regiment increased their height to impressive and intimidating proportions. On his cartridge sling the grenadier wore a small brass case, which, in the days when grenadiers actually threw grenades, held a slow-burning lighted match. The use of grenades had been discontinued since the mideighteenth century, but the brass case was still worn as a mark of distinction. As an extra weapon the grenadier wore a short sword.

The uniforms of the sergeants and officers were far more splendid than those of their men. Their coat was scarlet instead of brick-red, trimmed in either silver or gold. Each regiment had a designated metal, either silver or gold. The sword hilt, buttonholes, and lace on hat brims were also in the regimental metal. All officers wore one epaulet on their right shoulder, except those of a grenadier company, who wore them on both shoulders. Both sergeants and officers wore a sword and a crimson silk sash tied around the waist. Officers in the field usually carried the fusil, the smaller, improved version of the Brown Bess, with bayonet.

An officer on duty wore a gorget tied around his neck with a ribbon. This was a half-moon-shaped piece of metal in the approved regimental metal of silver or gold, engraved with the royal coat of arms and the regimental insignia.

Army regulations covered the uniform policy for drummers and fifers, as well, who wore bearskin caps like the grenadiers and coats the reverse of the regimental colors. For example, the Royal Welsh Fusiliers wore brick-red coats faced in blue; therefore, the drummers and fifers of the regiment wore blue coats faced with red. Waistcoats and breeches remained white. Drummers and fifers carried a short, scimitar-bladed sword. Unlike the drummer boys of a later era, these men were chosen for their strength and size, and the British enlisted many freed black slaves to serve as drummers.

Throughout the years some regiments won special privileges in dress as rewards for meritorious conduct during various campaigns. For example, all fusilier regiments wore a shorter version of the grenadier's bearskin cap. Thus in a fusilier regiment like the

23rd, no one wore the regulation three-cornered black hat. The grenadiers wore their tall bearskin caps, the battalion men wore their short bearskin caps, and the light infantry wore their black leather caps.

Army regulations specified the interesting list of necessaries to be furnished to each soldier:

> three shirts; two white stocks (or rollers), one black hair stock; one pair of brass clasps for hair; three pair of white yarn stockings; two pair of linen socks, dipped in oil, to be worn on a march, under spatterdashes (gaiters or leggings) when necessary; two pair white lined gaiters, if belonging to the guards; one pair of black long gaiters with black tops for ditto; one pair of half spatterdashes; one pair of linen drawers; one pair of red skirt breeches; one red cap; one cockade; one knapsack; one haversack; one pair of shoe buckles; one pair of garter buckles; black leather garters; two pair of shoes; one oil bottle; one brush and picker; one worm; one turnkey; one hammercap, and one stop.[1]

Regulations required that each regiment have at least two field days a week, for inspection of equipment and personnel. All officers wore full dress uniforms, and a strict accounting of men was required as to equipment and appearance. Missing pieces of equipment, buttons not polished, shoes not shined, hair not neatly queued and tucked under, musket dirty, any of a thousand small details could cost a soldier a flogging.

When the regiment was drawn up in regimental-front formation, the grenadier company was on the right, the light infantry on the left. Enlisted men, sergeants, corporals, and privates occupied their allotted places in the ranks, with Brown Bess held at the "order arms." Sergeants were the main unifying and disciplinary force of the British army. Men who had come up through the ranks from the very bottom of the ladder, they were tough, natural leaders in a merciless system of attrition. Each had won his stripes by hard, diligent work, devotion to duty, and courage in the face of the enemy. They ruled their men with an iron hand and were seldom reprimanded for their methods by their commissioned officers. The younger officers depended on the older sergeants to keep them out of trouble. The traditional British sergeant was a true leader and hard taskmaster with the voice and physical size to make good his threats. He was the vital force in combat.

The British foot soldier was equipped with a number of items in addition to his Brown Bess. Across his left shoulder he wore a two-and-three-quarter-inch white leather strap that held a black leather cartouche (cartridge box) on his right hip. This box was a block of wood covered with black leather and drilled to hold thirty cartridges. His haversack, made of linen, was fastened by another white strap across his right shoulder and hung on his left hip. This carried his food ration. On top of this haversack was his wooden canteen. The knapsack, of white or brown goatskin with the hair left on, was carried on his back and contained toilet articles, a change of clothing, and a blanket.

Despite reports to the contrary, the British worked hard during their stay in America to improve the marksmanship of the foot soldier. In awe of the sharpshooting ability of the Americans, British troops made great effort to develop confidence among the regiments in their own ability to shoot.

Loading and firing the Brown Bess and other military muskets of the eighteenth century were not easy skills to master and took months of intensive practice. To load the musket, the soldier extracted a paper round that contained both ball and powder from his cartridge box, bit off a small piece of the paper, and poured the powder down the barrel. He dropped the .75-caliber lead ball down the barrel on top of the black powder and followed that by crumpling the brown paper that held the round and stuffing it down the barrel. The metal rammer fastened beneath the barrel was used to tamp down the paper and charge, and then had to be replaced under the barrel. He pushed open the frizzen (or pan cover), which opened the flashpan, and pulled back the hammer to the half-cock position. He poured a bit of finely ground powder from the priming flask into the depression in the flashpan, closed the frizzen over the loose powder, and tilted his musket to his left. Tapping the base of the barrel allowed some of the priming powder to fall into the touchhole.

The musket was now loaded. To fire, the soldier pulled the hammer to full-cock and awaited the command to fire. When he pulled the trigger, it caused a spring to flip the frizzen upward just

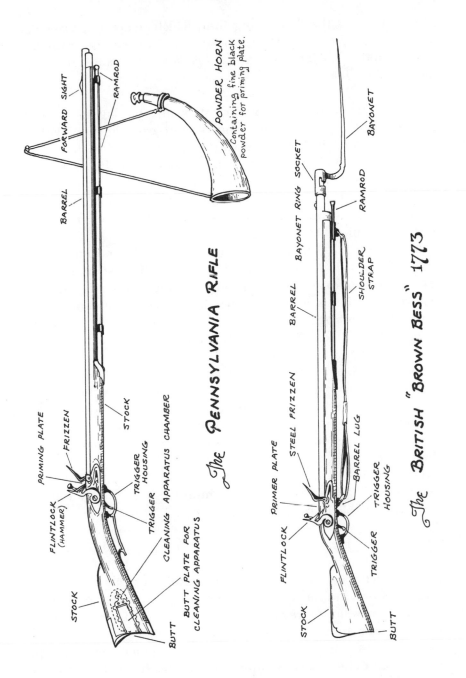

The PENNSYLVANIA RIFLE

FORWARD SIGHT

RAMROD

BARREL

POWDER HORN
Containing fine black
powder for priming plate.

PRIMING PLATE

FRIZZEN

STOCK

TRIGGER HOUSING

CLEANING APPARATUS CHAMBER

FLINTLOCK (HAMMER)

TRIGGER

STOCK

BUTT

BUTT PLATE FOR CLEANING APPARATUS

The BRITISH "BROWN BESS" 1773

BAYONET

BAYONET RING SOCKET

RAMROD

SHOULDER STRAP

BARREL

STEEL PRIZZEN

PRIMER PLATE

BARREL LUG

TRIGGER HOUSING

FLINTLOCK

TRIGGER

STOCK

BUTT

in time to meet the descending flint, which struck it a glancing blow that caused the sparks to shower into the exposed priming powder in the pan. The two explosions, one in the pan and one in the chamber, felt like one

Beginning in early 1775 the British army, hoping to achieve greater mobility in quick raids and pursuit, experimented with a new formation. The flank companies were taken from their own regiments and put together in a single strike force. It was a force of twenty-one flank companies that made what was supposed to have been the surprise assault on Lexington and Concord, and the force consisted of ten light infantry companies and eleven grenadier companies.

On paper each company consisted of thirty-eight men, but in practice it usually contained only twenty-five. By custom, the roster of each company carried three "contingency men" who received full rations and pay but did not, in fact, exist. They were fictional names legally carried on each company's roster, and their pay and rations went into a special fund controlled by the colonel of the regiment.

Since a regiment consisted of ten companies, the colonel had the monthly pay and rations of thirty men to disburse as he saw fit. Ostensibly the funds were to be used for support of widows and wounded men. Some corruption was inevitable, however, the colonels not being required to account to anyone for their handling of these funds.

The strength of the company was further reduced by the fact that normally at least 10 to 20 percent of the total force was ill or otherwise unable to report for duty.

The British army, like all European armies, provided for at least six women for each company. They were carried on the official rolls, subject to the same discipline, including flogging. They were given half pay and rations and were required to cook, clean, launder, and nurse in the regimental hospitals. Usually these women were married to men in the company or otherwise attached. A corporal or sergeant received enough monthly income to permit his wife and children to accompany him. Such families traveled with their men, sharing the hardships and sacrifices of military life.

The practice of allowing families to accompany their men was centuries old in Europe; officers believed it helped keep families together and reduced the desertion rate. However, as actually practiced in the regiments, the custom involved many more than six women per company. Various liaisons were arranged on a temporary or permanent basis, and often, the slumgirls who were thus promiscuously attached to the troops were the cause of dissension and other problems. Reports of the number of women and children officially carried by the British regiments stationed in colonial America indicate that these dependents or camp followers averaged over one hundred per regiment.

During the long history of the British army, corruption became institutionalized. The paymaster general invested the government funds at his disposal, usually pocketing a large sum annually. The paymasters of widows' pensions were similarly "rewarded." In addition to his income from the "contingency men," the colonel received his pay despite the fact that most colonels did not command their regiments but left that duty to a subordinate lieutenant colonel. Most political appointments to colonel went to men as commanders of barracks or governors of small garrisons, rather than to men actively engaged in armed conflict.

The meager pay due the men in the ranks was further reduced by a system of corrupt practices. A private's four and sixpence per week was reduced by charges for "clothing, medicine and armorers' services." He had a halfpenny taken out for the regimental paymaster and surgeon weekly, as well as other charges for washing and so forth. Consequently, the average soldier's weekly pay was usually a pittance.

Only the sons of wealthy men became officers, for the price of the commission was beyond the average man's means. Often a commission yielded little or no income, also, for officers sometimes sold their commission with the private understanding that the successor would turn the pay over to the retired officer. Consequently only men with private incomes could afford to assume an officer's commission, and the gulf between the average soldier and the officer was substantially increased.

NINE

Tensions Mount in Boston

FOR YEARS the colonial militia units around Boston had stored their powder in a stone building on Quarry Hill on the outskirts of Charlestown. During the intensive militia drills that began in the spring of 1774, most units had drawn their share of black powder from this supply, and only a small portion remained. In August the British decided to seize it as a gesture and remove it to Castle William for safekeeping.

At dawn, on September 1, 1774, a beautiful New England fall day, thirteen boats loaded with ten companies of light infantry slipped quietly away from Long Wharf. The 260 men, under the command of Lieutenant Colonel Maddison, were rowed around the top of Boston to the Mystic River and landed on the Charlestown shore at Temple's Farm. They sped over Winter Hill to the powder house and carried away 250 half-barrels of powder. Another detachment moved farther inland to Cambridge and captured two field guns belonging to the local militia regiment. Then the regulars returned to the waiting boats with their booty, and within an hour all were back at Castle William.

An exaggerated account of the affair soon swept New England, as horsemen sped out of Boston in all directions with the urgent news that the British fleet had bombarded the city. Bells pealed and beacon fires blazed through the day on hundreds of New England village greens.

While working his fields in Connecticut, Colonel Israel Putnam learned from a tired and sweating Captain Keyes that the city of Boston had been set on fire by a British bombardment. Putnam immediately sent out couriers to spread the alarm; then he rounded up his regimental staff and headed for Boston on the gallop, with orders for his regiment to follow. Within hours the roads leading to Boston were filled with marching militia units.

Over forty thousand such men had converged on Boston from within a fifty-mile radius when riders intercepted them to say that the original reports had been false. Putnam, who had reached Douglas, thirty miles from his home in Pomfret, turned around to halt the further flow of his men.

General Gage was stunned by the grim and efficient mobilization of forty thousand colonial militia. Convinced that his small force of less than three thousand was in grave danger if fighting broke out, he quickly ordered entrenchments dug on Boston Neck (also called Roxbury Neck) and a full regiment mounted there with field guns to strengthen the position. Then he casually announced that the fortifications had been erected to discourage desertions. The Americans did not believe this, just as the British had not believed American claims that they were drilling regularly in fear of another war with France.

The growing confrontation between Britain and New England was foreshadowed in the Minutes of the Selectmen meeting in Boston on September 6, 1774:

> Present Messrs. Scollay, Newell, Marshall, Austin, Wendell, Pitts.
>
> The Selectmen made the following application to the Governor which was read to him by the Town Clerk, viz.
>
> May it please your Excellency: The Selectmen of the Town of Boston now wait on your Excellency to acquaint you, that the inhabitants of the town are much alarmed to find that your Excellency has ordered the breaking up of the ground near the fortification on the Neck, and the Selectmen would beg of your Excellency to explain your design in this extraordinary movement that they may thereby have it in their power to quiet the minds of the people.

General Gage replied that he did not intend to obstruct the passage of people going into or out of Boston via the Neck, which was Boston's only link with the mainland, but had taken measures to fortify the Neck to protect the people of Boston and the British troops from presumably hostile forces. He did not mention his original reason relating to desertions.

Then on September 9 the selectmen sent another note to Gage:

May it please your Excellency: The Selectmen of Boston at the earnest desire of a number of gentlemen of the town and country, again wait on your Excellency to acquaint you that since our late application the apprehensions of the people not only of this but of the neighboring towns, are greatly increased by observing the design of erecting a fortress at the entrance of the town, and of reducing this metropolis in other respects to the state of a garrison. This with complaints lately made of abuse from some of the several persons who were peaceably passing in and out of town, may discourage the market people from coming in with their provisions as usual, and oblige the inhabitants to abandon the town. This event we greatly deprecate as it will produce miseries which may hurry the Province into Acts of Desperation.

We should therefore think ourselves happy, if we could satisfy the people that your Excellency would suspend your present design and not add to the distresses of the inhabitants occasioned by the Port Bill, that of garrisoning the town.

General Gage replied the same day:

Gentlemen: When you lately applied to me respecting my ordering some cannons to be placed at the entrance of the town, which you term the erecting of a fortress; I so fully expressed my sentiments, that I thought you were satisfied. People had nothing to fear from that measure, as no use would be made thereof unless their hostile proceedings should make it necessary, but as you have thus acquainted me that their fears are rather increased, I have thought proper to assure you that I have no intention to prevent the free egress or regress of any person to and from the town, or of reducing it to the state of a garrison, neither shall I suffer any under my command to injure the person or property of any of his Majesty's subjects — but as it is my duty, so shall it be my endeavor to preserve the peace, and to promote the happiness of every individual; and I earnestly recommend to you, and every inhabitant, to cultivate the same spirit — and heartily wish they may live quietly and happily in the town.[1]

Gage's men were not yet billeted in weatherproof barracks, and his concern increased when Whig workers refused to aid in the construction. He was also finding it increasingly difficult to get supplies from the countryside. Wagons that entered Boston with provisions were mysteriously set on fire or otherwise destroyed.

The general, however, tried hard not to anger the people of Boston. To the disgust of his men, in an attempt to forestall a confrontation he sided with American citizens in their complaints against his troops. Although the law gave him the power to arrest and send to England any of the rebel leaders, he held back. It is tempting to speculate what might have happened had Gage boldly seized Samuel Adams, John Hancock, and Joseph Warren and shipped them to England for trial. He had every opportunity and reason to arrest them, and his failure to do so infuriated his officers. But Gage was convinced that in any confrontation, his three thousand regulars would be annihilated, if confronted by fifty thousand well-armed Americans.

When Gage first came to Boston, he was able to close the port and shift the capital to Salem without much difficulty. Consequently, he was confident of his ability to handle the critical situation. But with the passage of the two Coercive Acts his position quickly deteriorated. He wrote to his superiors in September 1774 that trouble was increasing. In October he reported that the newly appointed members of the council had been terrorized into resigning, that the courts had been closed by mobs in the interior of the province, and that "civil government is near its end. Furthermore," he said, "conciliation, moderation, reasoning, is over; nothing can be done but by forcible means."

Gage warned that although it must come to force, he did not have enough men to do what was needed. Therefore he would "avoid any bloody crisis as long as possible, until his Majesty will in the meantime judge what is best to be done."

On November 18 Gage wrote the letter that later persuaded Parliament to replace him. In it, he declared that all of the northern colonies were supporting Boston, and rebellion was everywhere to a degree little imagined back in England. The only solution, he felt, was a military conquest of New England. Consequently, he recommended the repeal of the Coercive Acts, withdrawal of all British troops, and the subsequent landing of a large army, including German mercenaries, which could move in and conquer New England, assisted by the British fleet, which could clamp a complete blockade on the coast.

Gage's difficulties were amplified by the passage in May 1774 of the Quebec Act. Among its provisions this Act granted political freedom and equality to the Catholics of Canada and the colonies. To the intolerant eighteenth-century Protestants of New England, this was an extremely disturbing development, although not the main cause for their concern.

The provision that enraged all Americans was the ceding to the Province of Quebec of all territory north of the Ohio River and east of the Mississippi as far as the Appalachians. This territory, later known as the Northwest Territory, included land that Connecticut, Massachusetts, and Virginia claimed by solemn charter from England. Parliament had completely ignored those claims, and the Quebec Act simply confiscated this land. Edmund Burke advised the colonists that the true purpose of the Act was to restrict the old English colonies and limit their growth.

During December 1774, American intelligence agents discovered that General Gage was planning to reinforce the small Fort William and Mary in the harbor of Portsmouth, New Hampshire. The British garrison there consisted of only five men, and if the Americans struck quickly, they might be able to capture the military stores in the fort.

Paul Revere, probably the best rider in Massachusetts, was sent on a sixty-mile gallop over muddy roads to alert the militia to this opportunity. He arrived after dark at the home of Captain John Sullivan, who lived in Durham, not far from Portsmouth. Sullivan, an outstanding officer, was destined in coming months to become one of America's great generals.

He and his men set out immediately in several sailboats down the Piscataqua River. They waded ashore at the fort, rushed in and forced the commander, Captain Corcoran, to surrender. It was the first colonial capture of royal property in the history of the colonies, and it was a notable coup. They carried away ninety-seven kegs of powder and fifteen hundred small arms, including over a hundred highly prized Brown Bess muskets. Sullivan's men returned safely to Durham and hid the booty under their meeting-house.

The streetlights of Boston had not been lit since the day the Port Bill went into effect, but on August 31, 1774, money was appropriated by the selectmen to pay Edward Smith to light the lamps every night for the next year. Even when lit by flickering whale-oil lamps, however, the streets of Boston were very dark and narrow. They were patrolled every night by the Town Watch, a force of twelve constables, large and muscular, long experienced in handling drunken stevedores and sailors. Armed with a very effective weapon called a billhook — a four-foot staff of oak topped by a steel point from which a curved hook extended back toward the holder — a constable could jab with the point and jerk back with the hook.

Like many upper-class Englishmen of the period, some British officers were insatiable gamblers, and at Boston clubs they could bet enormous sums and drink large tankards of rum until the early hours of the morning. As they returned to their quarters, singing and roistering through the narrow streets, these drunken fun-lovers often had confrontations with the grim, tough constables.

On the night of December 21, 1774, between eleven o'clock and midnight, a British officer who later claimed he had been insulted unsheathed his sword and tried to attack a constable. Other constables and British officers soon arrived, and a general melee ensued. The officers swung and thrust with their swords, and the constables jabbed and hooked with their billhooks. Surprisingly, no one was killed. Hoarse shouts and the clang of steel on steel soon brought the main guard of British troops to the scene. By then one constable had his nose gashed; another had his thumb nearly severed, and an officer was cut in the neck by a billhook.

As luck would have it, Captain James Gore, the duty officer in command of the British main guard that night, was a man well known for his lack of judgment. He had been relieved of command of the light infantry company of the 5th Regiment by Lord Percy, his commanding officer, only five days before. Captain Gore was an impulsive and violent man, and on arrival at the scene of the riot, he immediately ordered his men to "present arms." In the British manual of arms, this preparatory command was followed by the order to fire. At the split-second between those two commands, two British senior officers arrived just in time to countermand the fatal command. Had they failed to intervene, the volley aimed at the Town Watch would have killed at least four men, and the revolution might well have begun that night on a dark Boston street.

A court of enquiry convened on Monday, the day after Christmas, to study the circumstances of the affair. The officers testified before the army court of enquiry, and the constables were examined by the selectmen. The constables claimed that a group of drunken officers had attacked them. The officers claimed that they had been insulted and attacked by the constables.

General Gage was furious with his officers for triggering the encounter. In a private order, he directed his three brigade commanders to assemble all of their officers and explain to them the impropriety of those who had disgraced the British army by their actions. He asked them to point out the delight with which the enemies of Britain would seize on this incident to discredit the entire army. The root cause for all the trouble, said Gage, was the frequent parties devoted to gambling and drinking.

Gage made it clear that in any altercation with the Town Watch of Boston or elsewhere, he would support the lawful authorities. He reminded the officers that the men of the Watch were appointed by law and protected by law. Therefore he would grant anyone who quarreled with the law no satisfaction for his injuries. He promised that in any similar situation he would make the most strict enquiries into the conduct of all officers concerned and try them by court-martial if they were found to be at fault.

The effect of the private order on the British officers was negative. Convinced that the members of the Town Watch were guilty of treason for insulting and attacking the officers of the king, they were incensed with Gage's support of the Watch and felt him guilty of cowardly appeasement of those who should have been punished. They were certain that Gage was too weak to handle the rapidly deteriorating colonial situation, and that he lacked the forceful determination to put down the treason that was all around them.

The officers argued that it was this same Town Watch that had arrested British enlisted men and put them in jail, while the British authorities bent over backwards to avoid trouble with the Watch. Finally, his officers felt that Gage was guilty of the ultimate act of subservience to the civilian authorities. He yielded to demands of the selectmen and ordered that no British officer or soldier appear on the streets of Boston with his side arm. Lieutenant John Barker's diary notation summarized the convictions of his fellow officers:

> Yesterday in compliance with the request of the Selectmen, General Gage ordered that no soldier in the future would appear in the streets with his side arms. Query: Is this not encouraging the inhabitants in their licentious and riotous disposition? Also orders are issued for the Guards to seize all military men found engaged in any disturbance, whether aggressors or not; and to secure them 'til the matter is enquired into. By whom? By villains that would not censure one of their own vagrants, even if he attempted the life of a soldier; whereas if a soldier errs in the least, who is more ready to accuse than Tommy?[2]

One of the cherished beliefs of members of Parliament was that most Americans were loyal to the king. In fact, there *were* large numbers of people in Massachusetts and the rest of the colonies who wanted no part of the Whigs or their political philosophy. But the fact that the only military force outside of Boston was under complete control of the Whigs made it impossible for those loyal to British rule to dissent openly. To do so would be interpreted as treason, and punishment was instantly meted out. Beatings, destruction of homes and property, public humiliation, and floggings were used by the militia to enforce the authority of the Whigs.

Those unfortunate men who accepted the king's appointments under the Coercive Acts were completely ruined. They suffered not only abuse and humiliation, but the loss of homes and possessions, for most were forced to leave the country during the British evacuation of Boston in 1776.

Late in 1774 the Loyalist leader General Timothy Ruggles formed a series of "Loyal Associations" of Americans who wished to oppose the "unconstitutional assemblies," committees, and congresses of the Whigs. These groups had constitutions binding those who signed them to oppose, even at the risk of their lives, the plans of the Whigs, whom they considered to be traitors.

In January 1775 a large number of people in the coastal town of Marshfield, thirty miles south of Boston, signed the constitution of the Loyal Association. The Whigs of nearby Plymouth then threatened to come to Marshfield and smash the association, whereupon the people of Marshfield applied to General Gage for protection. Immediately Captain Balfour, three junior officers, four sergeants, four corporals, two drummers, and one hundred privates of the King's Own 4th Regiment left on two armed schooners with provisions for fourteen days. They were joyously received by the Loyalists and billeted in comfortable quarters. For the next three months they had very enjoyable duty, leaving only when the news of Lexington and Concord reached Marshfield.

In spite of Gage's efforts to avoid altercations with the Americans in the streets of Boston, another fight took place on February 1, 1775. Lieutenant Thomas Hawkshaw of the 5th Regiment wounded an American with his sword. He claimed self-defense but was arrested and held for court-martial by General Gage.

Three weeks later another serious brawl broke out between British officers and civilians. Swords were used and there were casualties on both sides. Three officers were arrested and held for court-martial, all of them from the belligerent 5th Regiment that had been led by volatile Captain James Gore.

Another incident that might have triggered war took place in Salem on February 26, 1775. Loyalists living there informed Gage that several brass cannon and gun carriages were stored in the possession of the militia company. On an extremely cold Sunday afternoon, while the people of Salem were in church, Lieutenant Colonel Alexander Leslie, commander of the 64th Regiment, landed with a detachment at Marblehead Neck.

Leslie's mission was to march quickly to Salem, cross the Northfields Bridge to the north, and seize the brass cannon and gun carriages. However, the bridge had two leaves that could be raised to let ships pass, and when Leslie and the regulars reached the bridge, they found that the northern leaf had been raised. Demands that it be lowered were refused by militia Captain John Felt.

Two large barges were tied up on the western side of the bridge, and Leslie ordered some of his men to secure them to transport his men across. The owners of the barges were nearby, however, and they jumped into their boats to prevent this maneuver. In the ensuing struggle on the barges, one of the Americans, Joseph Whicher, was pricked by a bayonet. He was carried away by his friends as hundreds of people poured out of churches and homes and gathered at the bridge.

An ugly confrontation had developed. The British regulars were anxious to fire into the hostile crowd and charge across the bridge. On the other side, thousands of colonials jeered and dared them to do their worst. At this precise moment, militia companies from as far away as Danvers were crowding along the roads to Salem, armed and ready to fight.

Suddenly the Reverend Mr. Barnard, a Salem clergyman, approached Lieutenant Colonel Leslie and worked out a plan whereby the British could retain their honor and avoid bloodshed. Leslie promised that if the drawbridge were lowered, he would march only thirty rods (165 yards) beyond the bridge. Both sides agreed, and the bridge was lowered. The regulars marched over it the agreed distance, then countermarched and recrossed the bridge and marched back to Marblehead, where they embarked on their schooners late in the afternoon. As the British troops left Salem, militia companies entered the town from the surrounding countryside. Ironically, the two brass cannon the British sought had been hauled out of town earlier by a Quaker farmer named David Boyce.

The episode was commemorated in a poem written by John Trumbull and reprinted in American and British newspapers:

> Through Salem straight without delay,
> The bold battalion took its way;
> Marched o'er a bridge, in open sight
> Of several Yankees armed for fight;
> Then without loss of time or men,
> Veered round Boston back again,
> And found so well their projects thrive
> That every soul got home alive.[3]

After New Year, 1775, the British had begun a policy of pushing various brigades into the countryside for long marches with full equipment. Each time they moved out through Roxbury Neck (also known as Boston Neck), riders were dispatched by the colonists to warn the militia to take defensive positions in the event the regulars were out to capture military stores or Whig leaders. These expeditions kept the outlying towns in a perpetual state of alarm.

On one occasion the First Brigade, under General Lord Percy, who led them on horseback, left Boston at 6:00 A.M. and headed for Watertown, where the Provincial Congress was meeting. Mounted horsemen sped into the country ahead of them carrying the alarm to Watertown and other towns. At Cambridge, the militia pulled up the bridge to keep the regulars from crossing the Charles River, but the long column kept south of the river and crossed it farther up. When they reached Watertown, nine miles from Boston, the British found two unattended loaded cannon and hauled them away. Then, after marching around the countryside for nearly five hours and alarming towns within fifty miles of Boston, the First Brigade marched back to quarters.

There was a continuous traffic in stolen muskets and ammunition smuggled out of Boston to surrounding towns where the militia were drilling. A Brown Bess sold for a high price, and occasionally soldiers were found who were willing to sell their muskets. These were then smuggled through the British lines at Roxbury Neck or over the Charlestown ferry.

On March 8, 1775, Thomas Ditson, Jr., a farmer from Billerica, was discovered trying to buy a Brown Bess from a soldier of the 47th Regiment. Troops seized Ditson and stripped him, poured hot tar over him, covered him with feathers, fastened him to a chair in a cart, and paraded him through the streets of Boston, led by drummers and fifers of the 47th Regiment. Ditson was finally released at Roxbury Neck.

The Selectmen of Billerica appeared before the Selectmen of Boston, and both bodies protested to General Gage. There was great indignation among Boston citizens, and Gage, to the disgust of his troops, publicly apologized.

Ten days later, a farmer named Robert Pierpont was searched

as he left Boston by Roxbury Neck. The nineteen thousand ball cartridges secreted in his wagon were confiscated, but in view of General Gage's orders to avoid another incident, he was merely questioned by sentries and released. To everyone's amazement, Pierpont returned to Boston, strode into General Gage's headquarters at Province House, and demanded the return of his confiscated property, claiming that they were for his own use. He finally admitted that they were the last parcel of a large quantity that he had smuggled out earlier. Again, however, he was released without punishment.

Each year a commemorative oration was given in memory of the "Boston Massacre" of March 5, 1770. Because March 5 fell on a Sunday in 1775, the selectmen designated Monday, March 6, for the annual observation. Doctor Joseph Warren was the scheduled speaker.

The oration had never before been given when Boston was occupied by British troops, and Gage's officers considered it an insult to Britain to allow an inflammatory address to be presented under the circumstances. They decided to do something about it, and at 10:00 A.M. about forty officers reported to the Old South Meeting, where the oration was to be delivered. Conspicuous in their scarlet uniforms, they took front seats.

At 11:00 A.M. Doctor Joseph Warren resolutely entered the building, accompanied by the Selectmen of Boston and Samuel Adams, John Adams, Doctor Benjamin Church, Doctor Samuel Cooper, and other Whig leaders. Warren ascended the black-draped pulpit and began his address. The church was filled to overflowing, and a number of people, unable to find seats, congregated in the street in front of the building. There was great expectancy of trouble, due in part to the presence of the scarlet-clad officers.

Although Warren's speech was in keeping with the spirit of vilifying the British army and arousing the audience over their past actions, it was not as violent as the officers expected. The entire oration was delivered without interruption with the exception of a few hisses from some of the younger officers.

However, as soon as the address was finished, Samuel Adams

came forward from his seat with the selectmen and moved that, "The thanks of the Town should be presented to Doctor Warren for his elegant and spirited oration, and that another should be delivered on the 5th of March next, to commemorate the *bloody massacre* of the 5th of March, 1770." With that, several officers began to hiss and others shouted, "Oh fie! Oh fie!" These words sounded like "fire, fire" to some in the crowd, and a great commotion arose as people tried to leave the crowded building and pressed about the doors. Cries and screams broke out calling "Fire, fire!" and soon there was a full-scale panic.

By chance the 43rd Regiment passed Old South Meeting as the uproar began. Drums and fifes mingled with the steady tramp of the regulars marching into the countryside. This agitated the crowd trying to leave the building, many of whom believed it was all part of a plan to arrest the Whig leaders. Some people jumped out of the lower windows as others streamed from the doors, wild-eyed and disheveled.

Lieutenant Mackenzie, one of the officers present, wrote in his diary that night that the townspeople were evidently expecting a riot. He noted that nearly every civilian there carried a short stick or bludgeon of some kind, and he suspected that some carried a pistol or knife. The Whigs feared that the officers planned to make a public arrest of their leaders, and had that happened, there would certainly have been a full-scale riot. General Gage had also feared disorder and had made preparations for such an eventuality by ordering all regiments to be in readiness to march on Old South Meeting in case of an alarm.

Soon after this affair, all rebel leaders left Boston in case Gage should cease his mysterious forbearance and ship them to England for trial and possible execution for high treason. Only Doctor Joseph Warren stayed in town, and he expected to be arrested at any moment. Hostilities between Britain and New England were rapidly increasing, and in England Parliament struggled to cope with the realities of the situation.

TEN

The Struggle in Parliament

ON THURSDAY, January 19, 1775, a typically dark and rainy London day, the House of Commons met at noon in an atmosphere not unlike the weather. Prime Minister Frederick Lord North, a fat, friendly man who hated controversy, placed before the members all of the documents relevant to the current difficulties in America. There, in copies of proceedings of the First Continental Congress in Philadelphia, for all to see, was the voting record on various colonial proposals, including approval of the astonishing Suffolk Resolves. There were also petitions to Parliament seeking redress of grievances, notably an appeal from the First Continental Congress to repeal the Coercive or Intolerable Acts.

William, the Second Earl of Dartmouth, presented these documents to the members of the House of Lords, as well. When he introduced the material, a storm of anticolonial eloquence swept through the chamber. Sitting quietly through the turbulence, the sixty-seven-year-old First Earl of Chatham, William Pitt, finally rose and asked for the floor. Here was the man who, as Prime Minister, had led England from defeat to victory in the Seven Years' War. Now ill and infirm, he still commanded the respect of Parliament, and the room fell silent as he spoke.

He was convinced, Pitt said, that the troops now stationed in Boston must be removed. This was necessary at once in order to save the American colonies, which might otherwise be lost to England forever. He supported the Americans in their opposition to paying taxes, the legislation for which they had not been allowed to share. They did in fact possess legislative bodies that could have been consulted.

The Earl of Chatham was vigorously supported in the ensuing debate by several prominent Whigs, including the Duke of Richmond, the Marquess of Rockingham, the Earl of Shelburne, and Sir Charles Pratt, First Earl of Camden.

Some two weeks later, on February 1, Lord Chatham again took the floor to formally present his plan for settling the problems that existed. The plan, titled "A Provisional Act for Settling the Troubles in America and for Asserting the Supreme Legislative Authority and Superintending Power of Great Britain over the Colonies," consisted of eight sections dealing with the points of disagreement.

The first two sections reaffirmed the legality of England to rule the colonies and her right to send troops there should they be needed. However, those troops would never be used to deprive the people of their "just rights."

The third section supported the rights of the colonists to tax themselves through their provincial assemblies and provided that "no tax for his Majesty's service shall be levied from British freemen in America, without common consent, or by act of the Provincial Assembly there, duly convened for that purpose."

The fourth and fifth portions recognized the Second Continental Congress, scheduled to convene on May 10, 1775, as the supreme legislative authority of the colonies, provided that Congress recognize the supreme legislative authority of Parliament over their authority. In keeping with this recognition of Parliament's sovereignty, Congress would vote a specified sum of money to Parliament annually to help reduce the national debt. The amount was to be:

> in such honorable proportions as may seem meet and becoming from a great and flourishing colony toward a parent country, labouring under the heaviest burdens, which in no inconsiderable part, have been willingly taken upon ourselves and posterity for the defense, extension, and prosperity of the colonies.[1]

The sixth item declared that the American jury system would be restored, and no subject in America accused of a capital offense would be tried outside the colony where the offense was committed. No one was to be sent outside the colony or to England for trial. Also, the power of the vice-admiralty courts would be reduced to the limits in force before the passage of the Intolerable Acts.

This section of Pitt's proposal also would repeal all the earlier Acts deemed unjust by the colonies: the Sugar Act of 1764, the American Legal Tender Act, the Act Fixing American Postal Rates, the new American Import Duties Act of 1766, the Act for Setting Up an American Board of Customs Commissioners, and the Act of 1767, which provided for collection of revenues from those using the courts, in order to pay the civil servants involved. Actually this last Act had previously been repealed, except for the preamble and the duty on tea. Also to be repealed was the Act of 1772, which punished with special penalties anyone who destroyed military stores.

The seventh and most conciliatory of Chatham's provisions was aimed at the repeal of all the Acts termed Coercive or Intolerable by the colonists, passed in 1774: the Boston Port Bill, the Act for the Impartial Administration of Justice in Massachusetts Bay, the Act for the Better Regulating the Government in That Province, the Quartering Act, and the Quebec Act.

The eighth section proposed that judges in America be appointed for life or good behavior, just as in England. And all of the colonial charters in America were to be recognized as granting irrevocable privileges upon the people of the colonies.

Chatham's plan, which would have made the American colonies autonomous although subordinate to England, would have legalized the union the colonies had formed in the Continental Congress. His proposal was a preview of the organization adopted over 150 years later, in 1926, by the Imperial Conference, which established the British Commonwealth of Nations. That conference acknowledged that the various British colonies had changed from a status subordinate to the mother country, to a free association of equal partners.

Chatham's plan was a century and a half ahead of its time. Although it was heatedly debated, the majority of the members of Parliament, conservative and self-seeking men, were not ready for the larger concept embodied in the plan. Many of these men were in the actual pay of the king and could be counted on to vote his pleasure. Consequently, they were extremely conservative and opposed to any form of rebellion or opposition.

William, Earl of Dartmouth, supported Chatham's plan, as did the Duke of Manchester and many others. But the First Lord of the Admiralty, the very powerful Earl of Sandwich, led the fight against it. Addressing himself to the conservative members of Parliament, he stated that the Americans were not really interested in the principles of representation; they were in reality boldly planning to fight for independence and were only using the issues of taxes and representation as a mask to cover their preparations for war. In a vote of great historical consequence, Chatham's plan was defeated 61 to 32.

On February 2, Lord North introduced a motion for a joint resolution to the king on the question of the American colonies. This resolution, which asserted that a "rebellion" existed in Massachusetts and was being supported by other colonies, urged the king to force obedience to the authority of Parliament. Until a colony should apply to Parliament "in a due and constitutional manner," Parliament would not be ready to listen to their grievances. The resolution recommended the use of overwhelming military force to guarantee the respect and obedience of the colonies and said, in effect, the time for rhetoric was over.

The debate that followed this motion in the House of Commons was savage. Charles Fox, one of England's most remarkable political figures, had embraced the American cause and became her determined champion. He introduced a motion on an amendment which stated that it was Parliament who was to blame for the widening breach; that it was British stupidity rather than rebellion which was at issue.

John Wilkes, one of the most controversial figures of the age, a leader of the Whigs, and a popular champion of the common people of England, supported Fox's amendment. Despite Wilkes's devastating wit in its support, the move was defeated in the House of Commons, 288 to 105.

On February 10 Lord North introduced another fateful Act, the Restraining Bill, that would prohibit Massachusetts, New Hampshire, Connecticut, and Rhode Island from trading with England, Ireland, or the West Indies. Even more devastating to the trade of

New England, which lived mainly by fishing, these colonies were to be denied fishing rights off the Newfoundland Banks. This was a body blow meant to strangle the entire economy of New England, which was dependent on the Atlantic Ocean, whaling in the north and south Atlantic, and the export of lumber for fish barrels and shipbuilding. Much of her economy was tied up in the re-exporting business of importing sugar and molasses from the West Indies and exporting rum, as well as the re-export of British manufactured goods.

The Restraining Bill was a declaration of economic war on the colonies. One wonders if Lord North fully understood the implications of his suggestion.

In America, the thousands of Yankee fishermen, lumbermen, and workers who lost their jobs when Lord North's proposals went into effect became the solid base of colonial manpower reserves, which soon found their way into the militia. Charles Fox charged that the legislation was an attempt to "exasperate the colonies into open and direct rebellion," since it took from them all means of acquiring a livelihood and receiving provisions. It left no alternatives but starvation or rebellion.

Another friend of America, the famous conservative Edmund Burke, also fought the bill unceasingly, but he could not affect the numerical majority of the king, and the bill passed 215 to 61.

When the Restraining Bill went to the House of Lords, it was attacked by Lord Camden, who saw it as:

> a bill of war; it draws the sword and in its necessary consequences, plunges the empire into civil and unnatural war — To conquer a great continent of 18,000 square miles, containing three millions of people, all indissolubly united on the great Whig bottom of liberty and justice, seems an undertaking not to be rashly engaged in. What are the 10,000 men you have voted out to Boston? Merely to save General Gage from the disgrace and destruction of being sacked in his entrenchments. It is obvious, my Lords, that you cannot furnish armies, or treasure, competent to the mighty purpose of subduing America — but whether France or Spain will be tame, inactive spectators of your efforts and distractions, is well worth the considerations of your Lordships.[2]

Camden's efforts and those of other Whigs who supported the American position were to no avail. George III had absolute control of the necessary votes in both houses, and the Restraining Bill passed the House of Lords by a vote of 104 to 29, and quickly received the signature of the king.

On March 9, Lord North asked that Parliament extend the Restraining Bill to include New Jersey, Pennsylvania, Maryland, Virginia, and South Carolina. These colonies, like the New England provinces, were not to be allowed to trade with England, Ireland, or the West Indies, nor fish off the Newfoundland Banks.

It was during the debate on this measure that Edmund Burke delivered his famous "Pleas for Conciliation with the Colonies" on March 22, 1775. In his oration Burke declared that the colonies, despite the fact that they possessed legislative assemblies, had never been given the privilege of sending any members to Parliament. Although thus illegally deprived of representation, they had been required to pay taxes imposed on them by Parliament. These colonial assemblies had, at various times, said Burke, donated large grants and subsidies to the British government without being forced to do so. He was certain that if the colonies were allowed to raise revenue in whatever manner they wanted within their territory, the result would far surpass the method of taxation that Britain was using at the time and would eliminate the major cause of friction.

Burke demanded that the government repeal the Boston Port Bill, the Coercive Acts, and the Townshend Revenue Act; and he called for a change in the interpretation of the terms used in trials for treason. He further asked for a provision that would make judges immune to removal by the king except on the complaint of the colonial assembly or governor.

Burke's plan was voted down by the House of Commons, 270 to 78. Another attempt to save the cause of peace in America was made five days later by David Hartley, who proposed that the colonies be permitted to decide the amount of revenue to be sent to England, as well as the manner of collection. This proposal was also voted down. Hartley, a close friend of Benjamin Franklin, then proposed three more motions that were aimed not at repealing the Boston Port Bill and the Coercive Acts, but at their suspension. All were defeated by the solid strength of the king's votes.

The bill to restrain the trade of the Southern colonies was passed by both houses and received its final approval on April 13, 1775, five days before the British marched to Lexington.

The tragic lack of foresight and understanding on the part of the members of both houses of Parliament cannot be charged entirely to the millions of pounds with which George III bribed or influenced men to support his views. The handful of property owners and anti-intellectual, self-indulgent country squires who were elected from the "rotten boroughs" of England by voters who usually worked for them, insured an ultraconservative body totally out of sympathy with any projected change.

Although George III reflected the feelings of these men, it must be said in his favor that, unlike his brothers and the previous Georges, he was a moral man, a devout believer in the Anglican Church, a man of temperate habits and of courage, a devoted husband, and the father of fifteen children. His life was scandal-free, and when he became king of England in 1760, he was the most popular monarch England had enjoyed in over seventy years.

However, like so many of his supporters in Parliament, George was not given to intellectual examination of a subject. He adhered to ideas in which he believed with total rigidity; he was extremely stubborn and lost his temper quickly. What might have been an asset in others — his penchant for long hours of work — was his downfall and that of his nation. His labors, with his handful of blundering ministers, on behalf of his point of view, resulted in all manner of tampering with the votes in Parliament in order to make things happen the way he thought they should.

Horace Walpole, who as a member of Parliament had created the cabinet system, was a harsh critic of George III and his ministers. His evaluation of the British government at the time was considered extremely accurate and has been endorsed by history:

Lord North was a pliant fool, without system or principle; Lord George Germaine of desperate ambition and character; Wedderborn a thorough knave; Lord Sandwich a more profligate knave; Lord Gower a civilian capable of any crime; Elliot, Jenkinson, Cornwall, mutes that would have fixed bowstrings around the throat of the Constitution.[3]

The situation was complex, however. Both Lord North and the Earl of Dartmouth, while publicly calling for stern and coercive measures, secretly worked for conciliation with the colonists. They understood what the future would bring if war came, even if Britain defeated the colonies, and they quietly reached the conclusion, unknown to George III, that they would offer the Americans an end to direct taxation by England in return for the recognition by the colonies of the supremacy of Parliament's right to make general laws for the colonies. Early in December 1774 the two had begun secret negotiations with Benjamin Franklin in London. Meeting with Franklin under their direction was North's advisor, Thomas Villiers, assisted by two Quakers.

One of the most powerful men in all England during this period was Admiral Richard Lord Howe. At forty-eight, Black Dick, as he was called by his seamen, was at the pinnacle of power as a British naval officer. His daring and imaginative exploits during the Seven Years' War had won for him the love and admiration of all England. He had several times led his men in the storming of strongly held enemy positions. His ship was always in the thick of the fighting, and he had never lost a battle. By consistently facing danger with cool disregard, he won the loyalty of his hard-bitten English sailors, an admiration shared by fellow naval officers, who respected both his courage and his many technological improvements in the design of ships, sails, and anchors.

Howe was not only an admiral in the British navy, but, like his younger brother General William Howe, he was also an elected member of the House of Commons. As such he was a close friend and supporter of Lord Chatham, with whom he worked at the task of conciliation with the colonies. The Howe brothers felt particularly close to America. Their older brother, George, had died at Ticonderoga in 1758, and the General Court of Massachusetts had voted the large sum of £250 for a monument in his memory. Admiral Howe had supervised the work on the memorial and had read the eulogy at its unveiling in Westminster Abbey in 1762. He sincerely loved the American people, and the possibility of a war in which many Americans would be killed, wounded, or converted to abject and defeated enemies of Britain sickened him.

Through an accident of birth, this powerful admiral was even more influential than his military and political position would have entitled him to be, for the Howe brothers were the grandsons of George I. Their mother had been an illegitimate daughter of the king, and George III accepted them as his cousins and members of the royal family, showering them with gifts and honors. George III's brother sailed with Admiral Howe during the Seven Years' War, and the king consulted the admiral on all naval problems.

It was perhaps inevitable that the Howes would come to know Benjamin Franklin, the London agent for the Province of Massachusetts. Franklin had been publicly stripped of his post as postmaster general of the colonies and had been insulted by the king's party during an incident growing out of incriminating letters that had fallen into the wrong hands. He was living in London in semidisgrace when he was informed one day in early November 1774 that a certain lady wished to play chess with him, "fancying that she could beat him."

When he inquired who the lady might be, Franklin learned that she was none other than Caroline Howe, sister of Admiral and General Howe. An attractive widow of fifty-three and a sparkling conversationalist, Caroline Howe proved to be a formidable master of chess. She and Franklin played chess during the next several months and became close friends. On Christmas Day, 1774, Caroline introduced Franklin to her brother Admiral Howe. The two men liked each other at once and began an attempt to work out some of the difficulties of the impasse between England and America.

Howe began by asking Franklin to draw up a plan that would satisfy the colonies. Within several days Franklin sent a paper to Caroline for her brother. As an introduction Franklin wrote:

> It is supposed to be the wish of both sides, not merely to put a stop to the mischief at present threatening the general welfare, but to cement a cordial union and remove not only every real grievance but every cause of jealousy and suspicion.[4]

Franklin noted that Congress had previously explained the American grievances and had promised that if they were removed America would once again become a happy and loyal colony of Britain.

The paper then proceeded to specific points. Britain was asked to repeal laws that had caused the friction and to withdraw her ships and troops from Boston. If the British government would give authority to Congress in behalf of the Crown, it would be a welcome and satisfactory move toward permanent reconciliation. Congress would entertain such financial pledges as were requested, including payment to the East India Company for the loss of their tea. Franklin even offered to pledge his own fortune to pay for the tea.

Howe replied a week later, after having conferred secretly with Dartmouth and North, and asked Franklin if he could get Congress to pay for the tea first as a prelude to negotiations. Franklin replied that the Americans considered the tax as an injury before the tea was sent, but that Congress would be willing to pay for its loss if Parliament would pay the cost of the greater loss to the Port of Boston as a result of the Port Bill.

As a result of this correspondence with Franklin, Lord Howe was confident that if he went to America and talked on a person-to-person basis with the colonial leaders, he could successfully reconcile the differences developed in his negotiations with Franklin. Franklin heartily endorsed the idea, and Dartmouth agreed to sponsor a plan in the cabinet to send a delegation with Howe to America.

When, on February 10, 1775, Lord North introduced the Restraining Bill, which stated that only those colonies that acknowledged the authority of Parliament would be able to enjoy normal trade relations and fish in northern waters, the plans for such a delegation were dropped. Admiral Howe argued with the North ministry to try to suspend the Restraining Bill until negotiations could begin, but Lord North, afraid of the wrath of George III, refused. By March, Howe had conceded defeat and given up his plans for a peace commission. On March 21, 1775, Benjamin Franklin sailed for America.

Richard Howe's brother, General William Howe, also played an active role in the dispute between England and her colonies. Taller than his brother but with the same strong features and heavy brows that made both men impressive, William had risen in the army with the help of his powerful family, but had earned a solid reputation on the battlefield as an outstanding combat commander. He was well known as a strict disciplinarian whose regiments were always the best equipped and best trained in the British army. He had fought in North America during the Seven Years' War and was the officer who gallantly led the British detachment up the face of the cliff that led to the Plains of Abraham at Quebec. There, he and his regiment were in the thick of the volley and charge that destroyed the French army. Howe had been in the siege of Louisbourg, the victory at Belle Isle, and the siege and capture of Havana. He was admired for his fearless courage and ability to lead men in battle, and he was respected by his fellow officers for his superb knowledge of the military profession.

But William Howe's lack of moral qualities distressed those with whom he was associated. He lacked a sense of loyalty to those who depended upon him, and although a member of Parliament for twenty-two years, he took little interest in the affairs of his country. He rose to speak in Parliament only once, and that was to defend his conduct in the American Revolution. Married to an attractive and devoted wife, Howe took up with other women wherever and whenever he had the opportunity. He was a compulsive gambler who seldom went to sleep before 3:00 A.M. after a night of drinking with officers and one or more of his current mistresses.

However, William Howe agreed completely with his brother that negotiations could settle the dispute between England and her colonies. He too felt close ties of affection for the Americans, and many of the Provincial officers of the Seven Years' War were his close friends. When running for his seat in the House of Commons during the elections of 1774, Howe criticized the harsh policy of the ministry, declaring that it would be impossible for the army to enforce any solution that could be gained only by military force. He assured the voters on every occasion that he would refuse to serve in America if he were ordered to do so. This was accepted at face value by the people of his borough, for there were many officers who were of a like mind. General Jeffrey Amherst refused the command of the army in America; Admiral Keppel refused command of the navy; and many officers resigned their commissions rather than serve against their fellow Englishmen in America.

However, there are documents which prove that as he was promising his voters he would refuse to serve in America, William Howe was privately informing both North and Dartmouth that he wanted to be second-in-command to General Gage in Boston. Aware that Gage would soon be replaced, Howe knew that if he were in Boston, he stood an excellent chance of being named commander-in-chief. He convinced himself that as a friend of the Americans, he could accomplish by negotiations what had so far escaped the best efforts of his brother and others.

When Howe was finally offered the post, and accepted it, confusion was rife among the voters of Nottingham. In a letter to Howe a grocer named Samuel Kirk questioned his contradictory actions:

Sir: I cannot easily describe the discontent and disappointment which appears among a great number of your constituents here, on account of your having accepted a command in the expedition against our American brethren. From the opinion I had of your integrity in general, I voted for you at the late election, notwithstanding you had in some recent instances acted contrary to my sentiments. I took the liberty to tell you so, and asked you the following questions: viz.

Whether you thought our whole Army would not be insufficient to conquer America?

If you did not think the ministry had pushed the matter too far?

Whether if you should be appointed to a command, you would refuse?

Whether you would vote for the repeal of the four acts of Parliament, which you are now going to enforce?

If I am not mistaken, and I believe you will allow that I am not, you answered to every one of these queries in the affirmative. This out of pure regards to your interest here, I have made known to members who were in the same state of suspense with myself as to the propriety of our conduct at the election: and it has served to remove in a great measure the ill impressions, by which you yourself were very sensibly affected while amongst us.

We are however assured that General Howe is preparing to embark for America, in order to enforce the acts. Judge, if you can, the confusion this occasions among your friends. The most plausible excuse that is made among us, is that the King sent for you, and what could you do!

Now I must beg leave to say that I think you might have acted the part of a great man in refusing to go against this people on many accounts; but to say nothing of politics, your brother died there; they have shown their gratitude to your name and family by erecting a monument to him who bled in the cause of freedom amongst them; to him who dared to act in opposition to a court when his judgment informed him that opposition was right; and yet — he was a soldier. Our passions were wrought upon at the elections by the mention of his honored name in a paper which you may perhaps remember; and may I not mention it to you with a wish that you would follow so amiable, so disinterested, so revered a character? I believe you have not even an enemy who would impute your refusing to go for want of courage, nay, your courage would be made more conspicuous by the refusal.

If you should resolve at all events to go, I don't wish you may fall, as many do, but cannot say with success to the undertaking.

These, Sir, are the sentiments of many here, as well as of

Nottingham
February 10, 1775

Your obedient servant
[signed] Samuel Kirk

The letter must have stung General Howe, for he sent a prompt reply:

Sir: I have read your letter of the 10th with so much the greater degree of concern, as I had flattered myself I had removed all those prejudices that you had entertained against me when I had the pleasure of being with you at the election. The rancor and malice of some of those who were not my friends at the election fills me with astonishment, in the instance you mention, of their wishes for my fall in America.

My going thither was not my seeking. I was ordered, and could not refuse without incurring the odious name of backwardness to serving my country in a day of distress. So contrary are men's opinions here, to some with you, that instead of the grossest abuse, I have been most highly complimented upon the occasion by those who are even averse to the measure of administration.

Every man's private feelings ought to give way to the service of the public at all times; but particularly when of that delicate nature, in which our affairs stand at present. Whatever opprobrious names I may be called at Nottingham, I am encouraged to say that no such epithets will be put to it in any other quarter; I entreat you in particular to suspend your judgement in these matters, until the event approves me unworthy of your support.

One word upon America: You are much deceived, if you suppose that there are not many loyal and peaceable subjects in that country. I may safely assert that the insurgents are very few in comparison of the whole people.

There are certainly those who do not agree to a taxation from hence, but who do not wish to sever themselves from the supremacy of this country. This last set of men I should hope, by their being relieved from the grievance, will most readily return to all due obedience to the laws.

With respect to the few, who I am told desire to separate themselves from the mother country, I trust, when they find they are not supported in their frantic ideas by the more moderate which I have described, they will from fear of punishment subside to the laws.

With regard to trade, this country must now fix the foundations of its stability with America by procuring a lasting obedience to our laws: without which it can never arrive at that permanancy, so absolutely requisite for the well-being of this empire.

Queen Street	I am sir,
February 21, 1775	Your faithful and obedient servant,
	[signed] William Howe[5]

Howe felt that most Americans were loyal to England; he believed that only a few malcontents sought anything but a solution to the problem of being taxed without representation in Parliament. However, he sought first their recognition of the sovereignty of Britain, and he was convinced that he could solve the problem, once he was in Boston.

George III was delighted at the opportunity to appoint the highly capable Howe as Gage's second-in-command. He appeared to be the best-qualified officer in the army to restore discipline and confidence among the troops in America, and it was believed that the name of Howe would be well received by the Americans and would win Britain the support of the colonial veterans of the French and Indian War. Also, Howe was an expert in wilderness warfare and had conducted experiments on the Salisbury Plain in England with the newly organized light infantry companies. Perhaps he could teach the British soldiers to fight "Indian style" behind trees, walls, and hedges — in a manner far removed from the rigid formality common to the army of the times.

ELEVEN

The Spies of Gage

WHATEVER FAILINGS General Thomas Gage may have had as a military tactician, he understood well the importance of military intelligence. Even by modern standards of military espionage, his network of spies and undercover informers was impressive. It certainly excelled that of any other military commander of his time. Ironically, the colonial spy system, while less efficient, was just as effective.

It was rumored that within the inner sanctum of the foremost colonial leaders — the Committee of Safety — one man was a British spy. Could it be Doctor Benjamin Church, or even Paul Revere? Among those suspected at the time were Elbridge Gerry, Richard Devens, William Heath, Benjamin White, and Azor Orne.

This well-placed spy supplied Gage with prompt and accurate information about every plan or decision arrived at in the most secret colonial caucus. History would still be puzzled at his identity, had not George Washington unmasked him in September, three months after the Battle of Bunker Hill.

A second mysterious figure was revealed in documents that have surfaced within the last fifty years. John Hall, whose name appears in the confidential correspondence of Thomas Gage, sent Gage a comprehensive series of reports of American acquisitions of military supplies, food, and other necessities, and their exact location in and around the town of Concord. Hall was probably a farmer or merchant living in Concord, for he described the route taken by British deserters out of Boston, as well as their method of slipping around the sentries posted at Boston Neck.

It was Hall's report of April 6, 1775, that persuaded Gage to send the expedition to Concord that precipitated the battles at Lexington and Concord. In this report, Hall detailed the hiding place several miles out of Concord on the farm of the colonial militia commander of Concord, of four brass cannon stolen from the British at Boston.

On April 13 the spy in the Committee of Safety advised Gage that the Provincial Congress, in secret session, had decided — should British troops march out of Boston with artillery and baggage — to sound the alarm, whereupon the colonial militia would oppose the British forces "to the last extremity."

Other spies reported that British soldiers were selling their muskets to the Americans for four dollars each and described how the colonials were preventing food from reaching Boston. Through these spies Gage also learned that the Provincial Congress was planning to raise an army of 180,000 men.

Gage soon grasped the entire situation. There were, near Boston, two large American supply dumps bulging with accumulated military supplies, one at Worcester, forty-seven miles away, the other at Concord, twenty-two miles away. In view of his experience with General Braddock during the Seven Years' War, Gage decided to send out a small scouting party disguised as surveyors. Their mission would be to map the road systems between Boston and Worcester and between Boston and Concord, with special attention to military features of the terrain: possible ambush sites, bridges that could be torn down to trap a large force, bottlenecks, and other pertinent information. Gage believed that, armed with the proper information, he would be able to send a column of troops to one of the supply depots, destroy or capture the stores, and return to Boston without loss, as in the capture of the gunpowder at Charlestown.

In the General Orders of January 8, 1775, General Gage asked for volunteers from among the officers "capable of taking sketches of a country." Lieutenant John Barker of the 4th Regiment, King's Own, wrote somewhat petulantly in his diary that day:

> General Orders: if any officer of the different regiments are capable of taking sketches of a country they will send their names to the Deputy-Adjutant General. This is an extraordinary method of word-

ing the order; it might at least have been a more genteel way; at present it looks as if he doubted whether there were any such.

Such might have been the case, for Lieutenant Mackenzie's diary entry for that date also describes the order:

> It has been signified to the Army, that if any officers of the different regiments are capable of taking sketches of a country, they are to send their names to the Deputy-Adjutant General. I am afraid not many officers of this Army will be found qualified for this service. It is a branch of military education too little attended to, or sought by our officers, and yet is not only extremely necessary and useful in time of war, but very entertaining and instructive.[1]

As a result of the General Order, Captain William Browne of the 52nd Regiment and Ensign Henry de Berniere of the 10th were selected for the mission. De Berniere left a full account of the experience.

On February 22 the two young officers received their orders to travel through the counties of Suffolk and Worcester, sketching the roads as they went. With John Howe, a young corporal from the 52nd, who was to function as a servant, they disguised themselves as surveyors in brown clothes with red handkerchiefs tied around their necks.

On the morning of February 23, the three men crossed over to Charlestown on the ferry and walked through the town, Breed's Hill and Bunker Hill looming on their right. They then crossed Charlestown Neck to Cambridge and passed through the town and across the bridge to Watertown.

Shortly after Watertown they stopped for lunch at the inn of Jonathan Brewster, who had commanded a Ranger battalion in the French and Indian War. Browne and de Berniere ordered their lunch from a black serving girl and, as officers never ate with enlisted men in the British army, unthinkingly sent Corporal Howe to eat in the kitchen. Their waitress, noting this anachronism in colonial New England, became suspicious of the "surveyors" and examined them closely as they ate. Having worked at a Boston tavern frequented by British officers, she finally recognized Captain Browne.

As she was clearing the table, Ensign de Berniere remarked that it was a "fine country" thereabouts. She straightened up and looked him directly in the eye. "It is a very fine country and we have very fine and brave men to fight for it. If you travel much further you will find it to be true."

The three men paid their bill quickly and walked in apprehensive silence toward Weston. They accepted a teamster's offer of a ride in his wagon, but asked to alight in Weston at the Golden Ball Tavern because they feared traveling all of the way to Worcester with the man.

The Golden Ball was owned by a sturdy Loyalist named Isaac Jones, who they were told could be trusted. After dinner and a rest, the three left in a heavy downpour early the next morning for Framingham, nine miles away. Water-soaked, they trudged along the muddy road as de Berniere sketched possible defensive positions that might be used by American riflemen.

The three mud-caked men arrived at the Buckminster Tavern in Framingham late that afternoon. They now looked like American countrymen, and to avoid suspicion because of the officers' upper-class English accent, it was decided to let Howe do the talking. After dinner they climbed the stairs to their room, where a basin, sponge, and comfortable bed awaited them. They would not have slept so soundly had they known that their host, Joseph Buckminster, was a member of the Framingham Committee of Correspondence.

The next day was Saturday, February 25. The three decided to walk to Worcester, thirty miles away. They took along a lunch prepared for them by the tavern cook, and being very careful to treat Howe as an equal, they started southwest through Grafton.

The Loyalist Isaac Jones had recommended the tavern of a relative in Worcester, and when they arrived late in the afternoon, they found the innkeeper under great stress. His name was also Isaac Jones, and the Worcester militia had recently warned all loyal patriots to shun his inn. The British spies spent the night with their distraught host, only to find that they could not leave the next day — Sunday — because Massachusetts law prohibited anyone from being on the streets during the hours of church service. De Berniere spent his time reorganizing and detailing his sketches.

Unable to examine the supplies cache at Worcester because

Jones refused to act as their guide and be seen in their company, the officers decided to return to Boston as soon as possible. To the relief of the nervous innkeeper, they left early Monday morning, taking a northerly route through Shrewsbury so as not to retrace their earlier route. General Gage would thus have an alternate set of maps for a different itinerary.

Just outside Worcester they were passed from behind by a horseman who slowly looked them over and then, to their discomfort, kept looking back at them after he had passed. Suddenly he spurred his mount and galloped over the hill. Thoroughly alarmed, the three soldiers decided to turn back through Worcester toward Grafton and take refuge at the Buckminster Tavern in Framingham.

It was a wise decision, for the horseman was Timothy Bigelow, a Worcester blacksmith and member of the Provincial Congress. He was also captain of a militia company in Colonel Artemas Ward's regiment, and had followed the soldiers out of Worcester. When he passed them he raced on through Shrewsbury to Marlborough and organized a roadblock to intercept them.

Unaware of their narrow escape, the "surveyors" entered the Buckminster Tavern while three Minutemen companies drilled on the Framingham Green in front of the inn. No one paid any attention to the three men in muddy brown as they asked for a room at the inn.

Upstairs, their room overlooked the green and gave them an excellent view of the colonials at drill. After thirty minutes of marching to commands beat out on a drum, the Minutemen were called to attention, and their commander, Captain Simon Edgell, spoke of the imminent possibility of battle with the British regulars. He pointed out that Provincial militia had helped to defeat the French and Indians in the late war and that England would surely have lost the war in America had it not been for the valor and skill of the colonial troops.

Upstairs at the inn, the three spies quietly studied the intent, motionless men below and could not help noticing their lean and muscular appearance. In spite of themselves, they were impressed when Edgell said, "Americans are equal to the best troops in the world." He reminded his men to remain cool under fire, to be patient and brave. They must wait for the command to fire, then charge, but only as a disciplined body.

When the militiamen were dismissed they cheered their company commander and tramped into the taproom beneath the room of the "surveyors," where they drank hot mulled ale, smoked clay pipes, and talked until 9:00 P.M., while the three men above them slept.

The spies awoke to a beautiful morning. They had escaped serious dangers, and their youthful exuberance rose after a hearty breakfast served by Joseph Buckminster himself. They made short work of the nine miles to Weston and were soon back with their Tory friend, Isaac Jones, at his Golden Ball Tavern.

In their room each man enjoyed a hot bath standing in a large wash basin in the middle of the room. The bath began with a rinse of water mixed from two pitchers, one hot and one cold. A soaping with strong lye soap followed and was rinsed off with more water poured over by the other two men. After a brisk toweling with large, coarse towels, the three men dressed and went down to a hearty dinner served by Jones. The fare included roast beef, steak-kidney-oyster pie, and a favorite colonial dish, Indian pudding. Made from yellow cornmeal, the pudding was baked eighteen hours in a brick oven. Pewter tankards of excellent ale accompanied the meal.

Elated, the two officers decided to send John Howe back to Boston with the sketches that de Berniere had drawn, while they returned to Marlborough by way of Sudbury. The Weston–Sudbury Road was then the main road to Worcester, and they had missed it by going southwest through Framingham and Grafton to Worcester. They felt it was essential to sketch the route from Weston to Marlborough, which they had abandoned when they encountered the inquisitive horseman outside of Worcester.

They parted on the morning of Wednesday, March 1, a dark and threatening day. Howe left on the road to Boston, and Browne and de Berniere started for Sudbury and Marlborough. Had they understood New England weather, they would have seen the signs of an approaching, dreaded "northeaster" and postponed their journey.

Less than an hour after the officers left Weston it began to snow.

With each step they took, the wind, driving the snow horizontally, increased in violence. Their freezing feet, encased in heavy, buckled shoes, soon were large balls of frozen mud. Stubbornly, the young men pushed on for Marlborough sixteen miles away. Heads down, they concentrated on putting one frozen foot in front of the other, the freezing wind driving them on their way like sailing ships.

Finally they reached Sudbury and continued on through the howling storm to within three miles of Marlborough. Up to that point they had seen no other travelers. Now they found themselves being overtaken by a solitary horseman, who passed them and then pivoted his animal, blocking their progress. He asked them where they were headed, where they were coming from, and where they lived. They told him they were from Boston and were traveling to Marlborough to see a friend. The horseman looked at them somberly and, without warning, asked them if it were true that they were both British officers. The sudden question failed to unnerve them, and they both denied the charge, insisting that their story was true. They were going to see a friend. The horseman looked at them silently and, spurring his horse into a trot, splashed his way toward Marlborough.

The two officers were in deadly peril, and they knew it. Their diction was entirely out of character with their countryman disguises. Obviously the horseman did not believe their story and was now spreading the alarm. If they should be captured by the colonial militia they would be questioned by local officers. If they persisted in denying their positions as officers in the British army, they could be "sweated" in the colonial manner — hoisted by a rope attached to their wrists bound behind them — and thrown into prison or tarred and feathered and forced to walk back to Boston.

The blinding snowstorm obliterated the houses as they arrived in the main square of Marlborough, but they could discern people watching them along the side of the road. One man, a baker, judging by his apron, asked them where they were going in such weather. They replied that they were looking for the house of Mr. Henry Barnes; a wealthy merchant and prominent Loyalist, his name had been given to them by Isaac Jones. The baker pointed out the way to them, and as they left him they saw several dim figures run through the swirling snow.

When they arrived at the home of Barnes, he was waiting for them. He asked if they had spoken to anyone on the way, and when they mentioned the baker, his face turned pale. The baker was a leading militiaman in Marlborough and had a British deserter, a drummer named Swain, living in his home. At this Captain Browne, too, paled. Swain had been his drummer until less than a month ago.

At that moment a disconcerting knock sounded, and Dr. Samuel Curtis, a leading member of the Marlborough Committee of Correspondence, was at the door for a "friendly visit." Barnes had hardly spoken to Curtis for many years and begged to be excused, saying that he had visitors. Curtis was seen hurrying away toward the town meetinghouse.

The two Britons were invited to rest briefly while they recovered from their ordeal and dried their clothes. As they sat down to a steaming meal, a servant burst into the room saying that a large body of armed men was approaching. Snatching up several pieces of bread, the two officers sprinted out the back door, through the stables, and into a country lane that led to the Sudbury Road.

As they fled, militiamen forced their way into the house, demanding the surrender of the two British officers hiding there. They searched the house thoroughly, going through every room, peering under beds and closets, looking in every possible hiding place. Enraged, they cursed Barnes for being a "damned traitor" and threatened to burn his house down, but soon left without doing any damage.

The two fugitives ran down the Sudbury Road to the outskirts of town, where they wisely decided to take to the woods and eat their hasty meal of bread. This probably saved them from capture by American horsemen sent out to intercept them.

The storm was still driving the snow across the road as they resumed their trek. During the long day and evening they fought their way into the force of the wind, trying to shield their eyes and nostrils from the stinging snow. Several horsemen passed them, their heads, too, averted from the fierce wind, but they did not attempt to stop the officers.

At long last, much to their relief and that of their host, they stumbled into Isaac Jones's tavern in Weston and wearily ascended to their rooms. They strung their stiff clothes before the roaring fire to dry, bathed with pitchers of water sent up by Jones, and wrapped themselves in warm blankets. After several bottles of hot mulled Madeira wine, they dropped off to sleep before the warmth of the hearth. They had hiked and run over thirty-two miles in a blinding snowstorm since morning.

Early the next day they started for Boston and arrived at Roxbury Neck by noon. General Gage, who was inspecting the fortifications, did not immediately recognize the two men in their wrinkled and stained clothes. He was overjoyed at their arrival and was delighted with the quality of de Berniere's sketches.

Three weeks later Gage again sent for Browne, de Berniere, and Howe and directed them to undertake a similar mission to Concord, twenty-two miles away. The danger they faced had increased substantially in three weeks' time, and they armed themselves with pistols concealed under their coats. They left immediately, traveling through Roxbury and Brookline to Weston. From there they walked rapidly to Concord.

In Concord they asked to see Daniel Bliss, a leading Loyalist who had collected much important information about the location of colonial cannon and other military supplies stored there.

The news that three strangers of military bearing had asked for Bliss soon reached the local Committee of Safety. While the Britons talked to Bliss in his home, a knock sounded at the door, and a message was handed to him warning that if he tried to leave town he would be killed by the militia. The British officers told Bliss they were well armed, and he could leave with them. He gratefully accepted their protection and left Concord in their company without incident. However, he never saw his home or possessions again.

The information Bliss had collected was complete and invaluable. He described the terrain of Concord, which was situated between two hills through which the Concord River flowed. The river was bridged at two points, South Bridge and North Bridge. He pinpointed the hiding place of four brass field guns and ten iron cannon in the woods and houses of Concord. Other war supplies included cartridge boxes, harnesses, spades, pickaxes, bill-hooks, iron pots, wooden mess bowls, cartridge paper, powder, musketballs, flints, flour, dried fish, salt, and rice. There was also a magazine of powder and cartridges hidden on Colonel James Barrett's farm. All of this information was transcribed by de Berniere and marked on his maps.

Bliss directed them onto the road to Boston that led near the village of Lincoln and through Lexington. De Berniere noted that the road to Lexington was "very open and good for six miles," but that the following five miles were enclosed by hills and included several places that could afford an enemy good cover, for the road was very narrow there.

The four men walked back to Boston without incident, passing through Lexington and Menotomy (now Arlington), with Cambridge on their right, and turned toward Charlestown. They crossed over to Boston on the ferry and reported to General Gage at Province House. De Berniere's sketches, maps, and notes became an important factor in Gage's plans for the future.

Gage followed the colonial buildup of weapons and supplies, which continued at a frenzied pace as dispatches, sketches, and reports from his agents found their way into his possession. By the first of April he had an excellent picture of the situation in Concord but was uncertain of the extent of the American arms stockpile at Worcester.

On April 5, Gage sent for Corporal John Howe and Lieutenant Colonel Francis Smith, commander of the 10th Regiment. They were to disguise themselves as itinerant laborers looking for work and, with the enlisted man acting as guide, examine the measures that the Americans had developed for the defense of Worcester, including the size of the garrison that was available to defend the town.

The two dressed in clothing worn by workingmen of the time: leather breeches, gray coats, blue-and-white knit stockings, neckerchiefs, and the universally worn three-cornered hat. As was the custom, they carried their few extra articles in a homespun handkerchief in one hand, and a stout walking stick in the other. Their plan was to walk to Worcester, stopping frequently to ask for work.

At dawn on Thursday, April 6, 1775, they took the ferry to Charlestown and walked through Cambridge to Watertown. Howe remembered Brewster's Inn, where he and the two officers had eaten six weeks before, but he neglected to warn Colonel Smith about the alert black serving girl. Uneasily he watched her approach to take their order. Howe kept his pipe in his mouth as he muttered his order, but Smith, trying to play the role of an unemployed worker, asked her where two good but jobless men could find employment. Two bright eyes twinkled at him. "Colonel Smith, you will find employment enough for you and all of Gage's men in a few months."

The two men hastily ate their food and hurried to the door. The innkeeper, Jonathan Brewster, smilingly asked them how they had enjoyed their meal. Smith placed his coins on the counter and replied, "Very well, but you have a saucy wench here." Brewster, when told what she had said, murmured softly that she had been living in Boston and was probably confusing him with someone she had seen there. He advised them to walk to Weston, where they could ask for work and stay at the Golden Ball Inn.

Shaken by their experience, the two men hurried down the Weston Road until they were out of sight of the tavern. They started to trot, but Smith begged Howe to stop. They climbed over a brick wall to give Smith, a short-legged and overweight man streaming with perspiration in the morning sun, a chance to rest.

They decided that Colonel Smith, having been identified by the woman at Brewster's Inn, was useless for the mission and should return to Boston. Howe would continue to Worcester alone. Carrying letters of introduction to various Loyalists, a journal book, pencil, and ten guineas, he started out at a fast pace.

Howe soon arrived at an inn, where he questioned the innkeeper about the possibility of employment. When asked what kind of work he did, he said he would accept farming but preferred gunsmithing, as that was his trade. The innkeeper urged Howe to hurry to Springfield, for gunsmiths were desperately needed there. Howe proceeded to the Golden Ball at Weston, however, and gave Isaac Jones a letter of introduction from Gage.

The tolerant attitude toward strangers had changed since Howe's last visit to Weston. When he told Jones about the incident at Brewster's Inn and the innkeeper's suggestion that he spend the night at the Golden Ball, Jones insisted that he leave at once and spend the night in a nearby forest. Jones fed Howe and had his trusted black servant lead him deep in the woods on the outskirts of Weston, to the home of a Tory named Wheaton.

The next day Howe learned that a party of thirty Minutemen had invaded the Golden Ball at 11:00 P.M. and searched the entire building for two British spies that Jonathan Brewster reported serving at his tavern.

Howe spent the next day in hiding with Mr. Wheaton, using the time to record the information furnished by him and Jones's servant regarding the militia strength in Weston.

At 8:00 P.M. Jones's servant arrived from the inn by a circuitous route and led Howe through the forest, avoiding roads, until they reached Sudbury. Stopping there long enough to locate a fording place in the event the Americans destroyed the bridge over the Sudbury River, they proceeded to Marlborough.

They arrived at the home of Henry Barnes at 2:00 A.M., and Howe presented the letter from Gage, since he was a stranger to Barnes. Isaac Jones's servant ate and returned to Weston; Howe was fast asleep by 4:00 A.M.

Shortly past noon on Sunday, April 9, a greatly disturbed Barnes shook Howe awake. News was circulating through town that a woman had seen two men, one white, the other black, examining a bridge near her house late at night. She reported last seeing them walking on the road to Marlborough. Everyone was alerted to watch for the pair, who were assumed to be British spies. It was clear that Howe must remain hidden that day and be prepared to slip away into the swamp in the event of a visit from the local militia.

Late that night, he borrowed a horse from his host and rode into Worcester, arriving an hour before sunrise. There he found the house of a Loyalist recommended by both Gage and Barnes. His new host, an extremely capable and observant man, was able to furnish the British soldier with a complete list of the military stores collected in Worcester. After dark he led Howe to the area where the stores were kept, and keeping far enough from the cluster of buildings to avoid the suspicions of the sentries, the two studied various access routes. Howe noted in his journal that several wells were located nearby into which flour and cartridges could be thrown.

Near midnight the two men returned and, elated by the success of their dangerous mission, relaxed over some choice Madeira. Howe asked his new friend for his opinion of a raid from Boston by the British army to destroy the military stores at Worcester. "I do not think that a single man would dare lift a finger to oppose the regulars," said the Loyalist as he sipped his wine. He looked at Howe. "What is your opinion?" Howe took a long time to answer. "If you will promise to keep it a secret, I will tell what I think. It is this. If General Gage sends his entire force here with a train of artillery from Boston to Worcester, not one of them will get back."

It was long after midnight when Howe bade his friend goodbye and left on the road to Marlborough. The night was clear but bitterly cold, and his horse plodded over an icy road treacherous with miniature mountain peaks of frozen earth. The realization that he was fifty miles from the safety of Boston and that capture by American militia was a distinct possibility sent icy edges of fear through the young soldier. Despite his forebodings, however, he arrived at the home of Henry Barnes just as the sun rose. Barnes, relieved to see him, joined him in breakfast, followed by a lively discussion as Howe displayed his papers and notes. Barnes contributed additional information regarding colonial military preparations in the area from Marlborough to Worcester.

When Corporal Howe mentioned he was going northeast to Concord, Barnes advised him to wait until late that night and then head due east to Sudbury and from there north to Concord. Barnes led his guest to a garret with instructions to leave through the window at 8:00 P.M., because the front door was probably being watched. He then brought out a bottle of his finest brandy, and the two men drank each other's health and safety. Howe tied his belongings, including his papers, in his homespun handkerchief and placed it on a table ready to pick up quickly. As the two sat enjoying their brandy, a heavy knock at the front door resounded throughout the house. Both men sprang to their feet. Barnes told Howe to remain quiet, and if he did not return in one minute to leave by the window over the roof of the shed below.

From there Howe could lower himself to the ground and escape to the swamp.

The corporal heard a loud voice, "Esquire, we have come to search your house of spies," and Barnes's reply, "I am willing." With that, Howe threw his hat and bundle out of the window and followed them onto the icy roof of the shed. His feet slid out from under him and he sailed into the garden on his back. Shaken, he found his belongings and limped off into the frozen swamp as fast as he could. Glancing back at the house, he saw lights moving past the windows and heard the pounding of horses' hooves on the road in front of the house.

Fearful that he could be tracked through the snow that covered the frozen swamp, Howe alternately ran and walked for nearly four miles. In the center of a small clearing he came to a cabin and knocked on the door. A middle-aged black man answered, holding a candle to Howe's face. Claiming he had lost his way, the British soldier asked for directions to Concord. He was invited in, fed by the man's wife, and invited to spend the night. Though obviously exhausted, Howe was anxious to reach Concord that night. He offered his host a silver dollar to guide him there, explaining that he was eager to start work at his trade of gunsmithing. Assuring Howe that gunsmiths were needed, the man agreed to go. They trudged easterly to the river, where they spent the night at the home of Wetherby, a friend of the black guide. The next morning, Thursday, April 13, Wetherby accompanied Howe into Concord and introduced him to Major John Buttrick, one of the senior militia officers. Within a few hours Howe was hard at work repairing colonial gunlocks.

That evening he had dinner with a group of militia officers who were of the opinion that the regulars would soon be marching to Concord. They showed him the storehouse where muskets and large quantities of flour and ammunition were stacked. Surreptitiously Howe studied the gates and doors leading to the storehouse.

The next morning he informed his new employers that he needed to return to his home in Pownalborough to secure his tools, without which his ability to work on the muskets was limited. They agreed and urged him to get back as soon as he could.

Howe set out at once but stopped in Lincoln, four miles from

Concord, where he went to the home of an undercover Loyalist named Gove, who was expecting him. The two men compared notes on information that they both had, but Gove was nervous and insisted that Howe spend the rest of the day in a nearby shed. Late that night Gove brought two horses, and they rode into Charlestown and crossed by ferry into Boston. It was 2:00 A.M. when Howe finally reached his quarters.

Howe slept until late morning, and when he awoke he took his first good bath in days, shaved, and put on his corporal's uniform. He was walking happily down King Street looking forward to a hot breakfast, when he was intercepted by Lieutenant Colonel Francis Smith, his erstwhile traveling companion. Smith rushed him over to Province House and General Gage's quarters. A meeting of senior officers was in progress as they entered the room, but Gage rose and greeted Howe affectionately. He was delighted with the sketches and reports and asked him to sit down and recount his adventures to the assembled officers. There were many questions, and Howe kept his audience's attention for nearly an hour.

Gage asked him his frank opinion of the possibility of a successful march to Worcester to destroy the stores there. Howe replied that such an expedition, launched over forty-eight miles of winding roads, hampered with the necessary train of artillery and faced with the necessity of returning over the same roads, could only result in a military disaster. Worcester was too far away, in a countryside swarming with well-armed and fairly well-trained militia.

"What about Concord as a target?" asked Gage. Howe replied that five hundred mounted men could accomplish the feat easily, but he was far from optimistic about the chances of foot soldiers returning through the thousands of militiamen who would be waiting for them. When asked about the possibility of help from their Loyalist friends, Howe expressed his belief that they were a poor and terrorized group in no position to help anyone, including themselves.

The next day, Gage sent for Howe and ordered him to undertake his third mission as a secret agent. Later that afternoon, dressed as a farmer, Howe rode a farm horse onto the ferry for Charlestown. He was headed north toward Malden, Lynn, Marblehead, and Salem to report on militia readiness for the coming war.

TWELVE

Two if by Sea

BY APRIL 1, 1775, Samuel Adams and John Hancock had left Boston and were staying in Lexington at the home of the Reverend Jonas Clarke, whose wife was Hancock's cousin. John Adams was at his home in Braintree listening to the shouted commands as militia officers drilled their men on the Green. The three men looked forward to their trip to Philadelphia, where they would represent Massachusetts in the Second Continental Congress, scheduled to convene on May 10.

Back in Boston, only the extraordinary Dr. Joseph Warren still remained. Born in 1741 at Roxbury, Massachusetts, Warren had graduated from Harvard at age eighteen and opened his medical practice on June 15, 1763, shortly before a major outbreak of smallpox.

He was one of the handsomest young men in Boston, at five feet eight inches tall, with a barrel chest and the broad shoulders of a wrestler, and was the overwhelming favorite of all the ladies.

When the great smallpox epidemic broke out, Dr. Warren was twenty-two and the youngest doctor in Boston. Although hundreds of people packed their belongings and fled the city, the doctors of Boston fought the dread disease with the newly recognized weapon of inoculation. Despite great opposition from many doctors, the governor and council fought for and finally received permission to open two inoculation hospitals, one in Chelsea, across the Mystic River, the other at Castle William, in Boston

Harbor. Two doctors volunteered to serve in each of these radical departures from accepted medical practice; one of the men serving at Castle William was Doctor Warren.

During the months that he spent in quarantine at Castle William, Warren and his colleague Dr. Samuel Gelston treated over a thousand patients. By August 13, 1764, not a single person in Boston had smallpox. The two inoculation hospitals had inoculated 4977 people, of whom only forty-six had died. Of the 699 persons who had contracted the disease naturally, 124 had died.

As a result of his experience, Warren became the most sought-after physician in Boston. He married Elizabeth Hooton in the summer of 1764, and during the next ten years his reputation as a physician rose steadily. By 1774 Warren was treating twenty-five to fifty new patients each month, averaging 225 visits a month, which included people from every stratum of society, the wealthy to the workingman.

Warren was a close friend of Samuel Adams, and the two men were involved in politics from their youth. Of the two, Warren appealed to the general populace as the more civic minded and unselfish. His huge medical practice and understanding manner won him many friends, who saw in his political beliefs a wise and sincere man.

By April 1774 the official British government of Massachusetts Bay, as restructured by the Coercive Acts, had been repudiated by nearly all colonists. Their allegiance was to the Provincial Congress meeting in Concord, which was openly preparing for war with England.

Congress established rules and regulations for the "Massachusetts Army" and a general court-martial for enforcing them. On April 13 it voted to raise six companies of artillery and the money to pay for them. The next day it advised all citizens in Boston to leave the city and move into the surrounding countryside. On April 15 the Provincial Congress appointed a day of fasting and prayer and adjourned until May 10, when the Second Continental Congress convened in Philadelphia.

Since the First Continental Congress had voted to support Massachusetts in their opposition to the British attempt to alter their charter, the men of the Provincial Congress felt certain of the full support of the other colonies. They were also sure that there would soon be an attempt of force by General Gage, for news of the British reinforcements sailing for Boston had traveled through the colonies.

On Sunday, April 16, a newly arrived letter from England was handed to General Gage in Boston. It was a stinging reminder from his superior, the Earl of Dartmouth, to use the force that he had against the American "rebels." The letter reminded Gage that an "untrained and tumultuous rabble" had committed outrages in the colonies with no apparent punishment from the forces of the king. It promised him new reinforcements that were on their way which

> will enable you to take a more active and determined part . . . . The only consideration that remains is in what manner the forces you command may be exerted — the first essential step to be taken towards re-establishing government, would be to arrest and imprison the principal actors and abettors in the Provincial Congress — any efforts of the people, unprepared to encounter with a regular force, cannot be very formidable, and though such a proceeding should be according to your idea of it, a signal for hostilities, yet it will surely be better that the conflict be brought on, upon such ground, than in a riper state of rebellion.[1]

Gage did not record his reaction to this rebuke, but he had written to London on an earlier date:

> If you think ten thousand men sufficient, send twenty, if one million is thought enough, give two; you will save both blood and treasure in the end. A large force will terrify and engage many to join you, a middling one will encourage resistance and gain no friends.[2]

Now he had orders to move out with his "middling force" even before new reinforcements reached him. A good soldier, Gage prepared to obey and made plans to march to Concord and destroy the concentration of supplies located there.

The Americans had been expecting an attack for over a month and had carefully prepared to meet it by organizing an intricate network of spies under the leadership of Samuel Adams and his Sons of Liberty. This organization held secret meetings in the Green Dragon Tavern on Union Street in Concord. The towns of Roxbury, Cambridge, and Charlestown had teams of men moving every hour of the day and night through the streets and along the exits of the roads leading from Boston. Their orders were to report any unusual movements immediately to Dr. Joseph Warren in Boston. To that end a group of mounted messengers were ready at a moment's notice to ride for Boston from the outlying areas, or from Boston to Worcester or Concord. Paul Revere, an excellent horseman and one of Dr. Warren's favorite couriers, also headed a volunteer force of thirty artisans who patrolled the streets of Boston in pairs during the night. Officers were closely watched, every ship in the harbor was monitored through spyglasses, every movement of troops was carefully charted and reported. In addition, persons like servants, waiters, and barmaids who were in contact with British officers and men were organized into the intelligence network. All reports were channeled through Dr. Warren, who remained in Boston at constant risk to his life and who feared arrest at each knock on his door.

At the mouth of the Charles River across from Boston, Richard Devens commanded the colonial intelligence network in Charlestown. He had at his disposal a number of spies and couriers, should the British show signs of moving out in force through Charlestown.

On Saturday, April 15, as the Provincial Congress adjourned in Concord, sharp-eyed observers reported to Warren and Devens that the British man-of-war *Somerset* had been moved to a new mooring near the ship lane of the Boston–Charlestown ferry. Soon other reports came to Warren that ship's boats belonging to the British transports had been collected, ostensibly for painting and repair, and were now floating beneath the stern of British warships. Warren and his associates saw significance in these events and doubled their teams of observers.

On that crucial Saturday, a third piece of the puzzle fell into place on Dr. Warren's chart. The General Orders read to all British troops that morning contained an innocuous order from General Gage relieving all flank companies from guard or other extra duties:

April 5th, General Orders:
The Grenadiers and Light Infantry in order to learn Grenadier exercises and further new evolutions are to be off all duties till further orders.[3]

However, British Lieutenant John Barker noted drily in his diary: "This I suppose is by way of a blind. I dare say they have something for them to do."[4]

The General Orders for the next day, Easter Sunday, elaborated on the training for the new evolutions and announced that the light infantry companies would be instructed in "new maneuvers" by Lieutenant Frederick Mackenzie, adjutant of the 23rd Regiment.

It is possible that Gage actually intended to have at least one day's exercise in the new maneuvers that represented a radical departure from the British standard three-line formation and was an adjustment for fighting in the open country of America, which, unlike the terrain of continental Europe, contained large wooded areas. The previous year Major General William Howe had conducted exercises in these new maneuvers at Salisbury in England, and he was, that Easter Sunday, en route to Boston with over a thousand troops. Also aboard the British transports were two other major generals, Henry Clinton and John Burgoyne. It was widely rumored that Howe would soon replace Gage in command of the British army at Boston.

When Dr. Warren heard of these General Orders, he sent for Paul Revere and asked him to carry the news to Lexington the next day.

It was a little after 5:00 A.M. and still dark along the waterfront at Clark's Wharf when Revere slid his well-hidden boat from under the pier. Clark's Wharf was only a block from his house, so he did not risk being challenged by a British military patrol. As the first light of dawn streaked across the black waters of Boston Harbor, Revere smoothly rowed himself across the wide mouth of the Charles River to Charlestown. There a horse supplied by one of Richard Devens's men was waiting, and Revere was off for Lexington.

As the rising sun sent the shadows of Buckman Tavern across the village green, he trotted past the inn and meetinghouse. It was a cold morning, and although wrapped in his long surtout, or overcoat, Revere was glad to reach the warmth of the roaring hearth at the home of the Reverend Jonas Clarke, where Adams and Hancock were staying.

This painting, done in 1974, shows a typical scene along the Battle Road between Concord and Lexington, in what is now the Minuteman National Historical Park. The field-grown spreading oak and other leafless trees show the early New England spring. The house with its central chimney is typical of the time and place. The redcoats head back to Boston and safety, harried by patriots from the whole area.

American artist Don Troiani is a specialist in paintings of military subjects and is a past president of the Society of American Historical Artists. He has one of the largest collections of Civil War uniforms and weapons in private hands.

Clarke, his wife, John Hancock, Samuel Adams, Hancock's Aunt Lydia, and Lydia's ward, Dolly Quincy, were sitting down to an early Easter Sunday breakfast when Revere arrived.

The thirty-eight-year-old John Hancock, a bachelor, had been courting the beautiful Dolly for several years. His aunt intended to end the single state of her nephew and had driven Dolly and herself to visit him at Lexington the day before.

Over steaming mugs of coffee and stacks of corn cakes and sausages, Revere reported Warren's warning of the impending British raid. Having done so, he remounted and rode over the hills to Concord, where he warned Colonel Barrett that the British troops were coming in search of arms. Although it was Easter Sunday, carts, wagons, oxen, and horses were soon dragging cannon, stores, and ammunition along the crowded roads to Sudbury and Groton. Other supplies were taken into the adjacent woods and covered with freshly cut boughs. Colonel Barrett sent out mounted couriers to warn neighboring towns to have their Minutemen companies ready for a possible alarm within forty-eight hours. At the alarm they were to march to Punkatasset Hill north of the North Bridge of the Concord River, a mile from the center of Concord.

Revere returned to Charlestown, where he met Richard Devens and Colonel William Conant, commander of the Charlestown militia regiment, and arranged his now-famous signals in the event of a British expedition. If the British troops left Boston by land via Roxbury Neck, the militia companies of Watertown, Brookline, and Weston would have to try to stop them. They would probably head for Worcester, although they could still veer north to Concord. In that event, Revere arranged to hang one lantern in the belfry of the Old North Church on Princess Street across from his home. That would alert the Charlestown lookouts at their post near the Charlestown terminus of the ferry to warn the militia at Watertown, Brookline, and Weston.

If, instead, the British crossed the Charles River in the boats assembled under the sterns of the warships, it would appear that they were heading for Concord by way of Lexington. If that were the route, Revere would hang two lanterns from the belfry. He would then cross the river in the boat he had hidden and meet

Devens and Conant, who would be waiting for him with a good horse. Revere planned to carry the alarm to all of the Minutemen companies between Charlestown and Concord. If he were delayed more than half an hour, they were to dispatch another rider so that the militia could carry out the orders of the Provincial Congress, which were to fight.

On Tuesday, April 18, 1775, two days after the colonists of Concord hid their military stores, the cobblestones of deserted Marlborough Street echoed with the clip-clop of two horses as their scarlet-and-gold-clad riders approached the headquarters of General Gage at Province House in Boston. Brigadier General Hugh Percy and Major Edward Mitchell of the 5th Regiment had an early morning appointment with the commander of His Majesty's Forces in North America. They were shown into his quarters at precisely 8:00 A.M.

General Gage came to the point at once. He was sending the previously detached light infantry and grenadier companies to Concord for a dawn raid to destroy military stores collected there. Twenty-one elite companies would begin crossing the Charles River at 10:00 P.M. that night. After a brisk march they should enter Concord before dawn. Their work was to be completed before 8:00 A.M., and they should be back in Boston by noon.

To insure secrecy and surprise, Major Mitchell would lead a mounted party of six officers and six sergeants to Charlestown later that afternoon. From there they would proceed to Cambridge, detaching an officer and a sergeant above the Charlestown Neck to intercept anyone who rode out of Charlestown toward either Cambridge or Lexington after 10:00 P.M. So as not to excite suspicion, the remaining ten men would proceed in a leisurely fashion from Cambridge through Lexington to an area between Lexington and Concord. There they would set up a roadblock to insure that no one passed through their position toward Concord after 10:00 P.M. As an added precaution, General Percy was to be ready to leave Boston with his First Brigade upon receipt of orders from Gage and to march in support of the elite companies should they run into difficulties.

After the two officers left, Gage dispatched an order to Lieutenant Colonel Francis Smith, senior duty officer for the day:

> Sir: You will march with the corps of Grenadiers and Light Infantry put under your command with the utmost expedition and secrecy to Concord, where you will seize and destroy all the artillery and ammunition you can find.[5]

Gage summoned all regimental commanders to his quarters and ordered them to muster their grenadier and light infantry companies at their individual barracks shortly after 9:00 P.M. The men were to leave their knapsacks but were to carry one day's provisions in their haversacks. They would march quietly by companies to the beach near the magazine guard alongside the Boston Common, arriving there at exactly 10:00 P.M. If challenged, the password was "Patrole." Boats manned by the navy would be ready to take them across the Charles River.

At the moment that Gage sat down with Percy and Mitchell that morning, a joint meeting of the Provincial committees of Safety and of Supplies was getting under way at Wetherby's Tavern in Menotomy, seven miles away.

The Committee of Safety consisted of John Hancock, Joseph Warren, Benjamin Church, Richard Devens, Benjamin White, Joseph Palmer, Abraham Watson, Azor Orne, Artemas Ward, John Pigeon, William Heath, and Thomas Gardner.

The Committee of Supplies consisted of Elbridge Gerry, David Cheever, Benjamin Lincoln, Moses Gill, and Benjamin Hall. Several members of the two committees were absent, however, including John Hancock, who was in Lexington, and Joseph Warren, who was directing the surveillance of Gage's activities in Boston.

The meeting lasted into the late afternoon, and some members decided to eat together at the tavern. After dinner, over glasses of pale ale, they discussed the increasingly critical nature of the situation. Most of the members then left, but Elbridge Gerry, Colonel Azor Orne, and Colonel Henry Lee, who lived a considerable distance away, took a room for the night.

Richard Devens and Abraham Watson were returning along the

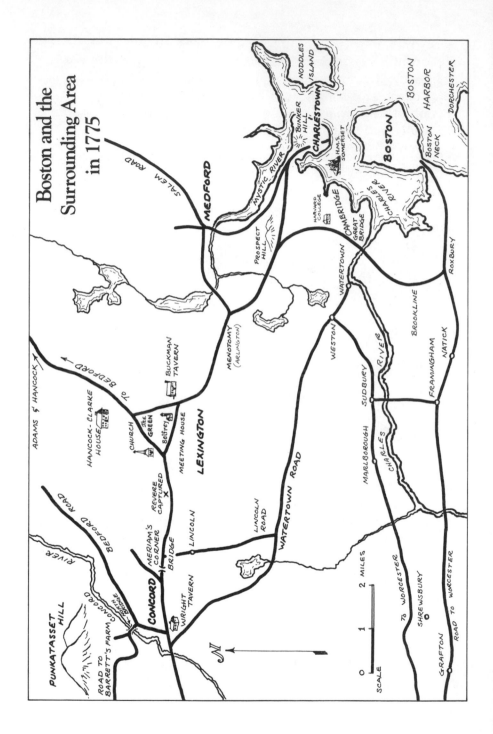

Boston and the
Surrounding Area
in 1775

dusty road to Charlestown in their chaise when they encountered
a party of ten horsemen plodding toward them along both sides of
the road. The riders were wrapped in heavy cloaks, but the colonists detected flashes of scarlet and gold and recognized them as
British officers. It was the group commanded by Major Mitchell,
en route to the area between Lexington and Concord.

Devens and Watson proceeded toward Charlestown for another
mile as they debated what to do. Deciding that the patrol might be
on its way to Wetherby's Tavern to capture the remaining members of the committees, they courageously turned their chaise
about in the road and, whipping their horses, overtook and passed
the British patrol. At the tavern they alerted their friends and
waited anxiously as the British patrol rode slowly by.

Devens and Watson then returned to Charlestown. Elbridge
Gerry immediately sent a mounted rider to Lexington, instructing
him to avoid main roads, with a warning to Hancock and Adams
that "eight or nine officers were out, suspected of some evil design." When the messenger reached Lexington, the militia posted
a guard of eight men under the command of Sergeant William
Munroe around the home of the Reverend Jonas Clarke.

Hancock sent the messenger back to Gerry with his hastily
penned reply, which, made at a critical moment, reflected his
breeding and courtesy:

Lexington, April 18, 1775

Dear Sir: I am much obliged for your notice. It is said the officers are
gone to Concord, and I will send word thither. I am full with you
that we ought to be serious, and I hope your decision will be effec-
tual. I intend doing myself the pleasure of being with you tomorrow.
My respects to the committee.

> I am your real friend,
> [signed] John Hancock[6]

Shortly after Devens arrived in Charlestown with Watson, he
received word from Joseph Warren that there was great activity
among the British troops; many men were marching to the beach
at the foot of the Common, apparently attempting to do so without being noticed by the inhabitants. It was reported that one
soldier had bayoneted a dog that barked at them.

Devens quickly called out his men and hurried to the ferry landing, placing himself so he could see across the rippling waters of the Charles and up the length of Princess Street. Soon two lighted lanterns appeared in the belfry of the Old North Church. Devens raced to the Charlestown Common, where he arranged for the use of Deacon John Larkin's best horse, should Paul Revere be able to evade the lookouts of the man-of-war *Somerset* and ride to sound the alarm.

At approximately nine-thirty that night, the twenty-one British flank companies began their march to the river. The boats, manned by sailors from the warships, lay off the beach, with no officer assigned to supervise the loading of troops. The first two companies to arrive were the grenadiers and light infantry of the 23rd Regiment. Lieutenant Mackenzie, the adjutant, commandeered the available boats to take them across. He soon returned with the empty boats, and the entire force crowded along the sandy shoreline as each company commander aggressively urged the navy to embark his own men.

Lieutenant Colonel Smith soon arrived with his second-in-command, Major John Pitcairn of the marines. Unfortunately, Gage had simply assigned the commander of the expeditionary force from the duty roster for the day. There were seven hundred men to transport, and Smith, noted for his slow and deliberate manner, allowed the crossing to take nearly two hours. Thus it was midnight before the troops were finally assembled on Lechmere Point in East Cambridge.

A young officer, Ensign Jeremy Lister of the 10th Regiment, had come down to the beach to see several of his friends off on their adventure. He found Captain Lawrence Parsons, the commander of the light infantry company of the 10th, highly agitated over the absence of a subaltern, Lieutenant James Hamilton. Parsons sent for Hamilton several times; finally, just as the 10th Light Infantry were filing into the boats, he received word from Hamilton that he was too sick to go. Lister, who volunteered to go in his place, was instantly accepted by the unhappy Parsons; Lister ran to his lodgings, gathered up his equipment, and returned just in time to take the last boat to Lechmere Point. Colonel Smith attempted to send him back because he had not participated in the necessary light infantry training, but Lister was permitted to go when he fluently argued that his absence would reflect on the honor of the 10th Regiment; if he did not go, it would be the only regiment in the detachment whose two flank companies did not contain their full complement of officers. (Hamilton was later dismissed from the service for his failure to join his regiment that night.)

Shortly after midnight, the 700-man column left Lechmere Point, wading through the swamps and inlets of Willis Creek until they reached a road. The officers on horseback remained dry, but the enlisted men emerged from the water with their shoes, gaiters, wool stockings, and trousers black with slime and soaked through to the skin. Smith, in surprising disregard for the welfare of his men, kept them standing along the road for over an hour when, forgetting that the men had the necessary one day's provisions in their haversacks, he sent back to camp for additional rations. Lieutenant Barker reported that when the provisions finally arrived and were distributed, most of the men threw the unnecessary extra weight away.

It was nearly 2:00 A.M. before the march to Menotomy and Lexington began through what is now the town of Somerville. Hoping to avoid wakening nearby farmers, Smith ordered the partially dried infantry and grenadiers to shun the wooden bridge that spanned an inlet of the Charles River and plunge up to their waists into the freezing waters of a long ford. To do so the troops cradled their cartridge boxes, priming flasks, and muskets in their arms. When they reached the main road to Menotomy, they formed into ranks with mounted Major John Pitcairn in the lead. The light infantry, their shoes awash with stagnant water, marched toward Menotomy and Lexington along what is now Massachusetts Avenue. Behind them rode Lieutenant Colonel Smith leading the grenadiers. It was after 2:00 A.M. on April 19, 1775.

As the British navy was rowing the troops across the Charles hours before, Paul Revere, summoned by Dr. Warren, entered his Boston home and nearly collided with William Dawes. In the event that harm should come to either one, Warren was sending two couriers to alert the countryside of the British troop movement. Dawes was to ride to Lexington by way of Roxbury Neck and warn Adams and Hancock that the regulars were heading toward them. From there he was to proceed to Concord and warn Colonel Barrett. Revere was to ride to Lexington by way of Charlestown and Menotomy with the identical warning, alerting all militia captains along the way.

Revere left Warren's house and hurried home, where he put on his riding boots and surtout. With a few belongings in his saddlebags he kissed his wife, Rachel, goodbye and left for his ride into history. He would not return to his home in Boston's North Square for nearly a year.

Revere ran to the home of a nearby friend and told him to hang two lanterns in the belfry of the Old North Church. As a result of this night's events, the church, a Congregationalist church and a center of Whig activity under the Reverend John Lathrop, was torn down and used for fuel by order of General William Howe nine months later, on January 16, 1776.

Revere retrieved his boat under Clark's dock and, joined by Thomas Richardson and Joshua Bentley, climbed aboard the small craft. Revere steered to avoid the *Somerset,* anchored in midstream, and they rowed across to Charlestown. The boat grounded to the east of the Charlestown ferry-way at a spot called the Sconce, a small fort located near the present Boston Naval Shipyard. It was 11:00 P.M., and the regulars were still crossing the Charles.

From there Revere hastened to Charlestown Square, where he was joined by a group of prominent Whigs, including Colonel Conant. They had a horse waiting for him at the barn of Deacon Larkin, near the Square. While the horse was saddled, Devens cautioned Revere and told him about his meeting with the mounted British officers.

Revere swung into the saddle and sped toward Charlestown Neck, the narrow stretch of land that connected Charlestown with Cambridge. Beyond the Neck the road forked. To the left lay Menotomy, to the right Medford. It was 11:45 P.M. as Revere crossed the Neck and veered left toward Menotomy.

Suddenly, the glint of metal caught his eye. As he reined his horse to a sliding halt, the animal reared high in the air, forelegs clawing for balance. Out of the shadows came two mounted figures with sabres glistening in the moonlight. Revere remembered Devens's warning — British officers. Spinning his horse around, he raced back toward the fork in the road, the two horsemen in determined pursuit. He reached the fork fifty yards ahead of them and cut sharply to his left on the road to Medford. One officer, who attempted to intercept him by crossing the space between the prongs of the fork, bogged down in a clay pond as Revere raced up the road, galloping across Ploughed Hill and over Winter Hill. Soon Revere reined his mount to a stop at the home of Captain Isaac Hall of the Medford militia; then he raced through West Medford and entered the main highway to Lexington at Menotomy.

He stopped at each house along the way, knocking at doors and shouting his warning. Shortly after midnight he galloped through the streets of Lexington.

Lexington, about fifteen miles northwest of Boston, was originally part of Cambridge and was called the Cambridge Farms prior to 1712. In the center of the village the road from Boston branched off sharply. To the left it led to Concord, to the right to Bedford. Between the roads lay a grassy area called the Green, and across the top of the Green a road connecting the Bedford and Concord roads created a triangle. At the apex of the Green, which faced toward Boston, stood the meetinghouse; to the right on the opposite side of the Bedford Road was Buckman's Tavern. On the Green, in front of the meetinghouse, was a small building known as the Belfry, which housed the town bell. Situated around the triangle that was the Green were ten large, white houses.

Revere took the Bedford fork, and within a few hundred yards he came to a halt before the parsonage of the Reverend Clarke. Tying his horse to the hitching post, he strode to the large door and pounded on it with his gloved fist. Sergeant William Munroe, in charge of the eight-man militia guard, came to the door and told him to keep quiet, as the family had asked him to see that they were not disturbed by unnecessary noise. "Noise!" shouted Revere. "You will have noise enough before long — the regulars are coming out!" The Reverend Clarke thrust his head out of the window above, and Revere asked for Hancock. He heard Hancock's voice, joking, "Come in, Revere, we are not afraid of you!"

Inside, Revere was explaining the situation to the robe-clad family and guests when there was another knock on the door and William Dawes, the courier who had left Boston shortly before Revere did, joined the group.

Sergeant Munroe sent several of his men to alert Captain John Parker to muster the Minutemen on the Lexington Green. The bell in the Belfry began to ring, and men ran onto the Green carrying their rifles and muskets. Seventeen-year-old Jonathan Harrington, who had taught himself to play the fife several months before, was fifing his shrill notes, while drummer William Diamond pounded out the pulsating rhythm of "Assembly."

By one o'clock that chilly, moonlit morning, 130 militiamen were formed into ranks on the Lexington Green. As they went through their manual of arms to keep warm, messengers were sent toward Boston to report the proximity of the British force.

At 2:00 A.M. Captain Parker ordered his men to load with powder and ball. Shortly thereafter, one of the messengers reported that there was no evidence of any troops on the road for a distance of seven miles. Parker thereupon dismissed his men, ordering them to reassemble when they heard the beat of drums. Many of them crowded into the Buckman Tavern to warm themselves with hot rum before the fire; others returned to their homes and beds. It looked like another false alarm.

In the meantime, Revere and Dawes decided to ride to Concord together, and shortly after 1:00 A.M. they headed toward Concord, passing the Lexington Green on their left. As they passed the Congregationalist church they were joined by a young Concord physician, Dr. Samuel Prescott, who had been visiting with Miss Millikan, a young lady of Lexington.

The three horsemen had trotted down the road to within three miles of Concord when they suddenly found themselves surrounded by a number of mounted British officers who had concealed themselves in the woods. With drawn pistols, Major Mitchell and his patrol forced Revere, Dawes, and Prescott into a fenced enclosure alongside the road for questions. As they slowly rode their horses into the meadow, Dr. Prescott suddenly dug his spurs into his horse's flanks, and the animal shot straight for a low stone wall. Horse and rider cleared the wall like a steeplechaser and the horse's hoofbeats disappeared down the Concord Road. Dawes attempted to do the same, but his horse reared, threw him to the ground, and galloped off. Dawes jumped to his feet and raced into the nearby woods, where he vanished among the trees.

Revere also tried to escape, spurring his horse toward a wall that skirted the woods a short distance away; but he was halted by a second group of officers who blocked his path. He was well known to the British of Boston, and Major Mitchell rode up and placed the muzzle of his pistol to Revere's head, quietly informing him that he was going to ask a few questions. If he felt the answers were false, he would blow Revere's brains out. Revere told him the time he had left Boston, that the British column had been badly delayed, and that there would be over five hundred Minutemen waiting for the column at Lexington, as he had alarmed all the Minutemen along the way. He was searched and, accompanied by three militiamen who had been captured earlier, was forced to travel in front of the ten officers as they rode toward Lexington. The sergeant guarding Revere had orders to kill him if he tried to escape.

Just as Major Mitchell and his prisoners were approaching the outskirts of Lexington, Captain Parker dismissed his company on the Lexington Green. As the exuberant militiamen were ordered to fall out, a number of them emptied their loaded muskets by discharging them into the night sky. It sounded like a volley to Major Mitchell, who halted his entire group and ordered his prisoners to dismount. Then, leading the Americans' horses by their reins, the British patrol galloped off toward Menotomy, leaving Revere and his companions standing in the middle of the road. In the darkness the men heard church bells ringing and the sound of more musket fire.

At the moment that Parker's company emptied their muskets, fourteen miles away along a road on the outskirts of Cambridge, Lieutenant Colonel Smith's column of grenadiers, after a wait of two hours, finally began to move toward Menotomy. Their wet, cold feet were rubbed raw in the damp, handknit woolen socks and sodden shoes, but the men were nevertheless glad to be moving. Around them they heard bells, dogs, horsemen, and musket fire through the moonlit night. Distant houses were lit up, and there was rushing and stirring throughout Middlesex County, as people and animals fled through the darkness.

Asleep in their rooms at the Wetherby Tavern in Menotomy were Elbridge Gerry, Colonel Orne, and Colonel Lee. About two-thirty in the morning they were awakened by the steady tramp of hundreds of marching boots on the road in front of the inn. When they rushed to the windows, there before them in the moonlight were serried ranks of men in scarlet and white, marching with practiced precision past the tavern. Behind the light infantry were a few mounted officers and ranks of grenadiers in tall bearskin caps.

To the consternation of the watching Americans, a file of the tall, burly soldiers suddenly left the column and turned toward the front door of the inn. The three colonists tumbled out of their room and down the stairs to escape through the back door. They remained hidden in the adjoining field as they listened to soldiers searching the tavern.

Mystified that the troops could have known they were there, the rebels steadfastly rejected the thought that a member of the two committees might be a British spy. We know today that there was such a member and that he had sent information about their meeting to General Gage.

The light infantry corps of ten companies was led by the light company of the 10th with Captain Parsons in the lead. Beside him was Ensign de Berniere, who had mapped this road nearly two months before. In the advance party was a volunteer from the 38th Regiment, Lieutenant William Sutherland; Lieutenant Adair of the Royal Marines; Ensign Jeremy Lister of the 10th; and Sergeant Richard Pope of the 47th. They rode their horses in a column of twos and ranged far ahead of the marching infantry. As they neared Lexington, they captured one by one three riders from Lexington who had been sent out by Captain Parker to find the British. The Americans were forced to give up their horses and accompany the column on foot.

Shortly before 3:00 A.M. the mounted patrol of Major Mitchell, leading the captured colonial horses, including that of Deacon Larkin, met the advance guard under Captain Parsons. Major Mitchell galloped down the line of marching men until he reached Smith. He reported that they had intercepted several American couriers, including Revere, and the entire countryside was awake and swarming with militia. It was evident that there was no opportunity for surprise, and there was every chance that they would meet with armed resistance from the Americans. There were several hundred armed militia waiting at Lexington.

Smith ordered Major Pitcairn to take six of the ten light infantry companies and press forward through Lexington to secure the two bridges at Concord. He then sent a mounted officer back to Boston requesting that Gage dispatch the First Brigade as reinforcements.

When the British released Revere less than a mile from Lexington, he hurried to the parsonage of the Reverend Clarke, where he found an argument in progress between Hancock and Adams. Hancock wanted to take his place with Parker's militia company; but Adams and Clarke argued that, as a member of the Continental Congress, he did not have the right to expose himself to danger. While Hancock's fiancée, Dolly Quincy, and his Aunt Lydia listened, it was decided that Adams and Hancock would take shelter in the nearby town of Woburn, which was out of the line of march. Dolly and Lydia wanted to return to Boston, but Hancock vetoed that plan and asked Revere to take the two ladies to the house of a widow who lived nearby.

At this point, John Lowell, Hancock's clerk, remembered that he had left Hancock's trunk in the upstairs room at Buckman's Tavern. The trunk, specially ordered by Hancock to fit on the back of his chaise, contained all the confidential papers required by Congress; if it were to fall into British hands, it could become a death warrant for many men.

Revere volunteered to return with Lowell to Buckman's Tavern. As they approached the Lexington Green, they heard drummer William Diamond beating out the call to assemble. It was nearly 4:30 A.M. Although only fifty Minutemen were lined up in a double line facing the meetinghouse, new men were appearing constantly to join the sparse ranks. Revere and Lowell passed through the forming men, went upstairs, and retrieved the trunk. They looked out of the window and saw the bright red ranks of the British light infantry crowding the narrow highway to Boston. Revere and Lowell, uncle of the future James Russell Lowell, muscled the heavy trunk down the narrow stairs, across the Green, and through the lines of waiting militia. They rushed to the waiting chaise and fastened the trunk by its custom-made straps behind the driver's seat. As they did so, in the pre-dawn darkness they heard a few shots, then a volley followed by the roar of shouting men. Samuel Adams, who was not far away, heard the volley, and his face shone as he joyfully cried, "Oh, what a glorious morning is this!"

Many of the 130 militiamen who had mustered earlier on the Lexington Green did not return at the second call for muster. Legend has it that as the British appeared opposite the Buckman Tavern, Parker faced his meager ranks of seventy-seven men and said, "Stand your ground. Don't fire unless fired upon, but if they mean to have a war let it begin here!"

When the light infantry had reached a half mile from Lexington on their fateful march into history, Major John Pitcairn had halted them, and every man was ordered to load his Brown Bess with powder and ball. Closing ranks, they marched briskly up the Bedford Road to Buckman Tavern. There they executed a "column left" across the Green behind the meetinghouse. From Major Pitcairn came the command, "Halt!" Another command, "Right face!" The British light infantry was now facing the thin line of Lexington militia. From tired and angry eyes the men in red peered through the gray darkness at the Americans. They had not slept since the night before, and there before them were the men responsible for their discomfort.

Major Pitcairn spurred his horse onto the Green between the two forces: "Lay down your arms, you damned rebels, and disperse!" There was a deathly silence. Dozens of spectators standing alongside the Green held their breath. Then a sharp command rang out from Captain Parker, and the militiamen filed off toward the Bedford Road and Buckman Tavern.

What happened next has been debated for over two hundred years. According to British troops, there was a flash of fire from a militiaman's musket, and then a shot rang out. Some British claimed it came from some Americans near Buckman Tavern. Others were certain it came from near the Congregational church on the far side of the Green.

Lieutenant Sutherland testified later that Major Pitcairn had shouted just before the fatal shot, "Soldiers, don't fire, keep your ranks and surround them." Immediately after that, according to Sutherland, a shot came from the American side. The British troops, tired, soggy, and furious, returned the fire without waiting for orders. Sutherland's frightened horse bolted straight through the Americans, who were falling back on either side of the Green. His horse carried him over six hundred yards beyond the Congregational church, and as he was returning to his men, he was fired on from the woods.

The first few shots triggered a volley that tore the darkness apart. The excited regulars followed that with a bayonet charge through and over the dead, wounded, and retreating Minutemen. Jonathan Harrington, the uncle of the young fifer of the same name, was standing among the ranks of the militia in front of his house. A bullet hit him in the chest and knocked him backward as his wife, Ruth, peered into the darkness from an upstairs window, their only son, a boy of nine, by her side. As she watched in horror, her husband attempted to crawl across the road. Screaming in anguish, she flew down the stairs and through the front door to help him. He raised up, stretched out his arms to her, and died before she could reach him.

Jonas Parker, older than the rest of the militiamen, was wounded by the British volley. He had vowed that he would never run from the British, and he was loading his musket when he was hit. Slowly he dropped to his knees and fired his musket. He was reaching for another charge when he was killed by the bayonet of a light infantryman.

American witnesses testified later that none of the militia had fired first. Sylvanus Wood and Robert Douglas of the Woburn militia had traveled to Lexington to help Captain Parker. Forty-nine years later Wood recalled that Major Pitcairn had said, "Lay down your arms, you rebels, or you are all dead men — Fire!" Lieutenant Barker of the 4th reported that:

> We still continued advancing, keeping prepared against an attack though without intending to attack them, but on our coming near them, they fired one or two shots, upon which our men without any orders rushed in upon them, fired and put them to flight. We then formed on the Common, but with some difficulty, the men were so wild they could hear no orders; we waited a considerable time there and at length proceeded on our way to Concord.[7]

Ensign Lister of the 10th Regiment reported that the Americans had fired several shots and then leaped behind a wall. Sergeant Richard Pope, there with the light infantry company of the 47th Regiment, wrote in his journal that the regulars paused before they reached Lexington, and:

> The whole then loaded till they were positively forbidden to fire without orders, and proceeding on their march perceived on Lexington Green a body of about 200, formed and seemingly determined to fight. Major Pitcairn ordered the Light Companies to surround them and repeating the orders not to fire. On approaching within 100 yards, the rebels filed off to the right and left, taking possession of walls, hedges, and houses, and began a scattered fire, which was returned by the troops. On the rebels breaking, Major Mitchell and seven or eight officers charged them, with great danger from our fire. The horse of Lieutenant Sutherland of the 38th ran away with him into a wood, where a large body of the rebels lay concealed, who fired at him; he, however got back safe. This brought on a heavy fire from the grenadiers which did great execution, and dispersed the whole.[8]

The Reverend John Clarke of Lexington, though not an eyewitness, disagreed with all other witnesses. He said:

> The foremost officer, who was within a few yards of our men, [Pitcairn] brandishing his sword and then pointing toward them, with a loud voice said to his troops, "Fire! By God! Fire!" which was instantly followed by a discharge of arms from the said troops, succeeded by a very heavy and close fire upon our part, dispersing, so long as any of them were within reach. Eight were left upon the ground! Ten were wounded. The rest of the company, through divine goodness, were preserved unhurt in this murderous action.[9]

Most evidence seems to substantiate the British claim that the Americans fired the first shot, which was followed by an emotional explosion on the part of the bone-weary British light infantry. There seems little doubt that the British troops went berserk, despite the frantic efforts of their officers. Robbed of normal sleep and marched the entire night through mud and water and over rutted roads, their murderous reaction was triggered by the sight of the rebellious Americans. When they heard the shot, they believed that they were being fired upon and reacted with pent-up desperation.

In addition to Jonathan Harrington and Jonas Parker, the American dead included Ensign Robert Monroe, killed as he crossed the edge of the Green trying to obey Captain Parker's orders to disperse; Caleb Harrington, shot dead as he tried to enter the meetinghouse; John Brown and Samuel Hadley, pursued across the road to a swamp north of the Lexington Green, behind the Reverend Clarke's house, and shot to death; and Isaac Muzzy, hit by the volley and killed instantly in the middle of the Green. Ashahel Porter had been captured by Lieutenant Adair five miles from Lexington several hours before, and had been released when the light companies had marched into Lexington. Unarmed, he was cautioned to walk, not run away. As soon as the firing began, he ran into the gardens of the Buckman Tavern and died when a British soldier shot him in the back.

In addition to the eight who were slain, nine were wounded, including Joseph Comee, John Robbins, Ebenezer Munroe Jr., and John Tidd, who had a saber cut on his head. Others wounded by musket fire were Soloman Pierce, Nathaniel Farmer, Thomas Winship, Jedediah Munroe, and Prince Estabrook, a black man who lived to serve in almost every major campaign of the war for the next seven years.

Very few of the seventy-seven members of the Lexington militia fired a shot at the British that morning. The names of those who did are recorded on an honor roll in Lexington: Solomon Brown, one of the men previously captured and released by Major Mitchell; Ebenezer Lock, Ebenezer Munroe Jr., Corporal John Munroe, Nathan Monroe, Jonas Parker, Lieutenant William Tidd, and Benjamin Sampson.

The British suffered very little. A soldier of the 10th Regiment named Johnson was wounded in the thigh, and Major Pitcairn's horse was hit by two bullets, although not seriously enough to disable him.

In the aftermath Major Pitcairn formed his advance force of two hundred men on the Concord Road and awaited Colonel Smith and the main body. It was still a half hour before dawn, and in the dim light the crumpled bodies of dead and wounded Americans lay sprawled upon the Green.

At 4:50 A.M. the remainder of the British column appeared on the Boston Road. Lieutenant Colonel Smith and his staff rode over to Pitcairn, and after a short conference the combined forces began to move on the Concord Road. With secrecy no longer necessary, the shrill fifes and crashing drums pierced the chill pre-dawn air, and the British troops broke into a series of rousing cheers. The fatigue of the past few hours was gone in the exhilaration of anger vented on the men of the Lexington militia. "That will teach the bloody bastards a lesson" was the sentiment heard from the marching men.

As the rear of the redcoated column disappeared behind the Congregational church on the road to Concord, people emerged from homes along the Green and began to remove the dead and wounded. The Reverend Clarke recited prayers over the dead, as friends and relatives tenderly lifted the wounded into nearby homes. Captain Parker reorganized his militia and kept them in readiness. The British would be returning through Lexington later in the day, and this time the militia would not hesitate to fire.

At this inopportune moment, five straggling British soldiers came marching into Lexington along the Boston Road. They were quickly captured and sent to Woburn under guard; their arms were eagerly divided among the militiamen. These five became the first prisoners of the American Revolution.

Thirteen

To Concord and Back

As BRITISH TROOPS were being ferried across the Charles River toward Lechmere Point, General Lord Percy crossed Boston Common in the dark to observe the operation. He overtook a group of Americans, and as he passed them he heard one of the men say, "The British troops have marched out, but will miss their aim." Percy, unable to ignore the remark, asked, "What aim is that?" "Why, the cannon at Concord," was the reply.

Percy hastened to Province House to inform Gage what he had just heard. It was clear that the Americans had somehow discovered the plans for the raid. Gage considered cancelling the expedition but decided that he had to go through with it. However, he ordered a tight security on all persons attempting to leave Boston.

As the hours passed Gage became increasingly apprehensive. If Lieutenant Colonel Smith were heading into the teeth of a forewarned countryside, his small force of slightly over seven hundred men could be inundated by over thirty thousand militiamen. Gage recalled the thousands of Americans who responded to the alarm occasioned by his raid on the powder magazine.

At 3:00 A.M., unable to sleep, he sent for a courier and handed him orders to be delivered to the First Brigade. The orders directed Lord Percy to muster his brigade on the Boston Common at 4:00 A.M. and march immediately toward Lexington and Concord. The courier left Gage at exactly 3:05 A.M. and, following the proper chain of command, delivered Gage's orders to the brigade

major of the First Brigade. As luck would have it, that gentleman
was not in his quarters, and the courier, rather than assume responsibility to find him and deliver the orders, simply left them
with the major's servant. The servant left the orders on the table,
and when the major arrived at 4:00 A.M., the servant forgot to
mention the orders, and the major went to bed.

Shortly before 5:00 A.M. the mounted officer from Smith's expedition came galloping through the town, covered with perspiration and wild with concern. His route back to Boston had taken
him around hundreds of militia marching toward Concord. Gage
sprang into action. The sleeping brigade major was routed out of
bed, and messengers to the four regimental commanders of the
First Brigade were soon spurring their horses through the darkened streets of Boston.

At 5:00 A.M. a messenger from Lieutenant Colonel Benjamin
Bernard, commander of the 23rd Regiment, knocked at Frederick
Mackenzie's house near Fort Hill. Nancy Mackenzie, seven months
pregnant, arose to fix a hot breakfast for her husband. Then, with
a hug and kiss for each of his three children and a smiling bearhug
for Nancy, Mackenzie raced to join his regiment.

At 6:00 A.M. Brigadier General Hugh Percy sat astride his
white horse facing three of the four regiments drawn up in scarlet
and white on Boston Common. The 23rd was on the extreme right
with Adjutant Lieutenant Mackenzie receiving reports from his
company commanders; the 4th was at center, and the 47th was to
the left. The 4th Regiment of the First Brigade, the battalion of
Royal Marines, for some unexplained reason was not there. Lord
Percy, a patient man, waited for them to make their appearance.

To the extreme left of the line were the blue-uniformed artillerymen of the Royal Artillery and their two six-pound cannon.
Behind the guns was a four-horse wagon driven by two civilian
teamsters, which carried 140 rounds of six-pound shot and powder.

When the marines had not appeared by 7:00 A.M. Lord Percy
sent one of his officers to the Marine barracks. There the surprised marine duty officer indignantly denied receiving orders to
muster with the First Brigade. When informed that orders had
been sent to him at 5:00 A.M. — two hours ago — the marine made
an instant denial. Percy's officer, furious, galloped back through

Boston's streets to the Common, where the brigade was waiting, and Percy directed him to Province House to report the fiasco to General Gage.

What had happened soon became clear. Forgetting that Major John Pitcairn, commander of the Royal Marines, had been assigned as second-in-command of the expedition to Concord, Gage had sent orders to muster with the brigade to Pitcairn's lodgings in North Square. There they had remained, while Pitcairn moved toward Concord.

The oversight delayed Percy's relief expedition nearly four hours in joining Lieutenant Colonel Smith's force. As a result, Percy felt that he would be further delayed if he took the ammunition wagon along, and he decided to go with only the twenty-four rounds that each gun carried in its side boxes. Colonel Cleaveland of the 4th Battalion of the Royal Artillery protested but was overruled on the grounds that "there could not possibly be an occasion for more ammunition than there was in the side-boxes."

The marines finally arrived, and shortly thereafter the First Brigade left Boston Common at 8:45 A.M. As the long column moved down Orange Street toward Boston Neck, the brigade band broke into the mocking "Yankee Doodle," a song that ridiculed the American Provincial soldiers during the French and Indian War. In a joke of the times, British military bands blared the word "dandy" to make it sound like the braying of a donkey.

Led by an advance party of four men under Captain Montresor of the Royal Engineers, the column marched across Boston Neck. Behind them came the two field guns drawn by their artillery horses, and astride the horses were the Royal Artillerymen led by Colonel Cleaveland. Left behind was the wagon with 140 rounds of shot and powder that would be sorely missed before the day was over.

Following were the 4th Regiment (the King's Own), the 47th, the Royal Marines, and the 23rd (the Royal Welsh Fusiliers). The four regiments were marching without their elite grenadier and light infantry companies, who were at that moment in Concord with Lieutenant Colonel Smith.

The advance guard, under Captain Montresor, soon reached the Great Bridge at Cambridge and discovered that the planks had been taken up. However, they were stacked neatly nearby, and it took Montresor and his men only a short time to replace them. When the artillery reached the bridge, the engineers watched them cross and then returned to Boston.

As the brigade moved through Menotomy, they became aware that the countryside was completely deserted. Houses and fields appeared empty of animals and people.

Gradually the scorching sun sent the temperature up to 85°, and the men began to perspire freely in their heavy wool waistcoats and coats. By noon they were still two hours from Lexington, and the officers urged the column to greater speed. By 1:30 P.M. they had moved to within a few miles of Lexington but had no inkling of what had transpired there.

The previous night, when Revere and Dawes were captured, Dr. Samuel Prescott had jumped his horse over the stone wall and galloped into Concord at 1:30 A.M. to give the alarm. The Committee of Safety and the militia officers hurriedly met on the Green and ordered the church bells rung. Lookouts were sent out on the Lexington Road to discover the proximity of the British. Minutemen and the remainder of the militia formed in ranks on the Green in front of the Town House, and the remaining population of Concord, under the supervision of Colonel Barrett and the Reverend William Emerson, began carrying all remaining military stores away. Men, women, and children, arms laden with materiel, hurried through the pre-dawn darkness into the nearby forest, where they covered the supplies with branches.

Just as the sun rose, Reuben Brown, one of the scouts sent out toward Lexington, returned to Concord to report that the regulars had fired into the ranks of the Lexington militia and killed a number of men only a short time before. As the British approached Concord, militia units from nearby Lincoln arrived and were aligned beside the Concord men. The regular militia was sent out on the Lexington Road to intercept the British, while the Minutemen under Captain Minot climbed the high hill overlooking the square and took up defensive positions.

It was still dark as the 10th Regiment's light infantry led the British column out of Lexington. The road to Concord was barely visible in the cheerless pre-dawn grayness. Far off, on top of a hill, a solitary horseman sat motionless. Then horse and rider slowly disappeared down the other side of the hill. The elated soldiers felt new vigor in their steps as the sun rose behind them and the gray light revealed hills and fields. Tramping through the dense forests near the village of Lincoln, their eyes searched the thick woods but saw only the dark shapes of the forest.

As the light improved, they could make out the hills and ridges that marked the outskirts of Concord, and Ensign de Berniere recognized the terrain he had sketched only two months before. He recalled the description of Concord in his report to Gage:

> Concord is a town lying between two hills that command it entirely. There is a river runs through it with two bridges over it. In summer it is pretty dry. The town is large, and contains a church, jail, and court house; but the houses are not close together but in little groups.

Where the road entered Concord, a steep hill rose gradually beside the road about a mile from the village, and veered sharply to tower fifty feet above the square in the center of town. The top of the hill was a flat and level area that offered an excellent view of the surrounding countryside. A half mile from the center of town, the Concord River flowed crookedly to the northwest. A mile north of the Town Green, the North Bridge crossed the Concord River near Old Manse, the home of the Reverend William Emerson. The road beyond the river led to the farm of Colonel James Barrett, several miles away, where de Berniere had reported the presence of a quantity of war materiel.

Just before entering the town, Colonel Smith split his force into two columns. The grenadiers marched up the main road, while the light infantry, under Major Pitcairn, was sent up the side of the hill that led to the flat area overlooking the town square.

As the grenadiers moved into Concord on the Boston Road, they were startled to see the colonial militia, led by a full band of fifers and drummers, marching toward them as if on parade. Suddenly the American column wheeled around in the middle of the road and led the British back into town, the fifes and drums filling the early morning air. The British musicians picked up the tune, and the two military bodies marched into the center of Concord.

The British halted in front of Wright's Tavern, but the militia continued out of town before stopping to re-form. They were joined by the elite Minutemen who had scrambled down from the plateau above the town as the British light infantry climbed the hill toward them. Both battalions of Americans marched north, crossed North Bridge a mile from Concord, and climbed atop Punkatasset Hill, which overlooked the bridge. From that vantage point they looked down on the bridge and the spire of the Concord church a mile beyond the trees.

Smith sent six of his ten light infantry companies toward North Bridge under command of Captain Parsons of the 10th, with orders to hold the bridge with part of his force, and he sent the remainder of his men to find the military goods secreted at Colonel Barrett's farm two miles away.

Meanwhile, the grenadiers searched for military stores concealed in town. Each home, barn, and shed was searched by small groups of men. They uncovered three cannons, several gun carriages, one hundred barrels of flour, and large amounts of assorted harness that were classified as military supplies. All such goods were placed on a rapidly growing pile in front of the Town House.

Most of the townspeople, unsure of what the regulars might do, caught up their most cherished possessions and fled to the nearby forests or to the homes of friends in the country. Mrs. Martha Moulton, a seventy-one-year-old widow living in a small house on the edge of Concord Green, suddenly found herself the unwilling hostess to over sixty officers and men who tethered their horses to stakes driven into the turf of her front yard. Perspiring redcoats tramped through her door calling for water for themselves and their horses. Her well behind the house was surrounded by thirsty men working the windlass.

Mrs. Moulton's house stood near the Town House, and when a grenadier sergeant set fire to the large pile of confiscated materiel, she feared that the flames would endanger her home. Suddenly, to her horror, she saw smoke seeping from the Town House. Seizing a pail of water she threw the water through the front door.

The British troops lounging on her lawn quickly formed a bucket brigade, led by Major Pitcairn, and saved the Town House as well as Mrs. Moulton's house, which would certainly have caught fire, along with a row of small houses and a small schoolhouse adjacent to the burning building. The following year the Town Council voted the elderly Mrs. Moulton a gift of three pounds for having heroically saved the buildings by her example. However, it is a matter of official record that during the entire episode in Concord, the behavior of the British army was exemplary. In addition to fighting fires, the soldiers molested none of the inhabitants, and each soldier paid for his food and drink.

It was nearly 8:00 A.M. when Captain Parsons and the light infantry arrived at North Bridge. Putting his own company of the 10th under the command of Lieutenant Waldron Kelly, Parsons took command of three of the light infantry companies and, guided by Ensign de Berniere, headed for Colonel Barrett's farm. The light company of the 43rd was stationed on the bridge under the command of Captain Walter Sloan Laurie. The 10th and 4th were sent part way up Punkatasset Hill to observe and contain the growing American force on top of the hill. Each of the three light infantry companies contained thirty-two men; thus a total of fewer than one hundred British regulars were expected to contain the larger American force, should it choose to attack the bridge.

An hour later, the British soldiers lying on their stomachs in the tall, comfortable grass along the lower slope of Punkatasset Hill were keeping their eyes open with difficulty. It was a pleasant, drowsy New England spring day, and the sweet aroma of new grass and wildflowers was everywhere. To their right, the beautiful blue and green water of the Concord River meandered through lush, fragrant foliage. The hum of countless insects in the motionless air encouraged the young Englishmen, already without a night's sleep, to doze. Lieutenants Edward Gould and John Barker of the 4th, positioned to the right of their men, kept a close watch on the hill above them. To their left were Lieutenant Waldron Kelly and Ensign Jeremy Lister, and men of the 10th were extended in a long line parallel to the base of the hill.

They could hear large numbers of men moving on the hill above them, as Minutemen and militia arrived in a steady stream from the surrounding towns. Contingents from Acton, Carlisle, Chelmsford, Westfield, and Littleton had arrived and now numbered over a thousand men. The men from Acton were the most numerous and arrived under the command of a rugged veteran of the previous wars, Captain Isaac Davis. As the number of Minutemen and militia companies increased, the colonists felt that they should take some action regarding the redcoated soldiers of Captain Laurie lounging on the bridge and the lower slope of the hill. Suddenly, beyond the trees that hid the town from view, black smoke began to rise in the morning air. The source was the burning materiel in front of the Concord Town House. The British efforts to save the Town House were not apparent to the colonial militiamen on the hill, and they believed that regulars were burning the houses of citizens known to be Whigs.

In this highly explosive atmosphere, a meeting was called of the militia company commanders. They proposed to lead their men against the British, rather than take no action while homes were being destroyed. Captain William Smith volunteered his company to lead an immediate attack on the troops below them, but Captain Davis leaped to his feet shouting that Acton men would lead the attack, as they had the largest contingent of any town there, and not a man in his company was afraid to meet the regulars in combat. A vote indicated that every officer present was in favor of immediate attack. Colonel Barrett agreed with the unanimous decision and appointed Major John Buttrick to lead the assault, but he cautioned the captains to hold their fire unless fired upon by the regulars.

Around 10:00 A.M. the drowsy British soldiers lying in the grass were suddenly aware that the hum of voices on the plateau above them had stopped. Something was about to happen, and the scarlet figures tensed in alarm. Then, slowly, just over the rim of the meadow above, the large-brimmed hats of the colonists appeared in two parallel files. With their rifles and muskets held at the "trail" position, the lean and determined men descended the slopes of the hill directly toward the two companies of light infantry at rest below them.

Lieutenant Kelly shouted orders for his men to move laterally to the right and close up with the 4th and retreat down the hill.

When Ensign Lister asked Kelly to order the men to retreat below a low stone wall close behind their position and form a firing line, he was brusquely overruled by both Kelly and Lieutenant Gould of the King's Own. Lister was certain that the regulars would be easy targets for the militia when they retreated down the slope, but the advancing colonials held their fire. Both British companies fell back to the bridge and rejoined the men of the 43rd, where the three groups were under the command of Captain Laurie of the 43rd.

With no apparent intention of stopping, the Minutemen slowly continued their advance, until they poured over the stone wall and onto the road that led to the bridge. They halted to re-form those lines that had become disorganized during the descent, and Captain Laurie sent Lieutenant Robertson galloping toward the town square to request immediate reinforcements from Lieutenant Colonel Smith. Robertson returned quickly with Smith's reply to the effect that three of His Majesty's light infantry companies should be sufficient to handle the situation at the bridge, but he would send some grenadiers to assist them.

No sooner had Robertson returned than the Americans, marching in parallel lines, advanced toward the bridge. Captain Laurie ordered his men to cross the bridge to the far side and draw themselves into a formation that the British army called "street fighting," wherein each thirty-two-man company formed four ranks of eight men. Three companies formed one behind the other would present twelve lines of eight men each. In a narrow street, the front rank of eight could fire a volley and drop off to either side to reform again in the rear, as the next eight-man line fired a volley and formed in the rear. As the process was repeated by each rank, they could reload while awaiting their turn to fire. In this way a continuous series of volleys was maintained. The maneuver was one of those that had been developed for the light infantry during the past year.

It was a poor choice for the moment, however, for Laurie did not have enough time to organize his ranks. A number of troops had stopped to take up some of the planks on the bridge but quickly gave it up as the Americans were only fifty yards away, well within musket range.

The Minutemen halted, formed a solid rank across the road, and started forward across the bridge. Several shots cracked out prematurely from the front rank of British troops on the far side of the bridge, followed instantly by a sheet of flame as a volley smashed into the Americans. Captain Isaac Davis and Abner Hosmer of Acton were killed instantly, and the Acton fifer, Luther Blanchard, was badly wounded. With a piercing yell, the Minutemen fired a volley, killing a sergeant and two privates of the 4th Regiment. Seven other men, including four of the eight officers present, were wounded. Lieutenant William Sutherland of the 38th, who had volunteered for the expedition, received a bullet in his chest; Lieutenant Waldron Kelly was hit in the arm; Lieutenant Edward Gould was hit in the foot and later captured; and Lieutenant Edward Hill of the 43rd was struck by several bullets in the body and died a few days later after intense suffering.

In Laurie's hasty formation, only a few men were able to fire at the advancing Americans, who were coming on with surprising speed. As the front rank retreated toward each side, the next rank quickly fired their muskets and joined the retreat, which turned into a general rout of the British troops. Some regulars, unnerved by the accuracy of the American fire, started to run. Others carried off the wounded, and the three companies fell back toward Concord, a mile away. The Americans, wild with excitement at the sight of the vaunted British regulars retreating, swarmed across the bridge in a torrent of men and guns. One of the wounded Englishmen, sprawled against the railings at the stone approaches to the bridge, groaned and tried to get up as the Minutemen streamed by. A young American, startled at the sudden move, instinctively swung his hatchet at the wounded man and cut off the top of his head.

As the retreating regulars reached the home of Elisha Jones a short distance up the road to Concord, the grenadiers of the 47th arrived with Smith in command. He insisted on leading his grenadiers to the bridge, Lieutenant Barker later wrote in his diary:

> The Colonel ordered two or three companies, but put himself at their head, by which means he stopped them from being on time, for being a very fat, heavy man, he would not have reached the bridge in half an hour.[1]

Consequently, Smith delayed his men long enough to enable the Minutemen to drive the light infantry back. However, on arrival, the grenadiers promptly fired a volley into the advancing militiamen and charged them with the bayonet. A number of Minutemen were killed or wounded, and the rest broke into two groups and fell back. One segment raced back across the bridge and up Punkatasset Hill; the other retreated into the hills overlooking the road to Concord. The grenadiers did not pursue them but returned to the center of town with the wounded light infantrymen, leaving several of the men of the 4th to watch for Captain Parsons and his men.

Unaware of what was happening back at North Bridge, Parsons and his three companies had been swarming over Colonel Barrett's farm seeking war materiel that was nowhere to be found, because it had been removed long before. Finally, at 11:00 A.M., Parsons and his hundred men arrived at the bridge on their return to Concord. They were horrified at the sight of three dead regulars sprawled along the sides of the road on the far side of the bridge. To the wide-eyed Englishmen it seemed obvious that one of them, with the top of his head laid bare, had been scalped.

As the regulars marched by, the hundreds of colonists on Punkatasset Hill and above Concord Road could easily have cut them off. But war had not yet been declared, and the colonial officers were unsure of what to do. While they debated, Parsons's men quickly moved past the danger.

On the Concord village Green, Smith concentrated his forces and waited for Parsons's return so they could begin their march to Boston, twenty-two miles away. Smith also needed to secure chaises and horses to transport the wounded. It was noon before Parsons returned and the fateful retreat began.

When it did, the narrow road to Lexington was filled with the short leather caps of the light infantry and the tall bearskins of the grenadiers. In the center of the column of grenadiers were the horse-drawn "chairs," an American adaptation of the French chaise, which Smith had appropriated to carry the wounded men. The light infantry was ordered to climb the ridge that loomed over the town and parallel the Lexington Road from above while the grenadiers marched along the main road. Where the ridge flat-

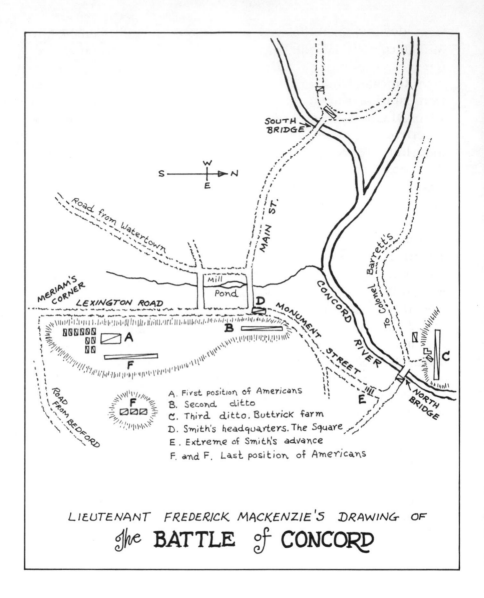

A. First position of Americans
B. Second ditto
C. Third ditto. Buttrick farm
D. Smith's headquarters. The Square
E. Extreme of Smith's advance
F. and F. Last position of Americans

LIEUTENANT FREDERICK MACKENZIE'S DRAWING OF
The BATTLE *of* CONCORD

tened down to meet the road at a bridge near Meriam's Corner, the two columns converged.

From the moment that the first shots were fired in darkness on the Lexington Green at four-thirty that morning, news of the British killing of Americans had traveled with astonishing speed throughout the countryside. Militia companies, in training for nearly a year, hurried toward Concord to strike back at the British. The Minutemen, trained to be the first to fight, were joined by regular militias composed of older men. The alarm companies, whose function was to remain and defend their villages, would not be held back as they, too, were anxious to share in the fighting. Throughout the early morning, on village greens within a radius of over fifty miles from Lexington, Minutemen, militia, and alarm companies formed and marched off to the music of fifes and drums. It was a mass migration of armed men.

As the British light infantry descended from the slopes and waited for the grenadiers to precede them across the bridge at Meriam's Corner, several long-distance shots sent lead balls humming into the ranks of the regulars. Suddenly they realized that they were completely encircled by large numbers of waiting riflemen. Minutemen had circled around from North Bridge and were waiting for the British columns to converge. Hundreds waited in the fields and lay concealed behind the walls of the Great Fields, a pasture adjacent to Meriam's Corner. The flow of newly arriving Minutemen and militia companies swelled the American forces to several thousand men.

As the leading column of grenadiers slowed to allow the chairs containing the wounded to cross the narrow bridge, occasional shots punctuated the traffic jam, but the column finally began to move. After the grenadiers and chairs had crossed the bridge, the light infantry led by Major Pitcairn followed, acting as the rear guard. As the last company of the column crossed the bridge, a command rang out and the last light infantry company halted, did an about-face, and fired a volley into the Americans who thronged the road behind them. Several colonials slumped to the ground, but others immediately returned the volley, and bullets ripped into the light infantry from all sides. Jeremy Lister's right elbow was shattered, and his scarlet coat turned black with blood. Wrapping his arm in his sash, he stumbled along behind his men. Just over the bridge, the bodies of two regulars were left in the road as the column marched off.

As it moved toward Lexington, musket and rifle fire struck at the marching men from every possible hiding place along the road. The militia, Minutemen, and alarm companies became hopelessly intermingled as men slipped behind trees or walls and waited for the column to pass. Then they fired their guns and quickly ran into the woods to reload, and sprinted ahead of the column for another chance.

Some of the colonial officers on horseback tied their animals to trees, raced in to get off their shot, ran back to their horses, mounted, and rode down the road to wait for the column. Near Hardy's Hill, Minutemen from Sudbury, under Captain Nathaniel Cudworth, attacked the regulars from dense woods that lined both sides of the road. The forests were swarming with American riflemen, and the light infantry was sent out as flankers to get in behind the colonials hiding alongside the road. On many occasions, however, British troops were themselves surrounded by scores of riflemen. Hand-to-hand struggles took place in the dismal woods, as neither side gave or received quarter. When the column approached the village of Lincoln, Major Loammi Baldwin joined in the fighting with 180 Woburn Minutemen. The musket and rifle fire doubled in intensity as more men arrived to replace those who had been killed or wounded. In the thick of the firing were the Minutemen from Lexington under Captain John Parker, getting a second chance at the men of the British army.

The troops at the rear of the column suffered the most. As soon as the column passed a given point, the colonists would leave their cover and converge on the rear of the receding column. British soldiers, trained to fire in volleys, were at a great disadvantage; there were no massed targets to volley against. Most of the British troops were young recruits in their first action, and they simply blazed away in the general direction of their tormentors. They had been told that Americans were cowardly creatures who became terrified at the smell of gunpowder and would run if fired upon.

Consequently the regulars wasted most of their ammunition firing into woods or walls. This unaimed firepower gave the Americans confidence in the inaccuracy of the British and inspired many to take risks they might otherwise not have taken.

The movement of the column was excruciatingly slow, as the furious troops kept stopping to reload. They offered easy targets for the hidden militiamen, and many young Englishmen joined Britain's roll of war dead buried thousands of miles from home in remote parts of the world.

By European standards, the colonial tactics of firing from concealment were murder committed by men too cowardly to stand up to fight. British officers and men were taught that war was conducted by brave men who faced each other in deadly but honorable combat, blazing away until one or the other was defeated. "Only a coward would hide behind cover and kill a soldier of the King without showing himself" might express the sentiment.

However, students of military science know that these tactics — the use of extended-order and the advantages of natural cover — were a foretaste of modern warfare. The eighteenth-century British style of formal evolutions has long since been discarded. From a tactical point of view, the British withdrawal from Concord was a contest between the tactics of the British, based on the formal practices of Frederick the Great, and the tactics of a light skirmish line founded on the pragmatic strategy of the American riflemen. Never again, after Concord, would British troops venture into the open country against the Americans around Boston. Several years later a British army under General John Burgoyne made history when it was forced to surrender on similar terrain at Saratoga. It was the first time that a British army had ever surrendered in the field. After the American Revolution, all European armies adopted the skirmish line as an improvement over the heavy infantry mass.

As the British marched toward Lexington through the hail of colonial fire, the column continually jerked to a stop as men reloaded. When it moved again, crumpled bodies lay in the road and had to be pulled to the side to make way for the living. The wounded were lifted into the chairs acquired in Concord, but these soon overflowed with bloody and moaning men.

The officers discovered that a mounted officer was a prime target and began to walk beside their horses. Wounded men were allowed to cling to the saddles or were strapped across the animals' backs to keep them from falling off.

The retreat through the area around Lincoln was brutal. There was a continuous crash of gunfire as regulars in sweat-stained red-and-white uniforms worked their way down to the bottom of the hill and across another bridge. Thick forests along the route concealed thousands of American marksmen, and one by one English soldiers were hit and fell in pools of blood along the dirt road. Colonel Smith was struck in the leg and limped along with the column, not daring to stop long enough to have the ugly wound attended to. However, as groups of light infantry slipped away from the column and got behind the Minutemen, many Americans were killed, as well. It was near Lincoln that Captain Jonathan Wilson of Bedford, Nathaniel Wyman of Billerica, and Daniel Thompson of Woburn were killed by British bayonets.

The regulars felt the effects of marching all night without sleep. They had hiked over twenty-five miles since 2:00 A.M., in addition to the distance covered during the maneuvering in Concord. Because of the running and climbing demanded by their flanking tactics, the light infantry companies were exhausted. Some men dropped from sheer fatigue and were lifted or kicked upright by furious sergeants and corporals. In general, however, the well-trained regulars kept their ranks.

It is difficult to understand why the entire British force was not captured or destroyed by the colonial militia. Had the Americans been led by a unified command, they could have easily set up roadblocks by felling trees and massing large numbers of the available militia to halt the progress of the column. As a collection of autonomous fighting units, their purpose appeared to be to kill as many individual British soldiers as possible, rather than to capture the entire column.

The redcoats soon entered open country and for a short distance had an opportunity to catch their breath. The wounded were rearranged among the various chairs, and the ranks were closed. The respite was brief, however, for ahead was an area of large boulders and three farmhouses full of armed men. Musket shots exploded from behind each boulder and from the houses.

More young Britons died, and of necessity the wounded were left to the mercy of the grim Americans, for there was no more room in the horse-drawn chairs. When the light infantry rushed one of the houses along the road, many Minutemen escaped, but the regulars were able to trap seven men inside, all of whom they shot and bayoneted.

To the men in the tormented column, the nightmare seemed to have gone on for many hours, but they had left Concord only two hours before. It was nearly 2:00 P.M. and they were close to Lexington. Marching over another hill, more colonial bullets thudded into flesh and bone, but the regulars did not return the fire. They had used up nearly all the thirty rounds of ammunition per man they had carried from Boston.

The heat of the day held at 85° for several hours, and many regulars stumbled or collapsed from fatigue and heat along the highway. A rocky ledge called Fiske's Hill near the entrance to Lexington concealed hundreds of colonial militia, and a hot though inaccurate fire rained on the distressed British. It was here that James Hayward of Acton met a British grenadier face to face. The grenadier leveled his musket at Hayward and yelled as he fired pointblank, "You are a dead man!" "And so are you!" retorted Hayward, and fired. The grenadier was killed instantly; Hayward died the next day.

The British regulars were near their breaking point when suddenly several of them broke into a wild race for the town of Lexington, not far from the bottom of the hill. Officers tried in vain to halt them as other men joined in the frenzied rush. In an instant the front of the column degenerated into a mad stampede of wild-eyed men.

Lieutenant Colonel Smith was too injured to take action, so Major Pitcairn seized his horse from several wounded men who were clinging to the animal, swung into the saddle, and galloped under intense fire to the head of the fleeing column. Musket shots from the rocky ledge startled his horse, which reared up and hurled the major into the middle of the road, where the panic-stricken mob surged over him. Other officers, however, followed Pitcairn's example and galloped ahead of the pack. Armed with their fusils, they dismounted and placed themselves in the road facing the on-rushing men. Coolly and courageously they pointed their fusils at the troops, and by the force of that discipline that so clearly marked the difference between officers and enlisted men, brought the wild-eyed herd to a halt. Ensign de Berniere reported later that the men were told that they would be killed on the spot if they refused to form into ranks. Sullenly, they obeyed and, under heavy fire, reformed their ranks.

At last Fiske's Hill was behind them and they were moving down toward Lexington. Below them, less than a mile away, was the town that they had left seven hours earlier amid victorious shouts. From their rear came the roar of musketry as several thousand militiamen marched on the open highway behind them, closing in on each flank and firing as fast as they could. The British force was now completely out of ammunition, and the colonials moved forward confidently, disdaining the need for cover. The end was in sight. The British would all be either dead or prisoners within a matter of minutes.

The village of Lexington lay before them: the church, the village green, the white houses around the green, the meetinghouse, Buckman's Tavern. And then, there on the other side of the meetinghouse, stretched across the road on a slight rise, stood three lines of redcoated British troops, bright bayonets held firmly to the front. It was Lord Percy's First Brigade, eight hundred strong, formed into a large square that enclosed Munroe's Tavern and the grassy ground around it. The British were saved!

The tired and bleeding men in the van of Smith's column broke into a tumultuous cheer that rippled down the line. The First Brigade opened its ranks and the exhausted, desperate soldiers entered and flung themselves thankfully onto the grass before Munroe's Tavern.

A six-pound cannon stood on the grassy knoll on either side of the road, blue-uniformed Royal Artillerymen at the ready. Below them, thousands of militiamen swarmed onto the Lexington Green from the Concord Road and from fields on each side. At a short command from Colonel Cleaveland, sharp flashes of flame and smoke roared from the guns. One cannonball smashed squarely into the meetinghouse and sent pieces of timber spinning across the Green. As the other ball hit the middle of the Green, the militia rushed for cover behind buildings and walls across the roads. Two more rounds slammed into the roads on each side of the Green, and suddenly there was not an American in sight.

The wounded regulars were lifted gently from their chairs and brought into the tavern. The walking wounded were helped into a large taproom, where regimental surgeons and their assistants set to work cleaning and bandaging the bloody wounds. The surgeon's mate of the 43rd Regiment looked at Ensign Lister's shattered right elbow and was able to extract the .75-caliber ball lodged there. Lister had lost a large amount of blood, and was able to stand only with difficulty.

General Percy and Major Pitcairn conferred with the wounded Smith while his leg was cleaned and bandaged. The entire British force, including the First Brigade, now amounted to fifteen hundred men. They were fifteen miles from Boston, and they had a large number of wounded. There were only twenty-two rounds for each of the two six-pounders. They were surrounded by over ten thousand confident, exultant militia, and new reinforcements were constantly arriving. Percy estimated that within an hour colonial forces would number twenty thousand or more. And there was real danger that the militia would bring up their cannon and barricade the road, forcing the entire British contingent to surrender.

Percy and the other officers decided that to delay would be fatal. They must get back to Boston before dark or soon after. Because the Americans were using houses along the route as fortresses, Percy ordered the buildings along his position beside Munroe's Tavern to be burned. A barn, two shops, and three houses were destroyed.

Percy then ordered the light infantry and grenadiers who had borne the brunt of the attack to retire and form behind the brigade. Immediately, however, they came under fire from the militia that were concealed behind trees and stone walls. Percy ordered the battalion men to advance on each flank to gain the protection of the walls themselves, and at 3:30 P.M., with flanking duties performed by battalion men of the brigade, the reinforced British column started for Boston. The 23rd Regiment was given the dangerous rear-guard position. Their adjutant, Lieutenant Mackenzie, lined his men along the walls on each side of the road to cover the brigade's withdrawal. The 23rd then dropped off by companies to pick up the flanks of the column farther down the road.

During the brief respite at Lexington, hundreds of new militia companies appeared along the road to Boston. Dr. Joseph Warren and General William Heath directed the flow of men to the Cambridge–Lexington Road but were unable to control the tactics of the various companies and regiments once they were within shooting distance of the regulars. However, they ordered a number of companies to concentrate at Menotomy in the one serious attempt to contain the British force and prevent their return to Boston.

A mile outside of Lexington, the now familiar pattern of musket and rifle fire came from both sides of the road and was particularly heavy from supposedly unoccupied houses along the road. Ensign Lister, lying prone atop his horse, decided that life expectancy there was not as long as it was below that elevated level. He dismounted and, though weakened, hung onto the saddle with his left hand. In the same manner, some horses were supporting four wounded men, and each of the artillery horses carried other men who were unable to walk. Occasionally, as Colonel Cleaveland ordered the cannon into action, the wounded slid off, the guns were wheeled into position, and a few balls whistled into concentrations of colonials, scattering them in all directions.

The mood of the British soldiers was murderous. They surged around houses along the route, instantly killing anyone found inside. Some of the regulars looted whatever they could find, and some were killed while looting by Minutemen who had concealed themselves in the houses.

Houses with fires in the hearth were burned down simply by spreading the embers about. Generally, those homes without fires on the hearth escaped destruction because it was too time-consuming to start a fire with steel and flint.

As the column approached Menotomy, the 23rd Regiment was relieved of rear-guard duty by the marine battalion. Colonial fire reached a bloody crescendo in Menotomy, and again British troops rushed house after house, killing everyone found inside, including an invalid named Jason Russell.

In response to orders from Warren and Heath, militia companies from Danvers and Essex had arrived at Menotomy earlier and taken up what they considered good defensive positions to halt the regulars, near the road behind walls and barricades of bundles of shingles. As the main column approached the American position, Percy sent a flanking force off to the left. The British surrounded the colonials, and giving no quarter killed and wounded many. Both Dr. Warren and General Heath were involved in the action. (Warren had a pin shot out of his hair without suffering a wound.) Dr. Eliphalet Downer, a physician from Cambridge, was charged by a young British soldier with leveled bayonet. He twisted the musket from the soldier and killed him with his own bayonet. Some regulars outflanked four militiamen hidden behind dry casks at Watson's Corner and, coming up behind the Americans, bayoneted and killed all four.

Meanwhile, newly arrived militia companies from Roxbury, Brookline, Milton, and Dorchester formed near the foot of the rocks in Menotomy, a good position from which to attack the right flank of the marching column. Again the British six-pounders went into action, as the wounded men were helped off and the guns were manhandled into position. A half dozen shots of the rapidly dwindling artillery rounds sufficed to send the Americans into retreat.

At this point, General Heath, who was attempting to direct the militia forces, received word that seven hundred Minutemen from Salem and Essex, led by Major Timothy Pickering, were marching down the Medford Road to Charlestown to engage the British when they got there. As luck would have it, Percy and his men reached and passed the junction before the colonials arrived, and the opportunity was lost.

As Lord Percy broke the colonial lines at Menotomy and approached Prospect Hill, he had to make a choice. He could return to Boston by way of Cambridge and Roxbury, or he could head for Charlestown, which was closer and would afford him the support of the navy's guns as he approached the Charles River. A return by way of Cambridge would necessitate crossing the Great Bridge, which was certain to be either heavily defended or destroyed by growing militia forces.

Correctly, Percy elected to take the road to Charlestown. General Heath had again removed the bridge timbers, and thousands of militiamen were massed along the bridge waiting for the British attempt to cross the Charles. Had Heath brought the many men at his command to meet the British instead of waiting passively at the Great Bridge, he could have surrounded and captured the entire British force. Given the British shortage of musket and field gun ammunition, Percy would have been forced to surrender. But Heath was unaware of the British shortage of ammunition and chose to make his stand at the bridge.

General Heath always blamed the Salem commander, Timothy Pickering, for not pushing his men down the Medford–Charlestown Road fast enough. Had the large American force been able to prevent the British forces from entering into the Charlestown Neck, they could have trapped them.

Heath defended his own actions on the basis of the two British field guns. The colonial troops, in his opinion, could not withstand artillery fire, and he was hesitant to send them into an attack. Without the two field guns, Percy would have been unable to extricate his force, however, and Heath's failure to order his men to concentrate their fire on the artillery horses has never been justified.

As Percy's men approached Prospect Hill, intent on taking the road to Charlestown, a large body of militiamen blocked the road and tried to force the British toward Cambridge. For the last time the British field guns rolled up the road, unlimbered, and sent the last of their solid shot screaming toward the colonials. The Americans fell back shouting, "King Hancock forever!" and retreated behind stone walls on adjacent pasture land. However, at the rear of the British column a large body of militia advanced, firing as they came. The Royal Marines, acting as the rear guard at this time, suffered many casualties.

The sun was setting behind them when the British approached the narrow Charlestown Neck. As dusk turned to darkness, flashes from colonial muskets revealed the rebel positions along both sides of the road. If the shots came from a house, it was immediately surrounded and all occupants put to death. Lieutenant Mackenzie reported that the last house seized as the regulars reached the Neck contained several men, including a black man, all of whom fought to the death.

The scene in Charlestown throughout the day had been one of great confusion and excitement. When news of Lexington arrived in the morning, large crowds of older men, women, and children gathered in the streets, and the Charlestown militia marched out to join the colonial forces heading for Lexington. Early in the afternoon, a message arrived from General Gage addressed to the Selectmen of Charlestown, informing them that he was aware that armed men had left the town to fire upon British troops. The message warned of the most disastrous consequences if one more armed man left Charlestown.

Late in the afternoon, news reached the town that the Great Bridge at Cambridge had been dismantled and that Percy's column was returning to Boston by way of Charlestown. Hundreds started to pack their belongings, fearful of the vengeful regulars. Every available wagon was put into service to remove the property of the frightened inhabitants. Those who believed that the troops would return by way of Roxbury decided to chance it and remain in their homes. Just before sunset, the sounds of distant firing reached Charlestown, and a lookout reported seeing redcoated soldiers on the road to Medford. Some crossed the Mystic River to Malden at Penny Ferry; others ran along the marsh toward Medford.

Just as darkness covered the town, the exhausted British troops poured into Charlestown. As rumors spread through the darkness that soldiers were massacring women and children, some people awaited the worst in desperate indecision, while others ran to hide in the clay pits behind Breed's Hill. The British, however, harmed no one. Officers directed the women to go into their homes and stay there, and asked them to hand out to the troops drinks that they had on hand. Officers crowded into the tavern on the square demanding beer.

When the British crossed Charlestown Neck to the peninsula, the firing stopped. Dr. Warren and General Heath followed Percy's men only as far as the Neck and then turned the militia back toward Cambridge.

As Lord Percy sat his horse in the square, directing his ex-hausted men to take up defensive positions on Bunker Hill, a courier handed him a most welcome message from General Gage:

> My Lord, Gen. Pigot will pass over with a reinforcement and fresh ammunition. The boats which carry him may return with the grenadiers and light infantry who must be most fatigued, and the wounded. I propose sending over Capt. Montresor immediately with intrenching tools to throw up a sort of redoubt on the hill, and to leave 200 men and guns on it, and if it's advisable during the course of the night, to bring your Lordship's men over. The fresh brigade may carry on the works. Fresh ammunition has been ordered long ago.[2]

Until they were relieved by fresh troops of the Second and Third Brigades, the exhausted regulars rested in defensive posi-tions that had been dug on Bunker Hill. The men of the grenadiers and light infantry, who had marched and fought over fifty miles in the last twenty hours, were the first to be loaded into boats and ferried across to Boston. Then the men of the battalion companies of the First Brigade were relieved from their positions atop Bunker Hill and returned to their barracks. It was after mid-night.

Lieutenant Mackenzie returned to his family several hours after midnight. Nancy had waited nearly six hours at the fleet landing and had endured the agony of watching the bloody and disfigured bodies of many friends as they were carried from the boats. She had no word from her husband's regiment until nearly midnight, when she learned that the adjutant of the 23rd had escaped both death and injury. It was with a heartfelt prayer of thanksgiving that she finally saw Frederick in the stern of one of the last boats to land from Charlestown. He jumped out as it touched the dock and enfolded her heavy, pregnant figure in his arms. They were soon back home, where the children joined them in a family celebration with tea and cakes that lasted until dawn.

It was less than twenty-four hours since he had left, but neither their world nor that of America or England would ever be the same again. The loss of many friends and the siege of Boston crowded upon them — events that defied all efforts to arrange their lives in an orderly and safe fashion.

Nancy was busy with the multitude of tasks performed by women at the time: preparing and cooking three meals daily; cleaning, washing, daily shopping trips for increasingly scarce supplies. Access to the area was completely severed, and each mouthful of food came by way of British naval vessels that often had to fight their way through American privateers attacking English ships.

In addition, Nancy took a position with the army supervising soldiers' wives in the new General Hospital. Established in an old building called the Manufacturing House, which had once been a linen factory, the hospital improved the care of the wounded, who had previously been farmed out to private homes. The doctors and surgeons of both the army and the town were able to concentrate their efforts to tend the large number of casualties, among them Ensign Lister.

When he was rowed across the Charles River that night, Ensign Lister learned that Captain Parsons had been badly wounded when a bullet smashed his knee, and Lieutenant Sutherland's chest wound was causing him great pain and suffering. As Lister tottered toward his lodgings, aided by a musician of the 23rd Regiment, he met the battalion companies of his own regiment of the 10th marching to be rowed to Charlestown to relieve the men on Bunker Hill.

When he reached his lodgings, dozens of people crowded into his room for news of their loved ones. Many were Loyalists who had been driven from their homes by the Sons of Liberty and were lodged in the house Lister lived in. He sat there, drowsily sipping a welcome cup of hot tea, and tried to answer the many questions. A woman behind him asked if he had seen Lieutenant Sutherland of the 38th Regiment. Without thinking he replied that he had just left him and supposed that he must be dead by this time. He turned his head just in time to see the woman, Sutherland's wife, slip to the floor in a faint.

Happily, Lister proved to be wrong. Sutherland recovered and was able to rejoin his wife and his regiment within a few months.

Lister's wound became progressively worse, however, and his arm was scheduled for amputation. A kindly surgeon took a personal interest in the case and fought successfully to save the arm. During the next seven months, while his arm healed, Lister was confined to the hospital and then to his lodgings. The arm remained stiff and would not bend, and in January 1776 Lister was excused from paying the usual stipend and received a promotion to lieutenant. He returned to England on recruiting duty.

In his diary, Lieutenant Frederick Mackenzie recorded the British killed, wounded, and missing from the raid on Concord. Among the officers:

4th Regiment	Lieutenant Gould, wounded in the foot, captured and exchanged.
5th Regiment	Lieutenant Baker, wounded in the hand.
	Lieutenant Hawkshaw, wounded in the cheek.
	Lieutenant Cox, wounded in the arm.
10th Regiment	Lieutenant Colonel Smith, wounded in the leg.
	Captain Parsons, wounded in the knee.
	Lieutenant Kelly, wounded in the arm.
	Ensign Lister, wounded in the arm.
23rd Regiment	Lieutenant Colonel Bernard, wounded in the thigh.
38th Regiment	Lieutenant Sutherland, wounded in the chest.
43rd Regiment	Lieutenant Hall, wounded in the chest, died May 2.
47th Regiment	Lieutenant McLeod, wounded in the chest.
	Lieutenant Baldwin, wounded in the throat.
Marines	Captain Souter, wounded in the leg.
	Lieutenant McDonald, wounded slightly.
	Lieutenant Dotter, wounded slightly.

Casualties among the British enlisted men:

Regiment	Killed	Wounded	Missing
4th	7	25	8
5th	5	15	1
10th	1	13	1
18th	1	4	1
23rd	4	26	6
38th	4	12	0

Regiment	Killed	Wounded	Missing
43rd	4	5	2
47th	5	22	0
52nd	3	2	1
59th	3	3	0
Marines	31	38	2
Artillery	0	2	0

Colonial losses were substantially lower. The militia lost forty-nine killed, thirty-nine wounded, and five missing. In addition to the eight killed at Lexington before dawn, two men from the Lexington militia died in the running fight later that day: Jedediah Munroe, who had survived the dawn encounter on the Green, and young Jack Raymond, who overslept the second muster but fought on the road to Boston.

The men killed and wounded came from a number of militia companies:

Lexington	Medford	Billerica
Concord	Charlestown	Chelmsford
Cambridge	Watertown	Salem
Needham	Framingham	Newton
Sudbury	Dedham	Danvers
Acton	Stow	Beverly
Bedford	Roxbury	Lynn
Woburn	Brookline	

Historically the battles of Lexington and Concord have been represented as fought by farmers who individually and spontaneously reached for their muskets and rushed out to fire upon the British regulars. In truth, no civilians were involved. Only members of organized Minutemen, militia, or alarm companies that had trained for nearly a year under company and regimental officers participated in the fight.

What astonished British officers and men was the apparent lack of concern with which the colonials accepted armed conflict with veteran British regulars. They had firmly believed that the colonists would never fight, and the American response to Gage's expedition profoundly shocked them. Lord Percy, who miraculously escaped injury during the withdrawal, wrote to a friend in London:

> Whoever looks upon them as an irregular mob will be much mistaken. They have men amongst them who know very well what they are about, having been employed as rangers against the Indians. Nor are several of the men void of a spirit of enthusiasm, for many of them advanced within ten yards to fire at me and other officers though they were mortally certain of being put to death themselves in an instant.

Like most of the British, Percy credited the Americans with acts of atrocity, including the "scalping" of the British soldier at North Bridge, a mistaken view held by the English people for many years.

Lord Percy's coup in bringing home fifteen hundred men, many of them wounded, over difficult terrain on a single narrow road surrounded by thousands of marksmen who kept up a continuous fire has justly entered the annals of British history as a splendid feat of arms. It was a military miracle, and it earned him a highly deserved commendation. Despite that, however, April 19, 1775, was a bitter, tragic day for England. Out of the total of 1500 men, 73 were killed; 174 were wounded, many of them mortally; 26 were missing, most of them prisoners of the colonists. There were 273 casualties in all, which represented 18 percent, or nearly one out of five men either killed, wounded, or captured.

In retrospect, however, it seems unbelievable that the continuous fire by thousands of militiamen, usually at close range, resulted in only 273 hits out of what has been estimated at 75,000 shots fired at the British.

Lieutenant John Barker was bitter in his appraisal of the entire expedition, which, in his opinion, was a military disaster, ill planned, and poorly executed from beginning to end. The three wasted hours, waiting on the Cambridge marsh for unnecessary provisions, gave the Americans time to assemble and squandered the element of surprise. Had it not been for that delay, the flank companies would have reached Concord soon after daybreak and thus have been able to destroy most of the military stores before the Americans could have removed them. According to Barker, they could then have returned to Boston with little or no opposition, because the colonial forces would not have had the time to intercept them. The cost in British lives would have been even greater had it not been for Lord Percy's timely arrival at Lexington.

In Lieutenant Mackenzie's analysis of the expedition, his criticism was directed toward the lack of real secrecy in the planning of the raid and the failure to use strategic misdirection. As he expressed himself in his diary, he believed that Gage should have sent the column toward Watertown as he had done once before, on what should have appeared to be another practice march. This would have created another "false alarm" reaction among the Americans and would have allayed their fears.

When the troops reached Watertown, they could have rested briefly, and then, instead of returning to Boston as they had done before, suddenly driven quickly toward Concord, eleven miles away. There, they would have found the stores still unmoved, due to the surprise of their sudden appearance. For even greater security, another column could have been sent in another direction, such as Medford, thereby preventing an American concentration at any one point. Such a plan would have insured the return of the main force with few if any losses.

Mackenzie was convinced that the ill-considered dispatch of mounted officers to position themselves along the road between Lexington and Concord served to warn the colonials as much as did the colonial couriers like Revere and Dawes.

Another tactical error, in the opinion of Mackenzie, was the selection of the overweight Colonel Smith to lead the surprise raid on Concord. Under the circumstances, a much more active officer should have been chosen. But the underlying cause of the British disaster, was, in the opinion of Mackenzie and other perceptive officers, General Gage's lack of understanding of the temper of the American people. Gage failed utterly to grasp the meaning of the American preparations begun the year before, to fight the British troops should they move out of Boston with hostile intentions.

FOURTEEN

The Colonial Call to Arms

DURING THE NIGHT of April 19, the British were still in position on Bunker Hill. The hills opposite swarmed with thousands of colonial militiamen separated from their companies during the running fight from Concord. Men from the surrounding country-side and the coast continued to flow into the American lines during the night, and by morning large groups of troops had arrived from Connecticut, Rhode Island, and New Hampshire, having marched throughout the night.

Thousands of armed men were encamped over the hills and fields surrounding Boston, and the responsibility to bring the multitudes under some semblance of control fell to Major General Artemas Ward and Brigadier General John Thomas, both of Massachusetts. (Eventually, the Committee of Safety under Dr. Joseph Warren would take over actual control of the Massachusetts army in the name of the Massachusetts Provincial Congress, sitting in continuous session in Watertown, five miles away.)

Artemas Ward was in bed in Shrewsbury suffering from a recurring case of bladder stones when an express rider galloped into town with the news of Lexington. In great pain, Ward nonetheless arose and raced over the rough road to Cambridge to take command of the American army.

Ward was headquartered in the Jonathan Hastings house in Cambridge, and the Committee of Safety shared the building with him. Together they acted as a directorate for all decisions relating to military affairs. By the time Ward arrived in Cambridge, the British forces had crossed into the lines of Charlestown. He immediately called a council of war at the Hastings house. Present were three generals, Ward, Heath, and Whitcomb; Colonel William Prescott; six lieutenant colonels; Samuel Osgood, acting as aide-de-camp; and Artemas Ward's second cousin, Joseph Ward, acting as secretary.

William Heath had been the first of the Massachusetts generals to arrive in Cambridge. From there he galloped to Watertown to bring Minutemen to Cambridge in time to take up the planking of the Great Bridge across the Charles, although the boards were easily replaced by Captain Montresor's men. When Percy's troops marched out toward Lexington, Heath and Joseph Warren collected all the Minutemen they could find and followed them, and during the British retreat toward Charlestown, both Heath and Warren were in the thick of the fighting at Menotomy.

Leading troops against the king and Parliament before the American cause had been endorsed by the Continental Congress was a daring act of rebellion. Heath, Warren, Ward, Thomas, and the others risked the hangman's noose at a time in history when rebellion against the king of England had never succeeded.

The problem that faced Ward that night was food and shelter for the sprawling army that had assembled overnight. Houses, barns, and sheds were overcrowded, with ten to twenty men sleeping on floors in each room. In the eighteenth century, men from the uneducated classes were believed to be by nature brutal, barbarous, and coarse, kept in control by the influence of wives, mothers, and sisters. The men themselves believed this to be true and acted accordingly. Consequently, many of the colonial troops did not attempt to find latrines or specific areas for the necessities of life, but simply relieved themselves wherever they happened to be. The filth and garbage generated by thousands of men ignorant of the rudimentary hygienic principles of army life presented the committee with a serious health hazard.

The first few days after Concord were therefore anxious and filled with feverish activity. Food was collected from the countryside; latrines and earthworks were dug; guards were posted; and messages were sent, begging for gunpowder and other supplies.

Officers in command were convinced that Gage was about to order an attack from Boston Neck aimed at Roxbury. General Thomas, in charge of the right wing of the Massachusetts army, was given what amounted to an independent command in Roxbury, for he was separated from Cambridge by the Charles River and several miles of land. By the morning of April 22 he had been reinforced by four additional regiments. Gage's attack, however, never came.

By then the American positions stretched in a great arc from Roxbury, north along the western shore of the Charles River, across its estuary to Cambridge, continuing along shore and marsh to Charlestown Neck and across the Mystic River to Chelsea. The line was twelve miles long, and it spanned hills, valleys, rivers, and marshes. Within its circling lines were three peninsulas that controlled the strategy of the siege: Charlestown Peninsula to the north, evacuated by the British the day after the battle at Lexington and Concord; the peninsula in the center, which was Boston itself; and Dorchester Peninsula to the south of Boston, unoccupied by either side. Admiral Thomas Graves wanted Gage to seize both Charlestown and Dorchester, because they outflanked the central peninsula of Boston.

When a courier galloped into Pomfret with news of Lexington, Israel Putnam was plowing one of his fields. Summoning his son from an adjoining field to take over, Putnam ran nearly a mile to his barns, saddled his best horse, and was soon on his way to Boston, a hundred miles away. He arrived in time to attend the war council in Cambridge the next afternoon. The password along the American lines that day was "Putnam" in his honor.

Within a few days, Putnam received an urgent message from the provincial legislature of Connecticut, then in session, asking him to return to Hartford to assist in dispatching the Connecticut regiments to Cambridge. He returned at once, organized the transport of men, animals, and equipment, and was promoted to brigadier general of Connecticut forces. Arranging for his troops to follow, he hastened back to Cambridge, certain that Colonels Knowlton and Durkee, old friends from the French and Indian War, would bring the troops to Massachusetts as swiftly as possible.

As a major general in the Massachusetts army, Artemas Ward outranked Putnam, who was a brigadier general in the Connecticut army. Consequently, in an outstanding example of interprovincial unity, Putnam accepted the post of second-in-command of the American forces headquartered at Cambridge. His command was the central position in the line between the Charles River and Lechmere Point. It was located across the estuary of the Charles River from that section of Boston that included the shoreline of Boston Common.

Among the Connecticut men who followed Putnam, or "Old Put," as he was soon known, to Massachusetts was a newly formed company of volunteers from New Haven under Benedict Arnold, a bold young captain who was a New Haven druggist and a former officer in the French and Indian War. The town of New Haven had placed obstacles in his way when he tried to supply powder to his men, and Arnold had furiously threatened to break open the magazines unless they gave him what he needed. The powder was released and the jubilant men marched off to Boston on April 24.

These troops belonged to the Connecticut militia but considered themselves an independent volunteer company. Each man signed a document or company charter that had been written by Silas Deane, a member of the Continental Congress. The document stated that they were loyal to George III but were driven by necessity to take up arms against the tyranny of Parliament. They were "fighting for the inalienable rights of mankind" and would avoid "such evil acts as drunkenness, profanity, gambling and plunder." Decisions would be made by a majority vote of the officers, and Captain Arnold would act as moderator. As his company hiked along the road to Boston, Arnold's nimble mind was busily planning strategy.

On their arrival in Cambridge, Arnold appeared before the Committee of Safety and proposed an expedition to Ticonderoga to seize the large numbers of British cannon there. The committee approved his plan, made him a colonel of the Massachusetts militia, and authorized him to raise a regiment to carry out his scheme. Arnold found, however, that he had been forestalled by Ethan Allen of Vermont, a former Ranger in the French and Indian War.

Allen and his brothers led an irregular army of guerrilla fighters against the Province of New York, which claimed part of the New Hampshire grants. The "Green Mountain Boys" had successfully fought against the New York militia for nearly nine years when the news of Lexington and Concord reached them in the northern forests. Allen immediately abandoned the provincial war and contacted the Connecticut Legislature with substantially the same plan that Arnold had brought before the Massachusetts Committee of Safety. Allen had his force ready, however, whereas Arnold needed time to recruit and train a regiment, so Arnold reluctantly waived his own claim to command and joined Allen as second-in-command. The joint expedition moved swiftly toward Ticonderoga from Castleton, Vermont. During the journey to the fort, Arnold and Allen agreed to a joint command, although most of the expedition consisted of Allen's two hundred Green Mountain Boys. On the night of May 9 the expedition reached Hand's Cove, across Lake Champlain from the fort and a few miles north. They found some boats and rowed themselves across the lake, and Arnold and Allen led their band of eighty-three men onto the shore in the pre-dawn darkness.

The British garrison consisted of only forty-two officers and men under Captain Delaplace of the 26th Regiment. The Americans slipped quietly along a path skirting the walls of the fort and reached a gate leading to the parade ground. Allen thrust his sword through the surprised sentry and ordered the wounded man to point out the way to Delaplace's quarters. Allen then leaped up the stairs shouting, "Come out, you damn old rat!" and threatened to kill every man, woman, and child in the fort.

The sleepy commander peered out of his door at the huge frontiersman waving his bloodstained sword. Behind Allen were dozens of disheveled men brandishing a variety of weapons. Delaplace promptly surrendered Fort Ticonderoga, which contained the largest artillery park in North America, with 183 cannon, 19 mortars, 3 howitzers, 51 swivel guns, 52 tons of cannonballs, and 40,000 musketballs.

From Ticonderoga, Arnold and Allen quickly moved across Lake Champlain and occupied Crown Point, which the British evacuated before they arrived. Arnold captured a schooner at

Skenesborough belonging to Major Skene of the British army, loaded it with some of his men, and sailed north toward St. John's on the Richelieu River, where he captured the fort, the garrison, and another ship. At Ticonderoga, in addition to Captain Delaplace the Americans had bagged a sergeant, a drummer, thirty-five privates, and twenty-four women and children. At St. John's, Arnold captured a sergeant and eight privates in addition to ten women and children.

One of the Connecticut volunteers who hurried north behind Israel Putnam was twenty-year-old Ebeneezer Huntington, a Yale senior due to receive his bachelor of arts degree in six weeks. On Friday, April 21, Huntington walked out of his classes at Yale. Two days later he was manning the lines at Roxbury as part of a militia company commanded by his brother in law. Three months later, in July, a month after the Battle of Bunker Hill, Ebeneezer received his degree from Yale in the trenches at Boston. He served throughout the war, rising from the rank of private to that of lieutenant colonel. In 1782, it was Lieutenant Colonel Huntington who marched toward Yorktown in the van of Washington's army. He participated in the siege of Yorktown as a member of Lafayette's division and was present at the surrender of Cornwallis. Huntington is among the officers pictured in John Trumbull's famous painting of the surrender.

John Stark was hard at work in his sawmill in Derryfield, New Hampshire, when a horseman brought the news of Lexington. Within ten minutes he had mounted his horse and was on his way toward the seacoast, stopping only long enough to direct his subordinate officers to form his 1200-man brigade and follow him to Medford. After forming the left wing of the American army, Stark put one of his regiments across the Mystic River to occupy Chelsea, thus extending the American lines around Boston.

North of Boston at Ipswich, Captain Nathaniel Wade received the Lexington alarm at 10:00 A.M. on April 19. Wade and his second-in-command, Joseph Hodgins, immediately formed their troops on the Common and marched toward Danvers and Salem. By the time they reached the Mystic River, Percy's men had crossed Charlestown Neck, so they camped at Medford and returned home the next day. After putting their personal affairs in order, the entire company left Ipswich to join the Massachusetts army at Cambridge.

Forty-two-year-old Simon Edgell had served five years as an infantry officer against the French and Indians. As captain of the Framingham militia, it was he who had impressed the spying British officers, de Berniere and Browne, while he lectured his men in front of the Buckminster Tavern. When he heard of the Lexington raid, Edgell saddled his horse, grasped his musket and cartridge box, and, unwilling to wait for his company, sent word for his men to follow him and raced his horse eight miles to Lexington. There he discovered that the Lexington Minutemen and militia companies were somewhere on the road to Concord awaiting the return of the regulars. He galloped toward Concord until he heard firing, then veered into the woods, dismounted, and worked his way up toward the British line of march to fire five shots into the passing regulars.

Edgell then ran back to his tethered horse and raced along the line of march and repeated the process; he spent the entire day paralleling the British column on its retreat to Charlestown. Reeling with fatigue by noon, he kept going nonetheless. Late that day, while attempting to cross a fence, Edgell collapsed on the other side. Spotted by a party of British flankers who shot at him, he lay still, and they assumed he was dead. Though wounded, he crawled away and continued his war with the British.

Because of his exertions on that hot April day, Edgell's health was nearly destroyed. He led his company through the Battle of Bunker Hill, but his health steadily declined and he was forced to leave the Continental army in 1776.

Amesbury, fifty-five miles north of Boston near the mouth of the Merrimac River, received news of Lexington late in the afternoon of April 19. Within two hours the fifty-four-man Minuteman company under Captain John Currier was on the road to Boston. They were joined by the Minutemen from Newburyport, a neighboring town, and the two companies hurried along behind their captains. They were among the thousands of men newly arrived in Cambridge on April 20, where they found an empty orchard and fell asleep on the welcome ground.

Because of the violence and unrest in Boston during 1773, thirteen-year-old John Greenwood was sent north to live with his uncle in Portland, New Hampshire. The uncle, a cabinetmaker and a lieutenant in the local militia company, encouraged John to play the fife, and he quickly became proficient enough to serve as the official fifer of the company.

During the two years he lived in Portland, John thought frequently of running away to return to his family in Boston. When the news of Lexington arrived, he quietly packed a few belongings, including his fife, and started out on foot for Boston 150 miles away. He did not know what he would do when he got there, but he was determined to be with his family during the critical time ahead.

The fifteen-year-old boy hiked doggedly all day, occasionally trotting on the downgrades. He held to a steady pace through the fragrant forests and covered forty miles by the end of the first day. After spending the night wrapped in an old blanket in a grove of trees, John started out as dawn filtered through the trees of the dense forest. He fell in with a company of militiamen from New Hampshire also on their way to Boston, and when they stopped at a tavern, John was invited to share their rations. He stayed with them the next day, then joined another detachment of marching men. No one questioned his presence on the highway, although he was obviously not old enough to be traveling alone, for there were many young boys among the ranks of militiamen headed for Boston.

John reached Cambridge in four days. There he attempted to cross over to Charlestown by way of the Charlestown Neck and find a boat to take him to Boston and his family. At the Neck, however, he faced three tough New Hampshire sentries who refused to let him pass unless he had a pass from General Ward. John tried to break past them but was easily collared and carried off to a nearby barn serving as a guardhouse.

The youth spent the night in the barn and in the morning was able to evade the sentries and reach the Charlestown ferry. He watched as a boatload of Boston families arrived with their meager possessions, distraught from the rigorous search they had undergone on the Boston side of the ferry. There, William Cunningham, the provost marshal of the British army, became notorious as a vengeful man who delighted in taking treasured articles such as pins, needles, and scissors from weeping women and throwing them into the river.

John tried to persuade the British sailors to take him across to Boston, but they merely laughed at him, so he wandered back into the nearly deserted town of Charlestown. Finally he met a group of young men nearly his age, members of a Minuteman company. They were housed in the deserted home of an Anglican minister who had fled to Boston when the British troops pulled out of Charlestown. When young Greenwood demonstrated his proficiency on the fife, the young militiamen persuaded him to join their company, and Captain Bliss swore him in as company fifer for eight months.

Simon Fobes had celebrated his eighteenth birthday on April 5, 1774, by joining the Amherst militia company. Nine months later he was selected for the elite Minutemen. On April 5, 1775, he was in Canterbury, Connecticut, to visit his sister and other members of his large family. He started home for Amherst, and on Wednesday, April 19, he was within thirty miles of home when a sweating courier rode by and shouted the news of Lexington and Concord. Spurring his horse, Fobes galloped home to change his clothes and collect a blanket, musket, and cartridge box. He then headed for Cambridge to join his company, which had arrived there the night before. The Amherst Minutemen were positioned at a breastwork called Fort Number 2, located along the marsh of the Charles River across from the Boston Common. Every night they heard British sentries hourly sing out, "All is well." Sixty years later, when recounting his wartime experiences, Fobes particularly remembered not the rigors of army life but the size of the voracious mosquitoes along the Charles River.

When David Perry was sixteen he marched to Ticonderoga as a member of Rogers' Rangers. An indentured servant who had been sold to his master to work as a tanner and shoemaker until he was twenty-one, Perry was permitted to join the Rangers, but all his pay went to his master. (In 1755 over half of the white inhabitants of the colonies were indentured, and nearly all of the blacks were either indentured or enslaved.)

When the Seven Years' War ended in 1763, Perry, then twenty-one, settled with his master and gained his freedom. He moved to Killingly, Connecticut, where he worked at his trade and eventually married and bought land on which he erected a tan-works. Hoping to increase his income, Perry went into partnership with another tanner, but within three years his crafty partner owned both tanneries and Perry was destitute.

When fighting broke out at Lexington, Perry enlisted in a Connecticut volunteer regiment and was accepted into the company of Captain Fleet, with a rank of lieutenant. The company, part of the Connecticut regiment of Israel Putnam, marched to Roxbury, where they were quartered in the abandoned home of Loyalist Joshua Loring. Within a short time, Captain Fleet, like many other soldiers at the time, died of the fever that swept the malodorous American camp, and Perry became the company commander.

Samuel Haws, a Minuteman from Wrentham, Massachusetts, was working in his yard when the alarm reached him at 1:00 P.M. on April 19. By 2:00 P.M. his company of Minutemen had mustered at the Moon Tavern and started down the road for Roxbury, thirty-two miles to the northeast. They did not halt for their first rest until they reached Walpole, ten miles away. Then they hurried on to Dedham, where the Congregational minister of the town joined their column, which continued on to Jamaica Plain without stopping. Six miles from Boston they were told that the fighting was over, and Major John Greaton, who had been in the thick of the battle, ordered them to proceed to Roxbury, where an immediate British attack was expected. They were deployed there facing Boston Neck and remained at their posts all night, without incident. During the night each man received three captured British biscuits, their first food in over fourteen hours.

Corporal John Howe of His Majesty's 52nd Regiment left Boston by the Charlestown ferry on Tuesday, April 18, to ride to Malden, Lynn, Marblehead, and Salem. Following Gage's orders he had disguised himself as a farmer and rode into the towns carrying letters of instruction to local Loyalists to use whatever influence they might have to restrain the local militia when hostilities broke out. Howe was not particularly eager to go on this assignment, but followed his orders.

He rode the Penny Ferry across the Mystic River to Malden, where he delivered his letter to a Loyalist named Goodrich and proceeded to Lynn. His ride to Marblehead was without incident, and he presented another Loyalist with the letter and headed for Salem late that night. He entered Salem at daybreak after a fifteen-mile ride. There he fed his horse and washed up, and climbed back in the saddle and rode wearily toward Lynn.

In Lynn, Howe stopped at a tavern and ordered breakfast. As he drank his third cup of tea he heard a commotion in the street, where scores of people had gathered around a horseman who excitedly related news of the British raid on Lexington. Thinking quickly, Howe volunteered himself to spread the alarm to Reading, Woburn, Billerica, and Bedford, and sped off toward Woburn, ten miles from Boston, with the news that the regulars were out and citizens should arm themselves and fight for their freedom.

He soon found the roads choked with armed units, and he proceeded through them slowly, playing the role of an American courier. Arriving in Charlestown as the British troops were fighting their way back from Lexington, Howe proceeded to the ferry and was soon back in Boston, where he reported to Gage.

Several weeks later, Corporal John Howe again dressed in his farmer's disguise and informed Lieutenant Colonel Smith that he was heading for Rhode Island to uncover preparations for resisting the regulars. As he left Boston, however, he turned his horse away from Rhode Island and toward Worcester and Albany. Howe found work as a teamster around Albany until September, then enlisted as a dragoon in the American army. When the war was over he purchased a tract of land on the Ohio River and later moved to a spot called Howe's Purchase or Hunter's Hill, where he set up a fur trading post and was eminently successful.

During the summer of 1774 thirty-two-year-old Nathanael Greene of Rhode Island made one of his major decisions when he joined the prestigious volunteer company of militia known as the Kentish Guards. The guards, formed in the East Greenwich district not far from Coventry, Rhode Island, consisted largely of Greene's lifelong friends and neighbors.

A wealthy and eligible bachelor, Greene owned a large, comfortable house on a hillside overlooking the bay at Coventry. His family, wealthy Quakers who had been established in Rhode Island for five generations, owned gristmills, sawmills, and a forge famous for its anchors.

When he was twenty-seven, Nathanael, the second son of his father's second wife, was chosen by his father to supervise a new forge built at Coventry. He was a voracious reader of every book available to him and often traveled to Boston to visit the bookstore of Henry Knox, an old friend.

Because the Greenes were pacifist Quakers, Nathanael's enlistment in the Kentish Guards caused his expulsion from the meeting of the Quaker church that he had attended since childhood in East Greenwich. He never regretted his decision, although like his bachelorhood, it caused his family great distress. His concern was that several members of the Kentish Guards were moving to expel him because a stiff knee put a slight hitch in his gait. After considerable discussion, however, the group voted to let him participate.

Members of the guard provided their own muskets, but Nathanael soon discovered that muskets had disappeared from the market and were impossible to find in Rhode Island. The royal government had placed heavy penalties on any colonial found transporting a military weapon, so he rode to Boston on a "business trip" ostensibly related to the forge; while there he hoped to purchase a musket and smuggle it back home.

In Boston, Greene visited his friend Henry Knox, who not only shared his consuming love of books but also his political views regarding the controversy between England and her colonies. Knox's bookstore was an unofficial officer's club, attracting many young British officers and scores of attractive young ladies from Boston's upper class. Knox, a physical giant, held a commission in the Boston Grenadier Corps, a militia unit famous throughout New England for its splendid uniforms, military precision, and bearing. The group had been founded and trained by British officers who liked Knox personally and frequented his shop. Consequently, he had invited Greene to visit the frequent military parades of the British regiments, and Nathanael had soon discovered within himself an unsuspected emotional involvement in military customs and tactics. He began to buy all the books on military science that he could find and carried them back to Rhode Island.

On this trip to Boston, he purchased additional volumes for his library, but he also returned with a newly acquired Brown Bess musket, which made the trip under a load of straw in a farmer's cart. As his companion, Greene took a disguised British deserter whom he was escorting to Rhode Island to become drillmaster of the Kentish Guards.

Once home, it became obvious that not all Greene's time in Boston had been spent on books, military parades, and the search for a musket. Among the young and attractive ladies in Knox's bookstore, he had found one whom he thought the most attractive and intelligent of all. He announced that he was going to marry Miss Kitty Littlefield, who was not quite eighteen years old.

Thus, at thirty-two, Private Greene of the Kentish Guards married Kitty, fourteen years his junior, at his father's mansion in East Greenwich. The marriage proved to be a happy one, although it marked Nathanael's complete break with the Quaker church.

When news of Lexington and Concord reached Providence, Rhode Island, the alarm swept quickly through the colony, and Nathanael Greene left at once for headquarters of the Kentish Guards in East Greenwich. Within a few hours this splendidly equipped and uniformed regiment was marching behind their excellent band toward the Massachusetts border. Passing through Providence, they were overtaken by a messenger from Governor Wanton with orders to return to East Greenwich. The message informed them that all fighting was over, and the British were besieged by a large army of Minutemen and militia encamped in a long line from Roxbury to Charlestown.

The Rhode Island Assembly met at Providence three days later and appointed a committee to arrange for the defense of New England in cooperation with Connecticut. One of the members chosen was Samuel Ward; when he was unable to attend because he was also a member of the Continental Congress then meeting in Philadelphia, Private Nathanael Greene was chosen as his replacement.

The committee reorganized the militia system of Rhode Island into a single brigade of nearly fifteen hundred men in three regiments. Rather than select the current major general of the Rhode Island militia, or any of the colonels of the regiments, to head the newly formed brigade, the committee chose Private Nathanael Greene of the Kentish Guards. He thus became a brigadier general and commander of all Rhode Island troops. Historians have speculated that there was a dispute whether to give command to a Congregationalist or an Episcopalian, and it was decided to select a Quaker as a compromise. Greene, the only Quaker available as a military man, was on the committee that made the choice, and consequently he was given the position. Greene is reported to have remarked, "Since the Episcopalian and the Congregationalist won't, I suppose the Quaker must."

Greene's appointment was recognized without question by the officers and rank-and-file of the new brigade, which suggests that his decisiveness and judgment were well known to the men of the militia.

After writing to his young wife of his spectacular promotion, Greene ordered a general's uniform to be made and delivered to him at Cambridge. With the aid of the British deserter he had smuggled out of Boston, he turned his energy and ability toward forming the brigade, and when the Rhode Island Brigade marched into the American lines in early June, they were the best-uniformed, best-equipped, and best-disciplined organization in the American army.

Greene's men were quartered on Jamaica Plain, and overnight the entire area changed dramatically. All the men were in uniform; long lines of neat white tents soon resembled the British camp; company streets were neat, straight, and clean; and sanitary arrangements were completed during the first three hours in camp. Muskets with fixed bayonets were neatly stacked in even rows along the camp streets, and sentries marched their posts at proper intervals in a military manner.

Greene had a happy reunion with his friend Henry Knox, who had escaped from Boston the night of the nineteenth by slipping through the British lines with his militia sword sewed in the lining of his wife Lucy's coat.

Greene was summoned to a council of officers at General Ward's headquarters in Cambridge, where he met Generals Israel Putnam and William Heath for a discussion of the problems of their various positions and the necessary army reorganization.

The New England army around Boston was, in reality, not one but five separate armies. Two were made up of Massachusetts men; each of the other three New England colonies had one army, each with its own commander. From headquarters at Cambridge, General Ward commanded fifteen regiments of Massachusetts troops, which formed the bulk of the force. Colonel John Stark, assisted by Colonels James Reed and Enoch Poor, commanded the New Hampshire force of three regiments, forming the left wing of the army. Israel Putnam commanded three regiments of Connecticut troops positioned between Stark and Ward in the Prospect Hill region. On the extreme right was General John Thomas, headquartered in Roxbury, with four thousand Massachusetts troops and four artillery companies equipped with field guns. The Rhode Island troops under Nathanael Greene were in reserve between Thomas and Ward on Jamaica Plain, where they were quartered in college buildings, churches, abandoned Loyalist homes, barns, sheds, and tents.

In contrast to the British, there were no women in the American camp. Observers blamed their absence for the profanity, gambling, and the general filth and lack of cleanliness found in all American camps except that of the Rhode Islanders. Men became ill and died because of inadequate diet and disease caused by poor hygienic practices. According to one observer, out of 4207 men stationed on Prospect Hill in May 1775, only 2227 were fit for duty one month later. The Committee of Safety toiled endlessly to alleviate the suffering and filth, but it seemed a hopeless task. The men were not really soldiers. They had no respect for their officers; they resented discipline; they were ignorant of the most elementary rules of hygiene; they had no sense of military life. In addition to the problems of disease and disorder, there were great scarcities of supplies: muskets, powder, lead, blankets, food, medicines, tents, tools, and money.

The militia units soon disintegrated into an undisciplined mob, disorganized as to size, equipment, or state of readiness. Many men left to return home, and others drifted in to take their place. No one was able to determine which men belonged to which companies, or under whose orders they were supposed to be.

Although drinking water was unsafe, orders to boil it went unobserved by the ignorant troops. Rum, however, was plentiful and resulted in noisy and disturbing incidents. In most areas around Cambridge and Roxbury, no hygienic precautions were taken; garbage and human waste lay in the open fields surrounded by clouds of flies and other insects. The stench from the American camp was carried across the Charles River into Boston on the late afternoon winds.

FIFTEEN

The New England Army

ON APRIL 20, 1775, while boats ferried the exhausted British survivors of the Concord raid across the Charles River, General Gage and Admiral Thomas Graves, the naval commander, considered the new strategic problems facing the British forces. Graves urged drastic measures: Both Charlestown and Roxbury should be burned to the ground, and the two heights that led to Boston — Bunker Hill near Charlestown Neck and Nook's Hill in Dorchester, which controlled the Boston Neck — should immediately be fortified.

Gage, however, believed that most Americans were loyal to the king, and he hesitated to use the harsh measures Graves proposed. He feared, too, that his force of fewer than three thousand was substantially outnumbered by the thousands of Americans whose campfires twinkled through the night in a solid semicircle from Roxbury to Chelsea. Gage was convinced that he would soon be attacked from either Roxbury or Charlestown, and he greatly feared an attack by citizens of Boston. He believed that should he disperse his small army to the perimeter of his lines, a sudden uprising of armed Bostonians could end in the complete destruction of his forces. Consequently, Gage adopted a defensive stance, to the disgust of his officers and Admiral Graves, pulling his troops back into Boston and thereby placing the British in a state of siege.

He ordered Roxbury Neck closed and an artillery battery established there to protect Boston from a land invasion from Roxbury. He had Graves place several warships near the Neck to supplement the firepower of the battery. Six-pound naval guns were fitted on flat boats to serve as floating batteries on the Charles River adjacent to the Common, where the water was too shallow for men-of-war.

In one of his greatest blunders, Gage withdrew the Second and Third Brigades from their temporary entrenchments atop Bunker Hill and brought them back to Boston. He directed the navy to transport a number of heavy 28-pound guns from the ships to the top of Copp's Hill. These guns, served by tough sailors of the fleet, would help defend Boston against any attack from Charlestown.

For the first few days after April 19, Gage put his men under orders to sleep with their clothes on, and all officers were to be with their troops at all times. Sixty cartridges rather than the usual thirty were to be carried by each soldier. Within a few days the 4th Regiment received orders to move into tents on Mount Whoredom north of Boston Common, and two battalions of marines under Major Pitcairn moved into tents on the Common. Lieutenant Mackenzie left his family to live with his regiment in tents on Fort Hill. Within a few weeks, the entire British force was living under canvas.

Few of the British soldiers and Loyalists in Boston understood the gravity of their situation or the long-range significance of the fighting. They were convinced that the colonists had blundered in taking up arms against the government and expected them to be promptly punished as soon as Gage's reinforcements, which were at that moment on the high seas, arrived. Fifteen hundred new troops were expected late in May, including three new major generals to assist Gage: Clinton, Burgoyne, and William Howe.

The Loyalists, many of whom had suffered at the hands of the patriots, eagerly anticipated punishment of the rebels and the arrival of the new troops, so that Gage could begin the necessary "clean-up." Some two hundred men volunteered to serve with the regulars under Loyalist General Timothy Ruggles. Their offer was gratefully accepted, and they were immediately stationed as guards at strategic areas in Boston.

In his concern for the possibility of an armed uprising within the city, Gage approached the Selectmen of Boston with a proposal to allow the departure of any citizen who wished to leave Boston with his belongings. Male inhabitants must promise not to take part in any hostilities against the regulars and must leave their arms at Faneuil Hall in the care of the selectmen. All carriages evacuating the city would be allowed to pass and repass across Boston Neck, subject only to search by the sentries to assure the absence of firearms. Gage promised boats from the navy for the use of those wishing to evacuate Boston by water.

In return, he demanded that Loyalists wishing to move into Boston be allowed to do so without interference from the military or civilian forces surrounding the city. To his annoyance, the Board of Selectmen requested that the Committee of Safety meeting in Cambridge first approve the agreement, which it did in a letter to the selectmen of April 22:

> Gentlemen:
> The Committee of Safety being informed that General Gage has proposed a treaty with the inhabitants of the town of Boston, whereby he stipulates that the women and children, with all of their effects, shall have safe conduct without the garrison, and their men also, upon condition that the male inhabitants within the town shall, on their part, so solemnly engage that they will not take up arms against the King's troops within the town, should an attack be made from without — we cannot but esteem those conditions to be just and reasonable; and as the inhabitants are in danger from suffering from want of provisions, which, in time of general confusion, cannot be conveyed into the town, we are willing you shall enter into and faithfully keep the engagement aforementioned, said to be required of you, and to remove yourselves, and your women, children, and effects, as may be.[1]

On April 27, the selectmen started to collect firearms from the citizens. Before the day was over, 1778 individual firearms had been assembled, including rifles, muskets, pistols, blunderbusses, and bayonets. That day the selectmen announced that inhabitants would be allowed to leave with all their effects except arms or ammunition, between sunrise and sunset by either land or water. Applications to leave were made to General Robertson, who was in charge. By the end of the day, several thousand applications had been received by harried army clerks working far into the night. As soon as their applications were approved, hundreds of families, their possessions piled high, began forming on Orange Street leading to Boston Neck. Others waited along the various docks for boats. Before sunset, most had left for the countryside, and coming into Boston from the Charlestown ferry were hundreds of Loyalist families.

In response to Gage's offer of evacuation, the Provincial Congress directed the towns to supply patriots leaving Boston with transportation and money to support themselves during relocation. To ease the emotional burden on the refugees, Congress directed that the recipients of this aid not be listed as "town poor," the normal designation used when giving out funds to the needy.

As long lines continued to form on Orange Street and inch their way toward the sentries on Boston Neck, Boston Loyalists began to have second thoughts regarding the mass exodus. Several expressed the opinion that the women and children of the patriots would better serve the town if detained as hostages against a possible rebel attempt to burn the city once the Whig families had left.

The powerful Tory faction pressured Gage to change his mind and discontinue the evacuation, and troubles soon developed at the checkpoints. Passes were refused; people with proper passes were allowed to leave but were forced to abandon their property; passes were worded in such a way as to separate husbands from wives and parents from children. A large group of the poor and helpless were collected, some with smallpox, and sent out into the country. More and more children were prevented from leaving in an attempt to use their presence to keep the city from being bombarded or attacked. Both the Board of Selectmen and the Provincial Congress angrily but futilely charged Gage with bad faith.

When the British troops evacuated Bunker Hill on April 20, the great majority of inhabitants evacuated Charlestown, certain that it was doomed. To those too poor to move, the Provincial Congress extended the same help they gave the refugees from Boston. Soon Charlestown was nearly deserted with the exception of a few citizens who returned occasionally to tend their gardens or remove belongings missed in the original scramble to evacuate. Colonial troops stationed on the Charlestown Neck had orders to stop anyone entering Charlestown unless he had a pass signed by General Artemas Ward.

After Concord, the Committee of Safety and the generals faced the task of reorganizing militia units into volunteer regiments officered by men appointed by the committee, while maintaining the existing forces in the lines around Boston. Dozens of men left hourly without permission to return home to sow crops or attend to personal affairs.

On April 29, 1775, the committee appealed to all New England towns to send substitutes to relieve men already on duty and to replace those who had left. Many militia companies had left western Massachusetts on the day of the Lexington raid and reached the lines after a march of over a hundred miles, only to find that the fighting had ended. After several days of inactivity and primitive living conditions, they marched back to their homes.

Joseph Warren and the Committee of Safety worked around the clock to reorganize the new regimental structures with new officers, and at the same time labored to maintain sufficient forces in position to meet an expected British attack.

Evidently unaware of these problems facing the Americans, Gage made no attempt to create difficulties for the colonists by threatening to break out of Boston from the Neck or from any other direction. By abandoning his positions on Bunker Hill and withdrawing into the peninsula of Boston, he allowed the desperate Americans sufficient time to complete the rebuilding of their army.

Day by day, most of the problems were solved and changes accomplished. Many of the militiamen were sent home with the understanding that they were to hold themselves in readiness to be called whenever necessary. Minutemen were encouraged to enlist in the new army, and most of them did. Those who did not returned home and became a part of the militia unit to which they legally belonged.

Slowly the new army came into being. Each man was required to swear an oath that he would serve until the end of 1775, and that he would submit to the orders of officers placed in command. After much infighting by various officers of disbanded Min-

utemen companies, the committee was forced to allow entire Minutemen units to enlist under their original officers. Many of them
had refused to serve under strangers from areas other than their
own.

There was, in some cases, a lack of qualified men available for
the position of colonel in some of the newly formed regiments.
Several captains were accordingly promoted to colonel. One of
those so honored, Captain John Nixon of Framingham, was the
captain of the second Minute Company of Framingham and had
fought throughout the bloody day of April 19. He was appointed
a colonel by the committee and given his beating orders. He raised
the required 590 men within a week, from Minutemen of Framingham, Sherborn, and Natick.

Colonel Nixon and his regiment would soon distinguish themselves at the Battle of Bunker Hill. With the arrival several months
later of General George Washington, Nixon was appointed a
brigadier general.

The newspapers referred to the new army as the Grand American Army, but it actually consisted of four armies. Of the total
of 16,000 men who had volunteered, Massachusetts furnished
11,500, Connecticut 2300, New Hampshire 1200, and Rhode Island 1000.

Each colony had an organization that supplied its own troops
with food, ammunition, and other supplies. Artemas Ward was
officially the commander of only the Massachusetts and New
Hampshire soldiers, but Connecticut and Rhode Island gave him
voluntary obedience by copying his orders and sending them on to
their own troops. After the Battle of Bunker Hill revealed the
weakness of this arrangement, Connecticut's Committee of War
instructed their generals, including Putnam, to take their orders
from Ward, and wrote to Rhode Island advising them to do the
same.

Although the Grand American Army had the inherent weak-
nesses of all divided commands, it was much stronger than the
British believed. Most of the officers and many of the older men
were veterans. The great majority were expert riflemen with a
good chance of hitting whatever they aimed at. They were determined men, volunteers from disbanded militia companies. Senior

officers were highly respected by their men, who looked upon them as heroes from the past. Such men as Israel Putnam, Artemas Ward, John Stark, John Thomas, William Prescott, and Seth Pomeroy were familiar by name and deed to all of the younger men in the army.

While the military leaders of both sides organized their forces and planned strategies for the forthcoming war, Samuel Adams was winning the propaganda war. He had labored throughout the night of April 19 composing a false and inflammatory report of the fighting at Lexington and Concord. Intended to win support for the radical Whig point of view, which was dedicated to complete separation and independence from Britain, the report described how brutal British troops had pulled women from their beds and driven them naked through the streets, and how old men had been butchered in their homes:

> The barbarous murders committed on our innocent brethren on Wednesday the 19th instant have made it absolutely necessary that we immediately raise an army to defend our wives and children from the butchering hands of an inhuman soldiery. These, brethren, are marks of ministerial vengeance against this colony for refusing with her sister colonies, a submission to slavery.[2]

The report, although written by Adams, was signed by Dr. Joseph Warren and went out over his signature to each of the colonies via hundreds of horsemen dispatched from the American headquarters at Cambridge. It sent a shock of revulsion against England throughout the colonies. When the dispatch reached New York it was quickly published in nearly all the papers and triggered violent anti-British riots during which much Loyalist property was destroyed. The huge equestrian statue of King George III was torn down by a large mob, which included a young college student from the British West Indies named Alexander Hamilton. Connecticut and Rhode Island stopped the shipment of all goods by sea to the British army in Boston. And from all over the northern English colonies, furious men marched along narrow dirt roads leading to Boston.

Samuel Adams was about to realize his life's ambition, and he was in full pursuit of his objective. He toured the Lexington and

Concord area collecting depositions from participants in or witnesses to the fighting. He interrogated several captured British soldiers, including Lieutenant Gould of the 4th Regiment. On April 23–25 hearings were held in Lexington and affidavits taken recounting remembered versions of events.

A letter was prepared by Adams and Warren using carefully selected reports and addressed to the inhabitants of Great Britain. Captain Derby was commissioned to sail his ship the *Quero* for England with the utmost speed. When the vessel arrived in England on May 29, the American letter was given to a colonial agent with directions to have it printed in all newspapers in the British Isles. Many papers carried the story the day after Captain Derby's arrival; within a week, it had appeared in nearly every paper in England.

The reaction was almost as violent in Britain as it had been in America. Speeches denouncing the British government thundered through the halls of both houses of Parliament. Crowds gathered in the larger cities threatening violent action to the ministry and promising aid to fellow Englishmen in America.

News of the supposed brutality of British troops shocked Londoners and provoked many editorials and letters denouncing the government's policy in America. There seemed to be no doubt in the minds of anyone except the men in government that the letter recounted the absolute truth regarding events in Massachusetts. The power of the printed word was as strong as any force in the unsophisticated world of the time.

The government attempted to counter the effects of the American letter by issuing an official notice to all British newspapers:

Secretary of State's Office, Whitehall, May 30, 1775

A report having been spread, and an account having been printed and published, of a skirmish between some of the people in the Province of Massachusetts Bay, and a detachment of his Majesty's troops, it is proper to inform the public, that no advises have as yet been received in the American Department of any such event.

There is reason to believe that there are dispatches from General Gage on board the *Sukey,* Captain Brown, which though she sailed four days before the vessel that brought the printed accounts, is not yet arrived.[3]

General Gage's dispatches finally arrived eleven days after the arrival of the *Quero*. Unfortunately and inaccurately, his account of the fighting agreed substantially with the American version. Unaware of the charges regarding the conduct of his troops, Gage had confined his report to the basic events and the objectives achieved, reporting that there were many dead and wounded.

A storm of criticism swept the entire nation. One hundred pounds sterling was collected for the relief of those Americans who had been wounded, as well as the widows and orphans of those killed.

In their race to reach England, both the *Quero* and the *Sukey* had passed the ship of the colonial ambassador, Benjamin Franklin, returning to America. For many years, Franklin had studied the problem of why American ship captains, such as Derby, were able to sail between America and England faster than English captains. He suspected that it was because the Americans understood the Gulf Stream and used it to increase their speed when sailing toward Europe. When sailing toward America, they steered so as to cross the stream at right angles, instead of running against it for days as the English did.

During the week of April 26 to May 3, 1775, sailing toward America, Franklin lowered a thermometer into the ocean for several hours each day. He noticed that the ship slid along the eastern edge of the Gulf Stream and then cut quickly across it to colder water. His thermometer supported his theory that the stream was not only warmer than the surrounding water but had its own color, contained more weeds, and did not sparkle at night. He immediately sat down and wrote a paper explaining his proposal:

> A vessel from Europe to North America may shorten her passage by avoiding to stem the stream, in which the thermometer will be very useful; and a vessel from America to Europe may do the same by the same means of keeping in it. It may have often happened accidentally that voyages have been shortened by these circumstances. It is well to have command of them.[4]

When Franklin's ship entered the harbor at Philadelphia on May 5, 1775, he learned for the first time of the bloody fighting at Lexington and Concord, which took place while he was in the mid-

Atlantic. His coming was celebrated as an omen of hope, and he was immediately chosen by the Pennsylvania Assembly as one of its deputies to the Second Continental Congress meeting in Philadelphia on May 10.

It took nearly a week for the news of Franklin's return to reach the American lines around Boston. British Lieutenant Barker noted in his diary:

> 16th. From 12 o'clock last night till 7 or 8 this morning, the rebels continued beating to arms, firing cannons and small arms, and making false fires; their reasons we have not yet learned.

> 17th. The reason for the above is said to be on account of Dr. Franklin's arrival at Philadelphia.[5]

On May 13, 1775, marching to the music of fifes and drums, twenty-two hundred men led by General Israel Putnam marched from Cambridge across Charlestown Neck and through the deserted streets of Charlestown to the top of Breed's Hill. From there, they marched to the ferry landing, massed along the shore, and yelled at the British aboard the warships, brandishing their muskets. Following this they formed into ranks and jauntily marched back to Cambridge. No shots were fired at them by the British, who stared at the display with amazement. Lieutenant Barker wrote that night:

> This afternoon between two and three thousand of the rebels came from Cambridge, marched over the Neck at Charlestown and up the heights above the town, where they kept parading a long time, then marched into the town and after giving a war-hoop opposite the *Somerset,* returned as they came.[6]

Putnam informed his officers that it was done to instill confidence in his men.

Gradually, the siege of Boston developed into a series of skirmishes involving the capture of livestock on islands in Boston Harbor. On May 17 a party of American riflemen fired on a British barge near Wheeler's Point, killing two sailors. Expecting retaliation from the regulars, four hundred militiamen were then sent to Lechmere Point to wait in ambush, but no British appeared.

Several days later a detachment of British troops in three vessels sailed for Grape Island seven miles southeast of Boston and north of Weymouth to procure a large quantity of hay stored there. The regulars landed on the island and started loading the hay on board their vessels. Suddenly, in the nearby village of Weymouth, church bells rang, guns were fired, and a large group of militiamen crowded onto a point of land near Grape Island. As the British ships fired on them the colonials answered with musket fire, although the range was too far. Three companies of General Thomas's troops soon arrived from Roxbury, and a number of boats were collected to transport them to Grape Island. However, the British left as the colonists closed in on the island; the Americans burned over eighty tons of hay to prevent its falling into British hands.

On Saturday, May 27, a detachment of forty New Hampshire troops under John Stark crossed over to Noddles Island and Hog Island by wading across from Chelsea. Their objective was to drive the livestock on the islands across to Chelsea through the shallow water or to destroy it and prevent seizure by British raiders. Stark's men arrived at 11:00 A.M. under a beautiful blue sky in which gulls wheeled overhead, wings spread against the gentle wind. The men waded chest-deep through the blue-green water onto the shining white sand and began to round up cows, horses, and sheep on Hog Island. Part of their force was dispatched to Noddles Island, where they set two Loyalist houses on fire and killed several cows.

Soon British naval vessels had spotted them, and a detachment of marines came wading through the white surf to drive them off. The Americans sprinted into a ditch as the marines opened fire and advanced a skirmish line across the island. When the British closed in on the ditch, the frontiersmen opened fire and drove them back, killing two men and wounding several others.

The tide was coming in and the Americans waded back to Hog Island through water up to their chins, British bullets kicking up bursts of spray among them. Under constant fire from marines on Noddles Island and from naval vessels, the New Hampshire troops on Hog Island finally drove off 300 to 400 horses, cows, and sheep through four feet of water to Chelsea. In the face of this continuous fire, John Stark sent a messenger to General Ward asking for reinforcements.

About 9:00 P.M. Israel Putnam arrived at the head of three hundred Connecticut troops with two artillery pieces. Dr. Warren, president of the Committee of Safety, arrived a few minutes later. When a British schooner ran aground within sixty yards of shore while attempting to come in close, Putnam waded out to the vessel and shouted for the crew to surrender. Two cannon shots sent him racing back across the beach. The Americans opened up with two field guns, and the British crew set fire to the schooner and abandoned it. At dawn a party of thirteen Connecticut men boarded the vessel and removed twelve new swivel guns and four four-pound cannon. The following day the British sent in reinforcements with artillery and began a sustained bombardment of the Americans on Hog Island. Under cover of the bombardment, they freed the burned-out hulk and towed it to Boston.

On May 30 a detachment of colonial troops again waded across to Noddles Island from Hog Island, burned the mansion of a Loyalist named Williams, and drove off six hundred sheep, twenty cows, and some horses. The next day the troops crossed to Peddocks Island and drove off five hundred sheep and thirty head of cattle. And on the night of June 2 Major Greaton took over eight hundred sheep and cattle from Deer Island and captured a barge and five British sailors from a man-of-war.

While these inter-island skirmishes were taking place, the British navy began capturing American-owned merchant ships on the Atlantic approaches to New England. On May 5 Captain Linzee of the man-of-war *Falcon* captured two American sloops in the harbor at Bedford. The Bedford militia promptly fitted out two sloops with thirty men and recaptured the captive ships after forcing the British sailors on board to surrender. Fifteen British prisoners were sent under guard to Cambridge.

On May 11 Captain Jeremiah O'Brien, an American schooner owner, fought a fierce sea-battle with a British schooner, the *Margaretta*, captured her, and brought his prisoners to Watertown.

A number of British officers and enlisted men captured during the Lexington-Concord fight were held in prison pens at Worcester. Artemas Ward offered these men a choice: they could be exchanged and return to their units in Boston, or they could join the Americans and seek work anywhere in the colonies. Three members of the Welsh Fusiliers and twelve Royal Marines chose to join the rebels and were released. They left Worcester seeking work, presumably never to return to England.

An exchange of prisoners took place on May 22, 1775, when Lieutenant Gould of the King's Own, wounded at Concord, was exchanged for an American militia lieutenant captured at Menotomy. Another exchange took place in Charlestown at noon on June 6. Dr. Warren and General Putnam met with Major Moncrief at the home of Dr. Foster in Charlestown to discuss the details. Moncrief and Putnam had fought together during the French and Indian War and were old friends. A friendly discussion took place over tea and sandwiches before the official exchange.

The British prisoners included Major Dunbar and Lieutenant Hamilton of the 64th, and Lieutenant Potter of the Royal Marines, who was wounded. Dunbar and Hamilton came down the road on horseback, with the wounded Potter riding in a chaise. Five wounded enlisted men followed in three chaises behind Potter. The eight Britons were taken to the ferry landing and rowed across the Charles to Boston.

After a short wait, a barge left the Boston ferry-way and eight Americans captured on April 19 stepped ashore at Charlestown: John Peck, James Hews, and James Brewer of Boston; Samuel Frost and Seth Russell of Cambridge; Joseph Bell, Elijah Seaver, and Caesar Augustus, a black man, from Dorchester.

HMS *Cerberus*, commanded by Captain Chads, arrived in Boston Harbor on May 25, 1775, bringing Major Generals Howe, Clinton, and Burgoyne from England. Additional ships continued to arrive with thousands of reinforcements, until Gage's force in Boston totaled nearly ten thousand men.

Boston papers reported that the *Cerberus* had met a ship leaving as she entered Boston Harbor. General Burgoyne shouted across the water, "What news of Boston?" When informed that Boston was surrounded by over ten thousand farmers, he asked, "How many regulars are there in Boston?" "Over five thousand," came the reply. Burgoyne shouted, "What! Ten thousand peasants keep five thousand King's troops shut up! Well, let us in and we will soon find elbow room." The phrase "elbow room" became a term of derision during the rest of the war and came back to haunt Burgoyne. Years later, after he surrendered his army at Saratoga, Burgoyne arrived as a prisoner in Boston. A large crowd gathered as he stepped onto the ferry-way from Charlestown, and an old woman perched on a shed above the crowd shrilled out, "Make way, make way, the General is coming! Give him elbow room."

General Gage met with the three newly arrived generals and discussed plans to break the colonial siege on Boston. After weeks of reconnaissance, the decision was reached on June 12 to land troops on Dorchester's Little Neck and Dorchester Heights, capture the town of Dorchester, and quickly encircle Roxbury to trap the American forces there against Boston Neck. To stop the attack the forces of General Thomas would have to come out into the open, where they could be cut down by artillery fire and attacked by the 17th Dragoons, whose arrival was expected shortly.

The assault was set for the night of Sunday, June 18. However, through some highly placed spy, the Americans received a copy of the complete British plan the night it was formulated. Artemas Ward called a meeting of the Committee of Safety the next day, and the committee appointed two officers, Colonel Palmer and Captain White, to proceed to Roxbury and confer with General Thomas regarding measures to forestall the British plan.

After considerable discussion between the officers and the Committee of Safety, it was fatefully decided to fortify Bunker Hill in order to forestall the coming British assault on Dorchester and Dorchester Heights. The consensus was that Gage would cancel his projected assault if American troops occupied and fortified strategic Bunker Hill.

At this time the reorganized American army consisted of three wings. The right wing under General Thomas was at Roxbury with four thousand Massachusetts troops and three artillery companies equipped with field guns and several heavy cannon. The center wing, under General Ward at Cambridge, contained fifteen Massachusetts regiments of infantry and a battalion of artillery loosely organized under Colonel Richard Gridley and quartered in various buildings at Harvard College. Connecticut troops under

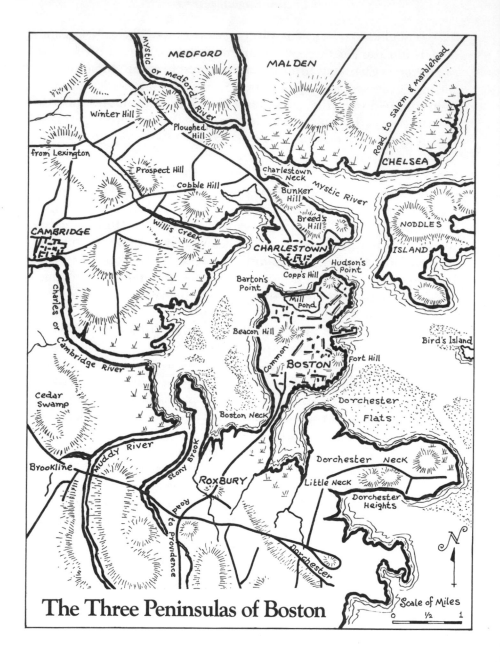

The Three Peninsulas of Boston

Scale of Miles

0   1/2   1

General Israel Putnam were stationed between Charlestown and Cambridge on Lechmere Point, Inman's Farm, Prospect Hill, and a tavern in West Cambridge. The left wing consisted of the New Hampshire brigade of two regiments: Colonel Stark's at Medford across the Mystic River from Prospect Hill and Colonel Reed's at Charlestown Neck with sentries at the two ferries to Boston and Malden. Charlestown Neck, an artificial causeway, was so low that it was frequently under water when the tide was in.

On Friday, June 16, a conference of colonial generals organized the occupation and fortification of Bunker Hill. Three Massachusetts regiments under colonels Frye, Bridge, and William Prescott — a total of 1264 men — were placed under the command of Colonel Prescott. A fatigue party of two hundred Connecticut troops drafted from several companies was under the command of Captain Thomas Knowlton. Major Scarborough Gridley's company of artillery and two field guns was included in the expedition.

Prescott was not to reveal his orders to anyone until his men had crossed Charlestown Neck. The entire force was ordered to proceed to Bunker Hill, build fortifications that would be planned on the spot by the chief engineer, Colonel Richard Gridley, and defend them until they were relieved. Colonel Gridley, a captain in the French and Indian War, had been responsible for bringing Wolfe's guns up the cliff to the Plains of Abraham.

The detachment paraded on Cambridge Common at 6:00 P.M. on Friday, June 16, and were addressed by President Langdon of Harvard, who closed with a solemn and inspirational prayer. At 9:00 P.M., the long column of men silently marched out of Cambridge toward Bunker Hill and what would be, for many of them, their last day on earth.

SIXTEEN

The Battle of Bunker Hill

ON THE NIGHT of Friday, June 16, 1775, Colonel William Prescott and a long column of men moved toward Charlestown and Bunker Hill, led by two sergeants carrying dark lanterns, open only in the rear. Several paces behind the sergeants marched Prescott, followed by his regiment, then those of colonels Frye and Bridge. They were followed in turn by two hundred Connecticut men under Captain Knowlton, forty-nine men of Major Scarborough Gridley's company of artillery, and two horse-drawn field guns. Wagons of entrenching tools brought up the rear. Obeying Prescott's strict orders to maintain silence, the men marched in file along each side of the road. Only Prescott knew the nature of their mission.

When they reached Charlestown Neck the men recognized the broad-shouldered frame of Israel Putnam among the mounted officers waiting for them. The wind whipped through their clothes as the column halted on the thirty-yard-wide causeway and Prescott ordered Captain Nutting to take his company of forty men and ten riflemen from Knowlton's regiment across Bunker Hill and Breed's Hill to the Charlestown waterfront a mile away. Keeping hidden, they were to observe the movements of the British warships.

Moving quickly, Nutting and his men were soon distributed along the shoreline. Across the Charles River, some 450 yards away, redcoated British sentries could be seen walking their posts, their fourteen-inch bayonets glistening with the reflections of nearby campfires. Riding their mooring chains nearby was a line of British warships. To the left, opposite Morton's Point, was the twenty-gun man-of-war HMS *Falcon;* farther south lay another twenty-gun ship, HMS *Lively.* Opposite the ferry landing was the powerful sixty-eight-gun HMS *Somerset.* Opposite the town of Charlestown, positioned to control the road leading from Charlestown Neck, were the twenty-four-gun HMS *Cerberus* and a number of floating batteries, including the armed transport HMS *Symmetry,* carrying nine-pound cannon and capable of coming in close through shallow water. Across the calm waters of the Charles the Americans heard reassurance that the British suspected nothing, as watches aboard ships called out, "All's well" at thirty-minute intervals through the night.

As Captain Nutting's men marched off to patrol the shoreline, Prescott led the remainder of his force across 113-foot-high Bunker Hill to the saddle-like ridge that connected Bunker and Breed's hills. Calling his field officers around him, he revealed his orders for the first time: to fortify Bunker Hill and defend it until ordered to withdraw.

An animated discussion then took place between Prescott, Putnam, and Colonel Richard Gridley, the chief engineer, regarding locations most suited to entrenchments. The orders specified Bunker Hill, but Putnam felt that to prevent the British from executing their planned assault on Dorchester, they must challenge them to an alternate course of action. He argued that fortifications on Breed's Hill, closer to Boston and visible to everyone in the city, would constitute a challenge that the British could not ignore and still preserve their pride.

Prescott, as commander of the operation, finally agreed to fortify Breed's Hill, provided entrenchments were also constructed on Bunker Hill in case a withdrawal to that point became necessary.

Quietly the men marched to the summit of Breed's Hill, only five hundred yards from the water's edge, and piled their packs and stacked their muskets by companies. It was midnight before the tools were distributed and the troops began their task. Colonel Gridley marked off the plan of fortification, a redoubt with four sides, each approximately forty yards in length. Soon over one thousand men were hard at work with spades and picks, digging into the rocky soil.

In four and a half hours of hard labor they had erected an earthen wall six feet high. Prescott, who also visited Nutting's men three times during the night to check on the watch along the river, joined in, as did the other officers. He knew that when the British discovered the fortifications at dawn they would bombard with intensive cannon fire from nearby ships as well as from the battery of twenty-eight-pound guns atop Copp's Hill across the river. Only strong, deep fortifications would protect his green men from the ordeal they would soon face.

The sun rose at 4:35 on June 17, and as it did a lookout on board HMS *Lively* spotted the fresh brown scars of the line of entrenchments against the green of Breed's Hill. The officer of the deck in turn notified the captain, who without waiting for orders swung his ship broadside to the target and opened fire at pointblank range.

The crash and concussion of the guns shook the city of Boston, and sleepy civilians and military men alike looked out their windows toward the hills of Charlestown. Soon hundreds of people poured through the streets toward the water's edge from Barton's Point to Hudson's Point, and hundreds more climbed atop roofs and church steeples, to watch the day's events unfold.

Admiral Graves, awakened by the pounding cannon, ordered the *Lively* to stop firing, but his orders were soon countermanded by General Gage, who ordered all ships in the harbor and the battery of heavy naval guns atop Copp's Hill to commence firing upon the American entrenchments. Anxiously the people of Boston watched as flashes from the guns sent black cannonballs arching across the water to fall like hail upon the Americans laboring on Breed's Hill. No men could be seen on the entrenchments; only spadefuls of brown dirt flying out of the trenches revealed the presence of the colonial troops. They were well protected by the deep ditches and were now strengthening the works by digging platforms of earth and wood for fire-steps. Disregarding the bombardment, they labored steadily until 8:00 A.M., when Private Asa

Pollard of Billerica, a member of Colonel Bridge's regiment, was decapitated by a cannonball. He was the first casualty, and his violent death shocked many militiamen into a realization of the imminent death and destruction. A junior officer rushed to Colonel Prescott to ask what should be done. "Bury him" was the terse reply. When a chaplain insisted on conducting services over the dead man, with a large number of soldiers gathered behind him, Prescott brusquely dispersed the group and ordered them to return to work.

Then, to inspire confidence in his shaken men, Prescott climbed atop the earthen parapet and walked leisurely around the entire length of the fortifications, inspecting the construction of new extensions from the redoubt. Viewers in Boston saw him outlined against the sky on top of the hill, and thousands of Bostonians cheered his courage as he calmly ignored the hail of fire from ships and batteries.

Turning to Councilor Willard, a Loyalist official standing behind him, General Gage asked if he recognized the officer who seemed to be in command of the entrenchments, which were visible from Gage's vantage point on the steeple of Christ Church. Using the glass Willard recognized his own brother-in-law. "He is Colonel William Prescott," he informed Gage. "Will he fight?" inquired Gage. "Yes sir, he is an old soldier and will fight as long as a drop of blood remains in his veins." Gage looked through the glass again and studied Prescott's tall, commanding figure. "The works must be carried," he said.

Soon other officers followed Prescott's example and mounted the parapet. The men were quickly back at work with renewed enthusiasm and became indifferent to the bombardment.

In spite of themselves, the British troops watching the hail of fire upon the American trenches were impressed. Later the *British Annual Register of 1775* stated, "The Americans bore this severe fire with wonderful firmness and seemed to go on with their business as if no enemy had been near."

As the morning wore on, the heat became intolerable to the exhausted men, laboring since midnight. Many had failed to bring provisions or water, and when no provisions arrived from Cambridge there was great discomfort from thirst and hunger. Colonel

Prescott later wrote in his memoirs, "Never were men in worse condition for action, exhausted by watching, fatigue and hunger, and never did old soldiers behave better."

Soon after the entrenchments were discovered, Gage called a meeting of his senior officers at Province House. The majority, led by Major General Clinton, favored moving a brigade by shallow-draft transports to the rear of the Americans on the Charlestown Neck. From the top of Bunker Hill they would have the entire American force atop Breed's Hill trapped as within a sack. Available for this action was the transport *Symmetry*, whose shallow draft and heavy nine-pound guns were ideal for the proposed landing upon the Neck.

Military men are agreed that Clinton's plan would have easily succeeded. Insufficient American forces were available to defend the Neck, and the attack could have resulted in the capture of Prescott's forces and possibly the end of American resistance.

Gage opposed Clinton's plan, however, for he quoted one of the military maxims of the period: "A commander should never place his army between two enemy armies." He argued that were he to land his forces on Charlestown Neck, he would be placing his own men between the American army strongly fortified atop Breed's Hill and the American army at Cambridge and Medford, which was superior to his in numbers.

Confident of the superior training and discipline of the British regulars, Gage decided to prove to the watching populace and the rest of the colonies that no resistance would defeat British courage and determination. To the dismay of many officers, he ordered a full frontal assault against the American position. Despite his recent experience at Concord and Lexington, Gage was certain that green American troops would not face and fight an orderly British attack.

At 9:00 A.M. Prescott called a council of war under the protection of the growing parapet. His officers reported that their men, worn out by the exhausting labor and lack of sleep, water, and food, were growing dissatisfied and mutinous. Some believed they were positioned in the middle of the British military forces as a sacrifice, to inflame the rest of the colonies against Britain. Ten days after the battle, colonial Private Peter Brown, a member of Prescott's regiment, wrote to his mother:

> The danger we were in made us think there was treachery, and that we were brought there to be slain, and, I must and will venture to say that there was treachery, oversight or presumption in the conduct of our officers.[1]

Prescott's officers urged him to request reinforcements and additional provisions, and to ask that his men be relieved by fresh troops, for they were in no condition to fight. Prescott rejected the advice to replace his men, but a messenger was sent to ask for fresh supplies. However, they never arrived.

Earlier, Putnam had asked Ward to send reinforcements, but Ward hesitated to weaken the rest of his army. He was certain that the British army would land troops on the Neck and trap the militiamen on the Charlestown peninsula. Thus he assumed that any fresh men sent to Prescott would also be captured by the British.

When Prescott's messenger, Major John Brooks, arrived at Cambridge with his request for provisions, Ward ignored the request and sent a messenger to John Stark at Medford asking him to send a third of his New Hampshire regiment to Bunker Hill. He then called an emergency meeting of the Committee of Safety and explained the danger of putting more men or material into the noose on top of Breed's Hill. His orders had specified the fortification of Bunker Hill, which would have commanded the Neck and made it impossible for the British to land there. Since those orders were disobeyed and Breed's Hill was chosen as the site, he would be unable to prevent a landing on the Neck, and any more men or supplies sent into Charlestown would only be sacrificed when the British made the logical landing behind them. Richard Devens argued that Prescott must be reinforced at whatever cost, because it appeared that the British were going to make a frontal assault. Devens convinced Ward that he must send more men to help Prescott, for the situation gave no indication that the British planned to land troops behind the peninsula. There was no activity among the British ships or transports except to bombard the Americans on Breed's Hill. HMS *Symmetry* was being used to fire on colonial reinforcements crossing the Neck rather than as a troop transport.

Consequently, Ward sent orders to Stark to bring two regiments of New Hampshire troops to Charlestown to join Prescott. Stark's own regiment and that of Colonel Reed immediately crossed the Mystic River and marched for Charlestown.

By 11:00 A.M. nearly all work had ceased on the entrenchments atop Breed's Hill. Tools lay stacked in the rear of the redoubt, and tired men slept in the trenches. Some wandered off and were not seen again. The main concern of everyone was the arrival of reinforcements and refreshments. In spite of the plan agreed upon eleven hours earlier, no work had been started on Bunker Hill.

Shortly after 11:00 A.M. General Putnam rode up to the redoubt and noticed a stacked pile of entrenching tools, which he asked Prescott to send to Cambridge, else they would be lost. Prescott replied that if he sent any of his men away with the tools, not one of them would return. When Putnam insisted, he sent a large party back with the tools, and while most of the men returned, some justified his apprehension.

Meanwhile, Major General William Howe, in command of the British attack on Breed's Hill, unhurriedly made his preparations. Ten companies of light infantry and ten of grenadiers were ordered to assemble on Boston Common, where they were soon joined by the battalion men of the 5th and 38th Regiments. The men were ordered to equip themselves with full field packs, blankets, extra ammunition, and provisions for three days. Howe's intention was to drive the Americans off the hill and pursue them into the countryside with grenadiers and light infantry, as other units drove toward Cambridge and destroyed the American army there.

In order to pin General Thomas and the American right wing in their positions, the British began a bombardment upon the Roxbury lines. The sun was directly overhead as British regulars marched to the music of fife and drum through the streets of Boston. Grenadiers, light infantry, and the 5th and 38th Regiments moved down King Street to board barges at Long Wharf.

The remaining grenadier and light infantry companies paraded with the 52nd and 43rd Regiments, then formed and marched along Ann Street, Fish Street, and Ship Street to the North Battery, six hundred yards north of Long Wharf. The 47th Regiment and 1st Battalion of marines under Major Pitcairn also proceeded to North Battery to await the return of the barges.

Organized into three divisions, each division's barges flew a different flag. Blue-flag division was ordered to land their troops first on Morton's Point. Yellow-flag division was to lay on their oars, and Red-flag division was to land their men as soon as Blue-flag pushed off from the Charlestown shore. Howe's orders were terse: "Any man who shall quit his rank on any pretense, or shall dare to plunder or pillage will be executed without mercy."

One sergeant, one corporal, one drummer, and twenty privates were left in Boston by each regiment to guard their respective encampments. As the regulars filed aboard the barges, several warships moved close to the Charlestown shore and opened a sustained fire on the American entrenchments. The guns of the *Falcon* and *Lively* swept the ground in front of the breastwork with grapeshot in order to kill any Americans who might be hiding in the tall grass. On top of Copp's Hill directing the fire of the naval battery were Major Generals Clinton and Burgoyne. The barges swept in unopposed, and high tide assured an easy landing.

With the renewed roar of artillery, everyone in Boston hurried again to their vantage point at the water's edge or on a rooftop. Many spectators had loved ones in the trenches atop the hill or among the red-uniformed men ferrying across the water.

The sky was blue and without a cloud as serried rows of naval barges, regulars standing at attention, slowly moved across the 450 yards of the Charles River. The long oars dipped and rose in perfect cadence, a picture of planning and precision. Americans watching from the top of Breed's Hill were apprehensive and impressed by the exact formations. As the barges moved majestically across the water, flashes of fire and smoke from the batteries and ships added to the awesome spectacle.

By 1:00 P.M. the British troops had completed their landings at Morton's Point, the northeast corner of the Charlestown peninsula. General Howe and Brigadier General Robert Pigot, his sec-

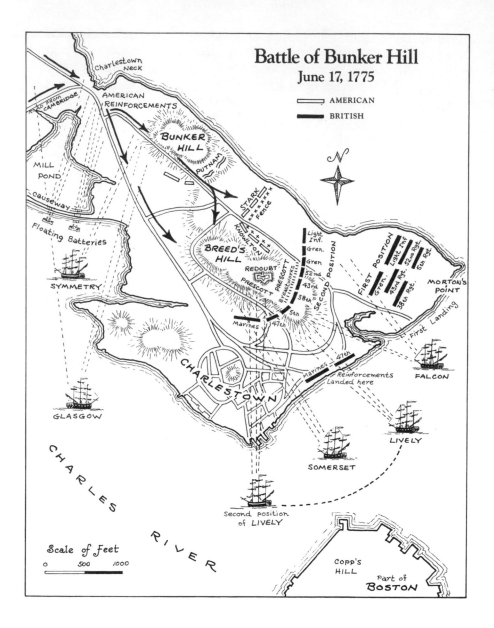

ond-in-command, carefully studied the American positions and sent a messenger to Gage requesting the 47th Regiment and 1st Marine Battalion as reinforcements. Howe carefully noted during his examination of the American positions that the area from the redoubt north to the Mystic River was unguarded and totally unfortified. Curiously, instead of immediately ordering an attack to take advantage of that American weakness, he ordered his troops to break ranks and eat lunch.

When Artemas Ward heard of the British landing from sweat-stained Israel Putnam, he ordered all but four regiments of his Massachusetts troops to march to Charlestown at once. Apparently, the British were committed to an inconceivable frontal attack upon Breed's Hill.

Similarly, Putnam ordered his Connecticut troops to race toward Charlestown. Unfortunately, however, many of the troops dispatched to the battle lines by Ward and Putnam never reached the fight. Some deserted, others dropped out to rest or moved so slowly that they arrived at the area under siege too late to participate.

Meanwhile, the colonial men atop Breed's Hill were sick with fatigue and the knowledge that they were facing death at the hands of the finest troops in the world. They felt deserted by their own army, for no reinforcements or provisions had appeared since they had begun work twelve hours earlier. At this crucial moment, several hundred new troops arrived, directed into the lines by Putnam, who was charging up and down the Cambridge–Charlestown Road to urge the laggard reinforcements on. Several members of the Committee of Safety also appeared, including Dr. Joseph Warren, clad in his best clothes and a fine, silk-fringed waistcoat. Although appointed a general several days before, he informed Prescott that he was there to fight as a private under his command. The appearance of reinforcements and the popular Warren boosted colonial morale and changed the mood of the men from deep dejection to one of confidence.

Prescott suspected that an attempt would be made to sweep around the undefended left flank, and at approximately 2:00 P.M. he ordered Captain Knowlton to move his two hundred Connecticut troops and the two field pieces of Major Gridley's artillery company from the redoubt down the northern slope of Breed's Hill to form a barrier there slanting diagonally toward Bunker Hill and the Mystic. Knowlton marched out and found a stone wall with two wooden rails along its top. Not far behind the wall was another similar wall, which Knowlton's men dismantled and used to strengthen the first fence. The openings in the fence were filled with grass, which would not stop a bullet but would effectively hide riflemen from view.

Meanwhile, high tide permitted the British floating batteries to come in close to the Neck from the south and sweep the narrow causeway with a hail of cannon fire just as Colonel John Stark entered the narrow Neck with his New Hampshire riflemen reinforcements. As cannonballs whistled by and hit the embankment, Captain Dearborn, one of Stark's company commanders, suggested that it might be wise to order the men to run across. In what has become a famous military maxim, Stark replied, "One fresh man in action is worth ten tired ones."

A vital factor in the defense of Breed's Hill was the fact that the area, owned by several farmers, was divided into many separate pastures, each barricaded with fences and stone walls. Yet nothing lay between the rail-and-stone fences and the rocky beach of the Mystic River nearly three hundred yards away. As Stark and Colonel Reed entered the area from Bunker Hill, Stark, the future victor in the Battle of Bennington, grasped the obvious need for fortifications and proceeded without orders.

He found a lane formed by two fences parallel to each other and had his men rip one apart to strengthen the other, while other men collected rocks lying along the beach and built a strong rock breastwork down to the water's edge. Additional rails were carried from other fences to reinforce the rock wall. Like Knowlton, Stark ordered his men to stuff armfuls of hay into openings in the fences to create an appearance of permanence.

Stark then measured off fifty yards from the front of the breastwork and had a number of stakes driven into the ground at that distance. Bits of cloth were tied to the top of the stakes.

By 3:00 P.M. the American positions were incomplete but defensible. On top of Breed's Hill stood the dirt redoubt built in the form of a square, each side about forty yards long. On the south side, facing the ferry, several projecting angles were dug in the wall to enable the defending colonial troops to enfilade, or fire laterally down the enemy line as it scaled the redoubt. A long trench dug at the front of the redoubt was piled with dirt to form a front line of defense. This breastwork, which allowed men to stand on firing steps behind the earth embankment and fire through slits cut into it, extended north a hundred yards and terminated in a sunken slough of brick kilns and clay pits. From the slough, Knowlton's rail-and-stone fence angled off 180 yards to the northwest, where Stark's rail fence ran three hundred yards northeast to the shore of the Mystic River.

South of the redoubt was a cartway along which a fence had been built. There, Captain Nutting's men constructed a fence similar to Knowlton's. Nutting assigned a number of men, including western Connecticut men with Pennsylvania rifles, to position themselves in the abandoned houses just below the redoubt to act as snipers. They were later joined by a number of New Hampshire riflemen.

Excepting Knowlton's men, the original detachment of men under Prescott was stationed in the redoubt. Just before the British attack began, Prescott was reinforced with numerous men from the regiments of Colonels Brewer, Nixon, Woolbridge, and Little, and Major Moore, in addition to a company of artillery under Captain John Callender. Firing from behind the breastwork proved to be extremely difficult for the inexperienced operators of Major Gridley's guns, who could manage only ineffective shots. It was decided to move both companies of artillery north of the redoubt to the right of Knowlton's rail fence. New reinforcements were sent behind the breastwork, where the thick walls offered good protection against cannonballs and musketry.

After the battle, it proved difficult to account for the positions of the various colonial companies and regiments that came across the Neck in the face of British naval gunfire, because as they reached Bunker Hill, Israel Putnam deployed them along the lines regardless of affiliation. Consequently the entire American force broke ranks and divided into small groups.

*

After finishing lunch, the main body of British troops waited patiently for the arrival of their reinforcements. Eventually, the 47th Regiment and 1st Battalion of marines, as well as several additional companies of grenadiers and light infantry, arrived by barge at the Sconce, where the Boston Naval Shipyard now stands. The total British force was then twenty-two hundred men.

Howe based his plan of attack in part on his earlier observations of the lack of troops on the American left. He would lead the grenadiers toward the right of the American breastwork, while light infantry companies swept to the right by columns along the shore of the Mystic River. The light infantry company of the 23rd, in the position of honor at the head of the rapidly moving columns, was to swing around the American left wing and move in between the rebels and Bunker Hill, to cut off their retreat. Howe and his grenadiers would penetrate the American line along the rail fence and swing in behind the undefended rear of the redoubt. Meanwhile, General Pigot, with the major force of the 5th, 38th, 43rd, 52nd, 47th, and the marines, would assault the breastwork and redoubt.

Before launching the attack, Howe sent out strong flanking parties and directed his artillery to pound the American lines. Immediately, the guns from the ships, the batteries on Copp's Hill, and the floating batteries began to fire as rapidly as the gunners could serve their guns, and a hail of iron rained down on the American positions.

Major Gridley's guns near the slough attempted to reply but were quickly knocked out of action by the accurate fire of the Royal Artillery. Before firing a shot, Captain John Callender pulled his troops out of their position behind Knowlton's fence and headed for Bunker Hill. When General Putnam ordered him to return to his post, Callender replied that the ammunition he was supplied with was too large for the bore of his gun. As the two officers discussed the situation, Callender's gun crews — actually riflemen unhappy with their role in the artillery — disappeared into the rank of Knowlton's Connecticut troops behind the rail fence. Callender left the guns where they were and fought with Knowlton's forces the rest of the day.

Nine days after the battle, Callender was tried by court-martial for cowardice in deserting his guns and was cashiered from the army. He instantly enlisted as a private in a company he had previously commanded, where his former fellow officers and enlisted men treated him with respect. A year later, fighting as a private at the Battle of Long Island, he distinguished himself and was recommended for a citation by General Washington, who ordered the court-martial sentence erased and restored Callender's commission to him. Callender, later captured by the British and exchanged, remained in the regular army of the new United States and was one of the few officers retained by Congress at the close of the Revolution.

As the storm of British artillery fire struck the American lines, British troops moved forward in a coordinated attack along the entire front in a line over a thousand yards long. On the extreme right the light infantry companies moved quickly along the rocky shore of the Mystic River and, unsuspectingly, headed straight toward the waiting New Hampshire riflemen hidden behind their fences. Advancing in column, the light infantry suddenly veered into a line as they became aware of the grass-covered barricade before them. The drums beat out the order to halt, and at another drumbeat the regulars fired a volley that went crashing over the heads of the concealed frontiersmen, who had the British in the sights of their deadly rifles. Again the British moved forward at a trot, and as they reached the line of stakes John Stark had planted in front of the breastwork, American drummers beat out the command to fire.

A solid sheet of flame flashed from the rail fence, and the entire front row of light infantry pitched forward into the grass, twisting and clawing in agony. Again a blast of fire burst from behind the fence, not in volleys but in steady sheets of flame, and the carnage increased. Marksmen behind the fence aimed at specific targets, particularly anyone wearing the epaulets of an officer. Nearly every British officer and sergeant was either killed or wounded within the first three minutes. The highly efficient rifle fire resulted because newly arrived colonial reinforcements went to work loading rifles and passing them forward to the frontier marksmen on the firing line.

The light infantry tried to advance but were methodically

slaughtered by the cool New Hampshire riflemen. John Stark moved about rapidly, pointing out targets, exhorting his loaders to quicken their delivery and occasionally firing his own rifle with telling effect. The remnants of the light infantry fell back in disorder from the deadly fire, stumbling over their dead and wounded, who only minutes before had represented the elite of the British army.

Some of Stark's men started to climb over the fence and pursue the fleeing troops but were prevented from doing so by their more prudent officers. However, the sight of the fleeing regulars caused wild excitement among the Americans, who jumped for joy and hugged and patted each other on the back.

As reinforcements arrived, Putnam ranged them alongside the Connecticut men. Captain Ford dragged Callender's abandoned guns to the rail fence and found some men who were able to load them.

General Howe, advancing at the head of the grenadiers, heard the firing to his right but was unaware of its outcome as he moved toward the rail fence concealing Knowlton's troops. When he and his men were one hundred yards from the fence, the colonial artillery opened fire, but the balls sailed over the heads of the disciplined grenadiers, who kept in perfect step as they marched to the tempo of their drums. Periodically these tall men in their bearskin hats were halted as they re-formed their lines, thrown into disarray as they scaled the many fences that enclosed the pastures on the hill. After regrouping, they would fire a volley, reload, and advance with studied deliberation at the regulation rate of eighty steps per minute. Among the Americans lying in wait, the tension became unbearable, and several men fired without orders. Putnam raced about, threatening to kill the next man who fired before ordered to do so.

As Howe and the grenadiers passed the 50-yard markers, Knowlton's rail fence seemed to explode in a continuous sheet of flame. The entire front rank of grenadiers fell, some hit by as many as three or four bullets. As the second rank tried to continue forward it ran into men who were dropping back. The result was a tangle of troops struggling before the merciless rifles of Knowlton's men, who dropped them in their tracks onto heaps of bleeding bodies.

The grenadiers refused at first to retreat but finally backed away, leaving the ground littered with dead and wounded. Howe himself was unhurt, but several officers were killed beside him, their blood spotting his white waistcoat and stockings.

Wild with excitement, the Americans watched as the grenadiers fled, and some, as the New Hampshire men had done, climbed over the fence to chase the retreating enemy; but Putnam, Knowlton, and other officers forced them back.

During the grenadier advance, the Royal Artillery had stopped firing, and a messenger soon informed Howe that twelve-pound balls had been sent to the artillery instead of the required six-pounders. Howe immediately ordered the guns to load with grape shot and move forward with the advance. When the gunners attempted to manhandle their guns over the muddy ground of the slough, they became stuck, so they dragged the guns into the brick kilns and fired grape at the Americans from there, although with little effect.

To the left of the grenadiers, the 43rd, 38th, 5th, 47th, and the 1st Battalion of marines moved forward in perfect precision to the beat of their drums. Advancing slowly, they kept in perfect alignment as they aimed for the breastwork and the redoubt. Soon, however, they ran into the maze of fences that had to be crossed, and the perfect lines disintegrated into groups of milling men scaling fences while weighted down with full packs, blankets, and provisions. They tried to push fence posts flat but found they had been sunk into the ground too deep.

Officers and sergeants were able to reorganize the men into straight lines only until they came to another fence. The first three hundred yards was a succession of such incidents. At one hundred yards' distance, the regulars fired a volley, then resumed their methodical advance.

The colonials waiting in the redoubt and behind the breastwork heard the roar of musketry and rifle fire off to their left but had no way of knowing what it all meant. Their officers were calling on them to hold their fire. "Do not waste your powder, fire low, aim at the spot where the white shoulder straps cross, pick off the officers." Captain Philip Johnson reported that it was there that Colonel Prescott called out, "Men, you are all marksmen; do not any of you fire until you can see the whites of their eyes."

As the regulars began to ascend the slope, the 38th Regiment, which was too far ahead, took shelter behind a stone wall near the foot of the hill. As the 5th marched up in regimental front of three ranks, the 38th moved out on their right flank. To the right of the 38th were the 43rd and 52nd, also in the regulation regimental front.

The British soldiers could see the round, crowned hats of the Americans waiting above the top of the parapet, but only a few scattered shots were fired at them. Prescott was furious at those men who could not control themselves and had fired without orders. Some of his officers jumped onto the parapet and kicked up those muskets that appeared to be prepared to fire too soon.

When the long red line reached the fifty-yard mark, Prescott gave the order to fire. It was repeated in a roll of drums, and with a flash and roar, a sheet of musket fire ripped from both the redoubt and the breastwork. Again, the entire first line of the advancing British regiments went down in agony, splattering the troops behind with blood, bone, and flesh. The second and third ranks held their ground with the ingrained valor of the British regulars, but the continuous fire from men protected by the earthworks soon covered the group with British dead and wounded. Sergeant Richard Pope of the 47th, who had marched to Concord with Lieutenant Colonel Smith, was in the front rank of his regiment. Although wounded, he survived to describe the scene in his diary: "The American fire resembled rather a continuous sheet of lightning and an uninterrupted peal of thunder than the explosions of firearms."[2]

When General Pigot reluctantly ordered his drummers to sound "retreat," his decimated regiments scrambled down the slope. The marines on the extreme left had been shattered by musket fire from the southern side of the redoubt in the same fashion as the other regiments, but in addition some men had been lost to sniper fire from the vacant houses behind them in the town of Charlestown.

Along the entire American position at the redoubt, the breastwork, and the rail fences of Knowlton and Stark, men with shining faces felt that they had met the supreme test of their lives, and won. They had faced the best soldiers in the world and sent them reeling in defeat.

ATTACK ON BUNKER'S HILL, WITH THE
BURNING OF CHARLES TOWN
American
National Gallery of Art, Washington
Gift of Edgar William and Bernice Chrysler Garbisch

This early painting by an unknown artist may be roughly contemporary
with a very similar print appearing in 1783 in Barnard's *History of England.*
We see in the foreground four British ships of war, Boston on the left
with firing from the British battery on Copp's Hill. Charlestown burns
spectacularly in the center, set alight by shells from Boston and by marines
from HMS *Somerset,* and the British troops advance up Breed's Hill
(mislabeled Bunker's Hill) toward the American redoubt.

The Garbisches, well-known collectors and patrons of art, were among
the earliest serious collectors of American primitives. They bought this
painting in 1949 and gave it to the National Gallery, where it is part of
the special Garbisch collection of more than three hundred paintings.

The leaders knew, however, that the British would be back, and they began to strengthen their lines. Putnam left the fence in an attempt to steer more men toward the battle lines.

At this juncture a lieutenant informed John Stark that his sixteen-year-old son, fighting with his father's regiment, had been killed. Stark ordered the man to be quiet, saying it was not the time to discuss personal affairs; happily, the report later proved erroneous.

Meanwhile, reinforcements braved the fire from British ships sweeping the Neck and arrived at Bunker Hill in the rear of the American battle line. Colonel Samuel Gerrish and his regiment were formed in ranks on the southern slopes of Bunker Hill waiting for orders to go into battle. But Colonel Gerrish evidently suffered a seizure and was unable to order the march down the slope. Putnam rode over and ordered him to move his men down to the rail fence, but the colonel fell to the ground, calling to his men to retreat before they were all killed. Putnam offered to lead the men forward himself, but many, unnerved by their colonel's actions, followed Gerrish back across the Neck to Ploughed Hill. However, Christian Febiger, the regimental adjutant, led a part of the regiment back toward the rail fence, where they joined Knowlton's men. Febiger, a former Danish lieutenant, had enlisted in the American army shortly after arriving from Denmark. He fought throughout the war, rising to the rank of colonel and winning a decoration for bravery in 1779 during the storming of Stony Point on the Hudson River.

Although a complaint was brought against him, Gerrish was not brought to trial, because General Ward refused to prosecute him. Several months later, however, Gerrish refused to fire on a floating battery that had attacked his position at Sewell's Point. General Washington had him arrested immediately, and when he was tried and found guilty of conduct unbecoming an officer on that occasion, as well as at Bunker Hill, he was dismissed from the army.

After the first British retreat at Breed's Hill, General Pigot reported to Howe that American riflemen hidden in some of the houses in Charlestown had fired into the flanks of the marines led by Major Pitcairn. Howe sent word to the battery at the top of

Copp's Hill to fire carcasses — hollow shells filled with incendiary material — into the town. Under the personal direction of Generals Clinton and Burgoyne this was quickly done. At the same time, a party of marines from HMS *Somerset* landed in the town and set fire to many of the houses. In a few moments Charlestown was ablaze, wooden church steeples burning like torches in the midst of a sea of fire.

The rooftops of Boston were solidly covered with people watching the tragic drama being played out across the river. The sight of tiny red figures advancing up the hill and falling into the grass as other small figures slowly retreated, accompanied by the crash and flame of gunfire, seemed unreal. Along the docks at Barton's Point, Perry's Shipyard, Grees's Shipyard, and Hudson's Point, thousands of people watched the battle with anguish and wonder. British soldiers not in action on the hill watched and cheered on their hard-pressed comrades. Among them were Lieutenant Frederick Mackenzie of the 23rd and Ensign Jeremy Lister of the 10th, who left his hospital bed to watch for hours from the dock at Hudson's Point.

Howe quickly reorganized his troops for a second attempt on the colonial fortifications. Marching in the same order as before, they were to continue the tactics of advancing, halting to fire and load, and then advancing again. This time, however, Howe ordered that the artillery, now supplied with the proper six-pound ammunition, move forward to within three hundred yards of the rail fence, in line with the breastwork on their left. From there they were to direct their fire down the length of the trenches as the 52nd, 43rd, 38th, and 5th Regiments attacked the breastwork from the front.

As the attack began, the precise red ranks again moved forward simultaneously along the front. Guns from the ships and batteries resumed their crescendo of noise and flame. This time, fully confident of their men, the colonial officers moved the stakes to within twenty-five yards of their position, ordering the militiamen to hold their fire until the British reached that point.

To spectators in Boston, the battle was an unforgettable sight.

To their left, the entire town of Charlestown was in flames. In the center, outlined against the grassy slopes of Breed's Hill, were precise lines of red-uniformed men advancing over green grass toward the entrenchments. On the crest of the hill, green- and brown-clad figures waited behind brown mounds of freshly dug earth, their long-barreled rifles and muskets extended across the parapets. Out on the brilliant blue water of the Charles River, white canvas–topped warships fired salvo after salvo into the American lines. Hundreds of spectators across the Mystic River on the Chelsea shore watched the British light infantry, what remained of it, courageously advance against American troops waiting behind the rock-and-rail fences.

As far away as the village of Amesbury, fifty-five miles to the north, people gathered on the Common as the wind brought the distinct boom of gunfire from the south. Worried friends and relatives who had men in Captain Currier's company tried to reassure each other. It was several days before they would learn that one man from Amesbury, David Harrington, had been killed and two others wounded.

Prescott believed that the British had set fire to Charlestown to use the smoke drifting across the American positions as a screen to protect advancing troops from American riflemen. If this was Howe's plan it was ineffective, for the wind blew the smoke in the opposite direction.

As the regulars advanced at their slow and deliberate parade-ground pace, they were halted every fifty yards to fire a volley. From its new position the Royal Artillery fired down the length of the breastwork, killing or wounding a number of Prescott's men. When the British reached the fifty-yard mark, they fired a volley that hit a number of men behind the rail fences and at the breastwork. The Americans, however, held their fire until the enemy reached the twenty-five-yard marker. At forty yards a British volley struck a number of Americans behind the fences. In addition to dozens of enlisted men, Colonels Brewer, Nixon, and Buckminster were wounded, and Major Moore was killed.

When the regulars reached the twenty-five-yard marker and the Americans opened fire, the position of the latter appeared to observers across the river as a solid line of flame. The effect on

British troops was devastating: Hundreds of men toppled forward into the flattened grass or were hurled backward, as though struck by invisible hammers. Survivors struggled forward as if pushing against the driving wind, but one after another fell, some silently, some in agony. On the right wing, General Howe led the light infantry in person against Stark's fence. Every man on his staff was either killed or wounded, but Howe miraculously escaped unharmed.

Finally, the British sounded retreat, and once again the British streamed down the hill pursued by the triumphant shouts of the Americans. On the left flank General Pigot's line had been nearly annihilated by the defenders of the redoubt; the surviving regulars retreated behind the covering fire of Major Pitcairn and his marines. Many men were hit by the deadly rifle fire still coming from the burning houses in Charlestown.

Atop Copp's Hill, Major General Clinton decided to intervene. Asking Burgoyne to explain to Gage that he felt compelled to act without waiting for orders, Clinton raced down the hill. He sent messengers speeding to the colonel of the newly arrived 63rd Regiment from Ireland and the commander of the 2nd Battalion of marines, ordering them to bring their men to him across the river. Commandeering a boat, Clinton had himself rowed across to Charlestown, where in a singular display of courage he landed on the beach under intense fire from American snipers concealed in the burning town. Two men of his boat crew were wounded, but Clinton, like Howe, was not to be hit that day. He raced along the waterfront collecting straggling troops, which he formed into units, issued fresh ammunition, and held in wait for the arrival of the 63rd and the 2nd Battalion of marines. In his "Narratives" Clinton writes:

> I then collected all the Guards and such wounded men as would follow — which to their honor were many — and advanced in column with as much parade as possible to impose on the enemy. When I joined Sir William Howe he told me that I had saved him, for his left was gone.[3]

Clinton had indeed saved the British army. Not only was Howe's left gone, but his right was virtually destroyed also. Both the light infantry and the grenadier companies had suffered over 90 percent casualties, and most light infantry units had fewer than seven men left out of thirty-five. The light infantry and grenadiers of the 23rd Welsh Fusiliers had been almost entirely destroyed.

Immediately after the second British charge, Israel Putnam seized a number of men, belatedly sent to Charlestown by Ward, and put them to work digging trenches on Bunker Hill behind Stark's rail fence. Major Henry Knox galloped across the fireswept Neck, bringing in new reinforcements. However, several regiments that were sent to Charlestown never arrived. Some claimed to have misunderstood their orders and gone to other areas. One regiment mistakenly marched to Lechmere Point, while another turned away from Charlestown and marched to Ploughed Hill. For several weeks after the battle, courts-martial were held charging various officers with cowardice and disobedience of orders.

Captain John Chester reported that when his company hurried out of Cambridge to Bunker Hill, there were three regiments ahead of him on the road. When Chester overtook them at Bunker Hill, the regiments had shrunk to company size as their men scattered "behind rocks, hay-cocks and apple trees." As he approached the battlefield, he passed small groups of men leaving. Some claimed that they had been up all night without sleep or food; others said that their officers had deserted them; and occasionally a large group of perhaps twenty men were seen escorting a single wounded man to the rear.

On top of Breed's Hill, however, Colonel Prescott had complete control of his men, and he encouraged them to hold the British one more time. If they could stop the next attack, he said, the British would never try again, and the battle would be won. But reports of the lack of ammunition made Prescott apprehensive for the first time. The only remaining sources of powder were several unfired artillery rounds left by Major Gridley. The men were ordered to break open the rounds and distribute the powder among themselves. Those whose muskets were equipped with bayonets were positioned at areas most likely to be breached. After warning his men not to waste any shots, Prescott ordered them to get as much rest as possible before the next attack.

*

Several of Howe's officers urged him to forgo another frontal attack and swing around by ship to land men on Charlestown Neck. But Howe, facing defeat and disgrace if he failed, was adamant. He reorganized his force and had the men divest themselves of their heavy packs. He then ordered that at no time during the assault were troops to be halted to fire. Only the bayonet was to be used, and they would attack in columns instead of in lines. The new objective was the breastwork and redoubt on top of Breed's Hill. The remnants of the grenadiers and light infantry would advance toward the rail fences as if to attack them, but at three hundred yards they were to veer left and join in the assault on the breastwork, avoiding getting entangled in the slough.

A division consisting of the 1st Battalion of marines and the 47th, reinforced by the 63rd and 2nd Battalion of marines, under Clinton and Pigot, were to assault the south face of the redoubt. The rest of the regiments were to drive straight for the top of the hill. The artillery was to move forward and rake the breastwork with grape until the regulars came within fifty yards, then change to solid shot so as not to endanger their own men.

As the drums began to pound out the charge, the British moved out against the enemy for the third time. Without the weight of their heavy packs, the regulars, in columns of companies instead of in lines, moved quickly up the hill like so many arrows. The Royal Artillery fired grapeshot and drove the Americans from the breastwork and into the redoubt. On the right, Howe led his light infantry and grenadiers toward the rail fence and then abruptly veered toward the now deserted breastwork. The Americans, down to their last few cartridges, waited until the British were within twenty yards and opened fire in a sheet of flame. Again the red figures pitched forward and the columns wavered, but this time others continued on and surged across the parapets.

The spectators in Boston saw a hail of rocks come from the American position, and the regulars, aware that the rebels were out of ammunition, crossed the parapet at three major points and, bayonets flashing, leaped into the crowded redoubt.

The fighting was hand to hand. Those few colonists with bayonets used them well; those without swung their muskets like clubs. Casualties on both sides were heavy. The first British soldier to cross the parapet was immediately shot and badly wounded. He was Lieutenant William Richardson, attached to the 18th Royal Irish Regiment fighting with Clinton's detachment. Thirty Americans were bayoneted to death in the redoubt. Leading his marines into the redoubt, Major Pitcairn was shot by Peter Salem, a black man from Framingham and a member of Colonel Nixon's regiment. Pitcairn fell into the arms of his son and died a few moments later after urging his marines on. British Lieutenant Colonel Abercrombie, a close friend of Israel Putnam during the French and Indian War, was badly wounded as he entered the redoubt on the northern side with his grenadiers. As he was carried away he said to one of his officers, "If you take Putnam alive, do not hang him, for he is a brave man." Abercrombie died later, as did many of the wounded. All the officers of Howe's staff were either killed or wounded, and of those wounded, only one — Lieutenant Page of the engineers — lived to return to England.

General Pigot was among the first to climb the parapet and leap into the redoubt. Dozens of his men followed. As the enclosure filled with the bayonets of the marines and battalion men, Colonel Prescott reluctantly gave the order to retreat. Some militiamen climbed over and down the western side; others squeezed through the northern outlet; and some fought their way through the British bayonets.

The close proximity of regulars and colonists ruled out the use of the musket by either side. Prescott, a superb swordsman and the last to leave the redoubt, cut his way out with his rapier, parrying repeated bayonets thrust at him by British marines. His clothes, pierced repeatedly by bayonets, were kept as a family treasure by his descendants. Clearing a way for several of his men, he escaped unhurt through the outlet.

Elements of the 47th Regiment circled around to the rear or west of the redoubt, while the grenadiers encircled the area from the north. Thus as the Americans raced between the two groups toward Bunker Hill, the regulars did not fire on them for fear of hitting each other. However, British troops inside the redoubt lined the western rim and fired upon the fleeing men.

Dr. Joseph Warren was hit by several bullets and killed instantly. Colonel Richard Gridley, chief engineer of the army, was badly wounded, and Colonel Ebeneezer Bridge, one of the original regimental commanders in the redoubt, was wounded by a saber cut in the neck. Colonel Thomas Gardner was torn apart by a cannonball as he tried to form a line to cover the retreat.

At Knowlton's rail fence, men closest to the slough started to drop back to their left as British troops swung in behind the redoubt. Keeping their line facing the enemy, they picked up other men along the fence as they worked their way slowly back toward the fortifications at Bunker Hill.

Soon after the British bombardment had started, General Artemas Ward sent Lieutenant Colonel Jonathan Ward's regiment to Charlestown. As a safeguard against a possible attack from the Boston Neck toward Roxbury, only half of the regiment was sent. Nineteen-year-old Private Simon Fobes marched in a double file of men toward the sound of the guns. No attempt was made to keep in step as they hurried along. Simon had been in the center of the column when they began, but upon reaching Charlestown Neck he was amazed to discover that he was now at its head, and half of the detachment had vanished.

They crossed the partly flooded manmade causeway under a hail of gunfire from the British floating batteries and ships. As they started across the slope of Bunker Hill, musketballs and cannonballs whistled by them, and a bullet struck Simon's musket near the lock, tearing off part of the wooden stock. Someone shouted for them to fall in behind a nearby rail fence stuffed with hay. Troops passed them on the way to the rear carrying badly hurt men covered with blood. Simon, controlling a wild desire to run away from the horrible scene, came to the fence and aimed his musket at the advancing British troops. When he fired and saw the man he had aimed at fall forward, Simon realized he was "as calm as a clock." He loaded and deliberately fired again, and he continued to fire until, while loading his musket, he happened to look around and to his astonishment saw his fellow soldiers running at full speed toward the rear. Having heard no orders to retreat, Simon turned toward his sergeant standing nearby to ask him what to do. At that instant the sergeant started to run.

Then Simon saw the company of British troops approaching

rapidly from his rear. He completed loading his gun, fired at the regulars, and sprinted up over the saddle toward the Neck. Musketballs screamed over his head as he raced down the other side of Bunker Hill.

Caleb Haskell of Newburyport was another militiaman whose regiment was sent to Charlestown after the British landing. He fought inside the redoubt and was able to scramble across the western parapet and escape. Haskell reported that cannonballs from the ships and batteries "were as thick as hailstones."

John Greenwood, the fifer in Captain Bliss's company, had been given a furlough pass to Andover to visit his aunt. On the day of the battle he returned to find his company gone. He briefly saw his mother, who had come over from Boston by special permission from General Gage, but could only spend a short time with her. Greenwood kissed his mother goodbye and hurried along the Charlestown Road toward the sound of gunfire. As the fifteen-year-old fifer crossed the Cambridge Common, he saw many wounded men brought back from the battle lying on the grass:

> Everywhere the greatest terror and confusion seemed to prevail. As I ran along the road leading to Bunker Hill it was filled with chairs and wagons bearing the wounded and dead, while groups of men were employed in assisting others, not badly injured, to walk. Never having beheld such a sight before, I felt very much frightened and would have given the world if I had not enlisted as a soldier; I could positively feel my hair stand on end. Just as I came near the place a negro man, wounded in the back of his neck, passed me and, his collar being open and not having anything on except his shirt and trousers, I saw the wound quite plainly and the blood running down his back. I asked him if it hurt much as he did not seem to mind it; he said no, that he was only going to get a plaster put on it and meant to return. You cannot conceive what encouragement this immediately gave me; I began to feel brave and like a soldier from the moment, and fear never troubled me afterward during the whole war.[4]

John Greenwood found his company attached to Colonel John Patterson's regiment stationed along the rail fence. Captain Bliss, who had given him permission to visit his aunt, was surprised but happy to see him. Men crowded around him and pounded him on the back when he told them that he had run all the way from Cambridge to be with them. With aid from two field guns, Patterson's regiment held their position on the road along the southern slope of Bunker Hill, leading toward the Neck. As retreating troops passed through their lines, the regiment withdrew across the Neck and began to fortify Prospect Hill.

Captain John Currier's company from Amesbury was stationed in the redoubt during the British attack. His company consisted of fifty-four men, including two black soldiers, Sipeo Grave, a slave belonging to Benjamin Barnard, and a servant of Eliphant Currier named Robert. During the retreat David Harrington was killed and Lieutenant Wells Chase was wounded, both by British bayonets. The rest of the men escaped under heavy fire. Currier was always proud of the fact that his men, unlike many under similar circumstances, carried away most of their equipment "with the exception of three muskets, one bayonet and only four blankets."

The Ipswich company of Captain Wade and Lieutenant Hodgins, part of Colonel Moses Little's regiment, were instrumental in the successful colonial retreat. They were ordered to march to Charlestown at 4:00 P.M., and when they arrived on the field, the British had just broken into the redoubt. Many timid and leaderless men atop Bunker Hill were reluctant to plunge into the tornado of fire. Stark's men were solidly holding their positions, but some of Knowlton's men were forced off their positions by British troops threatening to cut off their retreat. Hundreds of other militiamen streamed down the slopes of Breed's Hill behind the redoubt. In the face of this chaos, Colonel Little marched his regiment straight into the line of the British advance and set up a firing line that enabled most of the Americans to escape toward the Neck. Casualties in Little's regiment, which was fighting in the open, were extremely heavy. For example, Captain Nathaniel Warner's company lost seventeen men killed or wounded out of twenty-three in the field.

Other troops acquitted themselves with less merit. Colonel James Scammons's regiment from what is now Maine failed to advance beyond Bunker Hill. Scammons was tried for disobedience to orders but was not convicted. Colonel John Mansfield's regiment was ordered to Charlestown but marched to Cobble Hill instead and stayed there to "protect artillery." Mansfield was later tried for remissness and backwardness and sentenced to be cashiered and rendered unfit to serve in the Continental army. However, many felt his sentence was too severe, that he was guilty only of error caused by inexperience.

At the rock-and-rail fence of Stark and Reed, the long Pennsylvania rifles of the Scotch-Irish New Hampshire marksmen prevailed through all the British assaults. After the battle, the area in front of their position was littered with dead and wounded regulars to a distance of nearly two hundred yards. These men saved the day for the Americans, for they covered the retreat of the colonials behind Bunker Hill and on to the Neck and overcame a threat by the 47th Regiment and the grenadiers to encircle and cut off colonial troops. As the flood of running men swung behind them, the New Hampshire and Connecticut troops left their fence and slowly gave ground over Bunker Hill, still dominating the ground before them with the deadly accuracy of their rifles, which could kill a man at two hundred yards. By comparison, the Brown Bess musket of the British, useless beyond seventy yards, slowed the British pursuit and drained its momentum.

During the colonial retreat, Israel Putnam galloped from one side of the retreating line to the other, directing men to the safest route. Americans crossing the low-lying Neck came under fire from floating batteries, from the guns of HMS *Glasgow,* and from the armed transport *Symmetry* firing north from Charles River Bay west of Charlestown. Many were killed or wounded during this period, perhaps the worst in terms of American casualties.

By 5:00 P.M. the British had taken possession of Bunker Hill as well as Breed's Hill. Clinton tried to persuade Howe of the urgency for striking toward Cambridge immediately while the Americans were obviously disorganized and out of powder. Nonetheless, Howe was mindful of the firepower and accuracy of the American riflemen, and he decided to hold his present position and put his men to work digging a line of entrenchments atop Bunker Hill, where Percy had fortified on the night of April 19. There he set up two field pieces that fired on the militiamen who had retreated to Winter Hill.

Colonel Prescott, furious at what he considered the lack of proper support during the attack, galloped to Cambridge to confront General Artemas Ward. Prescott charged that had he received additional ammunition and a few more men, he would have had a victory.

Ward explained carefully that he had no assurance when the battle began that the British intended to make a frontal assault on Prescott. Thus he had to consider the possibility of a British attack on Cambridge by way of Charlestown Neck or Roxbury. Until the battle developed, Ward could not spare men or ammunition.

Prescott was entirely dissatisfied with Ward's explanation or the lavish praise that he received for his role in the siege. He demanded that Ward give him three regiments, a total of fifteen hundred men, with which he promised to retake Charlestown or die in the attempt. Ward refused, and the colonel stormed away. For the rest of his life Prescott felt that he would have won the Battle of Bunker Hill if his exhausted and hungry men had been properly supplied with ammunition. He pointed out that even during the final assault, the British had wavered under the first blast of American fire, and if the defenders had possessed the ammunition to sustain it, the British would have been driven back a third time and would have withdrawn to Boston.

Some military men are of the opinion, however, that had the British been forced down the hill they would have executed the maneuver appropriate in the first place — the occupation of the Neck to the rear of the American position. With the available firepower of the British ships and floating batteries, they would have been able to "bag" the entire American force and probably end the Revolution almost before it began.

SEVENTEEN

Aftermath of Battle

THE BATTLE OF BUNKER HILL opened with the British assault at 3:30 P.M. and ended ninety minutes later when they occupied the top of Bunker Hill overlooking Charlestown Neck. In that period the British lost 226 killed and 928 wounded, a total of 1154 men. Over one man in two was either killed or wounded, a casualty rate of 52 percent.

During the night the British wounded were collected by squads of men using lighted torches. The men were loaded into carts and driven through the still-smouldering streets of Charlestown to the ferry landing, where they were reloaded into waiting barges and rowed across to Boston. At the ferry-way located between Grees's Shipyard and Hudson's Point, hundreds of people waited, their pale faces shining in the light of flickering torches, as the bloody and dismembered bodies were gently loaded into waiting wood carts and chaises. Anxious eyes searched each face, handkerchiefs clenched in white-knuckled fists. Occasionally a scream of recognition pierced the torch-lit night.

Only the officers were brought to Boston to be buried. Enlisted men were buried in Charlestown in large pits along Breed's Hill. As the carts and carriages filled with wounded soldiers and dead and wounded officers trundled through the dark, narrow streets behind torch-wielding soldiers, Americans peering from behind darkened drapes were caught up in the pain and tragedy. A witness reported in a letter written several weeks later: "In the first carriage was Major Williams, bleeding and dying, and three dead captains of the 52nd Regiment. In the second were four dead officers."[1]

A total of twenty-seven British officers were killed and sixty-three wounded; of the wounded, many would die in the weeks ahead. Among them were Lieutenant Colonel Abercrombie, hit while entering the breastwork at the head of his grenadiers; Major John Pitcairn of the marines; and Major Spendlove of the 43rd. Spendlove, a forty-year veteran of the British army, had been wounded three times previously in his career and had been with Wolfe on the Plains of Abraham and with Israel Putnam at the capture of Havana.

On Monday morning, June 19, the dead officers were buried privately with appropriate services in various churches and churchyards of Boston. Pitcairn was buried in a vault under Christ Church on Salem Street.

The protection afforded by earthen breastwork and rock-and-rail fences considerably lightened the American casualties. The colonists lost 140 killed, 271 wounded, and 31 captured. The captured were nearly all badly wounded men who could not get away during the final retreat, and twenty of them died of their wounds or neglect and brutal treatment when they were taken to the Boston Gaol on Queen Street.

The man responsible for the treatment of American prisoners was Joshua Loring, an American Loyalist who fled his large home in Roxbury with his wife, Elizabeth, to escape the patriot mobs rampaging through the countryside. His abysmal treatment of captured Americans in Boston and New York earned him the hatred of all the colonies. He would have undoubtedly been hanged as a war criminal had he been captured by colonial troops.

Loring refused to send for doctors or to supply the men with bedding, food, water, or attention until forced to do so by General Gage, who was unaware of the conditions for nearly a month.

Many of the twenty who died under Loring's brutality might have been saved. One such was Lieutenant Amaziah Fawcett, captured while trying to escape the redoubt. His wounds were not serious, but the combination of a lack of soap and water, food, drinking water, and medicine soon caused his death.

Among the wounded in Boston Gaol was Lieutenant Colonel Moses Parker, second-in-command of Bridge's regiment. A musketball tore through his knee during the final assault on the redoubt, and he was allowed to lie on the floor of his bare cell without food, water, or medical attention for over a week while his leg became infected and swollen to twice its normal size. British surgeons, making a belated inspection, found him and amputated his leg to save his life. It was too late, however, and he died on the fourth of July at age forty-three.

The case of Captain Benjamin Walker was nearly identical. Walker led a party of riflemen to harass the British landings at Morton's Point. As he dropped back to the Mystic River bank to direct sniper fire, he was wounded in the leg and captured. Refused food, water, and medical attention for nearly two weeks, he died after a belated attempt by surgeons to save his life through amputation.

Even in the permissive society of the eighteenth-century British army, the actions of Joshua and Betsy Loring shocked the hardbitten British officers. Within a few days of his arrival in Boston, Sir William Howe had met Mrs. Loring at a gambling club frequented by British officers. Their mutual passion for gambling apparently drew them together, and several days later Betsy Loring moved into General Howe's quarters as his mistress. Not long afterward, the complacent Joshua Loring joined them, and within a week Howe had appointed him to the profitable post of commissioner of prisoners.

Three months after the battle, just before he was relieved by General Howe, General Gage appointed Loring chief auctioneer of the City of Boston. A great amount of confiscated rebel property was being disposed of by auction, and it was common knowledge that Loring found the position extremely lucrative. Although it was rumored that Howe received a share of the profits, that has never been substantiated.

When the British evacuated Boston in March 1776, the Lorings accompanied General Howe to Halifax. From there they all traveled to New York, where Loring again served as commissioner of prisoners until 1778. When Howe and his army went to Philadelphia, Betsy accompanied him and later returned with him to New York.

Loring's tenure as commissioner of prisoners in New York was marked by such wholesale cruelty to American prisoners that it earned him an unenvied place in history. He introduced the use of abandoned ship hulks to house prisoners, and there, amid filth, rats, neglect, and lack of food and water, American troops perished at a rate of over 90 percent. Little better was an infamous sugar warehouse in New York City, where hundreds of men died of disease and starvation.

Accounts of Betsy Loring, who flaunted her relationship with the commander-in-chief, appear in many journals and diaries of the period. A published poem called the "Battle of the Kegs" openly charged that Howe neglected his duties because of his inability to leave her bedroom. It was common gossip that he was unable to concentrate on the destruction of Washington's army because most of his time was spent with his "delectable Betsy." When Howe was recalled to England, both Lorings also left for England, where they disappeared into the British Isles.

In Charlestown the job of burying the American dead left on Breed's Hill was under the direction of British Captain Sloan Laurie, who commanded a large detachment of soldiers for this purpose. He was the same Captain Laurie who had commanded three light infantry companies at North Bridge at Concord on April 19. His men started to collect the bodies at a central point but gave it up as too time consuming and decided to bury them in pits wherever they were found.

Not far from the redoubt, some troops found the body of Dr. Joseph Warren. One of them stripped the expensive clothes from the body and brought them to Laurie, who removed several letters from the pockets and returned the garments to the soldier. Americans reported that several days later a soldier was hawking Warren's clothes in the town market.

Laurie ordered the naked body of Warren to be buried in a hole nearby that already contained the body of an American wearing a frock coat. The next day Laurie wrote a letter in which he said: "I stuffed the scoundrel with another rebel into one hole and there he and his seditious principles may remain."[2]

One of the letters that Laurie found on Warren's body incriminated a young man named John Lovell, son of one of the staunchest Loyalists in Boston. The letter, from young Lovell, included an accurate account of the strength of the newly arrived 17th Dragoons and 63rd Regiment and their positions of deployment. Further investigation revealed that John Lovell's brother Benjamin was employed by the British as a clerk at the artillery depot from which the wrong-calibered ammunition had been issued to the British artillery during the Battle of Bunker Hill. It also revealed that Colonel Cleaveland, chief of artillery, was conducting an intimate relationship with John Lovell's two younger sisters.

John spent the following nine months in Boston Gaol and was taken to Halifax when the British left. His brokenhearted father visited his imprisoned son and attempted to change his point of view, but without success. Ultimately John was sent to England as a prisoner and later exchanged.

The death of the highly respected Warren plunged all of the colonies in deepest mourning. He had fought as a volunteer soldier, even though appointed a brigadier general several days before by the Provincial Congress. Early on the morning of June 17 he returned to Cambridge and took to his bed with a splitting headache. When informed of the British landings on Morton's Point, Warren ignored his pounding headache and rushed to meet with the Committee of Safety. After trying to convince Ward of the need to send reinforcements to Charlestown, Warren secured a musket and ammunition and rode a horse to Bunker Hill.

There he met Israel Putnam near the rail fence where Knowlton's men were preparing for the British attack. Warren asked "Old Put" where he could be most useful, and Putnam pointed to the top of Breed's Hill, where they could see the redoubt bristling with riflemen. When Putnam remarked that it was protected by thick earthen walls, Warren looked him in the eye. "Don't think that I seek a place of safety; but tell me where the onset will be the most furious." Putnam hurled his finger toward the redoubt.

"That is the enemy's objective," he said. "If it can be defended, the day is ours!" Warren gripped his hand and started up the hill.

When Prescott met Warren entering the redoubt, he offered him command, but Warren refused, saying that he came only to fight and bring encouragement to the weary, hungry troops who had begun to feel forsaken. He also was there to tell them that over two thousand reinforcements were on their way. He felt that his presence was necessary, for it was the Committee of Safety that had put those men there, perhaps to die; as president of the committee the least he could do, Warren said, was to join them and share in their fate.

During the British assault, Warren fought shoulder to shoulder with the troops along the parapet, firing his musket at the advancing regulars from the fire-step until he had used all of his ammunition. He was one of the last to leave when Prescott ordered the retreat, and as he left the redoubt, British Major John Small, who later became a major general in the British army, recognized him from the top of the parapet and called him by name to stop and give himself up. Warren turned his head when he heard his name called and, at that moment, a ball smashed into his face, killing him instantly.

Following the British evacuation of Boston, an attempt was made to locate Warren's body and give him an appropriate burial. Dr. John Jeffries, while attending to wounded regulars on Breed's Hill the day after the battle, had seen Warren's body buried with another man "wearing a frock coat." Several days later he casually mentioned the incident to a friend, and after Jeffries left for Halifax with the British fleet the following year, the friend led Warren's brothers to the approximate area. Several graves were opened with no success before they came upon two skeletons, one with a crushed skull and no clothes around him, the other clothed in the remains of a frock coat. Unable to identify the body as their brother, Warren's brothers sent for his friend, Paul Revere, who immediately identified the body as Warren's by two ivory-and-wire artificial teeth he had personally fitted for Warren several days before the battle.

Warren was given a full Masonic funeral and was buried at King's Chapel Burying Ground beside many leading figures of

Boston. His remains were later placed in the family vault under St. Paul's in Boston.

Another officer who fought as a private soldier at Bunker Hill was seventy-year-old Colonel Seth Pomeroy, who rode a borrowed horse to Bunker Hill in time to join John Stark's men at their rock-and-rail fence. Like Warren, Pomeroy had been commissioned as a general by the Provincial Congress several days before, though he had not yet received the official document. He carried a hand-made musket that he had used thirty years before at Louisbourg. During the British attacks he fired his ancient weapon until a British ball shattered the stock, and he carried it back with him in the retreat across the Neck. When he heard of Warren's death, Pomeroy remarked:

> I think it very strange that Dr. Warren, the young and chivalrous soldier, the eloquent and enlightened legislator, should die, and I, old and useless, should escape.[3]

The American wounded that were removed from the battlefield at Breed's Hill by their companions were collected along Charlestown Neck and carted across under a barrage from British ships firing from the south. They were taken along rutted roads to Cambridge, where the houses of Governor Oliver and the Reverend Samuel Cook had been converted into hospitals. It was well after dark before the wounded began to arrive, and as long rows of desperately injured men were placed on the rough ground of the fields around the homes, moaning and hoarse cries for help filled the night. The eight doctors in attendance were swamped by the sheer numbers of men in need of care. Several doctors stumbled through the darkness aided by men holding flaming torches aloft. They tried to determine which men were capable of surviving. The others were left to die.

Most of those men died during the following two days, and a cemetery was begun Saturday night on the grounds in front of the Oliver house. For the next two months, men died of their wounds and were buried there.

During the bloody Battle of Bunker Hill, some men, like William Prescott, reached the heights of courage and adulation.

Others lived the rest of their lives in disgrace as a result of their actions.

On the British side, General William Howe is acknowledged as a most valiant soldier. Despite his questionable moral character, his courage and determination on June 17, 1775, have earned him a well-deserved place in English military history. The conduct of most British officers and men was unbelievably fearless. Marching into the teeth of a fiery stream of lead, few men flinched or failed to follow orders. One company of grenadiers had all of their officers killed or wounded, including sergeants and corporals. With only five men left, the most senior private took command and led his four surviving comrades toward the rail fence. When the order to retreat was sounded on the drums, they retreated in good order.

On the American side, perhaps no man in history had been more idolized during his lifetime than Colonel William Prescott. The tall, handsome soldier, cool and competent to the last, inspired his exhausted and hungry men to hold their fire until the proper moment and then destroy successive waves of the finest assault troops in the world. Prescott was the heart of the defense. In other areas of the battlefield men fought individually or in platoons. But within the redoubt and breastwork there was a unity of command under Colonel Prescott that astounded all who heard of it.

Israel Putnam also added to his luster on that bloody day. He met Prescott's detachment at midnight on Charlestown Neck, was instrumental in the conference that decided to fortify Breed's Hill, and galloped to Cambridge and back to Charlestown when the sound of cannon fire boomed across the early dawn. He rode his horse up Breed's Hill amidst the plunging shot and returned to Cambridge in an attempt to secure reinforcements and supplies for Prescott. Unable to convince Ward, he returned to Breed's Hill.

When Howe's regiments landed at Morton's Point and it became obvious that the British intended to launch a frontal attack upon the redoubt and had no intention of landing on Charlestown Neck, Putnam sped to Cambridge to explain the implications of the new situation to Ward. Starting the flow of reinforcements toward Charlestown, he dashed to the Connecticut encampment and ordered them to Bunker Hill. He then raced back to the battlefield to direct the arriving men into the lines.

As the first British assault swept across the green fields, Putnam took his place at the rail fence with the Connecticut troops under Knowlton. The first attack shattered, he returned to the slope on Bunker Hill, four hundred yards behind the line of rail fences, in an attempt to force the horde of reluctant men huddled there to advance toward the fences and take their places beside the fighting men. Only partially successful by the time the second assault was launched, Putnam returned to his place in the lines for the next attack.

During retreat he was the central figure on Bunker Hill, directing the rear guard that succeeded in slowing the British pursuit. He was one of the last to leave the peninsula, crossing the Neck under fire and leading several regiments of volunteers and a great many unattached soldiers up Prospect Hill. There he put them to work digging a line of entrenchments that discouraged General Howe from ordering the pursuit that might have ended the American Revolution. The sight of long lines of American muskets and rifles on earthen parapets pointing toward him from the dominating heights of Prospect Hill convinced Howe, shaken by enormous casualties, to stop and dig in against the possibility of a counterattack.

Also during the retreat, Colonel Thomas Gardner, a member of the Provincial Congress and a veteran of the French and Indian War, led part of his regiment, newly arrived from Lechmere Point, up toward Breed's Hill to provide a shield for the men abandoning the redoubt. While advancing, Gardner was struck by a cannonball that tore away part of his body. He was carried away and died several weeks later at the Oliver house in Cambridge.

Gardner's regiment continued up the hill under the command of Major Michael Jackson and stopped the British pursuit in a hand-to-hand struggle along the western slope of Breed's Hill. It was there that Major Jackson killed a British officer in individual combat and received a ball in his side that was partially deflected by his sword belt. The officer he killed had served with him sixteen years before during the war with France.

Colonel Richard Gridley, who had scratched out plans for the redoubt and breastwork with a stick the night before the battle, became ill shortly after 10:00 A.M. and was forced to leave the hill. However, when the first attack began he returned to the breastwork, where he was wounded by a piece of grapeshot near the close of the fighting. Gridley was carried to a sulky at the rear of the redoubt, but the horse was unable to pull the vehicle because one of the wheels was wedged between some large rocks. To lighten the load, Gridley was lifted out and placed on the ground while the men dislodged the wheel. Suddenly two cannonballs crashed into the sulky, smashing it to fragments and killing the horse. Gridley was carried to another cart and escaped capture.

Later, Gridley was promoted to major general, and on September 20, 1775, General Washington appointed him commander of the Continental artillery. He was subsequently reassigned to the position of chief engineer of the army, when young Colonel Henry Knox, the former bookseller of Boston, replaced him as commander of artillery.

One of the foremost colonial soldiers at the Battle of Bunker Hill was Captain Thomas Knowlton of Connecticut. When only sixteen, he had enlisted as a private in a Provincial regiment and fought throughout the French and Indian War. He rose through the ranks to become an officer before he was twenty-one, serving under the command of Major Israel Putnam. Following that war he had returned to Connecticut to become a successful farmer.

Knowlton was personally selected by Putnam to lead the 200-man fatigue party that accompanied Prescott on the night of June 16. When Prescott ordered Knowlton to extend the American left flank early in the afternoon, he constructed the improvised rail fence stuffed with hay that veered northwest from the breastwork. During battle he held the position with coolness and superb courage and handled his men with such tactical precision during the retreat that he made it possible for most of the defenders of the redoubt to escape from the encircling British forces.

Shortly after the battle, Knowlton was advanced to major and then to lieutenant colonel. He served as confidant and aide to General Washington until September 1776, when he was killed at the age of thirty-six in the Battle of Harlem Heights. Had he lived, there is little doubt that Thomas Knowlton would have become one of the foremost American generals.

One critical factor that determined the course of the battle on June 17 was the split-second decision by John Stark, acting without orders, to fortify the open space between Knowlton's position and the Mystic River. The makeshift fence built by Stark's men out of rocks and rails stuffed with grass was never breached, despite two desperate attempts by the assault troops of the British army. The deadly and accurate rifle fire of the frontiersmen simply blew apart the lines of light infantry and grenadiers. The astounding casualty rate suffered by the British right wing prompted Howe to remain on Charlestown Heights after the battle, instead of pursuing the American rear guard. The British distaste for charging entrenched American riflemen, prevalent throughout the war, was directly the result of the marksmanship and firepower demonstrated by the New Hampshire brigade at Bunker Hill.

On Monday morning, June 19, British troops in Boston and Charlestown listened to the General Orders read to them by their officers as they stood stiffly to attention in regimental formation:

> The Commander in Chief returns his most grateful thanks to Major General Howe for the extraordinary exertion of his military ability on the 17th instant. He returns his thanks also to Major General Clinton and Brigadier General Pigot for the share they took in the success of the day as well as to Lieutenant-Colonels Nesbitt, Abercromby, Gunning and Clark, Majors Butler, Williams, Bruce, Tupper, Spendlove, Small and Mitchell, and all the rest of the officers and soldiers who by remarkable efforts of courage and gallantry overcame every disadvantage and drove the rebels from their redoubt and strongholds on the heights of Charlestown and gained a complete victory.[4]

Five days later, American soldiers took time off from their digging to listen to General Orders from General Artemas Ward:

> The General orders his thanks to be given to those officers and soldiers who behaved so gallantly at the late action in Charlestown. Such bravery gives the General sensitive pleasure, as he is thereby fully satisfied that we shall finally come off victorious, and triumph over the enemies of freedom and America.[5]

Despite the expressions of satisfaction, a storm of criticism was directed toward both men for their tactics and stratagems during the engagement. The movement of over fifteen hundred American troops to Breed's Hill, deep into Charlestown peninsula, with its narrow, periodically submerged Neck the only line of communication, supply, or withdrawal, was characterized as a blunder that placed the New England army in a trap of their own making. A logical and far better position would have been the original objective — Bunker Hill. Tallest of the three hills on the peninsula, it dominated the approaches from both sea and land, and fortifications there would have allowed Prescott to protect the Neck, his only line of supply. Both the Committee of Safety and General Ward ordered the occupation of Bunker Hill, but the midnight conference chose Breed's Hill. In so doing, the Americans expanded the area they must defend to over five times what they would have had to hold at Bunker Hill. The choice also placed American forces five times as far from their source of supplies and their means of retreat. Significantly, most of the American casualties occurred within that extra distance during the colonial retreat toward the Neck.

Artemas Ward was also criticized for his lack of action in supplying the fighting men along the battle line. Neither food nor ammunition was forwarded to the front, and reinforcements were sent in piecemeal. At no time did he leave his headquarters at Cambridge, nor did he make any attempt to visit his men at the lines. In his defense, it was pointed out that he lacked a staff and had to find volunteers to carry messages that often went undelivered. Many orders were misunderstood, either intentionally or through inexperience, and some regiments, rather than march toward the battle lines, turned off in an entirely different direction.

Many officers proved incompetent in the stresses of battle. A number were guilty of cowardice and refused under various guises to bring their men into combat. It was a costly lesson in the need for a central command, for a staff that understood its job, for the necessity to weed out incompetents and promote those who could be depended upon under fire.

Would erection of American fortifications on Bunker Hill as originally intended have caused Gage to cancel his projected June

18 assault on Dorchester? The answer will never be known, but most likely Gage would have reacted in a similar fashion, because any American entrenchments on the Charlestown peninsula were a challenge to British power. Despite American mistakes, the entrenchments on Breed's Hill did abort the British attack on Dorchester Heights and the proposed encirclement of American forces at Roxbury. In the final analysis, the colonists were fortunate that Gage ordered the frontal assault. It gave American marksmanship and courage the opportunity to cut down the British with tremendous casualties, and it created new confidence in the ability of Americans to fight. Ultimately, it was this show of strength which encouraged the other colonies to join New England in a full-scale war against mighty Britain.

The effect of the battle upon the personality of Sir William Howe was greatly significant in the future conduct of the war. He became incapable of ordering an attack on American riflemen occupying fixed positions behind earthworks. In his memoirs written after the war, General Henry Lee wrote:

> The sad and impressive experience of this murderous day sunk into the mind of Sir William Howe; and it seems to have its influence on all of its subsequent operations with decisive control.[6]

An example took place fourteen months later. On August 27, 1776, Howe's superior British army had completely overwhelmed, outflanked, and outnumbered the American troops at the Battle of Long Island. Over a thousand Americans had been captured, including three generals, three colonels, and sixty-eight other officers. The remainder fled in wild disorder, and Washington's army degenerated into a mob of wild-eyed men feverishly interested only in saving themselves. Some nine thousand colonial survivors fell back on Brooklyn Heights and desperately dug entrenchments. The British and Hessian troops, smelling the sweet scent of complete victory, swarmed toward the partially dug American lines, and the Americans, low in ammunition and morale due to their long, disorderly flight, were ready to surrender. The wide East River behind them cut off further retreat, because the British navy controlled it. It looked as though only a miracle could save Washington's army and the Revolution.

The miracle arrived in the form of an order from General Howe to General John Vaughan, commander of the attacking force. Howe commanded Vaughan to halt his advance and dig in on the perimeter of the ground that they occupied at that moment. Unable to believe the authenticity of such an order, Vaughan sent a courier to Howe to say that the Americans were ready to surrender if his superior force was allowed to continue their present advance and overrun the uncompleted American redoubt.

Howe sent a second message to Vaughan repeating his order to halt and dig in, adding that he intended to use tactics that would achieve his objective at a cheaper price. The key word was "price." The unforgettable specter of dead and broken grenadiers, light infantrymen, and battalion men lying in shattered rows before the fences and parapets at Breed's Hill prevented Howe from paying a similar price to attack the deadly American riflemen at Brooklyn Heights. While he hesitated, Washington was able to extricate his army and cross the East River to Manhattan three days later.

At the parliamentary investigation into the conduct of the American war held in London in 1779, Howe's apparent timidity on Long Island was closely scrutinized, as were the strategy and tactics he and Gage used at the Battle of Bunker Hill. Depositions were taken, letters from participants were read into the records, and Howe spoke eloquently in his own defense. Gage, however, did not appear.

The investigation concluded that the British blunders at Bunker Hill were committed in a series of astounding actions that led to tragic and needless waste of life. The most serious error, according to Gage's critics, was his decision to ignore Clinton's plan to land behind the Americans on Charlestown Neck and quickly occupy the heights of Bunker Hill. That would have trapped Prescott's entire force in a bag like a sack of potatoes. British officers testified that American deserters had said the Americans would have begun an instant exodus from Charlestown Neck had they detected a British attempt to land anywhere along the Mystic River near Bunker Hill.

Officers reported that Gage had talked about "taking the bull by the horns" as a rationale for the fatal frontal attacks. Gage and others had strongly believed that Americans were cowardly soldiers by nature and would flee in wild disorder at the approach of the imposing red-uniformed ranks with drums beating and bayonets flashing.

Howe was vigorously criticized for a second serious error: his delay in delivering his assault once the decision had been made to attack. Had he moved toward the American left at 1:00 P.M., as soon as he completed his landing at Morton's Point, instead of waiting for reinforcements so that all men could advance at the same time, he would have met no opposition along the Mystic River. He could easily have swung around the American position on Breed's Hill and established a block on Bunker Hill to trap the entire colonial force in Charlestown.

By inexcusably waiting until 3:00 P.M., Howe gave Knowlton, Stark, and Reed the opportunity to construct the fences that resulted in the wholesale slaughter of British soldiers. This singular trait of indecisiveness became typical of Howe's conduct during the American war, and his officers blamed his addiction to gambling, rum, and Mrs. Loring for his lack of prompt and decisive action.

A third error of consequence made by both Gage and Howe was in ordering men to carry full field packs weighing 124 pounds up the hill during the assault. It reflected an inexcusable lack of consideration for the welfare of their troops and slowed the men down, restricting their freedom to move. Perhaps more important to the committee was the fact that this inexplicable order had been issued by the two men who had previously developed the light infantry concept of increased mobility through lightened equipment.

The committee found a fourth serious error in the tactics of halting the troops during the assault to fire volleys at the American position. It was obvious that the many fences and obstacles partly hidden by waist-high grass forced the regulars to halt in order to straighten their lines, but to pause to fire volleys at earthen breastwork simply gave the defenders time to reload behind the safety of the parapets while avoiding British fire.

This British practice of advancing in a long line of men was made to order for the American riflemen. It offered them a full field of fire and the opportunity to identify the officers. The parade-ground pace of eighty steps per minute and the frequent stops to realign the ranks and fire useless volleys created a slow, halting advance instead of a swift and swarming assault.

A letter written by a participating British officer was read into the official proceedings of the House of Commons investigation:

> In advancing, not a shot should have been fired, as it retarded the troops, whose movements should have been as rapid as possible. They should not have been brought up in line, but in columns with light infantry in the intervals, to keep up a smart fire against the top of the breastworks. If this had been done, their works would have been carried in three minutes, with not a tenth part of our present loss.
>
> We are all wrong at the head. My mind cannot help dwelling upon our cursed mistakes. Such ill conduct at the first outset argues a gross ignorance of the common rules of the profession, and gives us for the future, anxious forebodings. I have lost some of those I most valued. This madness or ignorance nothing can excuse. The brave men's lives were wantonly thrown away. Our conductor as much murdered them as if he had cut their throats on Boston Common. Had he fallen, ought we to have regretted him?[7]

The parliamentary committee further condemned both Gage and Howe for their failure to pursue the retreating Americans when Howe's troops reached the Neck. The committee ruled that Gage should have ordered Howe to drive past the defenders on Prospect Hill and march to Cambridge, and that his failure to do so justified his recall to England.

In September 1776 Gage was replaced by Howe as commander-in-chief of the British forces in America. Testifying before the House of Commons in 1779, Howe defended his decision to halt the pursuit on Bunker Hill, for his exhausted men were in no condition to have carried off an action requiring another assault and a forced march against fierce enemy resistance.

Howe's order for the deliberate destruction of Charlestown also created a storm of indignation throughout the colonies and in England. Most Americans and many Englishmen believed it an unnecessary and wanton act. Gage, however, had warned the Selectmen of Charlestown, during the British evacuation of that town the day after Lexington and Concord, that should American forces be allowed to occupy Charlestown, he would burn the town to the ground. Despite that threat, the selectmen had informed General Artemas Ward that they would risk the consequences if the Americans chose to occupy Charlestown.

To the thousands of spectators in Boston, the burning of Charlestown was a fiery drama, an awesome scene of destruction. The smoke was visible as far away as Salem and blotted out the entire western horizon at Boston. Over four hundred buildings burned to the ground, many with property deposited there for safekeeping by Boston citizens. Some people, such as Dr. Samuel Mather, lost entire libraries with thousands of priceless books and manuscripts. Many victims tried unsuccessfully to secure compensation for their loss from the Massachusetts legislature.

As the sun rose over Charlestown the day after the battle, it shone on a scene of desolation and death. Acrid gray smoke hung low over the brown-green hills marred with the bodies of soldiers lying in deep grass. On top of Bunker Hill overlooking the Neck, British troops labored with picks and shovels to fortify against the possibility of an American counterattack from Prospect Hill across the Neck. Howe had spent the night there with his men, supervising their work. Four women from each company were sent to Charlestown to clean and launder. Regimental tents sent from Boston soon rose as a tent city behind the entrenchments on Bunker Hill.

By late Sunday night, the British had constructed a line of entrenchments that extended from the mill pond on the left, across the top of Bunker Hill and down to the shore of the Mystic River on the right. Three gondolas — large flat boats with raised sides to protect the gunners from rifle fire — were towed up the Mystic River and covered the right flank with their heavy guns.

From houses along the Neck a number of American riflemen attempted to pick off the British troops at work, so Howe ordered the 47th and 52nd Regiments to burn all homes within gunshot of the British entrenchments. The following night, however, American snipers were back, firing from the ruins of the houses.

At dawn in Boston, hundreds of citizens who had waited patiently all night along the ferry-way below the battery atop Copp's Hill were still there as the loaded barges from Charlestown rowed across with their shattered cargoes of wounded men. The casualties were transferred to waiting chaises and wood carts, and long lines of vehicles rolled noisily down the cobbled streets to the general hospital. Gage ordered all regimental surgeons and assistant surgeons to attend to the wounded. Two women from each company, who had been previously trained as nurses, were sent to the hospital to help the hollow-eyed surgeons with their grisly tasks. Only three days after giving birth, Nancy Mackenzie volunteered to supervise other officers' wives. Lieutenant Mackenzie and his regiment had been stationed at Roxbury Neck during the battle, but were being sent across to Charlestown the next day.

Two miles from Bunker Hill across the Neck, General Putnam's corps of volunteers had labored all night atop Prospect Hill. Working hard alongside his men, the powerful Putnam had succeeded in erecting a formidable line of entrenchments by Sunday night. From the top of Prospect Hill, or Mount Pisgah as the British called it, Israel could see both the American and British lines spread out before him.

North of Prospect Hill, the New Hampshire troops under John Stark and James Reed had been up all night digging on Winter Hill. These two New Hampshire regiments soon were joined by a third under Colonel Enoch Poor, and their entrenchments appeared impregnable to attack.

At Roxbury, General Thomas had his men working in four-hour shifts around the clock to extend entrenchments across the base of Boston Neck. Across the roads leading into Roxbury, his men planted sharpened tree trunks with their points slanted toward Boston as protection against a possible cavalry raid by the newly landed 17th Dragoons. The chain of entrenchments was coordinated by Colonel Gridley acting as chief engineer in charge of fortifications. He worked out dimensions and characteristics for the various defensive positions with Lieutenant Colonel Rufus Putnam, Captain Joshiah Walters, Captain Jeduthan Baldwin, and Colonel Henry Knox. The entire American army was now busy with pick and shovel. Entrenchments were being dug from Cambridge toward the Charles River, their lines beginning at Harvard College and extending to the water's edge.

*

No sooner had the entrenchments, redoubts, and breastworks taken form than a continuous series of irregular skirmishes started between the two armies, confronting each other behind the rising parapets. Howe had constructed three powerful redoubts at the top of Bunker Hill housing heavy guns that soon opened fire on the American positions on Prospect and Winter hills.

An American light infantry company consisting of fifty Indian warriors of the Stockbridge tribe were positioned along the Charles River in front of Cambridge. On June 21, several British barges out of rifle range slowly cruised along the Charles taking soundings. The Indians let fly a shower of arrows that killed one man and wounded three others. Several nights later, a party of Indians ambushed a British outpost, killed four soldiers, and, according to British reports, "plundered the bodies." Following that incident, British batteries shelled the American positions almost every night.

In the eighteenth century, cannonballs carried a lighted fuse that exploded the round ball after it had landed. In an exciting game, Americans would race to the freshly landed missile and pull out the sizzling fuse before it ignited the powder inside. The cannonballs were easily visible as they arched through the sky overhead, and it was not too difficult, with a little experience, to determine where they would fall.

One night two Americans crawled up to a barn that British outposts were using as a shelter and tried to set it on fire. They were discovered and shot as they tried to get away. The British patrol pursued them and bayoneted the two wounded men as they lay on the ground only a few hundred yards from their agonized comrades. One of the watching Americans was Ebeneezer Huntington, the twenty-one-year-old private who had left Yale to enlist in Captain Chester's Connecticut company. In a letter to his father written the next day, he described the incident:

> About four o'clock two of our men very imprudently ran down upon the Neck to destroy the house their main guard was kept in, suspecting that they were out, but they were fired upon by about thirty regulars who killed them, then went up to the bodies of the dead and every one to a man thrust his bayonet into their bodies — they might

have easily taken them as they were both unarmed but they chose to destroy them than take them prisoners.[8]

Several days later another skirmish occurred in the same area near Boston Neck. A squad of regulars moved across the ground dividing the two lines and advanced quickly toward the American pickets posted near the George Tavern. The regulars fired a volley and charged, but were met with a withering fire from colonial reinforcements rushed to the scene. Several men were killed or wounded on each side before the British withdrew to their lines.

The Stockbridge Indians were moved north to Prospect Hill, where they made nightly raids upon the British sentries. One night they killed two British soldiers, and the British retaliated by sending a full company to burn some houses near the American position. The resulting battle raged for several hours and involved over a hundred men.

Although the Battle of Bunker Hill and its immediate aftermath were fought by a large but disorganized colonial force, efforts had been under way for weeks to bring the revolutionary army under a cohesive leadership. George Washington of Virginia was fated to assume the key role.

On May 10, 1775, over a month before Bunker Hill, the Second Continental Congress met in Philadelphia. Twelve of the thirteen colonies were represented, Georgia being absent. A majority of the delegates believed that the English Parliament had been misled by the machinations and corrupt practices of the Tory Party. They fervently hoped that George III, to whom they referred as "the best of kings," would make Parliament see reason and could dissuade it from its repressive and suicidal course.

Two days after the Congress convened, the Massachusetts Provincial Congress, with the advice of the Committee of Safety, drafted a letter to Philadelphia appealing to Congress:

> We tremble at having any army, though consisting of our own countrymen, established here, without a civil power to provide for and control it. We lay our distressed state before you, and humbly hope for your advice respecting the assuming of the powers of the civil government. And as the army is for general defence of the rights of

America, we suggest your taking the regulation and general direction of it, that the operations may more effectually answer the purposes designed.[9]

The letter was carried to Philadelphia by Dr. Benjamin Church, who rode through militia regiments marching to join the American lines at Boston. After weeks of fierce debate at Philadelphia, it became clear to the delegates that a decision had to be reached and, furthermore, the decision had to be unanimous. John Adams, Samuel Adams, and John Hancock were reminding them daily that a war had begun in Massachusetts. The New England colonies alone could not withstand the power of Britain, and if New England was defeated, all the colonies would be at the mercy of the mother country. The cause of the patriots must be adopted by Congress and the fight joined by all colonies.

John Hancock secretly believed that he would make an excellent commander-in-chief, should Congress take over the war. John Adams, however, was under no such illusions. Hancock's lack of combat experience and his ill health made him a poor risk. Adams liked George Washington and was determined that he become commander-in-chief of the revolutionary forces. He consulted with various delegates and found that most, though not all, agreed that Washington was an excellent choice. There were several reasons.

Virginia was the largest and most powerful colony in America, and Washington was her foremost military man. This made the choice of him almost essential from John Adams's point of view, for with Washington would come the support of Virginia, and with Virginia would come the rest of the colonies. The war would be viewed as a colonial war rather than a New England uprising.

Washington's reputation as a courageous and determined soldier in the French and Indian War was well known. He had been the leading American combat officer, had saved Braddock's army from destruction, and was known to be a man of quiet strength, courage, character, and courtesy. He was also thought to be the wealthiest planter in Virginia.

When Washington wore his blue and buff colonel's uniform of the Virginia militia — as proof, he said later, that Virginia was ready to fight if necessary — it was interpreted by the delegates as a hint that he would welcome his appointment as commander of the New England army. Washington was less optimistic than most but believed that American use of force in Massachusetts would make the king force Parliament to see the truth and come to its senses. Like other members of Congress, Washington referred to the British army in Boston as the "Ministerial Army."

Congress, however, refused to vote for war with England. On June 15, John Adams moved that Congress adopt the army at Cambridge and appoint a general to command it. He further urged that the general be George Washington of Virginia. After a debate, Washington was unanimously elected. Congress proceeded to appoint four major generals to assist him with the new Continental army: Artemas Ward; Charles Lee, a professional soldier and close friend of Washington who had fought in both the British and Polish armies; Philip Schuyler of New York, one of the richest men in America and a veteran of the French and Indian War; and Israel Putnam of Connecticut.

Eight brigadier generals were selected: Seth Pomeroy, Richard Montgomery, David Wooster, William Heath, Joseph Spencer, John Thomas, John Sullivan, and Nathanael Greene. Horatio Gates was chosen as adjutant general with rank of brigadier general.

Congress also voted to raise ten companies of frontier riflemen from Pennsylvania, Maryland, and Virginia to reinforce the men fighting in Boston.

Unknown to Washington, the Battle of Bunker Hill had been fought the day before as he sat down to write to Martha Washington at Mount Vernon:

Philadelphia

My dearest: June 18, 1775

I am now set down to write to you on a subject which fills me with inexpressable concern, and this concern is greatly aggravated and increased, when I reflect upon the uneasiness I know it will give you. It has been determined in Congress, that the whole army raised for the defense of the American cause, shall be put under my care, and that it is necessary for me to proceed immediately to Boston to take upon me the command of it.[10]

Washington left Philadelphia for Cambridge on June 21. When he reached New York City he was greeted by the news of Bunker Hill. Daniel Webster related the story many years later that when Washington first heard of Bunker Hill he asked how the American troops had behaved while under fire. He was told that they had held their ground until they ran out of ammunition, and had coolly held their fire until the regulars were almost upon them. They had then fired with devastating effect. Webster reported that Washington smiled and remarked softly, "The liberties of the country are safe."

Washington did not tarry in New York but pressed on for Cambridge. When his party reached Springfield, Massachusetts, he was met by a welcoming committee from the Massachusetts Provincial Congress. He arrived in Cambridge escorted by a large number of mounted citizens and a troop of light-horse cavalry. The next morning, Monday, July 3, 1775, under a large elm tree on Cambridge Common, the tall Virginian prepared to take command of the Continental army from General Artemas Ward.

EIGHTEEN

Washington Takes Command

THE WARM SUN felt good to the thirty-five hundred veterans of the Battle of Bunker Hill as they stood at parade rest in regimental formations. It was Monday morning, July 3, 1775, and six regiments from the various wings of the army had been collected at dawn to witness Washington's assumption of command and to be reviewed by their new commander-in-chief. Three regiments were from Massachusetts; New Hampshire, Connecticut, and Rhode Island had each furnished one.

The long ranks reached from one end of Cambridge Common to the other, and colonels and their staffs sat their mounts in front of the troops.

Opposite the center of the formation, on a slight elevation, a reviewing post had been established at the base of an enormous elm tree. General Artemas Ward, astride his horse, faced the massed regiments from under the shade of the tree. Ranged behind him were Generals Putnam, Greene, Thomas, Sullivan, Heath, and Spencer. If Ward had any thoughts about the ceremony that was about to demote him to second-in-command, he gave no indication of them.

Behind the mounted officers hundreds of spectators, including members of the Provincial Congress dressed in their finest, formed a background of vivid colors.

At precisely 10:00 A.M. a low throbbing of drums echoed from the town square, followed by the shrill sound of fifes. The pounding of the drums grew louder and more insistent, and a formation of musicians swung smartly onto the Common and marched in front of the reviewing stand in a thunderous tornado of sound. Reaching the end of the rigid lines, they countermarched to the center of the formation and, with drums muffled, formed to the right of the reviewing officers.

Moving rhythmically, three splendidly mounted general officers dressed in blue rode slowly across the sunlight and shadows of the Common toward the reviewing party. A squadron of mounted dragoons with drawn sabers clattered along behind them. The three officers drew abreast of Ward and his officers and exchanged salutes. Washington expertly wheeled his horse alongside Ward as his two companions, Major General Charles Lee and Brigadier General Horatio Gates, joined the other generals.

Men in the ranks strained for a glimpse of the man who was to command them. They had heard many things about him: that he was America's foremost soldier, the wealthiest man in America, serving without pay. It was their first glimpse of Washington, and despite their Yankee reluctance to look up to Southern aristocracy, they were impressed with what they saw.

Mounted upon a pure-blooded stallion sat a tall man with a tanned, slightly pockmarked face of great strength and regal bearing. He was dressed in a dark blue uniform with buff-colored facings and rich golden epaulets on each shoulder. Spotless white lace was at his throat, a black, three-cornered hat sat square upon his head, and an elegant sword hung from his belt. The aristocratic bearing and graceful manner with which he moved sent a surge of confidence through the army. They sensed that they were in the hands of a man who knew what he was about. That night Abigail Adams wrote to her husband, John, who was with the Continental Congress in Philadelphia:

> You had prepared me to entertain a favorable opinion of him but I thought the half was not told me. Dignity with ease and complacency, the gentleman and soldier, look agreeably blended in him. Modesty marks every line and feature of his face.[1]

It was the beginning of the lifelong love affair between George Washington and the American people.

For a few moments the ranks faced their commander-in-chief in silence. Then Washington moved forward and in a clear voice read his orders from the Continental Congress giving him command. When he finished, he reached across his body and swung his sword in a flashing arc, placing it before his right shoulder in the "carry" position. The new adjutant general, Horatio Gates, spurred forward and called out, "Pass in review." The drums and fifes broke into marching tempo and the regiments turned and marched to their right; they executed two left turns at the edge of the common and came swinging down toward the reviewing post.

Colonel William Prescott led the procession with his veterans of Breed's Hill in firm lines behind him. As his sword flashed toward Washington on his command of "eyes right," their eyes met in mutual respect. Washington brought the sword hilt to his lips and swung his blade to his right in a downward stroke.

In a few minutes it was over. After shaking hands with their new comrades-in-arms, Washington and his two companions left for an inspection of the army's positions, and the regiments returned to their fortifications.

A sincerely modest man, Washington believed that he needed all the professional help available to him, and he was delighted to receive the offer of assistance from two former high-ranking British officers making their homes in America. One was forty-three-year-old Major General Charles Lee, a member of the British nobility and a professional soldier since the age of fifteen. Extremely tall and thin, he had been nicknamed "Naso" in tribute to his long nose when he first entered the British army. Considered a brilliant student of warfare, he was graciously courteous when he wanted to be.

Washington had served with Lee during the French and Indian War and admired his thorough knowledge of military science and his clear, decisive mind. Lee always said what he felt, regardless of the effect, and he had been forced to leave England for America in 1773 after calling King George III despicable and stupid in a series of political articles.

In America Lee became a landowner and lived for a while at Mount Vernon, where he and Washington became reacquainted. Lee's military experience was extensive. He fought in America during the seven years of the French and Indian War and rose to the rank of colonel in the regular army. He later fought in Portugal, and during a period of peace in England he fought in Eastern Europe, where the king of Poland commissioned him a major general. Later, Lee fought with the Russian armies of Catherine the Great against the Turks. It was assumed by many, including Washington, that the Continental Congress would choose Lee to become commander of the American army. Lee thought so, too, and was secretly chagrined when Washington was selected.

Friends in Congress explained to Lee privately that Washington had been chosen over him because he was a native American, whereas Lee had lived in America for only a few years as a citizen. They suggested to him that he would in time become the real commander of the army and allow Washington to fill the role in name only. Lee unhappily concurred, and this would become a source of friction in the future.

Ambitious, proud, and quarrelsome, Lee was a complicated man. In person he was slovenly, crude, and profane, with an obsession for dogs, of which he owned many. They lived with him, slept with him, and ate with him. Lee often remarked that he preferred their company to that of humans. Washington, however, did not mind Lee's idiosyncrasies so long as his abilities were useful to the American cause.

The second professional, Horatio Gates, was a long-time friend of Washington's. The illegitimate son of a duke and his housekeeper, Gates entered the army at the age of fifteen when his father purchased him an ensign's commission. He became a splendid soldier who held many decorations and awards and had been honored for exceptional bravery during the capture of Martinique in 1762. He and Washington had served together with General Braddock in the French and Indian War.

Gates rose to the rank of major but found further promotion blocked by the circumstances of his birth. Discouraged, he resigned from the army and, at the urging of Washington, moved to Virginia, where he was helped to become a landowner. There Gates became a leading opponent of Britain's colonial policy and was one of the first to support independence.

When Washington was named commander-in-chief, he insisted

that Congress name the previously unknown Gates to the high post of adjutant general with the rank of brigadier general.

Strangely, Gates harbored a feeling of resentment toward his benefactor. He believed that if Washington had tried a little harder, he would have arranged for Gates to receive the rank of major general instead of brigadier. Like Lee, Gates felt superior to Washington in ability at the time, but kept his feelings to himself.

One of Washington's immediate problems upon taking command of the army was a crisis brought about by the military appointments of Congress. Brigadier General Spencer of Connecticut resigned because he was outranked by newly appointed Major General Putnam, whom he had previously outranked. John Thomas also resigned because he had been the commander of the right wing as a major general and was now demoted to brigadier general under Artemas Ward, now in command of the right wing. Washington spent several days explaining to the two men the need for cooperation with the table of organization, and he promised them future improvements in their status. Both men finally canceled their resignations and remained in the army.

Following the Cambridge ceremony the first task facing Generals Washington, Lee, and Gates was the inspection of the American fortifications and the camps immediately to their rear. The three men were shocked at the horrible stench permeating the entrenchments and living areas. It was obvious that digging latrines had not been a favorite activity of the American soldiers, and Washington placed this problem high on his list of priorities.

Food was plentiful and the men appeared to be well fed. However, they lived in a variety of makeshift wooden and brick huts, cabins, and lean-tos, abandoned homes, college buildings, barns, and numerous sailcloth tents. The inspecting generals were greatly impressed by the immaculate tent-city and well-uniformed, disciplined soldiers of the Rhode Island Brigade under Nathanael Greene. Thirty-nine years old, six feet tall, and broad shouldered, Greene made a favorable impression on Washington. In the Virginian's estimation, Greene was a natural soldier, destined for greatness, and when he promoted Greene to major general soon thereafter, he quickly lived up to Washington's expectations. Greene has been evaluated as one of the leading American generals of the Revolution, both under Washington and in independent command.

From Prospect and Winter hills Washington studied the British entrenchments and camps on Bunker Hill. The British lines extended 150 yards from the Neck toward the American lines. Howe's encampment presented a beautiful sight from the top of Prospect Hill; the green grass of the slopes was intensified by rows of perfectly aligned, clean, white tents. As Washington squinted through his long-glass, he saw precise formations of scarlet and white wheeling through intricate marching maneuvers. Across the Charles River and the ferry-way loomed the sinister heavy battery atop Copp's Hill.

On Winter Hill the three generals dined with the riflemen of New Hampshire. Washington was impressed with both officers and men, who reminded him of the Virginia frontiersmen he had fought with as a young man. On top of Prospect Hill they visited with Israel Putnam, who was directing his force of Massachusetts and Connecticut troops in strengthening their entrenchments.

Cambridge was garrisoned by Massachusetts regiments and two regiments of Rhode Island troops at Sewell's Point along the estuary of the Charles River. Two Connecticut regiments and nine Massachusetts regiments held the fortifications opposite Boston Neck at Roxbury, and seven hundred other men were scattered among the small towns south of Boston to provide protection against naval attacks. The British entrenchments around and beyond Boston Neck impressed Lee and Gates as being impregnable.

The night after arriving in Boston, Washington held a private conference with a man whose identity has never been revealed. This man left the general and slipped into Boston, from which he sent regular reports of British activities for the next eight months. Washington later asked Congress to appropriate a substantial sum of money to pay his unknown agent with no questions asked. It is probable that the spy was a British officer or a highly regarded Loyalist.

Among the most distressing conditions in the American army, in the opinion of Washington, Lee, and Gates, were the relationships between officers and enlisted men. It was apparent that the deplorable lack of necessary hygienic measures was caused by the weakness of officers whose commands were casually disobeyed with little fear of punishment. The generals agreed that this was a dangerous weakness and required immediate remedy.

On July 9, six days after taking command, Washington called a council of war with his brigadier and major generals. The first decision, which was resolved by unanimous vote, was to hold all present positions and not attempt the occupation of Dorchester Heights at that time, because the shortage of field guns and ammunition made it too hazardous. If a British attack succeeded in driving them from their present works, the army would retreat and reform their lines on Wales Hill to the rear of the Roxbury positions.

Washington then introduced the subject that he considered his principal problem. He charged, seconded by both Charles Lee and Horatio Gates, that the entire army and especially the officer corps was badly in need of reorganization. Discipline was lax or nonexistent. There was little general organization or chain of command. Disorders and riots among the men were frequent, and officers exercised little authority over their men. Furthermore, it was essential to weed out those officers who had proven themselves to be untrustworthy during the last battle. Charles Lee stated, in a letter that he wrote at the time:

> As to the materials, (I mean private men) they are admirable, young, stout, healthy, zealous, good humoured and sober. But there is much more cause for fear that the officers will fail in a day of trial than the privates.[2]

Inspection of company orderly books had revealed unbelievable degeneration in most of the units. Intoxication, theft, false returns on company rosters, disobedience of orders, disrespect for officers, and desertion were among the most common entries. Offenses were rarely punished except with occasional fines, standing in the pillory, or riding the wooden horse. In a few instances of flagrant crime, convicted men were drummed out of camp or given a whipping at the head of the regiment.

Washington was faced with the problem that democratic principles, when observed in the army, made it difficult to establish an officer corps with the authority necessary to command men in a manner essential to fight a war against first-class troops. He advocated that officers be lifted above their men socially as well as in their rate of pay. As an aristocrat, Washington firmly believed that the natural and social differences found between men in society must be carried into the military to insure that the troops obeyed their officers' commands without question.

After long discussion, the New England generals agreed to Washington's proposals, and the army was reorganized into three Grand Divisions, each headed by a major general. Each division contained two brigades commanded by a brigadier general. Each brigade consisted of six or seven regiments, each commanded, in most cases, by a colonel.

The left wing of the army, under Major General Charles Lee, consisted of the first and second brigades under Brigadier General John Sullivan of New Hampshire and Brigadier General Nathanael Greene of Rhode Island. Sullivan's three regiments of New Hampshire troops under Colonels Stark, Poor, and Reed, and three regiments of Massachusetts soldiers under Colonels Nixon, Mansfield, and Doolittle held the lines on Winter Hill. Greene's seven regiments on Prospect Hill were made up of three Rhode Island regiments under Colonels Varnum, Hitchcock, and Church, and four Massachusetts regiments under Colonels Whitcomb, Gardner, Brewer, and Little.

Major General Israel Putnam commanded the center of the army with headquarters at Cambridge. His fifth and sixth brigades were commanded by Brigadier General William Heath and the senior colonel of the sixth brigade. Heath had six Massachusetts regiments led by Colonels Patterson, Scammons, Phinney, Gerrish (soon to be cashiered), and Prescott. Heath's own regiment was under the command of his lieutenant colonel. The sixth brigade, under command of Colonel James Frye, consisted of Frye's own Massachusetts regiment, Putnam's Connecticut regiment under the command of Lieutenant Colonel Experience Storrs, and four other Massachusetts regiments under Colonels Bridge, Glover, Woolbridge, and Sargent.

The right wing, stationed at Roxbury and also responsible for the protection of the small towns to the south, included the third and fourth brigades under the command of Major General Artemas Ward. The third brigade, commanded by Brigadier General John Thomas, contained seven Massachusetts regiments under Colonels Fellows, Learned, Cotton, Davidson, and Brewer. Ward's and Thomas's regiments were commanded by lieutenant colonels.

The fourth brigade, under the command of Brigadier General Joseph Spencer, consisted of three regiments from Connecticut and three from Massachusetts. General Spencer's own regiment from Connecticut was commanded by his lieutenant colonel, the others by Colonels Parsons and Huntington. The three Massachusetts regiments included two led by Colonels Walker and J. Reed, and an independent regiment made up of various companies distributed among the southern dependent towns and commanded by their individual company commanders.

Washington immediately began the task of reorganizing the officer corps. A system of strict distinctions was established between officers and enlisted men, and the process of weeding out incompetent officers began. Within a short time it became a common sight to see men tied up and given the maximum sentence of thirty-nine lashes. Among the men, credit for the new severity was attributed to General Lee, who on one occasion threatened to use his cane on an officer for unsoldierly conduct.

The Reverend William Emerson remarked in a letter to his family in Concord:

> There is great overturning in the camp, as to order and regularity. New lords, new laws. The Generals Washington and Lee are upon the lines every day. New orders from his excellency are read to the respective regiments every morning after prayers. The strictest government is taking place, and a great distinction is made between officers and soldiers. Everyone is made to know his place and keep in it, or be tied up and receive thirty or forty lashes according to his crime. Thousands are at work every day from four till eleven o'clock in the morning.[3]

General Lee was the subject of much discussion among the men for reasons other than having instituted the British system of flogging. His profanity and laxity in his personal conduct outraged the devout New Englanders. It was common gossip that he had scoffed at a resolution made by Congress to set aside July 20 as a day of fasting and prayer to obtain the favor of heaven upon their cause. With his usual bluntness, he was reported to have remarked that "heaven was ever found favorable to strong battalions."

Washington was always scrupulous in keeping all the regulations imposed by Congress, including those days set aside for prayer and fasting. He required, however, that on such occasions officers and men remain armed and ready to answer any alarm.

The establishment of an elite by upgrading the officer corps soon showed gratifying results. As authority of the commissioned officers increased, the troops were forced to comply with regulations. The immediate effect was the digging of latrines; those refusing to use them were severely punished. After several harsh examples, results proved miraculous. Even the British noticed that the stench that had hung over the American lines for so long was gone at last.

The process of weeding out incompetent officers also began, and within six weeks of his arrival Washington had dismissed a colonel and two captains for cowardice at Bunker Hill, two captains for juggling the books of their companies to draw more pay and provisions than they had men, and another captain for being absent from his post at the moment that a British attack had struck his position. Under arrest and awaiting trial were a colonel, a captain, and two ensigns.

During this period, Washington and his staff lived in a house provided by the Provincial Congress. It belonged to Dr. Samuel Langdon, the president of Harvard, who generously turned it over to them. Thomas Mifflin was appointed aide-de-camp to Washington, and Joseph Reed of Pennsylvania became his secretary. Reed, president of the Provincial Congress of Pennsylvania, was an outstanding attorney who had studied at the Temple Bar in London. Samuel Griffin was chosen aide-de-camp to General Lee.

Within five days after Washington assumed command, the British noticed a new, aggressive spirit in the rebel army. At 10:00 P.M. on Friday, July 7, six volunteers under Majors Benjamin Tupper of Colonel Fellows's regiment and John Crane of Colonel Knox's artillery regiment crawled across the no man's land between the two armies opposite Boston Neck. They hid in the brush on each side of a house belonging to Thomas Brown, which was used as shelter by the British advanced pickets. Two brass field guns were

brought up at midnight and silently emplaced within three hundred yards of the house. At precisely 2:00 A.M. two rounds of solid
shot ripped through the house. The British sentries spilled out
and sprinted for the protection of their earthworks several hundred yards away. As soon as they left, the six volunteers jumped
from their hiding places and ran into the house, setting it and a
nearby building on fire.

On July 11 the Americans launched an attack on the burned-out
Brown house, drove back the pickets, and proceeded to burn
Brown's store. That night a raiding party from Roxbury crossed
over to Long Island in boats and surprised and captured fifteen
British soldiers. They took off 200 sheep, 19 cattle, 13 horses, and
3 hogs, a great loss to the British, living on salt pork and dried
peas.

Long Island was revisited on July 12, when Colonel John
Greaton rowed across Boston Harbor in eight whaleboats and led a
party of 136 men in a dawn attack. After landing, they burned
every house on the island and a large supply of hay that had been
collected for British artillery and cavalry horses. The British navy
sped an armed schooner and several armed barges to the scene
and tried to cut off Greaton's men by destroying their boats. After
a close and fierce fire fight, the Americans escaped with the loss of
one man. Greaton, who had previously raided Deer Island, where
he captured an armed barge, became one of America's foremost
soldiers and fought throughout the war; he was promoted to
brigadier general in 1783.

At dawn on July 20 — the day set aside for prayer and fasting —
Major Vose of General Heath's regiment landed on Nantasket
Point and set fire to the lighthouse that marked the southern edge
of the entrance to Boston Harbor and was an important naviga-
tional aid to British ships approaching Boston. The fire attracted
several men-of-war, who opened fire on the Americans. A number of barges loaded with regulars tried to land and intercept the
raiders, but accurate rifle fire drove them back to their boats. Vose
and his men proceeded to Point Shirley and drove off some young
colts. They returned the next day, burned some sheds and barns,
and brought back a thousand bushels of barley, furniture, lamps, a
large quantity of hay, and all the boats kept there. This was accom-

plished with the loss of only two men wounded, despite the fact they had to fight their way back to Roxbury past armed barges and a schooner.

British guns lobbed a continuous stream of cannonballs and shells into the American positions around Boston, with only an occasional reply. Washington's artillery was meager and his supply of powder was critically short. On one occasion a Connecticut soldier was killed in a street in Roxbury near the George Tavern. The cannonball, which drove the dead man over fifty feet, was discovered lodged inside his body.

Both sides developed trench warfare into a series of sporadic and deadly raids in which men were killed. As the weeks passed, the number of casualties increased, but men also died as the result of accidents and disease, and daily burial parties saw to the dead.

Samuel Haws of Wrentham paraded with his regiments nearly every day behind the Roxbury lines. One day in late July, following the parade, the regiment was given permission to sit on the ground to rest. As the men sprawled there, a soldier named Abel Petty accidentally fired his musket, barely missing Haws and striking Asa Cheany, a soldier sitting behind him. Cheany died in agony twenty-four hours later.

On July 20 Thomas Wood of Upton, a soldier in Colonel Reed's regiment, was killed in the same manner, and the following day a Connecticut soldier named Stephen Bueden died under identical circumstances. In fact, accidents involving firearms were frequent, for many men left their muskets in the full-cocked position before stacking arms. Experienced and competent officers began to ensure that their men obeyed regulations to avoid such accidents. Many soldiers, unable to swim, drowned in the Charles River while bathing. Such senseless deaths were generally laid to the lack of discipline among the colonial troops.

On July 30, a British force of five hundred men charged across the neutral ground on Boston Neck and drove back the American pickets. While British troops held their advanced positions, others behind them dug a small breastwork to protect their sentries. The American right wing of General Ward was alerted and placed in readiness for an attack. Washington and his staff rode over, and all men slept in the entrenchments under arms during the night. At dawn the British were found to have retreated during the night, leaving a new line of trenches to protect their forward outposts and two new floating batteries on the Charles River three hundred yards behind the British lines.

Using the diversion caused by the British attack, a working party of regulars had slipped over to Nantasket to rebuild the lighthouse. Major Tupper with three hundred men crossed over the next day and attacked the working party. He killed ten men and captured thirty-five regulars and Loyalists. After destroying the repairs of the working party, he was forced to fight his way back to his boats when a large detachment of regulars landed to capture him. A fire fight followed, and Tupper escaped with all his men and prisoners excepting one man killed and two wounded.

While Tupper was fighting on Nantasket, several hundred British troops charged out of their new entrenchments facing Roxbury, drove off the American sentries, and burned the George Tavern, a building used as an observation post by the Americans. During the attack one British soldier was captured and another deserted. Both sides reported deserters coming in from the other's army. Haws reported seeing three Connecticut soldiers being flogged for attempting to desert.

As in most human activities, life in the trenches on both sides evolved into established, organized routines. Daily drill began with the firing of a morning gun in the various forts. Men rose from their straw-stuffed bedding and filed into the trenches. Morning company drill in the American lines consisted of facing the fire-step in three ranks. The company commander cried out, "Make ready!" and the front rank stepped up on the fire-step or banquet while the other two ranks moved one pace forward. Muskets were thrust forward on the parapet and the men simulated taking careful aim. The next command was "Present," which in 1775 was the command to fire. The men simulated firing and turned to face right about and proceed to the rear behind the last rank. The captain then repeated the order, "Make ready," and the second rank stepped up on the fire-step and the process was repeated. After thirty or forty minutes of this, the men not on watch retired to their mustering areas for prayers, following which the orderly sergeants read the orders for the day, results of trials and courts-martial, and other announcements. This was followed by breakfast, which the men prepared individually or by groups who had pooled their daily rations. The rest of the day was spent in working on the fortifications, digging graves or latrines, and drilling in the complicated maneuvers required by the eighteenth-century field manuals.

The challenging procedure used by the sentries, which was identical to that of the British army, was a complicated system aimed at preventing unauthorized men from penetrating the security network. Every morning, General Orders announced the Parole and Countersign. For example, on October 7, 1775, the Parole was the word "Uxbridge," and the Countersign was "Williamsburg." At the sound of someone approaching, the sentry challenged him before he came closer than thirty yards by calling out, "Halt, who goes there?" If it was the inspection party, under command of a sergeant, making the tour of the camp called "Grand Rounds," the sergeant of the party would answer, "Rounds." "What Rounds?" the sentry would shout. "The Grand Rounds" was the answer. "Advance and give the Countersign." The sergeant would advance and whisper, "Williamsburg." Under the procedure, the sentry called for the sergeant of the guard, who marched out and shouted, "Who goes there?" "Rounds"; "What Rounds?" "The Grand Rounds"; "Advance, sergeant, and give the Parole." The sergeant advanced and gave the sergeant of the guard the Parole "Uxbridge." The sergeant of the guard called his captain and told him the Parole. The captain told him it was correct, and the sergeant of the guard called out, "Grand Rounds pass." The inspection party then passed through the men of the guard, drawn up in a double rank facing each other. When there was only a single sentry, only the Countersign was required.

This complicated ceremony was repeated hundreds of times a day and was difficult to master. Woe unto the sentry who failed to get his sequence of challenges correct. With the advent of Washington, Lee, and Gates, the use of flogging provided an incentive to get it straight.

Both American and British entrenchments were constructed in the manner taught by the British army. In building new fortifications in the face of the enemy, which soon became an American specialty, hundreds of men prepared fascines, gabions, and stakes. Gabions were stakes five feet high, interwoven with twisted bundles of reeds or switches like a basket without a bottom. Fascines were bundles of switches or light rods four feet long, fashioned into cylindrical bales three feet thick and tied with twine.

The next step was to mark out the lines of the fortification. The gabions were placed on these lines three to four deep, and a ditch was dug behind them. Men on top of the gabions supervised as the baskets were filled with dirt, which was tamped down, and the entire gabion held in place with stakes driven in. The fascines were then piled up in front on top of the gabions, and the entire construction covered with earth shoveled out of the adjacent ditch. When the structure reached the proper height, both inside and outside were covered with chunks of sod pinned down by stakes.

Proper intervals were left for embrasures, or openings with sides flaring out through which cannon could be fired. The inner part of the fortifications had to be higher than the outer, and the slope of fire must be in a direct line with the bank, or glacis, put in front of the breastwork.

In an attempt to mark distinctions between soldiers and officers despite the lack of uniforms, Washington, in his General Orders on July 23, directed field officers — majors and above — to wear red or pink cockades in their hats. Captains were to wear yellow or buff cockades, and lieutenants and ensigns green. Sergeants wore a strip of red cloth sewn on their right shoulder, corporals a strip of green.

The American lack of bayonets when the British stormed the redoubt at Bunker Hill remained a concern to officers who had witnessed it. Washington, in discussing the matter, suggested that if the men in the redoubt had been armed with long spears the British might have been stopped. He consequently issued orders to construct spears, and all of the entrenchments were equipped with them. Some did not measure up to the requirements, and on July 23 he covered that matter, also, in General Orders:

> The people employed to make spears are desired by the general to make four dozen of them immediately 13 feet in length and the

wood part a good deal more substantial than the others already made, particularly in the New Hampshire lines which are ridiculously short and slight and can answer no sort of purpose. No more are to be made on the same model.[4]

In August hundreds of tall, lean, and powerfully muscled men marched into Cambridge. Dressed in long, white-fringed shirts and wearing round hats, they moved with the effortless ease of the frontiersman. These were the riflemen from Pennsylvania, Virginia, and Maryland who had been called up by the Continental Congress. As they swept into the camps, hundreds of New England troops gathered to look at these legendary fighting men. When several companies had arrived, Washington called a review on the Cambridge Common for them to demonstrate their marksmanship with the long Pennsylvania rifles.

At a distance of over three hundred yards, a series of small targets seven inches in diameter were fastened to stakes driven into the ground. At the beat of the drums the riflemen charged toward the targets, firing on the run. To the amazement of the New Englanders, most of the balls found the center of the tiny targets. It was an awesome display.

Among those who took part in the review was the company of Captain William Hendricks of Carlisle, Pennsylvania. Hendricks, his three lieutenants, John McClennan, Francis Nichols, and Mathew Irvine, and ninety enlisted men left Carlisle, the county seat of Cumberland County in western Pennsylvania, on July 13. They marched through towns such as Harris Ferry on the Susquehanna, Hummelstown, Lebanon, Riding, Swan's Tavern, Allan's Town, and Bethlehem. After traveling 129 miles over wilderness trails, they crossed the Delaware River into New Jersey on July 25. From Oxford Meeting House they proceeded to Log Gaol, where they stopped to tar and feather one of the "ministerial tools who refused to comply with the resolves of [their] Continental Congress." After what may have been a pleasant diversion to the violent frontiersmen, the simple young men of Carlisle hiked by Sussex Court House, Dr. Hinksman's farm, and Brewster's Tavern and arrived in New Windsor on the Hudson River on July 30, a distance of 208 miles from Carlisle.

They spent a full day along the Hudson, washing clothes and

resting. The next day they crossed the river and pushed on for
Baker's Tavern and Litchfield, where they again "tarred and
feathered another ministerial tool." Crossing into Connecticut,
they reached Hartford, 311 miles from Carlisle, on August 4. After fishing in the Connecticut River, they pushed north through
Farmington and Mindon and entered Massachusetts near West
Springfield. Stopping at Ellis's Tavern, they marched into Cambridge on the evening of August 9. In twenty-six days the riflemen
had marched over mountains, through forests, along primitive
country lanes and dusty roads, and crossed wide, swift rivers for a
total distance of 432 miles.

Their presence at Charlestown soon became apparent to the
unsuspecting British regulars. On July 29 the British planted a
battery atop Bunker Hill, and under the protection of a bombardment they advanced their lines toward the American positions on
Prospect Hill. Many trees were cut down and sharpened to form
an abatis, or tilted fence of closely packed rows of sharpened
points, slanting toward the Americans. Washington ordered a
company of Pennsylvania riflemen from York County to cut off
the outpost and bring in a prisoner for questioning.

Captain Dowdie and thirty-nine riflemen slipped off to the right
of the new British position and crawled to the rear of the outpost.
Lieutenant Miller, with an identical party, slipped to the left of the
enemy and snaked his way around to the rear. Just as the two
groups were about to join, a party of regulars marching to relieve
the garrison blundered into the riflemen hidden in the tall grass.
The Americans opened fire and killed five regulars before taking
two prisoners and escaping. One Pennsylvanian was captured by
the British troops.

Intensely interested in the formidable captive, who said his
name was Creuse, General Howe spent several hours interrogat-
ing him. The next day Howe called some of his officers to witness a
demonstration of the prisoner's marksmanship. Amazed at his
ability, the British sent the American to England, where he gave
several exhibitions of his prowess.

As the Southern riflemen increased in number, they were introduced into the siege lines, where they exacted a steady toll of
British sentries. After several redcoats were killed by single shots
fired from a distance of over 250 yards, British soldiers became

understandably reluctant to expose themselves on the open areas of their fortifications.

The Southern riflemen, however, caused Washington a great deal of trouble unless they were continuously employed. They became bored easily and were extremely difficult to handle. On one occasion, one of their sergeants was arrested and placed in the guardhouse for failing to do his duty. His friends decided to free him, and thirty-two Virginia riflemen, armed and dangerous, marched toward the Main Guard in Cambridge to do so. Colonel Hitchcock's Rhode Island regiment, with fixed bayonets, and other troops cornered the mutineers. Washington appeared and personally ordered the riflemen to lay down their arms, which they instantly did. The men were arrested and confined, although they were later freed on payment of a twenty-shilling fine each.

Following the first general snowfall, a large group of sightseeing Virginia riflemen, recently arrived in Cambridge, wandered around the grounds of Harvard College, gawking at the buildings and peering through doors and windows. Their fringed hunting shirts, leggings, moccasins, and beaded, fringed hunting bags drew a series of whistles and remarks from a collection of off-duty soldiers from Marblehead, nearly all fishermen and sailors in peacetime. Their shouted references to the effeminacy of the Southerners' garb were followed by several well-aimed snowballs. A wild fistfight broke out that soon involved several hundred men as each group brought up reinforcements to join in the melee.

Suddenly, and without warning, General Washington appeared on the scene, dismounted, and seized two brawny combatants by the throat, roaring for everyone to leave at once before he had some of them shot. A witness reported that all the men dispersed within three minutes, and writing later he recalled:

> Here, bloodshed, imprisonments, trial by court martial, revengeful feelings between the different corps of the army, were happily prevented by the physical and mental energies of a single person, and the only damage resulting from the fierce encounter were a few torn hunting shirts and round jackets.[5]

British officers became increasingly concerned with the number of desertions from their ranks. Occasionally British sentries in forward positions would slip across the neutral ground and join the Americans. Major Charles Stuart of the 43rd Regiment wrote to his father, the Earl of Bute, on October 8:

> There is seldom a week that we do not lose a man or two by desertion, and I am sorry to say that it is seldom they desert from the enemy. Yesterday one of their deserters was confined for trying to persuade some of our men to desert to the enemy. It was no wonder, for the General instead of confining them like rebels, permitted them to walk about the town, nay, gave them their liberty.[6]

The Americans used various stratagems to encourage desertion among the regulars. Among the most effective was a series of handbills that were allowed to blow into the British camp by westerly winds. One titled "An address to the soldiers" made its point simply:

Prospect Hill	*Bunker Hill*
1. Seven dollars a month.	1. Three pence a day.
2. Fresh provisions in plenty.	2. Rotten salt pork.
3. Health.	3. The scurvy.
4. Freedom, ease, affluence, a good farm.	4. Slavery, beggary, and want.[7]

Colonel William Miller of the Rhode Island forces stationed on Prospect Hill as part of General Nathanael Greene's brigade wrote a letter on July 29, 1775:

> I also saw a gentleman that came out of Boston yesterday, who says the people of Boston and the soldiers are very sickly and much dejected; that General Gage had given orders for all the inhabitants of Boston that have a mind to depart by water to return their names and they should have liberty to depart.
>
>   We have three deserters from the regulars come into this camp since we came here, one of whom found his own brother here in the camp. Their meeting was very affecting. One hath deserted by way of Roxbury, who it is thought will prove a very serviceable man to our army, as he is able to give a plan of all the works and fortifications in Boston, and knows all their plans. He says he can direct the army to storm Boston, with the loss of very few men; that it has been in contemplation among the Gageites to set Boston on fire, and withdraw all of the troops and ships. But we ought not to catch at such shadows as that. We have nothing under God to depend upon but our own strength.[8]

During the early part of August 1775 there was little important fighting except for the usual British bombardment that took its weekly toll of American killed and wounded. Two men of Colonel Reed's regiment were killed one day while running after a rolling cannonball in an attempt to remove the fuse. The Americans were forced to withhold their return fire as the result of a disturbing development.

Upon taking command on July 3, Washington ordered an exact accounting of all military supplies available to him, including the exact amount of gunpowder on hand. He received reports that he had three hundred quarter casks of powder available. However, closer examination revealed that in reality he had only thirty-two quarter casks. Thoroughly alarmed, Washington called an emergency council of war on August 3 and exposed the state of their powder supply. The error was caused by counting the original amount of powder and failing to deduct what had been expended from June 17 to July 3.

Urgent messages were sent to Congress and the neighboring colonies, imploring them to explore all possible sources of powder. For a critical period, Washington's army was down to only nine cartridges per man, and he feared that Gage would launch an immediate offensive if he became aware of the facts. The situation was kept a closely guarded secret.

On one occasion Gage held the truth in his hands and did not know it. An American deserter was brought to Province House, where Gage questioned him about the American military strength. The deserter assured him that the colonial army was suffering from a shortage of powder and that each soldier had less than ten cartridges. Gage did not believe him and was convinced the story was an example of American guile — a deliberate attempt to trick the British into making an assault that would result in their wholesale slaughter.

In front of Winter Hill and only a few hundred yards from the British lines stood the small knoll called Ploughed Hill. Washington and his advisers planned to occupy this position as an additional obstacle against a possible British attack on Winter Hill. Rumors had been circulated that Howe was about to embark on an offensive against the Prospect Hill–Winter Hill line. There had been a series of parades behind the British lines, and American officers observed the regulars practicing embarking and disembarking with columns of boats that were rowed in formation back and forth along the Charles River out of range of the dangerous American riflemen.

Washington was eager to provoke a British attack and hoped that by occupying Ploughed Hill it would trigger the same kind of response that Prescott had accomplished when he occupied Breed's Hill. The enlistments of most of Washington's men were soon to expire, and he wanted to bring the enemy to action while he still had an army. New supplies of powder were reaching the Americans, and Washington was confident that if he could precipitate a British assault on his powerful defensive positions, he could destroy a major part of Howe's army.

At midnight on August 26 a detachment of twenty-four hundred troops from New Hampshire and Massachusetts under Brigadier General John Sullivan moved quietly down the slopes of Winter Hill and silently swarmed over Ploughed Hill in the darkness. An additional thousand men carried preconstructed gabions, fascines, and stakes. Working throughout the night with picks and shovels, the men built a strong series of fortifications in record time. As they labored through the night, hundreds of Southern riflemen were deployed close to the British lines to protect the men at the top of the hill.

When dawn broke at 5:26 on Sunday morning, August 27, the British discovered the fortifications and immediately began to fire upon them from their batteries on Bunker Hill. They hauled up a ship and two floating batteries on the Mystic River, and an intense rain of cannonballs descended upon the Americans hidden in the deep trenches they had just dug.

The bombardment continued all day long. The adjutant of Colonel Varnum's Rhode Island regiment was decapitated by a direct hit, and one of Captain Hendricks's men, William Simpson of Carlisle — who had hiked 432 miles to get there — was struck in the foot by a cannonball. Although his leg was amputated, he died several days later.

For six hours not a single shot was fired by the Americans as they hoarded their powder for the expected British assault. Finally, a nine-pounder mounted on Ploughed Hill zeroed in on the floating batteries on the Mystic River which had caused the injury of William Simpson. The American gunners scored several direct hits, killed two regulars, sank one of the barges, and silenced the other. It was a good example of the improved shooting skill of the newly reorganized colonial artillery.

The British bombardment finally stopped with nightfall. Early the next morning, American observers on the Chelsea side of the Mystic saw hundreds of British troops marching toward the lines on Bunker Hill. Messengers were sent to Washington, who deployed five thousand additional troops to Ploughed Hill. He was convinced that Howe would launch his attack from two directions at once: mounting an assault from the Bunker Hill lines and landing boats along the shore of Willis Creek north of Lechmere Point. In Washington's assessment of Howe's plan, the attack would come at high tide to allow the boats to land easily. It could therefore be expected around noon, and he was ready for them; extra ammunition had been distributed to the troops.

The New Hampshire regiments of Colonels Stark, Poor, and Reed held the left flank, and to their right the Massachusetts troops of Colonels Nixon, Mansfield, and Doolittle were ready at their entrenchments. It was going to be another Battle of Bunker Hill, but now the Americans were in stronger positions and were well supplied.

The two armies faced each other tensely. Twelve o'clock came and nothing happened. Nothing occurred at one or two. Then at 3:00 P.M. the British were observed marching back toward their base camps behind Bunker Hill. Gage and Howe had called off their response to the challenge of Ploughed Hill. The daily bombardments continued, however, until September 10.

Gage had apparently given up any real hope of dislodging the American lines around Boston. He wrote Lord Dartmouth that he believed the British should evacuate Boston and sail to New York, where the people were more loyal and the military situation offered the use of the Hudson River to buffer rebellious New England. Gage saw no advantage in storming the American lines; they would only retreat into the countryside and set up new lines.

The city of Boston had become a sickly and dismal area, due to the American blockade that kept fresh food from entering by

land. Provisions had to be brought in by ship, and, of late, these
were subject to capture by American privateers that swarmed the
seas off the coast. British troops and their dependents numbered
13,600, and the civilian population had dwindled to 6753, including most of the Loyalists of New England. One of the Loyalist
ladies wrote to a friend in England:

> We are in the strangest state in the world, and surrounded on all
> sides. The whole country is in arms and entrenched. We are deprived
> of fresh provisions, subject to continual alarms and cannonadings,
> the provincials being very audacious and advancing near to our lines,
> since the arrival of Generals Washington and Lee to command
> them.[9]

The extremely hot weather increased the suffering of the troops
sweltering inside their tents on the heat-drenched hills. A shortage
of straw for bedding and a diet of salt pork, fish, and beef, often
alive with maggots, combined with the heat to bring down many of
the troops with scurvy and other illnesses.

Alcohol became an ever-increasing problem. The wife of an
officer wrote to a friend on August 2:

> The fatigue of duty, bad accommodations and the use of too much
> spirits are causing problems in camp. The soldiers cannot be kept
> from rum; sixpence will buy a quart of West India rum, and four-
> pence is the price of a quart of this country rum. Even the sick and
> wounded have often nothing to eat but salt pork and fish.[10]

British soldiers were envious of the sailors in the harbor, who
had better living conditions aboard ship, where there was always
more breeze on the water than in the sweltering fortifications.
Also, sailors supplemented their diet by occasional raids on coastal
towns which yielded large quantities of spruce beer. Consequently,
there was much less sickness among the seamen and they appeared in good health.

Relations between British troops and Loyalists on the one hand
and the non-Loyalist population of Boston on the other grew increasingly bitter. A number of citizens were charged with spying
and signaling the rebels, and several were imprisoned. Many
wished to leave Boston but hesitated, fearing that everything they

owned would be confiscated or looted, if they left. Gage issued a proclamation that anyone who wished to go could do so, but would not be allowed to take away silver or other valuables. A number of Americans applied and left by way of Chelsea. Despite a body search, many were able to conceal valuables sewed into the linings of their clothes.

To ease their frustrations, a group of Loyalists and off-duty regulars armed with axes chopped down the huge elm the Whigs had dubbed the "Liberty Tree," and as it fell it struck and killed a soldier who, inebriated with rum, failed to avoid its path as it crashed to the ground.

A number of young Loyalists were formed into military units called King's Volunteers. Colonel Gorham was in command and the official name of the green-uniformed regiment became the Royal Fencibles Americans.

Amidst shortages of fresh food, Nancy Mackenzie did her best to feed her three older children and nurse her baby. She bartered possessions for fresh fruit and vegetables from the naval officers of armed coastal schooners.

Life in Boston and Charlestown became very difficult for the British troops and their families. Many lost relatives and friends in battle, and hundreds of wounded were dying in the hospitals. Life in the trenches became a nightmare as Southern riflemen took a daily toll from long range. Boston was under military siege, and death and tragedy became commonplace.

On September 13, 1775, Captain Chandless of the hard-fighting and hard-drinking Royal Marines committed suicide by cutting his throat. Three days later a soldier in the 4th Regiment lost his leg to an American cannonball. One morning, Captain Pawlett of the 59th was eating breakfast in the entrenchments at Boston Neck and a cannonball took his leg off neatly at the knee. A British squad of the 4th Regiment was searching an orchard for snipers in front of the lines when a soldier fell dead with a bullet hole in the center of his forehead. He had been shot from ambush nearly three hundred yards away.

Ensign Jeremy Lister of the 10th had survived a painful series of operations to save the arm shattered at Concord. The concern among the regimental surgeons who treated him was far from common. In most cases amputation was resorted to routinely in order to save the patient's life. Infection usually followed deep wounds, and by amputating the limb and searing the stump with a red-hot iron, the spread of infection could be stopped.

Lister found himself in a period of deep depression when he learned that his arm would always be stiff, and he was deeply affected by the death of many of his best friends.

Major Charles Stuart was the brother-in-law of General Hugh Percy, and with his ability and influence he would rise swiftly to become one of Britain's foremost soldiers. In 1790 he attained the rank of lieutenant general in command of the Mediterranean during the early years of the Napoleonic Wars. He captured Corsica, successfully defended Portugal against the French, captured Minorca and thirty-seven hundred prisoners without losing a man, and took Malta after a siege of many months.

Stuart arrived in Boston as a captain on June 18, 1775, the day after the Battle of Bunker Hill. In a letter to his father he graphically described what he saw:

> The day after this unhappy affair, I arrived, and it is impossible to describe the horror that on every side presented itself — wounded and dead officers in every street; the town, which is larger than New York, almost uninhabited in appearance, bells tolling, wounded soldiers lying in their tents and crying for assistance to remove some men who had just expired. So little precaution did General Gage take to provide for the wounded by making hospitals, that they remained in this deplorable situation for three days; the wounded officers obliged to pay the most exorbitant price for lodgings, when nearly 30,000 houses belonging to the proclaimed rebels, were uninhabited.[11]

With the money he received from his father, the influential Earl of Bute, Stuart purchased a position as major in the 43rd Regiment for £2600. In a practice common at the time, he agreed to accept a captain's pay, the remainder going to the previous holder of the commission, who had retired on half pay because of wounds and also needed the extra income.

British troops in the entrenchments around Boston were disheartened when British ships laden with supplies intended for them fell into the hands of the rebels. They were the victims of what was called "Washington's Navy."

When George Washington assumed command of the Continental army, he immediately began to plan the interception of the richly laden British supply vessels. After much inquiry he located John Glover, colonel of a Massachusetts regiment in the Sixth Brigade under Israel Putnam's command. Glover was a wealthy merchant of Marblehead in civilian life, and he owned a seventy-eight-foot coastal schooner, the *Hannah,* then tied up at Beverly. He offered Washington the use of his ship at one dollar per ton per month, and recommended that Washington employ Nicholas Broughton, one of his best captains, to sail out into the Atlantic and hunt for "richly laden prizes."

Washington accepted Glover's terms, and on August 24, 1775, the *Hannah,* with a crew of thirty-six men, many of them from Glover's Marblehead regiment, went into the employ of the Continental Congress as the first American warship. Washington issued orders to Captain Broughton to "find British ships that [were] available, unprotected and heavy laden" and bring in their cargoes to aid the American army. One third of the value of the cargo was to be divided among the captain and crew.

Within a month the *Hannah* was joined by four other ships. The British schooner *Industry,* carrying a cargo of turtles and pineapples from the Bahamas, and the brigantine *Dolphin,* with a cargo of cattle, sheep, and oatmeal sent by Tories in Quebec to the "sick and wounded in Boston," were captured and taken to Salem.

On October 16 a committee from the Continental Congress arrived from Philadelphia to confer with Washington. That day six ships were commissioned as part of the navy of the Continental Congress. By that time the *Hannah* had been driven ashore and abandoned to the British.

The six vessels commissioned by Washington sailed under the Pine Tree Flag, white with a green pine tree in the center over the motto "Appeal to Heaven." The *Hancock* was commanded by Nicholas Broughton; the *Franklin* by John Selman, an officer in Colonel Glover's Marblehead regiment; and the *Lee* was commanded by John Manley. The last was a forty-two-year-old rough and aggressive seaman who had served as a boatswain's mate on a British man-of-war and had been a merchant sea captain for many years, sailing from Boston and Marblehead. The *Warren,* commanded by Winborn Adams, a captain of the New Hampshire riflemen; the *Harrison,* commanded by Captain William Coit of the 6th Connecticut Regiment; and the *Washington,* commanded by Captain Sion Martindale, completed the flotilla of armed schooners.

Within two months the value of captured British cargoes was estimated at £20,000 sterling. One of the greatest prizes of the war was the British ordnance ship *Nancy,* which had left Ireland with military supplies for Boston. She carried over two thousand new Brown Bess muskets, a hundred thousand flints, over thirty tons of musket bullets, hundreds of barrels of gunpowder, a brass mortar, and hundreds of other military items that Washington's army desperately needed. The *Nancy's* armed escort, the warship *Phoenix,* left the *Nancy* two days out of Ireland. She was accompanied by several other warships until a storm separated them several hundred miles from America. Within fifty miles of the New England coast, the *Nancy* was sighted by the American schooner *Lee,* commanded by Captain John Manley. Without troops on board to defend her, she was easily captured and was sailed into the American port at Cape Ann. The coup was greeted with great joy by Washington and his entire army. Israel Putnam, in a wildly exuberant scene, straddled the large eighteen-inch mortar and, with a bottle of rum, christened it the *Congress.*

On December 4, 1775, Captain W. Glanville Evelyn of the 4th Regiment wrote of the loss, to his father in England:

> This brig, whose safe arrival was of the utmost consequence to us, and whose cargo was of most infinite importance to the rebels, because she contained the very things they were in the greatest need of, and could not be supplied with by any other possible means, was sent from England with other artillery ships, and she *was the only one of them* without a soldier on board, and totally unprovided with any means of defense.
>
> 'Tis impossible to consider the circumstances of this affair, and to call it an accident. Surely some inquiry will be made into it, and examples made, for there must be a fault somewhere, and it is a

matter of indifference to us whether it is by design or carelessness; the enemy are supplied, so we are to be sacrificed by it.[12]

If there had ever been any doubt of Washington's aggressiveness, among tough New England soldiers like Putnam, Prescott, or Stark, the weeks after his arrival dispelled them. On September 11, October 18, and January 16 Washington brought before his officers detailed plans for a two- or three-pronged attack upon the British army with the objective of capturing the entire British force or driving them out of Boston. His generals, however, convinced him that their troops, short of field guns, powder, and shot, were unprepared to mount such an offensive.

Thwarted in his plans to attack Howe, Washington decided to force a decision in the north, where Canada stretched across the horizon, a continuous source of danger during the French and Indian War. He feared that with the support of the French-Canadians, Canada would become a base for British attacks on the frontiers. With nineteen thousand men in his fortifications at Boston, far more than he needed, he thought it feasible to launch a quick invasion of Canada. The goal would be the capture of Montreal and Quebec, both poorly defended since the British forces had been denuded to reinforce Gage at Boston.

Since Benedict Arnold and Ethan Allen had captured Fort Ticonderoga in May, Washington advised General Philip Schuyler, whom he had placed in command at Albany, to invade Canada by way of the old invasion route of Lake George and Lake Champlain.

Schuyler's army was made up mostly of New Englanders, but he seemed to lack the desire to move north. Washington wrote him daily, encouraging him to begin the drive northward, and Schuyler answered each letter by emphasizing the problems of getting his army ready.

At that point, Washington met Benedict Arnold, the co-conqueror of Ticonderoga, for the first time. Arnold appealed to him as the tough, aggressive commander he needed to launch a second pincer upon the fortress of Quebec by a northwestern route. Arnold and his men would travel north to the mouth of the wild Kennebec River in what is now Maine, then westward up the

Kennebec and its tributaries and across mountainous terrain to emerge on the banks of the St. Lawrence River opposite Quebec. There they would become the right claw of a double envelopment; the left claw would be the army of Schuyler driving north from Lake Champlain to capture Montreal and then moving north to meet with Arnold in a joint assault on Quebec. Spies had informed Washington that General Sir Guy Carleton commanded a weak garrison there, fewer than a hundred regulars.

As August came to an end, Washington detached eleven companies of Massachusetts troops and ordered the Pennsylvania rifle companies to cast lots to choose three to go north with Arnold. The three companies chosen were those of Captains Smith and Hendricks of Pennsylvania and Daniel Morgan of Maryland. Nearly twelve hundred men marched off into the northern forests toward the Kennebec River. Arnold's force included many of the finest fighting men in Washington's army, such as a nineteen-year-old Princeton graduate named Captain Aaron Burr, Dr. Isaac Senter, Eleazor Oswald, and the powerful Daniel Morgan.

On September 25 they started up the Kennebec. Forty-six days later, on November 10, 1775, only five hundred survivors of Arnold's emaciated force reached Point Levis on the south bank of the St. Lawrence River across from Quebec, and they resembled scarecrows rather than men. One out of four men had deserted; many others had died from disease, drowning, or starvation.

Arnold waited three days at Point Levis, then crossed the river and climbed to the famous Plains of Abraham. That delay cost him the capture of the city, for during it British reinforcements arrived, and Arnold retreated to wait for Schuyler's army. Command of Schuyler's troops had been given to General Richard Montgomery, who advanced across Lake Champlain and captured St. John's and Montreal. On December 5 the two American armies of Montgomery and Arnold, numbering fewer than a thousand men, closed in on Quebec to begin the siege. By then, General Guy Carleton had over thirteen hundred men behind the walls of Quebec — including volunteers, militia, and one hundred regulars and marines from warships in the harbor.

On December 30, 1775, in a blinding snowstorm, the valiant but reckless Americans stormed the defenses of Quebec. Two feints

WASHINGTON AT THE BATTLE OF TRENTON
DECEMBER 1776
by Thomas Sully, 1783–1872
Used with permission of the Union League of Philadelphia Collection

British-born Thomas Sully was a leading American portraitist of the early nineteenth century, and spent most of his life in Philadelphia. He studied in the United States with Gilbert Stuart and in England with Benjamin West and Sir Thomas Lawrence. His own style was greatly influenced by the school of portraiture that Lawrence exemplified.

Sully painted Lafayette from life when he made his farewell tour of the United States in 1824 and 1825. In 1838 the newly crowned Queen Victoria sat for him. This portrait of Washington was commissioned in 1842 when the members of the Union League of Philadelphia raised a subscription for an equestrian portrait. Since Washington died in 1799, Sully's twenty or so paintings of Washington draw on the work of others, chiefly Gilbert Stuart. This is one of his finest.

One side of this gold medal shows a head of Washington, the reverse the scene on March 17, 1776, as the last of the British troops embark, watched by Washington and his officers from the heights above the city.

The medal was made in Paris, designed under the aegis of the Academy of Inscriptions and Belles Lettres, and carried out by Duvivier, royal engraver and the foremost medalist of France. The work was not completed until 1789.

After remaining for a century in the hands of the Washington family, the medal was bought by fifty eminent Bostonians and is permanently housed in the Boston Public Library.

(on the right)
WASHINGTON AT THE BATTLE OF TRENTON by Thomas Sully

THE EVACUATION OF BOSTON
print by M. Wageman
Courtesy of the New-York Historical Society

Once the Americans had captured the high ground above Boston and the British failed to dislodge them, the end was in sight. Sick and wounded, women and children, embarked on March 10. The troops worked on, destroying supplies, spiking cannon and dumping them into the harbor, and on March 17 the rear guard boarded and the fleet set sail for Halifax.

were first made against the upper part of the city near the Plains of Abraham. Then Arnold led his troops against the eastern works along the St. Lawrence River, while Montgomery and his men swept against the western end of the St. Lawrence River line. Running through the snowstorm, the Americans were undetected until they were inside the walls. But the British defenders reacted quickly and trapped Montgomery's force in a narrow enclave, where they slaughtered them with artillery and musket fire. Montgomery was killed, and many of his men surrendered.

The survivors retreated, leaving Benedict Arnold to carry on the attack on the eastern end of the fortifications without support. Arnold was badly wounded, and Daniel Morgan led the men in a series of hopeless attacks in which most of them were either killed or captured. Surprisingly, the wounded Arnold, rejoined by the remnants of Montgomery's army, led the battered troops in a continued siege of Quebec.

Washington rushed reinforcements to Arnold and sent General David Wooster to replace the slain Montgomery, but Quebec became a lost cause. Thousands of Americans died from smallpox in the American camp, and Wooster failed to fight.

The siege of Quebec lasted until June 1776. General John Thomas was sent to replace Wooster after Howe evacuated Boston; he died of smallpox and was replaced by General John Sullivan, who abandoned the attempt.

The Continental Congress tried to convince the French-Canadians to join the American colonies in their fight against Britain, and had they succeeded the British could have easily been driven out. But the French Catholics of Canada had not forgotten nor forgiven the anti-Catholic response of Protestant New England to Britain's Quebec Act of 1763. For a while at least, the Americans would have to fight alone.

NINETEEN

Stalemate at Boston

IN SEPTEMBER 1775 Washington moved from the Cambridge home of Samuel Langdon to the abandoned mansion of John Vassall, a wealthy Loyalist who had fled to Boston. The home was beautifully furnished and proved ideal for Washington and his staff, which included his secretary and military officers, two cooks, a kitchen maid, washerwoman, tailor, and six other servants, both black and white, who performed various duties. Fond of entertaining, Washington frequently invited his officers, members of both the Provincial and Continental congresses, and private citizens of New England.

Washington missed his wife, Martha, and wrote to her regularly urging her to join him in Cambridge. His letters dwelt on his longing for her and his need of her to manage his large household and to grace the social functions. Though apprehensive about making the long, arduous journey, she finally agreed to come. On November 20, she and her party left Mount Vernon in her personal coach, a splendid carriage drawn by four matched horses, mounted by four black postillions in scarlet and white livery.

Accompanying her on the long journey to Cambridge were her son, John Parke Custis and his wife, Mrs. Horatio Gates, and Mrs. Gates's nephew George Lewis, who wished to serve his uncle, General Gates, as an aide. The journey took almost a month, because the party was entertained by leaders of the Whig Party in nearly every large town along the way. They reached Cambridge in the middle of December during a snowstorm.

With the arrival of Martha Washington, style, elegance, and grace were immediately noticeable at Washington's headquarters. Prominent New England ladies such as Mercy Warren and Abigail Adams became frequent visitors and were entertained with wine and oranges at the fashionable hour of 2:00 P.M. Dinner parties in which scores of fashionably dressed men and women participated became frequent and highly prized occasions.

During August 1775 Godfrey Wainwood, who owned a bakery in Newport, Rhode Island, was visited by a former prostitute with whom he had lived. About to be married, he was greatly disturbed by her sudden appearance, but she told him she now lived in Cambridge and sought only a favor for "old times' sake." Could he arrange to deliver a letter to Captain James Wallace of the Royal Navy, commanding the man-of-war *Rose,* cruising off the Rhode Island coast? She suggested that he could convey the letter to Captain Wallace through George Rome, a Loyalist shipowner, or through Charles Dudley, the Royal Collector of Customs.

When Wainwood asked her about the letter's contents, she told him that she did not know, but that it was from the man with whom she was living in Cambridge and was addressed to a friend of his, a Major Kane of the British army in Boston. She refused to tell Wainwood the name of her lover, but pleaded with him to deliver the letter to Captain Wallace. Anxious to get her out of his shop and Newport, he assured her that he would take care of the matter and hurried her on her way back to Cambridge.

Though certain that the letter involved some form of treason, Wainwood did nothing about it for three weeks. When it continued to prey upon his mind, he carried it to Adam Maxwell, a schoolteacher friend. Maxwell broke open the letter and found three pages of strange, closely written characters, obviously in code. Instead of taking it to the local American military authorities, the two men put the letter away and tried to forget about it. They were afraid to become involved in what was possibly the work of a traitorous or demented woman.

Several weeks later, Wainwood received a letter from his former mistress which convinced him that the coded letter was an important message from a spy in Cambridge to the British army in Boston. In a childish hand she complained to him that he had not sent the letter as he had promised, and she begged him to return it to her at once, as she was uneasy about the letter not having reached Major Kane.

Wainwood wondered how she could have known that the letter had failed to reach an officer on General Gage's staff in Boston. He took the letter back to Maxwell, who advised him to contact Henry Ward, the patriot secretary of the Rhode Island Provincial Congress. After examining it, Ward instructed him to deliver the letter to General Nathanael Greene in Cambridge. Wainwood rode there bearing a letter of introduction from Ward to Greene, the letter from the young woman, and the coded letter.

When Greene read the letters and examined the curious writing, he asked Wainwood to accompany him to the Vassall mansion to see General Washington. There, they were immediately shown in to the presence of the commander-in-chief.

After reading the various papers, Washington questioned Wainwood about his relationship with the young woman. When told she lived in Cambridge, he ordered Wainwood to find her and bring her in. Wainwood spent several days trying to locate her, but she had evidently gone into hiding. Thus, when he reported back to Washington, the general instituted a general search and issued orders for her arrest.

Several days later, one of Putnam's regimental officers marched the elusive young woman into Old Put's headquarters near Harvard College. Then Putnam and the woman mounted his horse and left at a gallop for Washington's headquarters. He created a stir when he drew up before the Vassall house with a buxom young woman behind him, her arms wrapped about his ample midsection. The old warrior dismounted, helped her down, and hustled her into Washington's study.

The interrogation lasted over thirty hours. The woman stoutly denied everything despite a warning that her refusal to cooperate might take her to the gallows. Finally she admitted that the man she was living with had written the letter, but she refused to reveal his name. Only after additional hours of relentless questioning by Washington did she finally break down and reveal that the man she lived with, the writer of the letter, was Dr. Benjamin Church, the American surgeon and director general of the colonial hospitals and an original member of the Committee of Safety.

Church was promptly arrested, and under questioning he stated that he had written the letter to Major Kane, a friend who lived in Boston. However, he claimed that he wrote the letter purposely exaggerating the number of American troops in order to discourage the British from attacking the American lines. Washington turned over several copies of the letter to Elbridge Gerry, Reverend Samuel West, and Colonel Elisha Porter, three men familiar with deciphering. On October 3 Washington received two separate but identical versions of the deciphered message. It consisted of a detailed though exaggerated description of the American forces and contained no disclosures of importance and no remarks directed against the American cause.

Dr. Church wrote Washington a long report on the matter, in which he attempted to vindicate himself. Washington's generals assembled in a council of war and Church was brought before them. His statement was read and he confessed that he wrote the letter, but denied that he had any traitorous intentions.

After several hours of deliberation, the council agreed unanimously that Church was guilty of having carried on a criminal correspondence, particularly since the letter had been written in code. They referred the case to the Continental Congress and confined Church under close guard without visitors.

Congress voted to try Dr. Church before the legislative body of Massachusetts, the General Court. His trial took place on Friday, October 27, before hundreds of his old friends and companions. After his letter to Washington was read, he made a long, impassioned speech in his own defense. But his former associates listened impassively during the painful ordeal, and when they voted on November 2, it was clear that few had been impressed by his appeal. He was expelled from his seat on the General Court and sentenced to be confined for an indefinite period in the prison at Norwich, Connecticut:

Without the use of pen, ink or paper, and that no person be allowed to converse with him except in the presence and hearing of a magistrate of the town, or the sheriff of the county where he should be confined, and in the English language, until further orders of Congress.[1]

After the British evacuated Boston in March 1776, Church petitioned Congress for his release on grounds of ill health. His petition was granted, and he returned to Boston on parole after giving bond of one thousand pounds not to have correspondence with the enemy or to leave Massachusetts without permission of the legislature.

As a result of threats against him in Boston, Church was eventually removed to Waltham and placed in jail for his own protection. He was no safer there, however, for a mob broke into the jail intent on lynching him, and he escaped by jumping out of a window and fleeing into the nearby forest.

He was later returned to Boston and placed in the town gaol. While he was there, a mob broke into his home and looted everything he possessed; his wife reported that they left her "without a change of clothes or a bed for [her] children to lie on."

Church was exiled to the West Indies late in 1776, and he sailed on a schooner commanded by Captain Smithwick. It was presumed to have gone down during a storm with all hands, for no trace of the ship or her passengers was ever found.

Mrs. Church and her children sailed for England, where Parliament granted her a small pension of £150 a year for "services performed by her husband." In her petition for the pension, Mrs. Church stated that General Thomas Gage would know the extent of her husband's services.

For many years there were American patriots who believed that Dr. Church was innocent of treason, but was merely a victim of his own indiscretion. However, 150 years after the Revolution, correspondence found in the newly available files of Thomas Gage revealed that Church had been his secret agent since 1773.

On October 16, 1775, Congress appointed Dr. John Morgan of Pennsylvania as Director General of Hospitals to replace Church. Morgan graduated at Philadelphia in 1757 and received his M.D. in Edinburgh five years later. After practicing medicine in London, Paris, and Italy, he returned to Philadelphia and in 1765 founded the first medical school in America.

As soon as he was appointed to Washington's army, Morgan and his wife left Philadelphia for Cambridge. He set out to eliminate waste in the General Hospital and in the individual regimental hospitals. The latter were poorly staffed and equipped, and Morgan supplied them with medical supplies that had been hoarded at the large General Hospital in Cambridge. He arranged for the badly wounded and seriously ill men languishing in primitive regimental hospitals to be moved to the large hospital at Cambridge.

Morgan's struggle to upgrade the regimental hospitals by examining the qualifications of the surgeon's mates on duty there was hampered by the fact that many mates avoided his examination and were protected by their surgeons and colonels.

All persons suspected of smallpox were collected and sent to a special hospital where they could not infect other patients. Within a few months Morgan had inoculated every soldier in the American army who had not previously had the dread disease. Despite the risk in inoculation at the time, only one soldier died. Smallpox was never the problem to Washington's army that it was to the British across the Charles River.

Most American leaders, including George Washington, believed that the fighting at Lexington, Concord, and Bunker Hill had convinced Parliament that the colonists were determined to resist the British assault on their rights as Englishmen. Consequently they expected London to pass legislation that would initiate the necessary negotiations to settle the grievances. Thus, no one foresaw the need to recruit an army beyond 1775. Most of the enlistments of Washington's army were to expire on January 1, 1776, and thirty-seven hundred men from Connecticut were scheduled for discharge on December 1, 1775.

As discouraging reports continued to arrive from London, Congress reluctantly became convinced that the attitudes of both king and Parliament were stiffening and that they had no intention of negotiating the grievances. On the contrary, Americans were declared to be rebels, and there was abundant evidence that Britain planned to wage full-scale war to conquer them. Parliament voted to increase the British army to fifty-five thousand men and negotiated with Catherine the Great of Russia for use of Russian troops in America. When she refused, Parliament contracted with several German princes for the use of German mercenary troops, or Hessians.[2]

Faced with the necessity to confront the full military might of Britain and thousands of foreign troops, Washington was concerned about the probable disbanding of his army at the end of 1775. In effect, a new army would have to be enlisted, organized, and trained while holding the defensive lines opposite the British army on Boston Neck and Bunker Hill.

Early in October a Congressional committee consisting of Benjamin Franklin, Thomas Lynch, and Benjamin Harrison arrived in Cambridge to discuss the problem of a new army. Washington believed that the new force should consist of at least twenty thousand men recruited as Continental soldiers to serve for the duration of the war, a professional force patterned after the British army. Its nucleus would be the men who were then in the lines of the existing army.

A survey conducted among Washington's troops to discover how many men were willing to re-enlist indicated that half intended to remain. Most were from small villages and farms, and their concern lay with their families, whom they had left nine months before, expecting to return home shortly. During their absence their farms and crafts had been neglected; many families were in want; bills went unpaid; and many soldiers feared the loss of both home and family. The common feeling among the troops was that they had done more than their share; it was time for those who had remained safely at home to come forward and take up the burden.

Soon Washington was faced with what he would later call the crisis of the war. Unless he was able to persuade substantial numbers of men to re-enlist by January 1, 1776, he would have virtually no army. In mid-November eleven regiments reported a total of 966 men willing to remain, out of five thousand troops. Nearly 75 percent of the 3799-man Connecticut contingent refused to re-enlist.

As a means of keeping the Connecticut men a few days beyond their December 1 deadline, Washington issued his official interpretation, that their period of service was to count from the day that they had mustered, rather than the day they had been called up. He was thus legally enabled to keep them until December 10, although he had to enforce his dictum using other New England regiments, who were ordered to threaten to shoot anyone who left the camps.

Ensign Nathaniel Morgan's Connecticut regiment was ordered to parade before General Washington's headquarters on Friday, December 1. There, Generals Lee and Sullivan stepped forward, and amidst hushed silence Lee asked the men willing to serve ten days beyond their enlistments to withdraw. Approximately a fourth of the men stepped out and marched back to their barracks. The remainder were formed into a hollow square, which General Lee entered. Referring to them as "the worst of all creatures," Lee promised that anyone who continued his cowardly refusal to serve another ten days would be ordered to attack the British lines at Bunker Hill at noon. Those who refused to advance would be fired upon by sharpshooting riflemen.

In the face of this threat, company officers pleaded with their men to stay another ten days, and most finally agreed to do so. Those who refused were disarmed and marched to the guardhouse by a contingent of riflemen. Observing that one of the men being marched off was trying to get his companions to accompany him to the guardhouse, Lee leaped forward and struck him alongside the head. Each man who agreed to remain an additional ten days was given a cup of rum and told that he would receive another the next morning.

At parade the next morning, however, the colonel announced that new orders had been issued canceling all leaves and confining the men to camp. A notice was later posted on the colonel's door announcing that rations would not be issued to men who refused to serve another three weeks. The men, infuriated with this show of bad faith on the part of the colonel, voted not to stay the extra ten days. They milled about the camp, congregating in small groups, waving their muskets, and threatening mutiny, while officers tried to ease the dangerous situation. Other New England troops were brought in to restore order, which was done without bloodshed.

The rebellious Connecticut men were guarded by other regiments until December 9, when they paraded before General Lee. He announced that men willing to enlist for another year were to step out and return to their quarters. Nearly a fourth of the men did so. The rest were ordered to surrender their muskets and ammunition, which in many cases were owned by the men. Although the army paid for their muskets and cartridges, many felt the amount unsatisfactory.

Having disarmed the men, General Lee announced that because they could not be legally discharged until the next day, they were to march to Ploughed Hill and man the entrenchments there with spears that would be provided for them. The men indignantly refused to go and after a tense impasse were allowed to return to their quarters.

The next day, Sunday, the Connecticut militiamen once again formed in front of Lee's headquarters. There they were disdainfully counted out and dismissed, and they marched off to the jeers and boos of other New England troops who pelted them with refuse. Ironically, many of the men who hissed and jeered them would march off at the end of December, when their own enlistments expired.

On October 18, 1775, after giving the inhabitants of Falmouth, Massachusetts (now Portland, Maine), two hours to evacuate the town, four warships of the British navy opened fire at pointblank range from just off the beach. From 9:00 A.M. to 6:00 P.M., firing deliberately and accurately, the *Canceau, Halifax, Spitfire,* and the armed transport *Symmetry* blasted everything visible. The operation destroyed the entire town; over 130 homes were demolished, as were churches, warehouses, docks, and the courthouse. Late in the afternoon Captain Henry Mouat, the naval commander, sent several small parties of marines and sailors ashore to set fire to any houses that had survived. The operation was the idea of Admiral Thomas Graves, who considered it an object lesson against those towns that supported the ships of "Washington's Navy" in their attacks on British shipping.

Washington used news of the Falmouth raid to motivate his men to re-enlist, if only to prove to the British that such terror tactics would not succeed. He pleaded with them to meet their responsibilities at a time when Britain had clearly indicated her intention of burning down all New England towns, as the attack on Falmouth attested:

> When life, liberty, and property are at stake; when our country is in danger of being a melancholy scene of bloodshed and desolation; when our towns are laid in ashes and innocent women and children driven from their peaceful habitations, and a brutal and savage enemy, (more so than was ever yet found in a civilized nation) are threatening us and everything we hold dear with destruction from foreign troops, it little becomes the character of a soldier to shrink from danger and conditions for new terms of enlistment.[3]

Washington saw as his primary problem in building the new army the formation of a first-rate officers' corps. The total number of regiments was reduced from thirty-eight to twenty-six in order to have each one filled to its full complement. This created a surplus of officers from the disbanded regiments, but Washington solved the problem by forming all officers into a battalion which, through open discussion and voting, could decide which officers should command the various companies and regiments. The New England men, accustomed to town meetings and public discussions, found the solution acceptable.

New England men liked to be with friends and neighbors, and the rumored organization of a new Continental army made many fear that they would somehow find themselves under officers who were strangers. To encourage enlistments, Washington promised the men in the ranks that they would serve with men from their own areas. He also promised that any man signing for another year would receive a set of new clothes and a three-week furlough home. Young officers were sent home to recruit new men; and to take the place of the departing Connecticut men, Washington prevailed upon both the Massachusetts and New Hampshire provincial congresses to send their available militia units to Boston. Both colonies responded magnificently, and their regiments proved to be excellent troops. Many were men who had fought at Bunker Hill and returned home to their local militia companies.

Early in 1776, Washington found that his re-enlistments had created a Continental army of 8212. Without the men on recruiting duty and furloughs, he had 5582 ready for duty, in addition to newly arriving militia units. Washington then called again on the provincial congresses for men to fill the gaps, and militia companies materialized in large numbers. They saved the day for the colonial cause, for they took up the slack while one army mustered out and a new one was assembled to replace it. On December 11, Washington himself, who usually held a low opinion of militia, wrote:

> The militia are coming in fast. I am pleased with the alacrity which the good people of this province, as well as those of New Hampshire, have shown upon this occasion.[4]

The militia was holding defensive positions in the face of the professional British army. Their success was miraculous; the military world had never seen anything like it.

The organization of the new Continental army rested upon the basic unit — the company — composed of men and officers who were neighbors and friends. A company, commanded by a captain, was made up of a first lieutenant, second lieutenant, ensign, four sergeants, four corporals, a drummer, a fifer, and seventy-six privates, for a total of ninety men.

Eight companies comprised a regiment, which was commanded by a colonel and included a lieutenant colonel, major, adjutant, quartermaster, surgeon, and surgeon's mate. Thus a full regiment numbered 727 officers and men. At no time, however, during the Revolution did any company reach its full complement of ninety men; consequently, none of the regiments achieved its full strength.

On January 24, 1776, the American army was organized into six brigades of four to five regiments each, plus an independent regiment of Southern riflemen.

General Thomas's Brigade — *Massachusetts   First Brigade*
Colonel Learned's regiment
Colonel J. Reed's regiment
Colonel Whitcomb's regiment
Colonel Ward's regiment
Colonel Bailey's regiment

General Spencer's Brigade — Connecticut   Second Brigade
Colonel Parsons's regiment
Colonel Huntington's regiment
Colonel Webb's regiment
Colonel Wyllys's regiment

General Greene's Brigade — Rhode Island   Third Brigade
Colonel Varnum's regiment
Colonel Hitchcock's regiment
Colonel Little's regiment
Colonel Bond's regiment

General Heath's Brigade — Massachusetts   Fourth Brigade
Colonel Prescott's regiment
Colonel Sergeant's regiment
Colonel Phinney's regiment
Colonel Greaton's regiment
Colonel Baldwin's regiment

General Sullivan's Brigade — New Hampshire   Fifth Brigade
Colonel J. Reed's regiment
Colonel Nixon's regiment
Colonel Stark's regiment
Colonel Poor's regiment

General Glover's Brigade — Massachusetts   Sixth Brigade
Colonel Glover's regiment
Colonel Patterson's regiment
Colonel Arnold's regiment
Colonel Hutchinson's regiment

While the new army was being assembled, many sections of the colonial lines went unmanned. Had the British launched an attack, the effect on Washington's army would have been disastrous. The British failure to take advantage of the colonial vulnerability made the miracle possible.

On August 2, 1775, King George III summoned General Gage to London so he could:

Give his majesty exact information of everything that it may be necessary to prepare, as early as possible, for the operations of next year, and to suggest to his majesty such matters in relation thereto as your knowledge and experience of the service enable you to fur- nish.[5]

Gage immediately prepared for his journey. In speeches to his army and to the Loyalists, he said he intended to return as soon as he advised the king in regard to the situation. After turning over the army to General Howe on September 27, he left for England on October 10. There Gage quickly discovered that neither his advice nor his services were required in any capacity. The sum- mons had been a charade played out to save him embarrassment; he was being removed from command in America, and he never returned there.

On the eve of taking command of the British army in America, Sir William Howe wrote to Lord Dartmouth his honest assessment of the situation in Boston:

> I am of the opinion that no offensive operations can be carried on to advantage from Boston. On the supposition of a certainty of driving the rebels from their entrenchments, no advantage would be gained but reputation, victory would not be improved, through the want of every necessity to march into the country. The loss of men would probably be great, and the rebels be as numerous in a few days as before their defeat; besides, the country is remarkably strong and adapted to their way of fighting.[6]

The British army had long seen Gage as a man lacking in both desire and ability to come to grips with the Americans. They hated him for his leniency toward the people of Boston and were wildly enthusiastic when they learned he had been replaced. One officer wrote about Howe as their new commander: "Even the blunders of Bunker Hill were forgotten, so happy were many people at the change."[7]

Howe moved into his new headquarters in Boston, and General Sir Henry Clinton, the second-in-command, took over the forces on Charlestown Heights. Howe had completed a line of forts at the top of Bunker Hill that were so powerful that the outer lines on Charlestown Neck were abandoned as unnecessary.

On December 12, 1775, all the men on Charlestown Heights, with the exception of a garrison of six hundred left to man the forts, were brought back to Boston to live in barracks. It was correctly estimated that a garrison of that size was sufficient to stop the entire rebel army in the event of an attack. The garrison was relieved every two weeks.

Boston Neck was also strengthened; a canal was dug across the Neck and a drawbridge built over it. Many nearby buildings were torn down to improve the field of fire as well as provide firewood. Over six hundred men worked daily on the fortifications.

The possibility of an American attack across the frozen Charles River from Lechmere Point was not discounted, and a number of redoubts were constructed on Boston Common. These included a strong redoubt on a small offshore island called Fox Hill, and extensive fortifications atop Mount Whoredom north of the Common.

Before the Charles River began to freeze over, the British launched a large raid on Lechmere Point to carry off livestock. On November 9, Lieutenant Colonel Clark led six companies of light infantry and four companies of grenadiers across the Charles from Boston Common. At noon, as high tide inundated the causeway to the mainland and turned the peninsula into an island, barges were rowed across the river to land men on Lechmere Point. It was assumed that the American troops would be cut off while the regulars collected the animals.

The alarm was relayed quickly to the American camp, and Colonel Thompson's regiment of riflemen and part of the regiments of Colonel Woolbridge and Colonel Patterson raced to Lechmere Point, waded through two feet of water, and opened fire on the British troops.

By the time the Americans arrived, the regulars had collected the livestock and were leaving. Captain Evelyn, commanding the rear guard, was able to hold off the advancing Americans, and as he climbed aboard the last boat, grapeshot from the warship *Cerberus* raked the Americans advancing behind him, badly wounding two men. The regulars completed the raid with the loss of two men killed.

Colonial Ensign Nathaniel Morgan was sleeping in his tent behind the lines at Lechmere Point when he was suddenly jarred awake. He wrote:

The world seemed to be full of men and cannon roaring on both sides, and the small arms a-cracking and the cannon balls whistled through the air, and we saw them strike in the water and make it fly as high as the houses, and the regulars landed about 500 to get some of our cattle, and the riflemen waylaid them and fired and the regulars pulled on their oars and went off, and we stayed about half an hour and we had orders to return to our tents, and it began to rain and it rained all night.[8]

General Clinton praised his men the next day in General Orders, and Washington commended the riflemen and Patterson's regiment for their quick response in crossing the flooded causeway to attack the enemy. In his General Orders he praised the "men who had fought so well," but he took notice of some "who manifested backwardness in crossing," and he also reprimanded several officers whose men failed to show the proper desire to meet the enemy in combat.

During the night of November 22 Israel Putnam led a force of several hundred men down the slopes of Prospect Hill, across five hundred yards of meadow, toward the Charles River, and up a small elevation called Cobble Hill. Located on the northern bank of Willis Creek across from Lechmere Point, the hill would allow the Americans to bring field guns to bear, in the event of another British attack on that peninsula. Putnam's detachment brought gabions, fascines, and other entrenching equipment and worked all night without being detected. At dawn the exhausted men returned to their lines atop Prospect Hill.

The following night a detachment under General Heath returned to complete the fortifications. Several regiments of riflemen were posted between Cobble Hill and the shoreline as a safeguard against an attack that never came. To Heath's surprise, the entrenchments were completed without receiving any fire from British ships or batteries.

Heavy New England snow began to fall in November, and the weather turned bitterly cold. Howe brought in carpenters from New York and from ships in the harbor, and they hurried the construction of barracks for the men living behind fortifications at Bunker Hill and Boston Neck. Most of the American troops had moved into barracks built on Prospect Hill and Winter Hill, or at Roxbury and Cambridge. Over seventeen hundred men slept in the buildings of Harvard College. Others lived in snug cabins or in houses that had belonged to Loyalists.

There were serious shortages of firewood in both the American and British camps. At the start of the siege of Boston, large numbers of locust trees, famous for their fragrant white flowers that later turned to pods, were cut down for firewood by the soldiers. On September 2, 1775, Washington requested that the Massachusetts legislature send firewood to his army before regiments began to fight with each other over the remaining locust trees.

General Greene wrote to the Rhode Island Congress in December, "We have suffered prodigiously for want of wood. Many regiments have been obliged to eat their provisions raw for want of fuel to cook it."[9]

The presence of thousands of men along the battle lines, month after month, decimated the lush green farmlands of Cambridge and Roxbury. Fields and orchards were dug up and laid bare. Horses and cattle ate the available grass down to the bare ground, and most of the trees were cut for entrenching timber or for fuel. Fences had long since disappeared.

Moses Brown, a visiting Quaker, and Jeremy Belknap, a famous cleric and historian of the time, described Roxbury during the siege as a town with many deserted houses, windows gone, numerous buildings with holes caused by British cannon, and many houses torn down for fuel.

The lack of firewood in Boston was a major concern to the British army. Despite strict orders, the men kept dismantling fences and abandoned houses for firewood. On December 5, Howe issued orders that:

> The frequent depredations committed by soldiers in pulling down houses and fences, in defiance of repeated orders, has induced the commander-in-chief to direct the Provost to go his rounds attended by the executioner, with orders to hang upon the spot the first man he shall detect in the fact, without waiting for further proof by trial. The commanding officers are to take particular care that the soldiers are acquainted with this order.[10]

On December 13 Howe issued a plan he believed would provide firewood for his shivering troops. Each regiment was directed to furnish an officer and twenty men to collect firewood. Officers received an extra five shillings a day, and men received a gill of rum daily and had no other duties assigned to them. Armed with two iron crowbars, three crescent saws, handspikes, ten axes, six wedges, three mauls, and two fathoms of rope, the firewood details were to demolish such wharfs, houses, old ships, and trees as the major general commanding their barracks would point out to them:

> The wood to be placed where the commanding officer of the regiment may direct. When regularly piled up, it is to be measured, and the soldiers will be allowed 5 shillings sterling for each cord they so provide and pile. This will be delivered to the care of the regiment as a fund for their supply of fuel.[11]

Until they moved into their barracks on December 24, British troops on Bunker Hill had lived in tents around which snow swirled and piled up. Unable to have fires inside their tents, they huddled around open campfires in futile attempts to keep warm. Major Charles Stuart wrote to his father that two thirds of the men on Charlestown Heights were suffering from colds.

The daily life of the British soldiers consisted of constant parades and drills, hours of hard manual labor on fortifications, and long hours of sentry duty. Smallpox raged throughout the city and, with scurvy, brought fear and depression to the troops. Many men exhibited the telltale signs of scurvy: hemorrhaging in the skin and mucous membranes, and spongy gums that loosened their teeth. They became progressively weaker, until hundreds were incapable of physical activity.

To supplement their diet of salt fish and dried peas, officers and others who had money purchased fresh food from sailors who had access to it from nearby coastal towns. It was possible to buy whatever was needed if one had money, but the lot of the penniless privates, dying of scurvy for lack of fresh fruit and vegetables, was desperate.

Howe conferred with his regimental and divisional surgeons in an effort to discover some method of ending the nutritional deficiency. They recommended spruce beer, a drink popular with Americans as a good preventative of scurvy. Howe immediately ordered three pints daily for each man and prescribed the recipe for making the beer. A barrel of spruce beer, containing from thirty to thirty-two gallons, was brewed from five quarts of molasses and ten quarts of essence of spruce, which was obtained by boiling the twigs and leaves of the spruce tree. This mixture of molasses and spruce essence was boiled and then fermented with yeast.

Arrangements were made with Mr. Goldthwaite, a local brewer, to supply the spruce beer at one dollar per barrel. Howe insisted that a regimental quartermaster attend every brewing to be sure that the proper proportion of molasses and spruce was adhered to.

Another measure to combat scurvy was sauerkraut. The supply was limited, however, so it was issued only to regimental surgeons, who used it to treat men suffering from scurvy in the regimental hospitals. By late January, as supplies of sauerkraut arrived from Ireland, Howe announced that quartermasters were to draw one hundred pounds for the officers of each regiment. Near the end of February, sauerkraut was available to each soldier at the rate of one half-pound a week. Spruce beer and sauerkraut cleared up scurvy among the regulars, and inoculations finally decreased the number of cases of smallpox.

In spite of brutal punishments, the crime rate among British troops remained high. Private Henry Drake of the 18th Regiment, the Royal Irish, was sentenced to one thousand lashes for desertion; Private William Croan of the 17th Light Dragoons was sentenced to be hanged for the same offense. Since one thousand lashes was in reality a sentence of slow and painful death, the hanging was considered more humane.

Private Richard James, a sentry, broke into a store and was caught with a bucket, a bottle, and a jar of molasses in his possession. He was sentenced to receive five hundred lashes on his bare back. Two other privates, Thomas Owen and Henry Johnston of the 59th Regiment, were captured while disposing of a number of articles they had stolen from the store of a merchant named Coffin. The two were hanged two days later.

Private Thomas McMahon and his wife, Isabella, were both found guilty of buying stolen merchandise, and the court-martial ruled that both were aware that the articles were stolen. Eighteen-year-old Thomas McMahon was sentenced to one thousand lashes and sixteen-year-old Mrs. McMahon was sentenced to one hundred lashes, "on the bare back at a cart's tail in different portions of the most conspicuous part of town and to be imprisoned for three months." Isabella, a slight girl, did not serve the latter part of the sentence, for like her husband she did not survive the lashing.

Two privates of the 59th, Thomas Jones and William Ives, were found guilty of forcibly breaking and entering a house while drunk and stealing various articles of food and clothing. They were sentenced to eight hundred lashes each.

The savage justice accorded to privates was in marked contrast to that meted out to commissioned and noncommissioned officers. Anyone below the rank of corporal was considered an animal to be disciplined with severe physical punishment; it was therefore considered to be the only method by which he could be made to understand. One can visualize the upper-class British officers, sons of England's leading families, their childhoods spent on country estates or in large London townhouses, seated on a court-martial board in a neat row of scarlet and white splendor. Before them, awaiting their verdict with downcast eyes, stood the product of workhouses, foundling homes, and orphanages. The gulf between them made compassion or understanding virtually impossible.

Lieutenant William Hamilton of the 63rd Regiment was charged with being drunk while on duty. When his captain put him under arrest, Hamilton offered to fight him and refused to go to his quarters when ordered to do so. Hamilton was charged with behaving in "a scandalous, infamous manner unbecoming the character of an officer and a gentleman." The court found him not guilty of being drunk but guilty of refusing to go when placed under arrest, offering violence against his superior, and actions unbecoming the character of an officer. He was sentenced to be discharged.

Lieutenant Terrance Macgrath of the 45th was tried by court-martial for assaulting Lieutenant Houghton of the same regiment. It was charged that Macgrath insulted Houghton in an attempt to get him to fight, and when Houghton refused, Macgrath attacked him in "a scandalous and infamous manner, such as unbecoming an officer and a gentleman." The court ruled that Macgrath had not acted "with scandalous behavior" but only with "improper and unwarrantable behavior." He was suspended from all duty and pay for three months and was sentenced to be publicly reprimanded by the commander-in-chief. After reviewing the case, General Howe did not choose to reprimand.

On November 10, 1775, King George III announced that all regiments in North America with the exception of the 18th and 59th were to be augmented, i.e., the number of companies in each regiment increased from ten to twelve. Each regiment henceforth contained one grenadier company, one light infantry company, and ten battalion companies instead of eight.

The table of organization for a regiment required one colonel, one lieutenant colonel, one major, nine captains, fourteen lieutenants, ten ensigns, one chaplain, one adjutant, one quartermaster, one surgeon, one surgeon's mate, thirty-six sergeants, thirty-six corporals, twenty-four drummers, two fifers, and 672 privates. The roster continued to carry the names of the nonexistent thirty-six contingency men who drew pay and rations through the colonel. The regiment's true strength was set at 819 officers and men.

Augmentation provided immediate promotion for many officers, who could be advanced by direct appointment from General Howe without payment for the new rank. Lieutenant John Barker of the 4th was promoted to captain. When Captain Thomas McCann of the 23rd was made commander of one of the two new companies in the 23rd, Lieutenant Frederick Mackenzie, on November 23, at last was promoted to captain and given command of Captain McCann's previous company. Five years later, after thirty-five years of continuous service, Mackenzie was promoted to the rank of major.

With the arrival of freezing weather, the British troops moved into barracks for their second winter in Boston. Howe ordered that all women drawing half-rations were to find lodgings close to the barracks of their regiments. He directed General Clinton to return all of the women who had been quartered on Bunker Hill after the battle, to Boston, where they were to reside near their respective regiments. The only force in the fortifications of Charlestown Heights was to be the 600-man garrison.

The 23rd Regiment moved back to their barracks on Fort Hill, and Nancy Mackenzie found a fine house on Olivers Street only two hundred yards from the barracks. With the abundance of abandoned homes, it was not difficult, and although General Howe required officers to serve more time in barracks with their men, Frederick Mackenzie was able to spend a great deal of time with his family. He and Nancy worried that the children might contract smallpox, and he had the entire family inoculated.

Howe's General Orders for November 3 sounded a somber note:

> No more graves are to be made in the burial ground upon the left of the Marine encampment. Soldiers dying in the General Hospital may be buried in the ground at the back of the upper Hospital and those dying in the regimental Hospitals, will be interred in the nearest burying ground.[12]

On December 12, 1775, despite bitter cold, American troops began construction of a causeway across the arm of the Charles River that isolated Lechmere Point during high tide. To protect the workmen, two eighteen-pound guns were brought from the Roxbury lines and hauled up Cobble Hill. Early in the morning of December 17, in a heavy fog, three hundred men under Israel Putnam marched across the new causeway and climbed to the top of a hill on Phipp's Farm on Lechmere Point. Under protection of the fog, they immediately began to build fortifications, working less than half a mile from a British warship off the beach.

Shortly after 12:00 noon, however, the fog cleared away to reveal the Americans on top of the hill. The warship *Scarborough* commenced firing immediately at pointblank range with grape and round shot. One man was wounded, and the Americans were driven from the hill.

General Heath was ordered to return to the hill the next day to finish the work begun by Putnam's men. Expecting a large number of casualties, Heath ordered one of his surgeons to accompany his detachment of three hundred men. Fortunately, the capable Captain Smith of the American artillery commanded the eighteen-pounders on Cobble Hill. As dawn rose, he opened fire on the *Scarborough* and scored several direct hits. While the Americans on Cobble Hill cheered, the warship weighed anchor and dropped down toward Barton's Point and the ferry-way.

Heath halted his detachment below the summit of the hill and had his men ground their muskets. Moving by companies, the men filed into the various unfinished areas to which they had been assigned. Once the men were within the protection of the gabion-raised walls, two sentries were posted to watch the British batteries on Charlestown and Barton's Point in Boston. They had orders to shout, "A shot!" when they saw the flash from the British guns, whereupon everyone was directed to drop flat and stay that way until they heard the ball hit.

The men started to work and within a few minutes the sentries cried, "A shot!" and all three hundred men hit the ground. It was a shell from one of the large thirteen-inch brass mortars on Charlestown Heights, and it burst with a roar as it hit the side of the embankment. Dirt rained down over nearby men, and a piece of metal struck the hat of one prone soldier. The bombardment continued the rest of the day, shot and shell smashing into the fortifications on the hill. Strangely, not a man was hit, and the troops worked steadily, interrupted only by the cry of the sentries. That night they moved out of the nearly completed works, picked up their arms, and marched back to Cambridge.

Work on Lechmere Point continued for the next several days until the fortifications were completed. The day before Christmas, Washington and his staff visited the hill and inspected the two new redoubts erected there. They enclosed several guns and mortars with which Washington planned to bombard Boston when his long-delayed plan to assault the city from across the Charles River was put into action.

On the night of December 28 an attempt was made to surprise the British sentries on Charlestown Neck. The plan called for crossing the frozen Charles River from Cobble Hill and dashing across the solidly frozen mill pond to the rear of the British positions. The audacious raid might have succeeded had not one of the attackers slipped and fallen on the ice, discharging his loaded musket. This warned the British of their danger, and the raid was called back.

By Christmas Day, Washington's apprehension about being left without an army had disappeared. Although many Massachusetts and Connecticut troops had left, the influx of thousands of sturdy militiamen from Massachusetts and New Hampshire more than compensated for their loss. Many entrenchments were held by relatively green troops, but enough veterans had re-enlisted to hold them together. As military materiel captured by Captain Manley from the British ship *Nancy* started to arrive from Cape Ann, the number and quality of supplies improved. Unlike the British that winter, the Americans were well supplied with food and firewood. Barracks had been built, and as word arrived of early successes in Canada, many new men enlisted in the Continental army.

During the lean years ahead, Washington would wistfully recall the wealth of food available to the Americans in New England. The Provincial Congress kept long trains of cattle and wagons headed for the American lines. On December 24, 1775, Washington directed that the rations for each soldier were:

Corned beef and pork, four days a week.

Salt fish one day, and fresh beef two days.

As milk cannot be procured during winter, men are to have one pound and a half of beef or eighteen ounces of pork per day.

Half pint of rice, or a pint of Indian meal, per week.

One quart of spruce beer per day.

Six pounds of candles to one hundred men per week, for guards.

Six ounces of butter, or nine ounces of hog's lard per week.

Three pints of peas and beans per man per week, or vegetables equivalent.

One pound of flour per man each day; hard bread to be dealt out one day in the week, in lieu of flour.[13]

At the opening session of Parliament on October 26, 1775, King George III had made a memorable speech in which he declared that the Americans were not fighting for a redress of grievances as they had publicly proclaimed; they were, in reality, fighting to establish "an independent empire." Consequently, the British government was determined to put a speedy end to disorders in America. To this end, the army and navy were enlarged and negotiations begun with foreign governments for the use of their troops to supplement British forces in America.

Word of George's historic speech reached the colonies January 1. It was sent to Washington under a flag of truce the day after it arrived at Howe's headquarters. Washington's answer to the speech was to raise the Union flag atop the fortifications on Prospect Hill in what was that flag's first appearance anywhere. The flag had thirteen red and white stripes with the Union Jack in a small field in the upper inside corner. The waiting British troops on Bunker Hill believed at first that the flag indicated a desire on the part of the Americans to surrender in the face of the king's unyielding speech. But the cheering soon dwindled away as the significance of the Union flag was realized.

January 1, 1776, was a critical day for the American army. Officers and men were joining their regiments in the new army, and hundreds of others were leaving for home. The departing men were asked to sell their muskets or rifles, if they owned them, to the army at a price determined by a board of officers. Some men refused to sell for the offered price, but the officers were determined to obtain the arms, and in most cases they were successful.

Despite their critical position regarding troop replacement, Washington and his army had weathered the storm. On January 4 he proudly wrote:

> Search the volumes of history through, and I much question whether a case similar to ours is to be found; namely, to maintain a post against the flower of the British for six months together, without powder, and then to have one army disbanded, and another to be raised, within the same distance of a reinforced army. It is too much to attempt.

And General Nathanael Greene wrote:

> We have just experienced the inconveniences of disbanding an army within cannon shot of the enemy, and forming a new one in its stead. An instance never before known. Had the enemy been fully acquainted with our condition, I cannot pretend to say what might have been the consequence.[14]

Twenty

The Fortification
of Dorchester Heights

WHEN GENERAL ARTEMAS WARD took command of the American militia after the British return from Lexington and Concord back in April 1775, he was faced with the problem of designing the American strongholds around Boston, which would necessarily rely heavily on artillery. To assist him, he secured the services of the Boston bookseller Henry Knox.

Knox, like John Stark, was descended from Scotch-Irish people who had emigrated to America from Northern Ireland. His parents had ten boys but lost six in childhood. Of the four surviving brothers, the oldest died at sea. At nine, Henry was apprenticed to a bookseller to help support his family. Three years later, his father, a sea captain, died in the West Indies, leaving Henry the sole support of his widowed mother and three-year-old brother.

At nineteen Knox was present at the Boston Massacre on March 5, 1770. Standing only a few feet from the British troops when they opened fire, he tried to convince their captain to keep his men from shooting.

When he completed his apprenticeship in 1772, Knox opened a bookstore on Cornhill Street that soon became a favored meeting place for educated young people in Boston, as well as young Nathanael Greene of Rhode Island. A member of the smart Boston Grenadier Corps, Knox reached the rank of lieutenant and, at six feet five inches and weighing 250 pounds, the heavily muscled Knox was an impressive figure.

He fell in love with Lucy Flucker, the buxom and beautiful daughter of Thomas Flucker, Royal Secretary of the Province of Massachusetts Bay and one of the leading Loyalists of America. Through Lucy's brother, a lieutenant in the British army occupying Boston, Henry was offered a commission in the regular British army, which he refused.

During the fateful year of 1774, twenty-four-year-old Henry and twenty-year-old Lucy were married. The union meant an end to Lucy's claim to her family's fortune as well as its political beliefs, so far removed was her husband from her social role. On the night of April 19, 1775, during the return of Lord Percy's regiments from Lexington and Concord, the couple escaped from Boston.

Knox's bookstore, left in the care of his nineteen-year-old brother, William, was soon looted and wrecked by off-duty British troops assisted by enthusiastic Loyalist militants. Knox, however, proved very capable in aiding General Ward in fortifying American positions around Boston; and when Washington took command of the army after the Battle of Bunker Hill, he was so impressed with Knox's knowledge of artillery and fortifications that he wrote Congress recommending him to be commissioned a colonel and given command of the American artillery, which was then suffering from its ineffective performance at the Battle of Bunker Hill and was, in fact, practically nonexistent.

The twenty-five-year-old Knox received his commission as a full colonel in November and took command of colonial artillery, replacing Major General Richard Gridley, who was reassigned as chief engineer.

Within a week after his appointment, Knox suggested to General Washington that he be allowed to go to Fort Ticonderoga and bring some of the guns there to Cambridge. Washington enthusiastically endorsed the plan and issued orders for him to leave at once:

> You are immediately to examine into the state of the artillery of this Army and take an account of the cannon, mortars, shells, lead and ammunition that are wanting. When you have done that, you are to

proceed in the most expeditious manner to New York; there to apply to the president of the Provincial Congress and learn of him, whether Colonel Reed did any thing or left any orders respecting these articles, and get him to procure such of them as can possibly be had there. The president if he can, will have them immediately sent hither; if he cannot, you must put them in a proper channel for being transported to this camp with dispatch before you leave New York. After you have procured as many of these necessaries as you can there, you must go to Major Genl. Schuyler and get the remainder from Ticonderoga, Crown Point, or St. John's. If it should be necessary from Quebec, if in our hands; the want of them is so great that no trouble or expense must be spared to obtain them. I have wrote to General Schuyler, he will give every necessary assistance that they may be had and forwarded to this place with the utmost dispatch. I have given you a warrant to the Paymaster General of the Continental Army for a Thousand Dollars to defray the expense attending your journey and procuring these articles, an account of which you are to keep and render upon your return. Given under my hand at Headquarters at Cambridge this 16 day of November . . . 1775.

[signed] G. Washington[1]

Accompanied by his brother William and a servant, Knox left for New York City. After arranging there for available cannon to be sent to Cambridge, they traveled up the Hudson to Albany and delivered Washington's letter to General Philip Schuyler, commander of the northern territory. Washington's letter persuaded Schuyler to lend Knox his wholehearted support, and largely as a result of his efforts, the two brothers arrived at Ticonderoga in four days with men and equipment. They were soon joined by scores of other men recruited by Schuyler.

Most of the British cannon were located along the walls of the fortress, set into embrasures, and held in place by iron bars and concrete. The weather was bitterly cold, and the waters of Lake George were beginning to freeze. Working in icy winds along the parapets, they began to cut the bars and break out the concrete by using sledgehammers and chisels.

After weeks of backbreaking labor, forty-three cannon, three howitzers, and fourteen mortars had been lowered to the frozen ground below the parapets. The total weight of the guns was

120,000 pounds, or sixty tons, and presented a formidable task to men charged with dragging them to the shore of Lake George and loading them on flat barges, or bateaux. In addition to the guns, they loaded thirty thousand flints and thousands of musket- and cannonballs packed in kegs.

Gangs of men used hundreds of oxen pulling heavy ropes to drag the massive guns to the north landing of Lake George and onto the bateaux by rolling them along the frozen ground over tree trunks that the men laid in front of the load. Other men would carry the logs that had just been traversed and reposition them in front of the heavy, rumbling guns. Earthen ramps were constructed at the lake to help ease the guns onto the bateaux.

The kegs of musket- and cannonballs were trundled over "corduroy roads" made of logs laid side by side and covered with earth. They finally succeeded in loading the heavier guns into three large bateaux, and the lighter items were loaded onto smaller boats.

When all was ready, Henry Knox headed south with the smaller vessels for Fort George, thirty-three miles to the south at the southern terminus of Lake George. There he organized local citizens and the troops sent north by General Schuyler into an army of ox-drawn sled teams under the direction of experienced drivers.

Young William Knox was given responsibility for floating the three heavily laden bateaux down the length of Lake George. His flat-bottomed, tapered boats rode dangerously low in the water as they sailed away from the frozen shoreline into the open water by breaking a channel through the ice. The sails used to propel the bateaux failed to move the overburdened craft with any appreciable speed, so the men were forced to row with long-handled wooden sweeps.

At the narrowest part of the lake, above Tongue Mountain at Sabbath Day Point, one of the bateaux ran aground, ripping out the bottom, and it started to settle with its heavy load of iron. The other boats pulled into a landing and, working in the icy waters, the men began the difficult and dangerous task of removing the guns onto the rocky shore. After several days of unbelievably brutal work, the vessel was repaired and the guns reloaded. On days when the men labored in the freezing waters of Lake George, a nearby encampment of Tuscarora Indians of the Iroquois Confederacy furnished warm food and shelter.

With icy water swirling only inches below the gunwales of the boats, they moved slowly into the rapidly narrowing open water. Heading into the wind, they laboriously rowed past the north arm of Lake George and First Narrow, near present-day Bolton Landing. They finally reached Fort George on December 15 after ten hours of backbreaking rowing.

Henry Knox was waiting for them with an army of men and animals. In addition to the hundreds of men, oxen, horses, and sleds that had arrived from Schuyler's army in Albany, Knox had contacted local citizens, such as Squire Charles Palmer of Stillwater, and had signed individual contracts with each team that agreed to haul one gun. In order to move a single gun that fired a ball weighing nine pounds, a four-oxen sled was required. An eighteen-pounder or twenty-four-pounder required eight oxen. Each team was manned by four to six men per sled.

The men toiled night and day in the bitter cold to unload the guns from the bateaux and lash them onto the waiting sleds. The kegs of balls and flints were packed into sleighs carrying the lighter guns. Finally, a total of fifty-five ox-drawn sledges with eighty yoke of oxen attended by their drivers were loaded and ready to go. On December 17 an optimistic Knox wrote to Washington, estimating that he should arrive in Cambridge, three hundred miles away, within sixteen or seventeen days.

Their first objective was Fort Edward, ten miles away over the old French and Indian War military road. The snow was packed hard, and the sledges slowly crunched their way through the white-sheathed forest. Some of the sleds broke through the top crust of ice to become locked in depressions below the surface. When this happened, everyone stopped and helped to extricate the sledge that was in trouble. Knox was strict in demanding that the entire three-mile-long caravan stay together.

Finally the procession reached Fort Edward, on the banks of the Hudson River, and on Christmas Day 1775 they crossed the frozen Hudson to the west bank. From there the caravan moved south over a winding, narrow wilderness road through Saratoga toward Albany, over thirty miles away. New Year's Eve found them within ten miles of Albany, in their usual night-camp. At dusk the expedition halted, and the animals were unhitched and led into a large enclosure where they were fed and watered. Armed men guarded the animals during the night, relieved at two-hour intervals. The heavy sleds with their tons of iron and brass were left in the road, guarded by mounted men who rode up and down the long column.

In an enclosure near the animals three hundred men cooked their evening meal, smoked long clay pipes, and slept around the many campfires bundled in long fur coats and caps. The temperature was 5° below zero.

Knox planned to cross the Hudson River above Albany to the east bank so that he could avoid crossing the Mohawk River and then face a second crossing of the Hudson below Albany. His attempt failed, for the ice was too thin; one sledge went through it and would have pulled the oxen in with it, had it not been for a quick-thinking driver who cut the harness with his hatchet. Both the gun and the sledge were subsequently recovered.

Knox chose to cross the Mohawk and go into Albany, recrossing the Hudson from there. They crossed the Mohawk at Sloss's Ferry over ice that was dangerously thin, and one gun and sledge were lost. Somewhat behind schedule, the long column reached Albany on January 4 and was greeted by an anxious General Schuyler.

A thaw then set in; the snow disappeared from the roads, and the ice on the Hudson became too thin to bear the weight of the heavy sledges. There was nothing to do but wait for colder weather; but fortunately, within a few days it turned bitterly cold again, and the Hudson began to ice. To insure thicker ice Knox sent his men out on the frozen river to chop holes that would allow the water to seep to the surface. With this extra thickness he hoped the ice would be strong enough to bear the terrible weight of the loaded sledges.

On the morning of January 7, while hundreds of Albany citizens watched, the column of sledges moved out onto the surface of the river. Ten sleighs moving across the ice at 200-yard intervals had reached the east bank when a sledge containing a heavy, twenty-four-pounder broke through the ice near the Albany shore. Again the driver saved his animals by cutting the harness with his hatchet, but the sleigh and gun broke a hole in the ice fourteen feet in diameter.

Dozens of citizens rushed out on the ice to help, and with their assistance, both gun and sleigh were recovered. By the end of the following day, January 8, the entire column had crossed the Hudson and camped for the night near the town of Green Bush, where Knox negotiated for several new heavy sleighs and a spare string of horses and oxen.

The column snaked its way south toward Kinderhook and on to Claverack nine miles away. That night Knox waited for his column to close up before unhitching the animals and making camp.

They were now in an area of steep and forbidding mountains that would test the endurance of both men and animals to the utmost. On January 10 the teams pulled their ponderous burdens up steep slopes covered with hip-deep snow. The weary men and animals reached Hillsdale in New York and crossed the border into Massachusetts. There began a painful struggle through deepening snow and over rugged mountain passes, from whose heights, Knox noted, they "might have seen all the kingdoms on earth."

On January 12, the column was deep in the heart of the Green Woods, an area containing steep grades that undulated in an endless succession of snow-covered ridges. Painfully they moved toward Blandford, where the sledges faced the steep drop into the valleys of the sheer Glasgow or Westfield mountains.

On this descent, the teamsters, fearful that the heavy guns would cause the overloaded sleighs to plunge down upon their animals and riders, refused to proceed until convinced that it could be done by using long ropes tied to the sledges and anchored to tree trunks. Using blocks and tackles, each sleigh was eased down, aided by hundreds of men who helped hold back each one with the long ropes.

Not until mid-January did the long caravan reach Westfield. The following day they were in Springfield, faced with the problem of crossing the wide Connecticut River. Luckily it was frozen solidly and the heavy sleds streamed across the ice. On the east bank Knox paid off his New York teamsters and hired Massachusetts teams to complete the journey.

During a fierce snowstorm on January 25, the long and weary procession struggled into Framingham, twenty-one miles from Boston. There the heavier guns were unloaded onto the ground along what is now Waverly Boulevard, and the sleds with the lighter-calibered guns continued toward Cambridge.

Well into early February, hundreds of soldiers labored to load the big guns on scores of ox-drawn carts to transport them to Cambridge. Other men worked constructing gun carriages and gun mounts for the new weapons. One by one, the guns were placed in the fortifications ringing Boston. Some of the new twenty-four-pounders went to arm new redoubts built at Sewell's Point, Brookline Fort, and Lamb's Dam along the Roxbury lines.

Knox's feat in bringing the guns of Ticonderoga to Cambridge has justly gone down in history as one of the great accomplishments in American military annals. He and his crew brought fifty-five guns of brass and iron weighing over 120,000 pounds, twenty-three kegs of cannon- and musketballs, and one barrel of flints over three hundred miles of wilderness, half-frozen lakes, virtually impassable mountains, and frozen rivers. He kept a careful account of his expenditures and submitted a bill, including expenses of himself, his brother, and their servant, to the Continental Congress for slightly over £520 sterling, roughly $2600 in 1776 currency, two and a half times his original budget.

On January 16, 1776, perhaps in anticipation of Knox's success, General Washington called a council of war of his commanders. The Honorable John Adams and James Warren were in attendance as Washington argued for the adoption of a plan to attack the British army in Boston. He believed that, despite his green troops, the situation demanded a bold, offensive stroke. The formidable Atlantic Ocean had kept reinforcements from reaching Howe during the winter months, but with the advent of April the four British regiments waiting in Ireland would most certainly arrive.

Owing to the shortage of adequate troops, the generals and members of Congress opposed the plan in practice, despite the fact they agreed with it in principle. The council suggested, however, that Washington ask Congress to petition Massachusetts, Connecticut, and New Hampshire to provide thirteen regiments of militia at Cambridge by February 1. Congress later approved Washington's request, and the provincial governments responded promptly.

By this time, news of the American failure at Quebec and of the death of Montgomery had reached Washington. At another council of war the question arose of sending reinforcements to Benedict Arnold, still besieging Quebec. Because of his own shortages, Washington could not send more troops, but it was voted to divert three of the thirteen militia companies marching toward Cambridge, and send them to Quebec by way of Albany.

Sir William Howe and Sir Henry Clinton did not work well together. Clinton's lack of tact made him a difficult officer to work with, particularly for one of Howe's temperament. Clinton did not approve of many things that Howe did, and although second in command, he did not hesitate to express his disapproval.

Both men were therefore relieved when Clinton embarked in January aboard two armed sloops transporting two light infantry companies to Cape Fear, North Carolina. The two light companies of the 4th and 44th Regiments under Captains Evelyn and Kennedy were to be the nucleus of a force coming from England under Admiral Sir Peter Parker. Their purpose was to support and rally the large number of Loyalists that Parliament believed existed in the South and who needed only minimal military support to form themselves into a powerful army that would overrun the South. The combined forces rendezvoused at Cape Fear and sailed to Charleston, South Carolina, where they seized Sullivan's Island in the harbor. However, the Loyalists failed to materialize, and the entire expedition proved a fiasco.

When Washington was informed by his spy in Boston that Clinton was sailing south on a mysterious expedition, he logically assumed that Clinton was leading an expedition to seize New York City. Consequently, Washington sent General Charles Lee to New York to organize the New York and New Jersey militia, directing him to "disarm all disaffected persons and collect the arms and ammunition in their possession." Lee traveled to Connecticut, where he quickly recruited twelve hundred militiamen; with these men he marched into New York City and began to fortify it.

On February 2, 1776, Admiral Thomas Graves was replaced as commander-in-chief of the Royal Navy in America by Vice Admiral Molyneux Shuldham, who had arrived several weeks before. The king, dissatisfied with Graves for many months, had sought someone to replace him. However, Shuldham too would soon be replaced by Sir Richard Howe, who had maneuvered for command ever since his brother succeeded General Gage.

Below the 600-man British garrison on Bunker Hill lay fourteen houses along the Charles River that had escaped destruction in the fire; they were now used by off-duty regulars as a recreation area offering women, drink, and gambling.

On the night of January 8, 1776, General Israel Putnam sent a detachment of two hundred men under the command of Major Knowlton to destroy the houses and deny their use to the British troops. At 9:00 P.M. the Americans left Cobble Hill, crossed the icy field, and filed silently across the narrow mill dam south of the mill pond. Each man carried a bundle of straw in addition to his musket, for Knowlton had directed Major Carey to proceed with half the force to the farthest group of houses and set them on fire. Major Henly's group was to wait until the houses were ablaze and then set fire to the houses nearest the mill pond. Some of Henly's men, however, failed to contain their impatience and started the fires prematurely.

The flames alarmed the British garrison above them on Bunker Hill, and the British guns promptly opened fire on the burning houses. The Americans held their fire and coolly went about the task of torching the other houses. Ten houses were burned to the ground, and Knowlton's detachment returned across the mill dam without losing a man.

They brought back eight prisoners found in the houses, including one woman. Overcome with fear and fatigue, she became a problem to the troops crossing the narrow mill dam, and was finally carried across by two soldiers. General Putnam was waiting for them as they filed onto the mainland and, noticing the exhausted men carrying the woman, cried out, "Here, hand her up to me!" As soon as she was seated behind Old Put, the woman threw her arms around his waist and was heard to exclaim as they cantered off, "Jesus bless you, sweet General! May you live forever!"

The American raid created great consternation in Boston that night. Major General Burgoyne, an amateur playwright, had organized an active theatrical program which was extremely popular in recreation-starved Boston. Faneuil Hall had been converted into a theater, and on the night of January 8 an audience composed of off-duty officers, including General Howe and his companion, Betsy Loring, and the wives or mistresses of the rest of the officers were witnessing a series of one-act plays.

They had just applauded politely for "The Busybody," and "The Blockade of Boston" was beginning, when an actor playing General Washington strode onto the stage with an awkward gait and an oversized wig, carrying an unusually long, rusty sword. Behind him followed an actor portraying a country bumpkin carrying a rusty old musket seven feet long.

As the audience broke into appreciative applause, a sergeant rushed out from the wings and shouted, "The Yankees are attacking our works on Bunker Hill!" A ripple of laughter rose from the audience, who assumed that the sergeant was part of the play. General Howe ended the hilarity when he rose quickly and called out, "Officers, to your alarm posts!"

Instant pandemonium broke out as women screamed and officers rushed out to rejoin their units. The drumbeat of horses' hooves thundered through the streets of Boston, mingling with the roar and thunder of gunfire from Bunker Hill.

Constant raids and counterraids continued in small, sharp actions that killed and wounded men on both sides. In an attempt to obtain firewood, a number of British troops on Bunker Hill slipped down to the mill pond and pulled off the planks of the deserted tide mill. They were spotted by American gunners on Cobble Hill, and a few well-aimed shots wounded several regulars. The next day fourteen Americans crossed the mill dam under intense musket and artillery fire and set fire to the tide mill to prevent its use for firewood by the enemy.

Several days later, a small herd of cows wandered close to the British outposts along Charlestown Neck. A detachment of regulars emerged from the fortifications to drive them into their lines on Winter Hill, and a fierce struggle took place with casualties on both sides.

General Artemas Ward had established an outpost of seventy men on Dorchester Neck to observe the British lines on Boston Neck, less than half a mile across Boston Harbor. At 4:00 A.M. on February 14, a force of two hundred light infantry and grenadiers under the command of Colonel Leslie and Major Musgrave landed quietly along the shore and surprised the Americans, nearly capturing the entire group. After a brisk exchange of musket fire in the pre-dawn darkness, all but two of the Americans succeeded in escaping. Houses and sheds used by the colonials were destroyed. The Americans retaliated a week later by capturing two British sentries on Boston Neck in a similar pre-dawn raid.

On February 14, twenty-one-year-old Lieutenant Samuel Shaw wrote a letter to his father from his regiment's position on Prospect Hill.

> Our life in camp is confined. The officers are not allowed even to visit Cambridge, without leave from the commanding officer, and we are kept pretty closely to our duty. The drum beats at daybreak, when all hands turn out to man the lines. Here we stay until sunrise, and then all are marched off to prayers. We exercise twice a day, and every fourth day take our turn on guard. Opinions are various, whether Boston is to be attacked or not. I think it is a difficult question to answer. However, if it should be judged expedient to do it, I hope our troops will act with sufficient resolution to command success. Should it be my lot to go, I trust that a sense of what I owe my country, my parents, and myself, will induce me to behave in a suitable manner.[2]

By the middle of February, Washington and his generals had completed their plan of attack. With the guns brought to Cambridge from Ticonderoga, Washington now had the means to press for the decision that he had been forced to postpone. The American army's strength was more than fourteen thousand Continental soldiers in addition to six thousand New England militia.

The plan consisted of three parts: The Colonials were to take immediate possession of Dorchester Heights and construct fortifications to protect the twenty-four-pounders that would command the harbor and the ships in it. Washington was certain that Howe would have no other option than to attack Dorchester Heights as he had previously attacked Bunker Hill. Unlike the situation at Bunker Hill, however, the Americans would now be well supplied with powder and grapeshot to meet the attackers.

The second phase of the plan involved an extension of the Dorchester batteries to a spur of Dorchester Heights called Nook's Hill. From this promontory, which jutted out to within six hundred yards of the British entrenchments on Boston Neck and the southern shoreline of Boston, guns would command the entire rear of the British fortifications on Boston Neck.

Since they first arrived in Boston, Washington, Lee, and Gates had appreciated the strategic importance of Dorchester Heights and Nook's Hill, but they had no value to the Americans unless they possessed artillery. Now, thanks to Henry Knox, Washington had the artillery. Why Gage, and then Howe, had not occupied Dorchester Heights and Nook's Hill remains a mystery. Failure to do so became the major cause of bitter attacks on Howe in Parliament and the British press for years to come. Gage ascribed his reluctance to his unwillingness to fragment his army. But after the Battle of Bunker Hill demonstrated the need to protect Boston by occupying peninsulas that could be used to control the harbor and its shipping, the obvious threat of Dorchester would logically have persuaded Howe to take the necessary measures.

The third part of Washington's plan was a direct assault across the Charles River the moment Howe was committed to his attack on Dorchester Heights. As soon as British troops were landed at the foot of Dorchester Heights to begin their climb up the hill, two brigades of American troops under Generals Greene and Sullivan would be rowed across the river from Sewell's Point and Phipp's Farm in scores of flat-bottomed barges. The four thousand men in the attack would be preceded by two floating batteries mounting twenty-four-pounders that could deliver a steady fire at the point of the assaults.

Sullivan's First Brigade was scheduled to land along Boston Common and seize the Powder House, Mount Whoredom, and Beacon Hill. The Second Brigade under General Greene, coming from Phipp's Farm, would land slightly south of Barton's Point between Leveret's and Windsor streets. One regiment would move across the mill dam and drive up Snow Street to capture the battery atop Copp's Hill. The other regiments of the Second Brigade were to move south to join the First Brigade. The combined brigades would then thrust down Orange Street toward Boston Neck. There, they would capture the fortifications from behind and allow the forces at Roxbury to pour into the city.

Generals William Heath and Artemas Ward were both violently opposed to the third phase of the plan that involved the landings in Boston. Speaking out against it, Heath stated:

> It would most assuredly produce only defeat and disgrace to the American army. The British General must be supposed to be a master of his profession; that as such, he would first provide for the defence of the town, in every part, which was the great deposit of all his stores; that when this was done, if his troops would afford a redundance, sufficient for a sally, he might attempt it; but it was to be remembered that, at any rate, the town would be defended; that it was impossible for troops, armed and disciplined as the Americans were, to be pushed down in boats, at least one mile and a half, open to the fire of all the British batteries on the west side of the town, and to their whole park of artillery, which might be drawn to the bottom of the Common long before the Americans could reach it, and be flanked also by the works on the Neck; that under such a tremendous fire, the troops could not effect a landing.[3]

In spite of the opposition of Heath and Ward, the plan was adopted. Everything was in readiness on February 27.

Thousands of gabions and fascines were woven and collected by hundreds of soldiers. Wagons and carts were collected from as far away as Worcester, and stocks of ammunition were stored that had arrived from the Royal Arsenal in New York, from ships captured by Washington's navy, and from other colonies. Cases of cannonballs, shells, and grapeshot were stockpiled behind the lines. Hundreds of kegs of powder had been hoarded for this moment.

Officers who tested the ground on Dorchester Heights at night reported that the ground was frozen to a depth of eighteen inches, and it would be difficult to dig enough dirt to cover the fascines. It was decided to improvise a new device called a chandelier, a heavy wooden frame in which fascines could be stacked. The entire structure when filled with fascines would be held in place by stakes and covered with earth, but it was believed that it would require less dirt to cover than when the fascines were laid on the ground in piles.

On February 26, the eve of his offensive to drive the British out of Boston, Washington issued his General Orders:

> All officers, non-commissioned officers, and soldiers, are positively forbid playing at cards, and other games of chance. At this time of public distress, men may find enough to do in the service of their God and their country, without abandoning themselves to vice and immorality.
>
> As the season is now fast approaching when every man must expect to be drawn into the field of action, it is highly important that he should prepare his mind, as well as everything necessary for it. It is a noble cause we are engaged in; it is the cause of virtue and mankind; every temporal advantage and comfort to us, and our posterity, depends upon the vigor of our exertions; in short, freedom or slavery must be the result of our conduct; there can, therefore, be no greater inducement to men to behave well. But it may not be amiss for the troops to know, that, if any man in action shall presume to sulk, hide himself, or retreat from the enemy without the orders of his commanding officer, he will be instantly shot down as an example of cowardice; cowards having too frequently disconcerted the best formed troops by their dastardly behaviour.[4]

Nine of the thirteen regiments on Winter and Prospect hills received their orders on February 22, to move out of the quarters that they had occupied for nearly eight months and march to Roxbury with full packs late that night. Their old positions were occupied by militia regiments from Massachusetts and New Hampshire called up for three weeks of duty.

Dr. James Thatcher, the regimental surgeon of Colonel Whitcomb's regiment, accompanied his regiment during the night march and wondered how many of his comrades would require the use of the two thousand sets of lint and bandages used for fractures and gunshot wounds, which he had been secretly ordered to prepare.

There was no suspicion within the British lines of the impending American assault. Perhaps they missed the services of Dr. Benjamin Church. General Howe had decided months before to evacuate Boston, and he was awaiting the arrival of sufficient ships to enable him to embark in the mild weather of June. More ships were needed to remove the vast accumulation of military stores that had been amassed during the past two years. In addition, he had to provide for the evacuation of thousands of Loyalists and their possessions.

British unawareness of the coming blow was reflected in a letter written by a British officer in Boston on Sunday, March 3:

> For these last six weeks or near two months we have been better amused than could possibly be expected in our situation. We had a theater, we had balls, and there is actually a subscription on foot for a masquerade. England seems to have forgotten us, and we have endeavored to forget ourselves. But we were roused to a sense of our situation last night in a manner unpleasant enough. The rebels have been for some time erecting a bomb battery, and last night began to play upon us. Two shells fell not far from me. One fell upon Colonel Monckton's house, but luckily did not burst until it had crossed the street. Many houses were damaged, but no lives lost. The rebel army is not brave, I believe, but is agreed on all hands that their artillery officers are at least equal to ours.[5]

This was high praise indeed for American artillery that had performed so miserably at Bunker Hill. Colonel Knox, since his return from Ticonderoga, had been toiling day and night to form the American batteries into highly efficient units. His new guns enabled him to treble the artillery around the American perimeter.

By the first of March, the American lines were bristling with men, guns, and hundreds of pieces of equipment. Hundreds of oxen occupied a large park at Jamaica Plain, their hundreds of teamsters camped beside them. Thousands of new chandeliers, gabions, and fascines were stacked behind the Roxbury lines. Large quantities of hay had been twisted into bundles resembling modern bales that weighed nearly three hundred pounds. Not far from the Dorchester lines were several hundred heavy carts and twenty-four-pound cannon riding on newly built gun carriages.

Below the Great Bridge of the Charles River at Cambridge floated forty-five flat-bottomed boats, each capable of carrying eighty men. Several large barges had been fastened together, and heavy planking placed across them formed gun platforms for twenty-four-pound cannon. The floating batteries were protected by heavy timbers on each side and a roof of logs.

On Prospect and Winter hills, militiamen who had replaced the Continental soldiers had settled into the normal routine of entrenchments. To the British, there were the usual number of men to be seen through the long glasses with which British officers studied the American positions.

On the night of Saturday, March 2, the American guns around the city opened a furious and accurate bombardment of Boston. Shells and bombs arched high into the cold night sky to burst and smash into the streets of the frightened city. The shells and solid shot shattered many houses, and one cannonball seriously wounded six British soldiers when a direct hit was made on a guardhouse. Many Boston citizens hid in cellars, and to Loyalists the shock of discovering the rebels were capable of mounting such a bombardment was as frightening as the actual missiles.

British batteries returned the fire and scored a direct hit on Prospect Hill, normally considered beyond artillery range. During the bombardment, the thirteen-inch brass mortar that Israel Putnam had christened the "Congress" burst, as well as three other guns. The mishaps were due to American inexperience with the weapons, for the frozen ground did not permit proper bedding of the base of the mortar sufficient to absorb the shock of the recoil.

Abigail Adams was sitting at her desk in the study of the family home in Braintree, ten miles from Cambridge. It was Saturday night, and she had just begun a letter to her husband, John, attending the Continental Congress in Philadelphia:

> I have been in a constant state of anxiety since you left me. It has been said tomorrow, and tomorrow for this month, and when the dreadful tomorrow will be, I know not. But hark! The house this instant shakes with the roar of cannon. I have been to the door, and I find it a cannonade from our army. Orders, I find, are come, for all of the remaining militia to repair to the lines Monday night by 12 o'clock. No sleep for me tonight.

She left the unfinished letter upon her desk and went to bed at midnight, but she could not sleep. Early the next morning, when guns were quiet, she went down to the north Common to watch the militia company of Braintree march off with three days' rations in their haversacks. They were headed for the Roxbury lines to take the place of the Continentals who were moving forward for their attack.

She returned to her desk and resumed her letter:

> I went to bed after twelve but got no rest; the cannon continued firing, and my heart kept pace with them all night. We have had a pretty quiet day, but what tomorrow will bring forth, God only knows.

It was quiet all day Sunday, but just as the sun went down the American guns resumed their bombardment. Again the house shook, but Abigail was exhausted from the night before, and she went to bed despite the barrage. Unable to sleep in spite of her fatigue, she rose, dressed, and climbed to the top of Penn's Hill to watch the fiery display over Boston. It was shortly before midnight when she turned again to write on the open pages that lay waiting before her:

> I have just returned from Penn's Hill, where I have been sitting to hear the amazing roar of cannon, and from whence I could see every shell which was thrown. The sound, I think, is one of the grandest in nature, and is of the true species of the sublime. "Tis now an incessant roar; but oh, the fatal ideas which are connected with the sound! How many of our countrymen must fall!"

Again that night, Abigail Adams found herself unable to sleep and returned to her letter:

> I went to bed about twelve, and rose again a little after one. I could no more sleep than if I had been in the engagement; the rattling of windows, the jar of the house, the continual roar of twenty-four pounders and the bursting of shells gives us such ideas, and realize a scene to us of which we could scarcely form any conception. I hope to give you joy of Boston, even if it is in ruins, before I send this away.[6]

TWENTY-ONE

The Capture of Boston

THE NIGHT OF MONDAY, March 4, 1776, was the moment that thousands of American troops had been waiting for. Artemas Ward, in charge of the details, ordered the movement to begin at dusk. As the sun set behind the Roxbury lines, American artillery began their third continuous night of bombardment. The British guns took up the challenge, and the bright, moonlit night was alive with the continuous roar of guns and the explosion of shells. Overhead, the flight of streaking shells and solid shot crisscrossed under a luminous moon to plunge toward the ground in a shrieking crescendo of sound.

A group of eight hundred specially selected riflemen was first to move up the lonely road to Dorchester Heights. Gliding like slim shadows through the night, they cradled their five-foot-long Pennsylvania rifles in their arms, their eyes squinting through the ground fog that hung over the hill. The weather — bright sky above, fog-shrouded hills below — was perfect for the American plan; the fog would hide activities on the hill from British observers.

The riflemen split into two groups as soon as they reached the summit at 8:00 P.M. One group moved toward Nook's Hill, the point on Dorchester Heights that overlooked the British entrenchments less than a quarter mile away. The other moved to the eastern point overlooking Castle William. The men felt strange as they moved through the silent fog, the thunder and crash of artillery tearing the night apart only a half mile away. Should they be spotted by the British, they would soon become the vortex of the bombardment.

Twelve hundred Continental troops led by gallant General John Thomas followed behind the riflemen. Behind them came a long train of horses and ox-drawn carts and wagons, containing the entrenching tools and materials, their drivers silently urging their animals along. As the carts moved up the hill, men placed a wall of twisted hay between them and the British positions on Boston Neck. The large blocks of hay masked them from view and helped to muffle the sounds of the creaking wheels, but the roar of the bombardment drowned out the noise of their ascent and probably made other precautions unnecessary.

The roar of the guns increased as American and British batteries redoubled their rate of fire. House after house in Boston was hit and shattered by the Yankee artillery, and there were a number of casualties among the British troops and their dependents. It occurred to no one among the British to look up at the fog-shrouded top of Dorchester Heights that dominated Boston from the south.

Among the twelve hundred Continentals marching behind the riflemen was twenty-one-year-old Ebeneezer Huntington, who had left his classes at Yale only eight months before. Now a first lieutenant in Colonel Samuel Wyllys's regiment, he was in the van as the 336 men of his regiment marched silently to the ridge at the top of the hill.

When they reached the summit, they found that the ground was so frozen it was difficult to dig, even with the use of picks and crowbars. The gabions were soon in position, however, and were gradually filled with frozen chunks of earth.

Major General Richard Gridley had chosen the long saddle part of the Heights on which to build the entrenchments. At the eastern end he laid out a large redoubt that was to anchor the lines; the other redoubt was located toward the side of the Heights closest to Nook's Hill. Between the two redoubts a long parapet was built ten feet high, with firing steps for the troops.

The men labored magnificently throughout the night. At precisely 4:00 A.M. a relief party of three thousand men marched up to relieve them. By then the entire line of fortifications had taken shape, and the new men pitched in with a will as the exhausted troops returned to the Roxbury lines. General Gridley remained on the hill all night supervising the construction of the works.

The chandeliers proved a success, because the fascines, when placed within their frameworks, formed a massive series of earthen walls that were soon covered with frozen earth and sod. Troops went into the adjoining orchards and cut down hundreds of trees; their sharpened trunks formed the abatis that fronted the parapets.

A novel feature of the fortifications atop Dorchester Heights grew out of an idea presented to Washington by William Davis, a former merchant of Boston then living in Cambridge. Rows of heavy barrels filled with earth and rocks were placed around the base of the parapets at the edge of the steep cliff below. They appeared to be part of the forward edge of the entrenchments, but their real function was to be rolled down the hill toward ascending troops. The steep slope of the hill guaranteed increased velocity when they hit the advancing formations and promised havoc and substantial casualties among the attackers.

At dawn on Tuesday morning, March 5, the British were completely astounded to see the powerful redoubts on Dorchester Heights looming through the early morning haze. One British officer wrote that, "They were raised with expedition equal to that of the Genii belonging to Aladdin's wonderful lamp."

On March 4 General Archibald Robertson of the Royal Engineers wrote:

> By daybreak we discovered that they had taken possession of the two highest hills, the tableland between the Necks, and run a parapet across the two Necks, besides a kind of redoubt at the bottom of Sentry Box Hill near the Neck. The materials for the whole works must all have been carried. Chandeliers, fascines, gabions, trusses of hay pressed and barrels, a most astonishing night's work must have employed from 15 to 20,000 men.[1]

In a letter to his father, Major Charles Stuart vividly described the American bombardment and the occupation of the Heights:

> Their shells were thrown in an excellent direction, they took effect near the center of the town, and tore several houses to pieces; the

cannon were unusually well fired, one shot killed eight men of the 22nd Regiment, and houses were pierced through and through with balls they fired from Phipp's Farm. Our lines were raked from the new battery they had made, and though we returned shot and shell, I am very, very sorry to say with not quite so much judgement.

The bombardment continued for five nights, and a nobler scene it was impossible to behold; sheets of fire seemed to come from our batteries; some of the shells crossed one another in the air, and then bursting looked beautiful. The inhabitants were in a horrid situation, particularly the women, who were several times driven from their houses by shot, and crying for protection.

At daybreak the next morning, we perceived two posts upon the highest hills of Dorchester peninsula, that appeared more like magic than the work of human beings. They were each of them 200 feet long on the side next the town, and seemed to be strong cases of packed hay about ten feet high with an abatis of vast thickness around both. We discovered near 6,000 people, most of them at work; they opened embrasures before 9 o'clock and about 2 o'clock had made a ditch and connected the two hills by a breastwork.[2]

Howe believed the fortifications had been the work of twelve thousand men, but he did not plan to waste time in contemplation. He realized that the fate of the British army in Boston would be decided within the time it took to drive the Americans off Dorchester Heights. Every British ship in the harbor was in deadly peril, as were the fortifications on Boston Neck. As General Robertson put it:

I think that most serious step ever an army of this strength in such a situation took considering the state of the rebels works are in and the number of men they appear to have under arms. The fate of this whole army and the town is at stake, not to say the fate of America.[3]

Howe ordered twenty-four hundred men to embark on transports and drop down to Castle William, from which point they would land at midnight under the protection of a bombardment from the warships and the batteries on Boston Neck. The landings, under the command of Major General Hugh Percy, were scheduled to be made at high tide along the beach at the base of Dorchester Heights. Under a heavy bombardment from warships and the batteries on Boston Neck, the British assault forces would storm the American fortifications.

By nightfall Long Wharf was a crowded scene of troops clambering into barges to be taken out to transports anchored in the harbor. To the muffled beat of drums and the rhythm of flashing oars, the regulars of the 40th, 44th, 49th, 52nd, and 55th Regiments moved across the rippling waters of the harbor to their ships, the *Goodintent, Sea Venture, Venus, Spy*, and *Success*. Each man carried provisions for one day in his haversack, and their canteens were filled with a mixture of rum and water. Men who were too ill to go remained in the barracks for guard duty.

Howe had learned a bitter lesson at Bunker Hill. For this assault, the men were ordered not to load their muskets, but to rely exclusively on the bayonet, supported by artillery.

Meanwhile, Washington ordered two thousand new troops to join the three thousand men working steadily on the rapidly growing fortifications. As the new regiments climbed the hill and filed into the newly erected trenches and parapets, thousands of spectators began to gather on surrounding hills to witness the coming battle.

Across the Charles River at Sewell's Point and Phipp's Farm, four thousand assault troops of General Putnam were nervously awaiting the signal to cross. The signal would come at the moment the British regulars landed in the darkness at the foot of the hills on Dorchester Peninsula. The opening cannon fire from the American redoubts was to be the signal for the brigades of Greene and Sullivan to move out in their boats.

By 8:00 P.M. the British troops on Castle William numbered thirty-five hundred, having been augmented by the grenadier and light infantry companies of the 23rd and 38th Regiments. These men had been rowed across the harbor to the Castle in the darkness as the waters of the harbor rose and fell in sickening convulsions, constantly threatening to swamp the barges. As the troops climbed onto the wharf at the Castle, they were soaked to the skin and shivered in the driving wind sweeping in from the sea. The sailors strained to hold the plunging boats against the pilings and enable the troops to disembark. The barges scheduled to land the regulars along the beaches a half mile away were pitching and tossing like a herd of wild horses.

Atop Dorchester Heights the American troops were ready.

Guns loaded with canisters of grapeshot were trained on the beaches, and other guns were aimed offshore, loaded with solid shot to destroy the barges that would soon appear laden with soldiers. As the wind lashed the men behind the parapets, they covered themselves with blankets and sheets of canvas. By 11:00 P.M. heavy gusts of rain were driving across the harbor from the southeast, and the winds soon rose to hurricane force. Windows were smashed, houses, sheds, and fences were blown down, ships were driven ashore, and the plunging barges tied to the wharfs on Castle William broke loose and smashed against one another.

The newly dug trenches atop Dorchester Heights began to fill with water. The Americans of Putnam's assault force, riding in barges lashed together along the Charles River near Sewell's Point, scrambled ashore to avoid being crushed or swamped by the lurching, pitching, flat-bottomed craft. The storm was one of the worst to hit New England in over twenty years.

Just before midnight, Howe called off the assault. It was obvious his men would never survive the crossing, even if he were able to embark them. He ordered the assault to be made twenty-four hours later, but the next day the storm increased in fury, and the wind and rain howled across the sea and against the unprotected fortifications sheltering the sleepless, soaked, and shivering Americans, who continued to work in the mud to strengthen their positions. Oxen labored to pull carts whose mud-caked wheels made progress almost impossible.

On March 6 Howe's General Orders to his troops read simply:

> The General desires the troops to know that the intended expedition last night was unavoidably put off by the badness of the weather.[4]

In the colonial camp, General Putnam's assault force was taken ashore, and the boats were moved upriver to protect them from the surging waves. William Heath always believed that the storm had been sent by God to prevent the Americans from embarking on that foolhardy assault on Boston Common.

By Thursday, March 7, the storm began to abate, but Howe's situation was difficult. The American positions on the Heights were now impregnable, a result of two extra days' work. Admiral Shuldham informed Howe that his ships could no longer remain in the harbor, for they were at the mercy of American artillery. British positions on Boston Neck opposite Roxbury were now thoroughly exposed. To remain in Boston, Howe recognized, was to expose his army to disaster; yet to leave now, instead of three months later as planned, was to abandon a wealth of materiel and property due to his lack of ships. And the Loyalists in Boston, wild with concern, demanded that he provide the protection promised them for their persons and property.

Late that day, Howe called a council of his senior commanders and laid out the situation. Lord Percy and others advised the immediate evacuation of Boston. Howe replied that he also believed that to be necessary, but had hesitated because of the honor of the troops. It was agreed, however, by nearly everyone, that evacuation was the only solution to the problem. The first priority was to save the army from disaster.

It was a difficult decision for Howe to make. He had written a letter to the ministry earlier outlining in logical detail why the army should not move from Boston until he received reinforcements in the spring. He had denied then that he was in danger from Washington's army, saying his lines were too strong.

The 40th and 44th Regiments relanded from their transports; other troops were kept on their transports by rough water that followed the storm. Work parties were immediately formed to remove heavy artillery and other heavy equipment for evacuation. Ammunition of every caliber was removed from magazines and trundled toward the wharves to be loaded aboard ships. Heavy artillery was dismantled or thrown into the harbor. Some of the impregnable works that had taken so long to build were demolished. Regiments were instructed to bring barracks furniture to the storehouse on King Street and put it in the custody of officers who would arrange to disassemble it and store it aboard ship. Hand carts were brought in to be disassembled and stored. Regimental commanders sent work parties to their brigade quartermasters to receive provisions for the coming sea voyage to Halifax, which were then stored on assigned ships. Each regiment received eighteen large casks or butts of porter to be put aboard the transports and issued to the troops after they were embarked.

Dram shops, which sold liquor, were to be shut down until the army had left. Anyone found selling liquor was to be arrested and his wares destroyed. Troops were to be held in their quarters in the evening, and musters were to be held at tattoo, five minutes before taps. Howe was determined to carry off all the rum the ships could hold, and he issued orders that rum not brought in for the use of the military was to be destroyed.

Grenadier and light infantry companies, released from all garrison duties, were used to supervise the loading of the ships. Working parties from all regiments mustered at 5:00 A.M. and began to load the ships. Regimental commanders polled their regiments and submitted a list of men capable of rowing boats. These men were kept together and close at hand to be available for instant call.

On Sunday, March 10, all the sick and wounded were loaded aboard the transports assigned to their regiments. On that day, all women and children of enlisted men were ordered to form alongside the wharves adjacent to the ships of their regiment. They were to be on board by 6:00 P.M., and any woman who did not comply was to be taken to the Boston Gaol and left behind when the fleet sailed for Halifax. All soldiers sent their bedding and knapsacks aboard their ships before 6:00 P.M.

Officers' wives and children were received on board their ships after other women and children were below decks. Frederick and Nancy Mackenzie, unable to find anyone who would buy their furniture, abandoned everything they owned, excepting some clothes, valuables, and family heirlooms. Taking a chaise to the wharf, Nancy and the children were soon installed in a cabin similar to the one in which they had traveled to New York on the *Friendship,* three years before. Captain Mackenzie left to return to his regiment.

The decision to evacuate Boston struck the Loyalists like a lightning bolt. They were utterly unprepared for the total loss of everything they believed in or possessed. Many were well-to-do members of New England's upper class: government officials, wealthy merchants, landowners, and Anglican clergymen. Everything they owned in the countryside had already been confiscated, and they had been waiting in Boston for the inevitable British triumph that would restore their "stolen" property to them. Now within a matter of days, everything they left behind would be lost forever.

Thus began a mad scramble to salvage some goods by getting

them aboard one of the British ships. With varying degrees of cooperation from army or navy officers, based on friendship or bribery, desperate Loyalists entirely filled some ships with their belongings, and large quantities of military stores had to be left behind as a result. A letter written by one of the Loyalists to friends in London described the chaos:

> The necessary care of the women, children, sick and wounded, required every assistance that could, be given. It was not like breaking up a camp, where every man knows his duty; it was like departing your country, with your wives, your servants, your household furniture, and all your encumbrances. The officers, who felt the disgrace of a retreat, kept up appearances. The men, who thought they were changing for the better, strove to take advantage of the present times, and were kept from plunder and drink with difficulty.

Lord Dartmouth, when first apprised of the possible evacuation of Boston as early as August, had written to Gage:

> If we are driven to the difficulty of relinquishing Boston, care must be taken that the officers and friends of the government be not left exposed to the rage and insult of rebels, who set no bounds to their barbarity.

In consideration of the plight of the Loyalists, Sir William Howe did his utmost to enable them to take as many of their possessions as they could. The shortage of transports, however, forced him to make agonizing decisions. Had he been able to leave three months later, as he had intended, the problems would have been minor. In his report to the Earl of Dartmouth, Howe wrote:

> A thousand difficulties arose on account of the disproportion of transports for the conveyance of the troops, the well-affected inhabitants, their most valuable property, and the quantity of military stores to be carried away.[5]

About this time the non-Loyalist inhabitants of Boston became concerned with the possibility that the British would mark their final withdrawal by burning the city to the ground. Word reached the selectmen that General Howe had announced that if he were bombarded by American cannon fire during his withdrawal, he would assuredly burn the city. The ruins of Charlestown across the river underscored the British willingness to do so. The selectmen called on General Robertson to verify Howe's statement, and after conferring with Howe, Robertson stated the general had no intention of burning Boston unless the rebels attacked the evacuation effort. In that case, Howe had told him, he did not know what he might do.

Anxiously the selectmen sent a letter to General Washington under a flag of truce, asking him to honor Howe's request. Washington replied through Colonel Learned that he was unable to take notice of their message, as it was unauthenticated, unaddressed, and therefore not obligatory on General Howe. Consequently, Washington continued his preparations for the attack.

During the night of March 9, a strong detachment of American troops marched to Nook's Hill, a position that dominated the British lines on Boston Neck. They brought the usual equipment for setting up a redoubt — gabions, fascines, and chandeliers — and worked expertly to build the parapets. It was a cold night, and some of the men foolishly built a fire on the far side of the hill in order to keep warm. The red glow silhouetted the figures of the men atop Nook's Hill and brought a fierce bombardment from British batteries on Boston Neck and Castle William. Five colonial soldiers were seriously wounded, and the remainder of the detachment abandoned the half-completed entrenchments.

Abigail Adams described the bombardment to John in a letter she wrote the next day:

> A most terrible and incessant cannonade from half after eight till six this morning. I hear we lost four men killed and some wounded in attempting to take the hill nearest to the town, called Nook's Hill. We did some work, but the fire from the ships beat off our men, so that they did not secure it, but retired to the fort upon the other hill.[6]

Sunday, March 10, was a full working day for the troops of the British army. While British horse transports loaded hundreds of horses belonging to the artillery, cavalry, and officers, the grenadiers and light infantry spiked cannon by hammering iron spikes into the cannon vent, the opening into which the slow match was inserted in order to explode the charge. They also smashed gun carriages and tossed cannonballs and cannon into Boston Harbor from the end of the wharves.

One of the Loyalists preparing to leave Boston was a man

named Crean Bush, who had migrated north from New York. He
was an ardent friend of George III, and Howe commissioned him
to form a detachment of Loyalists to search out what Howe believed to be large quantities of war materiel stolen by Boston
Whigs.

Bush and his detachments went to work enthusiastically, early
Monday morning. They busily stripped rebel stores and homes of
their possessions and carted them off to the schooner *Minerva* and
the brigantine *Elizabeth.* Early the next day they were back at what
was turning out to be a pleasant and profitable task. They had
competition, however, from large bands of volunteer sailors and
soldiers who wanted to join in the fun of legally looting the unfortunate Americans at their mercy. In order to stop what was be-
coming an orgy of wholesale looting, Howe canceled Crean Bush's
assignment and issued a General Order:

> The Commander in Chief finding notwithstanding the orders that
> have been given to forbid plundering, houses have been forced open
> and robbed. He is therefore under the necessity of declaring to the
> troops, that the first soldier who is caught plundering, will be hanged
> on the spot.[7]

To the dismay of Crean Bush and the Loyalists, the ship
Elizabeth, which sailed for Halifax loaded with plundered posses-
sions of Boston citizens, was captured several weeks later by an
American privateer.

On March 14 the streets of Boston were barricaded as the British
began to contract their lines. Grenadiers and light infantry patrolled the streets of the city seemingly deserted since most Loyalists had been embarked on transports.

Mistakenly, Washington began to suspect that Howe was guile-
fully pretending to evacuate Boston. Perhaps large British reinforcements were about to land below Boston at some place such as
Quincy Bay and outflank the American lines. A council of war was
summoned which included Washington, Ward, Putnam, Thomas,
Sullivan, Heath, Greene, and Gates. They decided that unless Boston were evacuated by Friday, March 15, it would be advisable to
occupy and finish the fortifications atop Nook's Hill on Friday

night. They agreed that if Howe was planning to leave, the new fortifications atop Nook's Hill should give him a final push.

When Howe had still not evacuated the city by Friday, the order was issued to march to Nook's Hill and establish a strong battery there. The detachment was unable to get started that night, but early the next morning they moved onto the hill from which they had been driven six days before. Many of the British guns had been removed from the lines on Boston Neck, and British gunfire was too feeble to affect the renewed colonial entrenchment. However, as the redoubt took shape, the British kept up a desultory fire to which the Americans refused to reply. Not a single gun of the batteries surrounding Boston fired. That was Washington's answer to Howe's unwritten agreement not to burn the city.

The moment was historic. On St. Patrick's Day, Sunday, March 17, 1776, at 4:00 A.M., those soldiers and officers of the British army not already on board ship were lined up along Boston's wharves ready to evacuate Boston and the Massachusetts Bay colony. As additional provisions, each brigade received one large cask of biscuit from Major Campbell as it filed onto the wharf to wait for barges to take them to ships riding at anchor in King's Row Channel.

At 9:00 A.M. the garrison of Bunker Hill marched down the now-famous slope and through the ruined streets of Charlestown. On the ferry landing they took their places in barges that were rowed by soldiers assigned to the duty by their colonels. The long line of barges was pulled past North Battery to their regimental transports. Meanwhile, other boats left the wharves of Boston for King's Row Channel to bring the rear guard of grenadiers and light infantry from Boston Neck.

A British officer of the 17th Dragoons recounted the historic retreat, to a friend in England:

> According to my promise, I proceed to give a brief account of our retreat, which was made this morning between the hours of two and eight. Our troops did not receive the smallest molestation, though the rebels were all night at work on the near hill which I mentioned to you in my last letter, and we kept a constant fire upon them from a battery of twenty-four pounders. They did not return a single shot.

It was lucky for the inhabitants now left in Boston that they did not; for I am informed everything was prepared to set the town ablaze, had they fired one cannon. The dragoons are under orders to sail tomorrow for Halifax, a cursed cold wintry place, even yet; nothing to eat, less to drink. Bad times, my dear friend. The displeasure I feel from the very small share I have in our present insignificancy is so great, that I do not know the thing so desperate I would not undertake, in order to change our situation.[8]

As the British withdrew, the Americans quickly moved to occupy Boston. General Ward, followed by Colonel Learned and his 386-man regiment, crossed Boston Neck and entered the city by the causeway that led to Orange Street. Men and horses had to beware of hundreds of caltrops, or crow's feet, which had been scattered over the ground. These small iron balls were similar to present-day jacks, with sharp points about an inch long. No matter which way they fell, one point always reached upward to pierce the feet of men or horses.

Atop Bunker Hill, before the British pulled out they had dressed wooden figures in red uniforms with muskets on their shoulders and placed them at various posts to look like sentries. Several colonial riflemen crawled over and quickly discovered the truth, and within ten minutes the formidable fortifications were swarming with cheering men. Putnam launched his flatboats across the Charles and led his two brigades under Greene and Sullivan into the city just as the last British regulars left the wharves on the east side of town.

Washington and his officers, concerned with the danger of smallpox that had been raging in Boston for months, issued orders forbidding officers, soldiers, and others from entering Boston without a pass:

> As soon as the Selectmen report the town to be cleansed from infection, liberty will be given to those who have business there to go in. The inhabitants belonging to the town will be permitted to return to their habitations, proper persons being appointed at the Neck and at Charlestown Ferry, to grant them passes.
>
> [signed] Brigadier for the day,
> General Sullivan[9]

On March 20 the regiments of Colonels Whitcomb, Phinney, and Hutchinson marched into Boston with their drums and fifes throbbing. As they swept through the narrow streets, with General Washington and some of his officers at their head, the men noticed that the inhabitants were reluctant to come out of their houses, but watched from behind their windows. Dr. Thatcher, among the marching men, described the Bostonians as happy but not free from a "melancholy gloom," which they seemed to have acquired during the British occupation.

However, the following day hundreds of Boston refugees who had been living outside the city flooded into Boston. Friends and relatives who had not seen each other for many months were reunited in emotional scenes.

The three regiments were ordered to remain in Boston to guard the town and public stores and to help the civil authorities promote peace and good order. They were also charged to take every precaution necessary to destroy the "infection of the smallpox."

During the fighting, Boston had not been injured as much as many who fled had feared. Dr. John Warren, brother of the slain Dr. Joseph Warren, entered Boston within two hours after the British left, and he noted in his diary:

> The houses I found to be considerably abused inside, where they had been inhabited by the common soldiery, but the external parts of the houses made a tolerable appearance. The streets were clean, and upon the whole, the town looks much better than I expected. Several hundred houses were pulled down, but these were very old ones.[10]

John Hancock's palatial home had not been damaged; even the family pictures on the walls were untouched. The fact that the house had served as General Clinton's headquarters probably contributed to its preservation.

However, many public buildings had been treated brutally. Old South Church, or Old South Meeting as it was called by its Congregationalists, had been used as a riding school because of its past associations as the seat of Whig activities. The British had cut its hand-carved pews and silk furniture to pieces. The handsome floor was covered with dirt and gravel several feet thick to permit horses to jump a bar at full gallop. A stove set up in winter to heat the massive structure had been fueled with many books and manuscripts from the fine library.

The Old North Church, or Old North Meeting, built in 1677 and used by Paul Revere to signal his friends in Charlestown during his famous ride, had been demolished for fuel on January 16, 1776, by order of General Howe.[11] Episcopal churches such as Christ Church on Salem Street, where British officers and men worshiped, were undamaged and well cared for. Most of their clergy, however, had left for Halifax with General Howe.

Dr. Samuel Cooper returned to Boston on March 19 and found his own home a shambles, with all of his beds, bedsheets, blankets, and quilts gone. Hundreds of other houses had been pulled down for firewood; Cooper reported in his diary that he received permission from General Greene to go to any of the many houses deserted by Loyalists and take what he needed of their furniture and furnishings to use in his own home. Such looting of Tory houses soon began.

Beautiful Boston Common had changed radically during the past two years. The stately elms had been cut, and only the stumps remained to mark their former positions. Many level areas had been dug up to form redoubts with sod-covered parapets and trenches. Faneuil Hall had been converted to a theater, and both the Brattle Street Church and Hollis Street Church had been used as barracks.

Having left Boston Harbor, General Howe and his fleet dropped down to Nantasket Road, where they remained for ten days before setting sail for Halifax. British engineers were sent out from the fleet to blow up Castle William before sailing. Howe's military forces aboard the ships totaled over eleven thousand soldiers and sailors.

More than a thousand Loyalist refugees also left Boston with Howe. In spite of the fact that many Loyalists were wealthy officials, landowners, and merchants, an official description of their occupations reveals that many were merely middle- and lower-class British subjects loyal to their king:

Government officials	102
Anglican clergy	18
Farmers and landowners (large)	105
Merchants and townsmen of Boston	213
Small farmers, traders, and mechanics	382
Unspecified	200

The continued presence of the British fleet worried Washington and his officers. On March 24 General Orders were read to all American troops:

> The enemy still continuing in the harbor without any apparent cause for it, after winds and weather have favored their sailing leaves abundant reason to suspect that they may have some design of aiming a blow at us before they depart. The General therefore, in the strongest terms imaginable recommends it to the commanding officers of every Corps to prevent their men that are off duty from straggling but to have them ready to turn out at a moment's warning with their arms and ammunition in good order. For this purpose a strict examination is to be paid at Rollcalling and delinquents severely punished.
>
> The General Officers in their several departments are to take care that proper alarm posts are assigned every Corps that no confusion or disorder may ensue in case we are called out.[12]

As it developed, the British navy maintained warships off Nantasket for several months after the main fleet sailed north. On July 14, 1776, the fleet was finally off, much to the relief of the citizens of Boston.

The day after Howe's troops evacuated Boston, General William Heath marched out of Cambridge with his brigade, which included Colonel Thompson's regiment of riflemen, the regiments of Colonels Greaton, Stark, Patterson, Bond, and Webb, and a detachment of artillery, nearly three thousand Continental troops. Bound for New York, they marched through Watertown early in the morning on their way toward Worcester. From there they proceeded through West Springfield and Hartford and arrived within a week at New London, Connecticut, where they waited for ships to take them to New York City. Loading guns and troops aboard American transports, they sailed into New York Harbor on April 17.

On March 27, after Howe sailed for Halifax, Washington sent Sullivan's brigade to New York, also; on April 1 he sent another brigade, followed on April 4 by Spencer's brigade, which Washington himself accompanied. The siege of Boston was over.

Washington left Boston with a well-equipped army which had profited greatly from the staggering amount of military equipment abandoned by the British. They had left over a hundred cannon and mortars, hundreds of solid shot and shell, immense numbers of cartridges, great quantities of wheat, hay, oil, medicines, horses, and other military hardware. Nearly all the cannon were made serviceable, despite being spiked. American craftsmen were able to drill out the spikes and clear the vents, after which the cannon functioned as though new.

Dr. John Warren led American medical teams to various abandoned hospitals, including the large "Manufactury House" where Nancy Mackenzie had worked with the wounded. From these the colonists recovered large numbers of blankets, beds, and rugs. With Washington's authority, Warren also took possession of a large supply of drugs, enough to make up completely equipped medical chests for each regiment in the army leaving for New York.

General Thomas Mifflin, quartermaster general of the American army, reported the following inventory of captured materiel on March 20, 1776:

A brigantine, about 120 tons burden, loaded with oil and pearl.

A schooner, about 80 tons, scuttled with 200 hogsheads of salt on board.

150 hogsheads of salt found in a store. 100 bundles of iron hoops.

Long Wharf: 157 pack saddles, 123 water-casks. A brigantine scuttled, about 140 tons. A sloop scuttled, about 70 tons. A schooner scuttled, about 40 tons. 1000 chaldrons of sea coals. 52 iron grates. General Gage's chariot taken out of the dock, broken. A quantity of cordage and old cable, broken. Five anchors.

Green's Wharf: 200 blankets. Four and two-thirds large jars of sweet oil.

Hatch's Wharf: Three cannon, double charged and spiked.

Hancock's Wharf: A new ship, about 300 tons, scuttled. About 1000 bushels salt. 3000 blankets. 30 water casks.

Tudor's Wharf: A ship, about 350 tons, scuttled.

Dummet's Wharf: 5000 bushels wheat in store. A sloop, about 60 tons, scuttled. A fishing boat.

Webb's Wharf: A sloop, about 60 tons, scuttled.

Fuller's Wharf: About 500 bushels of salt.

Fitch's Wharf: A schooner, 70 tons, scuttled.

B.M. Generals Office: About 1000 bushels sea coal and one clock, and lumber. About 150 hogsheads of limes, four barrels of flour, 100 empty iron-bound casks, ten 24-pound-cannon cartridges.

Tileston's Wharf: 300 hogsheads of salt. Three brigantines: one, 150 tons; one, 120 tons; and one, 130 tons. The brig Washington (captured earlier by the British) commanded by Captain Martindale, with all her guns, in the dock. One and a half hogshead of sugar. A quantity of pickets, fascines, and gabions, in store. About 5000 feet of board.

Griffin's Wharf: A number of iron grates.

Hubbard's Wharf: About 1500 rugs and blankets. 50 water-casks, iron bound. One cask of deck nails. About 200 cords of wood. About 200 chaldrons of sea coals.

South Battery: 52 pieces of cannon, trunnions broken off and spiked. 600 feet of boards. About 30 iron-bound casks. A number of ball and empty shells. A brigantine, 120 tons; a schooner, 60 tons.

Wheelwright's Wharf: 14 anchors. Three and a half hogshead of brimstone. 300 hogshead of sea coals. One 13 inch mortar, with an iron bed; a number of shells, carcasses, and cannon shot, in the dock.

Hall's Wharf (and in his possession): 600 bushels of corn and oats; 100 sacks of bran; 8 hogsheads of molasses; 100 empty iron-bound casks. Two schooners, about 60 tons each. One sloop, about 40 tons. Ten horses, teams and harness.

Hutchinson's Wharf: A new ship, about 350 tons, scuttled. Two brigs, about 120 tons each, scuttled. Two sloops, about 60 tons each, scuttled.

Winnismet: A new ship, building, thrown off the stocks, 200 tons. About 100 bushels salt. Store pulled down.

Peck's Wharf: About 100 hogsheads of essence of spruce. 10 hogsheads of beef. 6 hogsheads of molasses not quite full. 5 barrels of molasses. A sloop, about 50 tons, two thirds full of molasses.

At Mr. Lovell's: General Gage's coach, a phaeton and harness complete. 20 iron pots and kettles.

Joy's Yard: A parcel of lumber, tools, and joists.

Hill's Bake House: 20 barrels of flour.

North and South Mills: 10,000 bushels of wheat and flour, not bolted. 1500 bushels of bran.

King's Brewery: 13 empty bound butts; 14 hogsheads spruce beer; two iron pierced trucks.

Town Granary: 1000 bushels of beans; 100 bushels of horse beans.

Vincent's Stable: 10 tons hay.

Love's Lumber Yard: 50,000 shingles, 35,000 feet of boards; 1000 clapboards; 20 hand-barrows.

Henderson Inches Store: About 6 tons of hay.

Stable at the Rope-Walk: 10 tons of hay; 110 horses.

Boston   By return this day,
March 20, 1776   [signed] John G. Frazer,
                                          D.G.M. General

Ezekial Cheever, the commissary of artillery, gave an account dated March 22, 1776, of the ordnance stores left by the British:

North Battery: Seven 12-pounders, two 9-pounders, and four 6-pounders, all spiked.

On Copp's Hill: Three 28-pounders, one 8-inch shell, 177 28-pound shot, 273 wads, 2 handbarrow levers, 2 drag ropes, half a side of leather.

At West Boston: Three 32-pounders, 39 shot, 154 wads, one 13-inch mortar, 1 large chain.

On Beacon Hill: Two 12-pounders, 23 shot, 23 wads.

82 cannon in different places, ten swivels in the Washington, a lot of shot and shells, and cannon wheels.[13]

On an inventory dated May 10, Assistant Quartermaster General John C. Frazer listed the materials his men had retrieved from the water alongside the wharves. He counted large numbers of anchors, cannon, gun carriages, shot, shell, and tools. There were two thirteen-inch mortars, 390 twenty-four-pound shot, 645 twelve-pound shot, eighty six-pound shot, 358 thirty-two-pound shot, 402 eighteen-pound shot, 271 grapeshot, and 162 shells.

For years to come, the failure of Gage and Howe to occupy Dorchester Heights during the long months of British occupation was the subject of bitter criticism and recrimination in the British Parliament and press. John Wilkes, the brilliant critic of the Tory Party, spoke on the subject on November 18, 1777:

> Let us recollect, sir, what passed after Boston was taken by the British forces. Our general was soon besieged in that capital of New England, ignominiously cooped up there many months with twenty regiments, and at last driven from thence. I know the coloring given to this retreat by the court party among us, and have been nauseated with the cant terms of our generals' changing their quarters, and shifting their positions. All the military men of this country now confess that the retreat of General Howe from Boston was an absolute flight, as much so, sir, as that of Mahomet from Mecca.[14]

The Duke of Manchester summed it up in a speech in the House of Lords:

> The army of Britain, equipped with every possible essential of war; a chosen army, with chosen officers, backed by the power of a mighty fleet, sent to correct revolted subjects; sent to chastise a resisting city; sent to assert Britain's authority — has for many tedious months been imprisoned within that town by the Provincial army; who, with their watchful guards, permitted them no inlet to the country; who braved all their efforts, and defied all their skill and ability in war could ever attempt. One way, indeed, of escape, was left; the fleet is yet respected; to the fleet the army has recourse; and British generals, whose names never met with a blot of dishonor, are forced to quit that town which was the first object of the war, the immediate cause of hostilities, the place of arms which has cost this nation more than a million to defend.[15]

The evacuation of Boston elevated Washington to the level of a world-famous figure. From July 3, 1775, to March 17, 1776, he had, despite colonial poverty, exasperating annoyances, personal and class dissensions in Congress, jealousy, and stupidity, forced the finest troops in the world to sail off in utter defeat. Washington was not a great man when he went to Cambridge, but he learned under the necessity of his awesome responsibilities. As the British sailed north to Halifax, from that time until his death Washington was admittedly the foremost man of North America.

In Philadelphia, John Adams, Benjamin Franklin, Thomas Jefferson, and others were arguing for complete independence. Washington's victory at Boston seemed to make it wildly possible, and those who had felt that a military decision would lead to inevitable disaster for the colonies found new courage.

On July 4, 1776, only 109 days after General William Howe and his army sailed from Boston, Congress adopted a declaration for independence. The war would not end, nor would independence be achieved, easily. Ahead lay the terrible defeat of the Americans at Long Island; Washington's skillful retreat from Brooklyn to Manhattan; defeat, retreat, and defeat again at Harlem Heights, retreat and defeat at White Plains; and retreat again across the Hudson and across New Jersey, with an army that lost hundreds of men daily to desertion.

Then, on December 26, 1776, with Colonel Henry Knox leading the attack, Washington turned and struck his pursuers at Trenton and Princeton and, throwing up a block at Morristown, prevented the British march on the colonial capital at Philadelphia. Thus ended the cataclysmic year of 1776.

Notes

CHAPTER 2

1. Arthur Meir Schlesinger, Sr., *The Birth of the Nation,* with an introduction by Arthur M. Schlesinger, Jr. (New York: Alfred A. Knopf, 1968), p. 26.

CHAPTER 3

1. Richard Hofstadter, William Miller, Daniel Aaron, *The American Republic,* Vol. I, rev. ed. (Englewood Cliffs, N.J.: Prentice-Hall, 1970), p. 184.

CHAPTER 4

1. William Heath, *Memoirs of Major General William Heath* (New York: William Abbatt Publishers, 1901), p. 4.
2. Lieutenant John Barker, *The British in Boston,* the diary of Lieutenant Barker of the 4th Regiment of King's Own, from November 15, 1774, to May 31, 1776 (Cambridge, Mass.: Harvard University Press, 1924), p. 14.
3. Ibid., pp. 10–27.
4. Board of Selectmen of City of Boston, *A Report of the Record Commissioners of the City of Boston,* containing the minutes of the Board from 1769 to April 1775 (Boston: Rockwell & Churchill, 1893), pp. 237–43.
5. Ibid., pp. 234–37.

6. Richard Frothingham, Jr., *The History of the Siege of Boston and Bunker Hill* (Boston: Charles C. Little and James Brown, 1849), p. 9.
7. Lawrence Henry Gipson, *The Triumphant Empire*, Vol. XII: *Britain Sails into the Storm, 1770–1776* (New York: Alfred A. Knopf, 1965), p. 153.

CHAPTER 7

1. Charles Knowles Bolton, *The Private Soldier under Washington* (New York: Charles Scribner's Sons, 1902), p. 92.
2. Captain W. Glanville Evelyn, 4th Regiment, King's Own, *Memoirs and Letters from North America, 1774–1776* (Oxford: James Parker and Company, 1879; printed for private circulation), pp. 27–28, 38–39.

CHAPTER 8

1. Lieutenant Charles M. Lefferts, *Uniforms of the American, British, French, and German Armies in the War of the American Revolution, 1775–1783* (New York: New-York Historical Society, 1926; in Special Collection, University of California at Los Angeles), pp. 203–4.

CHAPTER 9

1. Board of Selectmen of the City of Boston, *A Report of the Record Commissioners of the City of Boston*, pp. 227–28.
2. Lieutenant Barker, *The British in Boston*, p. 3.
3. Frothingham, *The History of the Siege of Boston*, p. 48.

CHAPTER 10

1. Gipson, *Britain Sails into the Storm, 1770–1776*, p. 280.
2. Ibid., p. 299.
3. Horace Walpole, *England as His Letters Picture It*, edited by Alfred Bishop Mason (London: Constable and Company Ltd., 1930).
4. Carl Van Doren, *Benjamin Franklin* (New York: Viking Press, 1938), p. 506.
5. *An Enquiry into the Detail and Conduct of the American War Under Generals Gage, Howe, and Burgoyne, and Vice Admiral Lord Howe, Before the Committee of the House of Commons, and of the Celebrated Fugitive Press Which Are Said to Have Given Rise to That Important Enquiry*, 3rd ed. (London: Richardson and Urquart, 1780), pp. 11–12.

CHAPTER 11

1. Lieutenant Frederick Mackenzie, Adjutant 23rd Royal Welsh Fusiliers, *A British Fusilier in Revolutionary Boston: The Diary of Lieutenant Mackenzie, January 5 to April 30, 1775* (Cambridge: Harvard University Press, 1926), p. 27.

CHAPTER 12

1. Gipson, *Britain Sails into the Storm, 1770–1776,* pp. 320–21.
2. Allen French, *The First Year of the American Revolution* (Boston and New York: Houghton Mifflin, 1934), p. 15.
3. Lieutenant Mackenzie, *A British Fusilier in Revolutionary Boston,* p. 48.
4. Lieutenant Barker, *The British in Boston,* p. 32.
5. French, *The First Year of the American Revolution.*
6. Frothingham, *The History of the Siege of Boston,* p. 57.
7. Lieutenant Barker, *The British in Boston,* p. 32.
8. Sergeant Richard Pope, 47th Regiment, original diary on file in Rare Manuscript Section, Henry E. Huntington Library, San Marino, California, p. 8.
9. Related by Samuel Haws, "Personal Journal of Samuel Haws of Wrentham, Massachusetts, 1774–1775," manuscript on file, Henry E. Huntington Library.

CHAPTER 13

1. Lieutenant Barker, *The British in Boston,* p. 34.
2. French, *The First Year of the American Revolution,* p. 19.

CHAPTER 15

1. Frothingham, *The History of the Siege of Boston,* p. 94.
2. Benton, *The Annals of America,* Vol. II: *1755 to 1783,* p. 548.
3. Ibid.
4. Van Doren, *Benjamin Franklin,* p. 522.
5. Lieutenant Barker, *The British in Boston,* p. 47.
6. Ibid.

CHAPTER 16

1. Franklin B. Dexter, *The Literary Diary of Ezra Stiles* (New York: Charles Scribner's Sons, 1901), pp. 595–96.

2. Sergeant Pope, original diary, p. 17.
3. Lieutenant General Sir Henry Clinton, *The American Rebellion, 1775–1782*, edited by William B. Wilcox (New Haven: Yale University Press, reprinted 1954), p. 19.
4. Isaac J. Greenwood, *The Revolutionary Services of John Greenwood of Boston and New York, 1775–1783*, edited from the original manuscript in 1809 (New York: privately printed, 1922), pp. 12–13.

CHAPTER 17

1. Frothingham, *The History of the Siege of Boston*, p. 194.
2. Richard M. Ketchum, *Decisive Day: The Battle for Bunker Hill* (Garden City, N.Y.: Doubleday and Company, 1973), p. 195.
3. Frothingham, *The History of the Siege of Boston*, p. 174.
4. Ibid., p. 199.
5. Charles Martyn, *The Life of Artemas Ward* (New York: privately printed by Artemas Ward, 1921).
6. Frothingham, *The History of the Siege of Boston*, p. 157.
7. *An Enquiry into the Detail and Conduct of the American War*, pp. 14–15.
8. Ebeneezer Huntington, *Letters of Ebeneezer Huntington* (New York: privately printed for Charles Fred Heartmen, 1914), copy number 155 in the possession of Henry E. Huntington Library, p. 16.
9. French, *The First Year of the American Revolution*, p. 66.
10. John C. Fitzpatrick, editor, *The Writings of George Washington, 1745–1799*, from the original manuscript sources (Washington, D.C.: United States Government Printing Office, 1931–44).

CHAPTER 18

1. Frothingham, *The History of the Siege of Boston*, p. 222.
2. Bolton, *The Private Soldier Under Washington*, p. 133.
3. Frothingham, *The History of the Siege of Boston*, p. 221.
4. Captain William Coit, *Orderly Book at Siege of Boston April 23 to August 7, 1775*, kept by Moses Fargoes for Captain Coit's Company, 4th Company of 6th Regiment under Colonel Samuel Holden Parsons of Connecticut (Connecticut: privately printed, 1899), pp. 58–59.
5. Israel Trask, a memorandum quoted by Washington Irving in *Life of Washington*, Part I, 1859.
6. Lieutenant General Sir Charles Stuart, *The Letters, Manuscripts, and Documents Sent by Lieutenant General Sir Charles Stuart to His Father, the Earl of Bute 1775–1779* (London: privately printed by L. Kashnor, 1927), p. 5.

7. Frothingham, *The History of the Siege of Boston,* p. 228.

8. Ibid., p. 229.

9. Ibid., p. 235.

10. Ibid.

11. Lieutenant General Stuart, *The Letters, Manuscripts, and Documents,* p. 3.

12. Captain Evelyn, *Memoirs and Letters,* pp. 71–72.

CHAPTER 19

1. Frothingham, *The History of the Siege of Boston,* p. 284.

2. Ibid.

3. James Thomas Flexner, *George Washington in the American Revolution* (Boston: Little, Brown and Company, 1967), p. 54.

4. Frothingham, *The History of the Siege of Boston,* p. 273.

5. Ibid., p. 247.

6. Ibid., p. 248.

7. Ibid., p. 251.

8. Ensign Nathaniel Morgan, "Journal, April 21, 1775, to December 11, 1775" (in Orderly Books and Journals Kept by Connecticut Men While Taking Part in the American Revolution, Connecticut Historical Society, 1899), p. 125.

9. Martyn, *The Life of Artemas Ward,* p. 187.

10. General Sir William Howe, *General Sir William Howe's Orderly Book, June 17, 1775, to May 26, 1776,* edited by Benjamin Franklin Stevens. First published in 1890 with a historical introduction by Edward Everett Hale (Port Washington, N.Y.: Kennikat Press, 1890; reissued by Kennikat Press, 1970), p. 160.

11. Ibid., p. 169.

12. Ibid., p. 127.

13. Frothingham, *The History of the Siege of Boston,* p. 275.

14. Ibid., p. 285.

CHAPTER 20

1. William Bell Clark, *Naval Documents of the American Revolution,* Vol. I (Washington, D.C.: United States Navy Department, 1964), p. 1040.

2. Major Samuel Shaw, *The Journals of Major Samuel Shaw, Including the Siege of Boston,* with the life of the author (Boston: William Crosby and H. P. Nichols, 1847), p. 8.

3. Heath, *Memoirs,* p. 31.

4. Frothingham, *The History of the Siege of Boston,* pp. 296–97.

5. Washington Irving, *Life of George Washington*, Knickerbocker Edition, Vol. III (New York and London: G. P. Putnam's Sons, 1857), p. 27.
6. Ibid., p. 28.

CHAPTER 21

1. General Archibald Robertson, *His Diaries and Sketches in America, August 1775 to April 1777*, private journal edited by Harry Miller Lyndenberg (New York: New York Public Library, 1930), pp. 73–74.
2. Lieutenant General Stuart, *The Letters, Manuscripts, and Documents*, p. 6.
3. General Robertson, *His Diaries and Sketches in America*, p. 74.
4. General Howe, *His Orderly Book*, p. 226.
5. Frothingham, *The History of the Siege of Boston*, pp. 302–3.
6. Ibid., p. 306.
7. General Howe, *His Orderly Book*, p. 237.
8. Frothingham, *The History of the Siege of Boston*, pp. 308–10.
9. Colonel William Henshaw, *The Orderly Books of Colonel William Henshaw, October 1, 1775, through October 3, 1776* (Worcester, Mass.: American Antiquarian Society, 1948), p. 103.
10. Frothingham, *The History of the Siege of Boston*, p. 327.
11. James Thatcher, M.D., *Military Journal of the American Revolution* (Hartford, Conn.: Hurlbut, Williams and Company, American Subscription Publishing House, 1862), p. 42.
12. Colonel Henshaw, *The Orderly Books*, p. 105.
13. Frothingham, *The History of the Siege of Boston*, pp. 406–8.
14. Ibid., p. 326.
15. Irving, *Life of George Washington*, p. 46.

Selected Bibliography

PRIMARY SOURCES

Barker, Lieutenant John. *The British in Boston, the Diary of Lieutenant Barker of the King's Own Regiment.* Cambridge: Harvard University Press, 1924.

Clinton, Lieutenant General Sir Henry. *The American Rebellion, 1775–1782.* New Haven: Yale University Press, reprinted 1954. William B. Wilcox, editor.

Coit, Captain William. *Orderly Book at Siege of Boston, April 23 to August 7, 1775,* kept by Moses Fargoes for Captain Coit's Company, 4th Company of 6th Regiment under Colonel Samuel Holden Parsons of Connecticut. Privately printed, Connecticut; 1899.

Curwen, Samuel. *The Journal of Samuel Curwen, Loyalist,* edited by Andrew Oliver. Cambridge: Harvard University Press for the Essex Institute, Salem, 1972.

Evelyn, Captain W. Glanville, 4th Regiment (King's Own). *Memoirs and Letters from North America, 1774–1776.* Oxford: James Parker and Company, 1879; printed for private circulation.

Fobes, Simon. *Simon Fobes Narrative,* given by himself and narrated to his son, Joshua, in 1835. Tarrytown, New York: William Abbatt, 1922.

Greenwood, Isaac. *The Revolutionary Services of John Greenwood of Boston and New York, 1775–1783,* edited from the original manuscript in 1809. Privately printed, New York, 1922.

Haskell, Caleb. *Caleb Haskell's Diary, May 5, 1775, to May 30, 1776.* Tarrytown, New York: William H. Huse and Company, 1881.

Haws, Samuel. "Personal Journal of Samuel Haws of Wrentham, Massachusetts, 1774 to 1775." Manuscript at Henry E. Huntington Library, San Marino, California.

Heath, Major General William. *Memoirs of Major General William Heath.* New York: William Abbatt Publishers, 1901.

Hendricks, Captain William. *A Journal of the March of a Party of Provincials from Carlisle to Boston, July 13 to December 1775.* Personal journal of the author. Glasgow, Scotland: B. Chapman and A. Duncan, 1820.

Henshaw, Colonel William. *The Orderly Books of Colonel William Henshaw, October 1, 1775, through October 3, 1776.* Worcester, Massachusetts: American Antiquarian Society, 1948.

House of Commons. *Committee on the Detail and Conduct of the American War under Generals Gage, Howe, Burgoyne, and Vice Admiral Lord Howe. An Enquiry.* Third edition. London: Richardson and Urquart, 1780.

Howe, John. *A Journal Kept by Mr. John Howe While He Was Employed as a British Spy During the Revolutionary War.* Concord, New Hampshire: Luther Roby, 1827. Reprinted by William Abbatt, Tarrytown, New York, 1927.

Howe, General Sir William. *General Sir William Howe's Orderly Book, June 17, 1775, to May 26, 1776,* edited by Benjamin Franklin Stevens and with a historical introduction by Edward Everett Hale. New York: Kennikat Press, 1890. Reissued, Kennikat Press, 1970.

Huntington, Ebeneezer. *Letters of Ebeneezer Huntington.* 320 copies privately printed; copy 155 in Henry E. Huntington Library, San Marino, California. New York: Charles Fred Heartmen, 1914.

Knox, Henry. *Diary of Henry Knox.* New England Historical Genealogy. Quoted in Henry Steele Commager and Richard B. Morris, *The Spirit of Seventy-Six,* New York: Harper and Row, 1958.

Lamb, Sergeant Roger. *An Original and Authentic Journal of Occurances during the Late American War.* Dublin, Ireland: Wilkinson and Courtney, 1809.

Lister, Ensign Jeremy. *Concord Fight.* Cambridge: Harvard University Press, 1931.

Mackenzie, Lieutenant Frederick. *A British Fusilier in Revolutionary Boston: the Diary of Lieutenant Mackenzie, January 5 to April 30, 1775.* Cambridge: Harvard University Press, 1926.

———. *An Account of a Voyage to New York in a Troopship in the Year 1773.* Cambridge: Harvard University Press, 1926.

Pope, Sergeant Richard, 47th Regiment. Original diary, written 1775–1776. On file in Rare Manuscript Section, Henry E. Huntington Library, San Marino, California.

Robertson, Lieutenant General Archibald. *His Diaries and Sketches in America, 1762 to 1780.* New York: New York Public Library, 1930.

Serle, Ambrose. "The American Journal of Ambrose Serle, Lord Howe's Secretary." The original on file at the Henry E. Huntington Library, San Marino, California.

Stark, Caleb. *John Stark, Memoirs and Official Correspondence.* Concord: G. Parker Lyon, 1860.

Stuart, Lieutenant General Sir Charles. *Letters to His Father, 1775 to 1779.* Privately printed London: L. Kashnor, 1927.

Thatcher, James, M.D. *Military Journal of the American Revolution.* Hartford, Connecticut: Hurlbut, Williams and Company, 1862.

Williams, Major Ennion. *Journal of Major Ennion Williams on His Journey to the American Camp at Cambridge, 1775,* edited by William Henry Engle, M.D. Harrisburg, Pennsylvania: E. K. Meyers, State Printer, 1893.

SECONDARY SOURCES

Alden, John Richard. *The American Revolution, 1775–1783.* New York: Harper and Row, 1954.

Aptheker, Herbert. *The American Revolution, 1763–1783.* New York: International Publishers, 1960.

Army, Department of. *American Military History, 1607–1958.* ROTCM-145–20, Headquarters, Department of the Army, 1959.

Aylmer, Keven J., and Harold Murdock. "The Banker and the Battle of Lexington." *American History Illustrated,* October 1973.

Bailyn, Bernard. *The Ideological Origins of the American Revolution.* Cambridge: The Belknap Press, Harvard University Press, 1967.

Bakeless, John. *Turncoats, Traitors and Heroes.* New York: J. P. Lippincott Company, 1959.

Bartlett, George B. *Concord: Historic, Literary and Picturesque.* Boston: D. Lothrop Company, 1886.

Bernstein, Barton J. "Toward a New Past." *Dissenting Essays in American History.* New York: Random House, 1967.

Berthoff, Rowland. *An Unsettled People: Social Order and Disorder in American History.* New York: Harper and Row, 1971.

Billias, George Athan. *George Washington's Opponents.* New York: William Morrow and Company, 1969.

Billington, Ray Allen. "The Interpretation of Early American History." The Huntington Library, San Marino, 1966.

Blumenthal, Walter Hart. *Women Camp Followers of the American Revolution.* Philadelphia: George S. MacManus Company, 1952.

Bolton, Charles Knowles. *The Private Soldier under Washington.* New York: Charles Scribner's Sons, 1902.

Boorstin, Daniel J. *The Americans, the Colonial Experience*. New York: Vintage Books, a division of Random House, 1958.

Board of Selectmen of City of Boston. *A Report of the Record Commissioners of the City of Boston*, containing the minutes from 1769 to April 1775. Boston: Rockwell & Churchill, City Printers, 1893.

Brown, Gerald Saxon. *The American Secretary: The Colonial Policy of Lord George Germain, 1775–1778*. Ann Arbor: University of Michigan Press, 1963.

Brown, Wallace. "The British Press and the American Colonies," in *History Today*, May 1974.

———. "The Loyalists and the American Revolution," in *History Today*, March 1962.

Cary, John. *Joseph Warren: Physician, Politician, Patriot*. Urbana: University of Illinois Press, 1964.

Chidsey, Donald Barr. *The Siege of Boston*. New York: Crown Publishers, Incorporated, 1966.

———. *The Loyalists: The Story of Those Americans Who Fought Against Independence*. New York: Crown Publishers, Incorporated, 1973.

Clark, William Bell. *George Washington's Navy, Being an Account of His Excellency's Fleet in New England Waters*. Baton Rouge: Louisiana State University Press, 1960.

———. *Naval Documents of the American Revolution*, Volume I. Washington, D.C.: United States Navy Department, 1964.

Clermont-Crèvecoeur, Comte de (Jean-François-Louis). "The Observant French Lieutenant," in *American Heritage*, October 1972.

Coburn, Frank Warren. *The Battle on Lexington Common, April 19, 1775*. Published by the author, limited edition of 254 copies. Lexington: 1921.

Coleman, John M. "How Continental Was the Continental Congress?" in *History Today*, August 1968.

Commager, Henry Steele, and Richard B. Morris. *The Spirit of Seventy-Six*. New York: Harper and Row, 1958.

———, and Allan Nevins. *The Heritage of America*. Boston: Little, Brown and Company, 1939.

Cummings, William P. and Elizabeth C. "The Treasure of Alnwick Castle, Revolutionary War Maps of Hugh, Earl Percy," in *American Heritage*, August 1969.

Cummins, D. Duane, and William G. White. *The American Revolution*. New York: Benzinger Brothers, 1968.

Cutter, William. *The Life of Israel Putnam, Major General in the Army of the Revolution*. New York: Kennikat Press, 1850. Reissued 1970.

Degler, Carl L. *Out of Our Past: The Forces that Shaped Modern America.* New York: Harper and Row, 1959.

De Tocqueville, Alexis. *Democracy in America,* translated by Henry Reeve. Cambridge, Massachusetts: Sever and Francis, 1863.

Dexter, Franklin B. *The Literary Diary of Ezra Stiles.* New York: Charles Scribner's Sons, 1901.

Douglass, Elisha P. *Rebels and Democrats.* Chapel Hill: University of North Carolina Press, 1955.

Dow, George Francis. *Every Day Life in the Massachusetts Bay Colony.* New York: Benjamin Bloom, 1935.

Duncan, Louis C. *Medical Men in the American Revolution, 1775–1783.* Carlisle Barracks, Pennsylvania: Medical Field Service School, 1931.

Encyclopedia Britannica, eleventh edition.

Encyclopedia Britannica, 1965.

Falls, Cyril. *Great Military Battles.* New York: Spring Books, 1964.

Farrington, Charles C. *Paul Revere and His Famous Ride.* Bedford, Massachusetts: Bedford Print Shop, 1923.

Fleming, Thomas J. "The Enigma of General Howe," in *American Heritage,* February 1964.

Flexner, James Thomas. *George Washington in the American Revolution.* Boston: Little, Brown and Company, 1967.

Forbes, Esther. *Paul Revere and the World He Lived In.* Cambridge: Houghton Mifflin Company, the Riverside Press, 1942.

Franklin, John Hope. *From Slavery to Freedom.* New York: Alfred A. Knopf, 1965.

French, Allen. *The First Year of the American Revolution.* Boston and New York: Houghton Mifflin Company, Riverside Press, 1934.

Frothingham, Richard, Jr. *The History of the Siege of Boston and Bunker Hill.* Boston: Charles C. Little and James Brown, 1849.

———. *Life and Times of Joseph Warren.* Boston: Little, Brown and Company, 1865.

———. "The Alarm on the Night of April 18, 1775," letter to the Honorable Samuel C. Cobb, Mayor of Boston, and to the Gentlemen of the City Council of Boston, December 28, 1876. Original manuscript in Henry E. Huntington Library, San Marino, California.

Furneaux, Robert. *The Pictorial History of the American Revolution.* Chicago: J. G. Ferguson Publishing Company, 1973.

Garrison, Webb. *Sidelights of the American Revolution.* New York: Abingdon Press, 1974.

Gipson, Lawrence Henry. *The Coming of the Revolution, 1763–1775.* New York: Harper and Row, 1954.

————. *The Triumphant Empire,* Volume XII: *Britain Sails into the Storm, 1770–1776.* New York: Alfred A. Knopf, 1965.

Greene, Jack P., ed. *The Reinterpretation of the American Revolution.* New York: Harper and Row, 1968.

Gruber, Ira D. *The Howe Brothers and the American Revolution.* New York: Atheneum, 1972.

Gurney, Gene. *A Pictorial History of the United States Army.* New York: Crown Publishers, Incorporated, 1966.

Hamilton, Edward P. *The French and Indian Wars.* Garden City, New York: Doubleday and Company, Incorporated, 1962.

Hart, Albert Bushnell. *American History Told by Contemporaries,* Volume II: *Building of the Republic, 1689–1783.* New York: The Macmillan Company, 1890.

————. *Commonwealth History of Massachusetts,* Volume III: *Commonwealth of Massachusetts, 1775–1830.* New York: States History Company, 1929.

Higginbotham, Don. *The War of American Independence.* New York: The Macmillian Company, 1971.

Hofstadter, Richard. *The Age of Reform.* New York: Vintage Books, division of Random House, 1955.

————, William Miller, and Daniel Aaron. *The American Republic,* Volume I, revised ed. Englewood Cliffs, New Jersey: Prentice-Hall, 1959, 1970.

Irving, Washington. *Life of George Washington,* Knickerbocker Edition, Volume III, London and New York: G. P. Putnam's Sons, 1857.

Judson, L. Carroll. *Sages and Heroes of the American Revolution.* Philadelphia: Moss and Brother, 1853.

Kaplan, Sidney. *The Black Presence in the Era of the American Revolution, 1770–1800.* New York: New York Graphic Society, Ltd., 1973. National Portrait Gallery, Smithsonian Institution.

Katcher, Philip R. N. *Encyclopedia of British, Provincial and German Army Units, 1775–1783.* Harrison, Pennsylvania: Stackpole Books, 1973.

Ketchum, Richard M. *Decisive Day: The Battle for Bunker Hill.* Garden City, New York: Doubleday and Company, 1973.

Langdon, William Chauncy. *Everyday Things in American Life, 1609–1776.* New York: Charles Scribner's Sons, 1939.

Leckie, Robert. *Warfare.* New York: Harper and Row, 1970.

Lefferts, Lieutenant Charles M. *Uniforms of the American, British, French, and German Armies in the War of the American Revolution, 1775–1783,* edited by Alexander J. Wall, librarian of the New-York Historical Society. New York: The New-York Historical Society, 1927; 500

copies, copy no. 231 in the Special Collection, University of Southern California.

Lloyd, Christopher. *The British Seaman, 1200 to 1860 Survey.* London: Granada Publishing Ltd., 1968.

Lossing, Benson J. "The Fifer at Lexington, the Story of Jonathan Harrington," in *Hours with Living Men and Women of the Revolution in 1848.* New York: Funk and Wagnalls, 1889.

Main, Jackson Turner. *The Sovereign States, 1775–1783.* New York: New Viewpoints, a division of Franklin Watts, Incorporated, 1973.

————. *The Social Structure of Revolutionary America.* Princeton, New Jersey: Princeton University Press, 1969.

Martin, Joseph Plumb. *Private Yankee Doodle, Dangers and Sufferings of a Revolutionary Soldier,* edited by George E. Scheer. First published in 1830. Boston: Little, Brown and Company, 1962.

Martyn, Charles. *The Life of Artemas Ward.* New York: privately printed by Artemas Ward, 1921.

Merrill, Joseph. *History of Amesbury.* Haverhill, Massachusetts: Press of Franklin P. Stiles, 1880.

Miers, Earl Schenck. *Crossroads of Freedom, the American Revolution and the Rise of a New Nation.* New Brunswick, New Jersey: Rutgers University Press, 1971.

Mitchell, Broadus. *The Price of Independence, a Realistic View of the American Revolution.* New York: Oxford University Press, 1974.

Montross, Lynn. *Rag, Tag and Bobtail, the Story of the Continental Army.* New York: Harper and Brothers, 1952.

Moore, Frank. *The Diary of the American Revolution.* New York: Washington Square Press, 1967.

Moore, Warren. *Weapons of the American Revolution and Accouterments.* New York: Promontory Press, 1967.

Morgan, Edmund S. "The Puritan Ethic and the Coming of the American Revolution," in *The Reinterpretation of the American Revolution,* Jack P. Greene, ed. New York: Harper and Row, 1968.

Morris, Richard B. *The American Revolution, 1763–1783.* New York: Harper and Row, 1970.

————. *The American Revolution Reconsidered.* New York: Harper and Row, 1967.

Namier, Sir Lewis. *Personalities and Power.* New York: Harper and Row, 1965.

Newcomer, Lee Nathaniel. *The Embattled Farmers, A Massachusetts Countryside in the American Revolution.* New York: King's Crown Press, Columbia University, 1953.

Oliver, Peter. *Origins and Progress of the American Rebellion, A Tory View.* Stanford, California: Stanford University Press, 1961.

Pancake, John. "American Militia in the War of Independence," in *History Today*, November 1972.

Pearson, Michael. *The Revolutionary War, an Unbiased Account.* New York: Capricorn Books, 1972. (Also published as *Those Damn Rebels.* London: William Heinemann Ltd., 1972.)

Peckham, Howard H. *The War for Independence, a Military History.* Chicago: University of Chicago Press, 1963.

Perry, Clay. "Big Guns for Washington," in *American Heritage*, April 1955.

Perry, Captain David. *The Life of Captain David Perry.* Written in 1822. Reprinted Tarrytown, New York: William Abbatt, 1928.

Peterson, Harold. *The Treasury of the Gun.* New York: Golden Press, 1962.

———, and Robert Elman. *The Great Guns.* New York: Madison Square Press, Grosset and Dunlop, Incorporated, 1971.

Plumb, J. H. *In the Light of History.* Boston: Houghton Mifflin Company, 1973.

Preston, Richard A., and Sidney F. Wise. *Men in Arms.* New York: Praeger Publishers, 1970.

Quennell, Peter. "The Rampant Fox, Charles James Fox," *Horizon*, May 1960.

Quincy, Josiah. *The Journals of Major Samuel Shaw, Including the Siege of Boston.* Boston: William Crosby and H. P. Nichols, Publishers, 1847.

Rankin, Hugh F. *The American Revolution.* New York: G. P. Putnam and Sons, 1964.

Richardson, A. E. *Georgian England, A Survey of Social Life, Trades, Industries and Art from 1700 to 1820.* New York: Charles Scribner's Sons, 1931.

Robertson, Diana Forbes, "Lady Knox," *American Heritage*, April 1966.

Rossiter, Clinton. *The First American Revolution.* New York: Harcourt, Brace and World, Incorporated, 1956.

Sabine, Lorenzo A. M. *Framingham in the Revolution,* an address read before the Middlesex South Agricultural Society on March 14, 1853. Framingham, Massachusetts: Framingham Historical and Natural History Society, 1933.

Scheer, George F., and Hugh F. Rankin. *Rebels and Red Coats.* New York: World Publishing Company, 1959.

Schlesinger, Arthur Meir, Sr. *New Viewpoints in American History.* New York: Macmillan Company, 1934.

———. *The Birth of the Nation.* New York: Alfred A. Knopf, 1968.

Smelser, Marshall. *The Winning of Independence.* Chicago: Quadrangle Books, 1972.

Smith, Page. *John Adams,* Volumes I and II. Garden City, New York: Doubleday and Company Incorporated, 1962.

Sparks, Jared. *Library of American Biography,* Volume I: *Life of John Stark.* Boston: Hilliard Gray and Company, 1834.

Stout, Neil R. "The Spies Who Went Out in the Cold," in *American Heritage,* February 1972.

Thane, Elswyth. *The Fighting Quaker, Nathanael Greene.* New York: Hawthorn Books Incorporated, 1972.

Train, Arthur, Jr. *The Story of Everyday Things.* New York: Harper and Brothers, 1941.

Trevelyan, G. M. *The Eighteenth Century, Illustrated English Social History.* Harmondsworth, Middlesex, England: Penguin Books Ltd., 1944.

Tunis, Edwin. *Colonial Living.* Cleveland: World Publishing Company, 1957.

———. *Colonial Craftsmen and the Beginnings of American Industry.* Cleveland: World Publishing Company, 1965.

Van Doren, Carl. *Benjamin Franklin.* New York: Viking Press, 1938.

———. *Secret History of the American Revolution.* New York: Viking Press, 1941.

Ver-Steeg, Clarence L. *The American People, Their History.* Evanston, Illinois: Row, Peterson and Company, 1961.

Wade, Herbert T., and Robert A. Lively. *This Glorious Cause, The Adventures of Two Company Officers in Washington's Army.* Princeton: Princeton University Press, 1958.

Wallace, Willard M. *Appeal to Arms.* Chicago: Quadrangle Books, 1951.

Walpole, Horace. *England as His Letters Picture It,* edited by Alfred Bishop Mason. London: Constable and Company Ltd., 1930.

Weigley, Russell F. *History of the United States Army.* New York: Macmillan Company, 1967.

Wigginton, Eliot. *The Foxfire Book.* Garden City, New York: Anchor Press/Doubleday, 1972.

———. *Foxfire Two.* Garden City, New York: Anchor Press/Doubleday, 1973.

Windrow, Martin, and Gerry Embleton. *Military Dress of North America, 1665–1970.* New York: Charles Scribner's Sons, 1973.

Woodward, W. E. *A New American History.* New York: The Literary Guild Incorporated, 1937.

Wright, Louis B. *The Cultural Life of the American Colonies, 1607–1763.* New York: Harper and Row, 1957.

Young, Brigadier General Peter. *George Washington's Army.* Reading, Berkshire, England: Osprey Publishing Ltd., 1972.

Index